PLANNING, POLITICS AND
THE STATE

PLANNING, POLITICS AND THE STATE

Political foundations of planning thought

N. P. Low

London
UNWIN HYMAN
Boston   Sydney   Wellington

Published by the Academic Division of
Unwin Hyman Ltd
15/17 Broadwick Street, London W1V 1FP, UK

Unwin Hyman Inc.,
955 Massachusetts Avenue, Cambridge, MA 02139, USA

Allen & Unwin (Australia) Ltd,
8 Napier Street, North Sydney, NSW 2060, Australia

Allen & Unwin (New Zealand) Ltd
in association with the Port Nicholson Press Ltd
Compusales Building, 75 Ghuznee Street, Wellington 1, New Zealand

First published in 1991

British Library Cataloguing in Publication Data

Low, Nicholas
    Planning, politics, and the state: political foundations
    of planning thought.
    1. Environment planning. Political aspects
    I. Title
    711

ISBN 0-04-351075-2
ISBN 0-04-445897-5

Library of Congress Cataloging-in-Publication Data

Low, Nicholas.
    Planning, politics, and the state: political foundations
    of planning thought / by Nicholas Low.
        p.   cm.
    Includes bibliographical references and index.
    ISBN 0-04-351075-2 (HB) : $49.95.
    ISBN 0-04-445897-5 (PB) : $17.95.
    1. Planning.   2. Political planning.   3. State, The.   I. Title.

HD87.5.L69   1991   90-12819
320'.6-dc20   CIP

Typeset in 10 on 11 point Bembo.
Printed in Great Britain by Billing and Sons, London and Worcester

To Elizabeth,
without whom this book would have been
written much quicker

Contents

List of figures

Acknowledgements

Thanks are due to my colleagues at the University of Melbourne who gave me encouragement and intellectual challenge, in particular to John Power, who showed me the difference between sociology and politics, to Brian McLoughlin for whom theoretical endeavour is the essence of academic life, and to Trevor Tyson with whom I have co-taught for many years and who made me realise that a deeper understanding of politics can be gained from study of the small group. My thanks also go to the University of Melbourne itself for providing funds for travel and the time to write this book, and to the School of Environmental Planning. There are also many from whom I have benefitted in discussion and hospitality and who contributed indirectly – whether they know it or not; Tony Eddison, Robin Hambleton and Susan Barrett at the School for Advanced Urban Studies in Bristol, Andreas Faludi at the University of Amsterdam, Rod Rhodes and Bob Jessop at the University of Essex, Peter Saunders at the University of Sussex, Melvin Webber and Judith de Neufville at the University of California (Berkeley), Neil Smith and Bob Beauregard at Rutgers University, Gordon Clark, formerly of Carnegie-Mellon University, Pittsburgh, now of Monash University, Melbourne, Patsy Healey at the University of Newcastle upon Tyne, John Dee at the School of Environmental Planning here in Melbourne, Colin Campbell at Georgetown University and Guy Peters at the University of Pittsburgh – co-organizers of the Structure and Organization of Government Research Group of the International Political Science Association, and many others associated with that group, especially Ulrich Klöti and Erwin Rüegg at the University of Zürich.

Morag van der Zee patiently typed an earlier draft with great good humour and precision. Dorothy Bugg and Maggie Francis both provided excellent secretarial assistance. My thanks also go to Gordon Smith at Unwin Hyman who was always helpful, efficient, friendly and sympathetic and who must sometimes have wondered if the book would ever be finished, and to the anonymous reviewer for a stringent and correspondingly useful critique.

I have needed academic guides through the complexities of political and state theory. I would like to mention in particular Robert Waste's book (*Power and Pluralism in American Cities. Researching the Urban Laboratory*, 1987, New York: Greenwood Press) which helped unravel American pluralism for me, Bob Jessop's book on Marxian state theory (*The Capitalist State. Marxist Theories and Methods*, 1982,

Oxford: Martin Robertson) and David Held's book on the Frankfurt School of critical theory and on Jürgen Habermas (*Introduction to Critical Theory. Horkheimer to Habermas*, 1980, Berkeley and Los Angeles: University of California Press). Robert Dahl's work continues to inspire me and I thank him and his publishers for permission to reproduce the extract from *A Preface to Democratic Theory* (Chicago and London: The University of Chicago Press, 1956) on pages 99–100 of this book. I, of course, remain responsible for the use to which I have put these excellent texts.

PLANNING, POLITICS AND THE STATE

1 Introduction

This is a book about theory, the theory of the state, of politics and of planning. Its focus is planning as a political practice.

A large body of *planning theory* has grown out of the need to generalize and explain that practice. But this theory is a recent development. It grew up close to planning practice, almost as a by-product. 'Within urban and regional planning', writes Beauregard (1986, p. 172), 'the theoretical practice of academics is overwhelmed by the practical business of professionals. As a result, planning ideas are buffetted by unstable and unpredictable political and economic forces rather than discussed with scholarly deliberation.' Planning theory has been characterized by rapidly changing fashions, so that there appears to be a variety of competing models or 'paradigms' of planning (Hudson, 1979; Alexander, 1984; Hoch 1984a). Here it will be argued that the variety of planning models is traceable to varying assumptions and propositions from political thought. These in turn arise from different political practices emerging in different national and regional contexts. Ultimately, we encounter intractable dilemmas inherent in all human organization.

Lindblom's (1959) 'disjointed incrementalism' and Davidoff's (1965) 'advocacy planning' were both grounded in the American pluralist tradition (Bentley, [1908] 1935; Dahl, 1956). Faludi's (1973b) 'process' model of planning owes more to the European view of the state as a corporate entity under parliamentary control (see Mannheim, 1940). And, of course, the Marxist work that laid siege to the mainstream of planning theory in the 1970s and early 1980s threw the whole question of political 'ideology' into sharp relief (Scott and Roweis, 1977; Harvey, 1985). But, despite a fairly widespread perception of the political nature of planning, there have been few attempts to confront the theoretical implications of this perception. Instead, planning theorists have sought to weld together the theory of the activity of planning with theories of spatial development. In fact, it is only in the last thirty years or so that planning theory has been anything other than a collection of ideas about cities and urban development (see Clawson and Hall, 1973, ch.8; Cherry, 1974; Krueckeberg, 1983; Beauregard, 1984). In 1955 the American planner Dennis O'Harrow pointed out that the central theme to which planners from different disciplines contributed was 'interest in the city, the development of the city, the operation of the city, the problems of the city (see Berger, M. S., 1981, p. 290).

McLoughlin (1969, p. 95) pursued this theme in arguing that 'the planning process must have a similar shape to the human eco-system'. More recently, Cooke (1983) connected theories of planning with theories of spatial development and wrote with disapproval of the separation of planning theory from 'theory of the socio-spatial development processes with which it interacts in the external world' (ibid., p. 1). Faludi (1973a) who did much to promote the idea that the theory of planning could be separated, conceptually, from theories of the urban process (theories 'in' planning) found himself roundly condemned by Marxist geographers and sociologists. Planning thus conceived was 'a generic and universal human activity for which no special training and qualifications are required' (Paris, 1982, p. 6). Theory of the planning process was 'non-scientific, normative, speculative, theorizing' (Scott and Roweis, 1977). Planning theory divorced from its supposed object was 'contentless' (Thomas, 1982). On procedural theory: 'not only is it purely prescriptive, but in the assumptions which it makes concerning the political and social context, it is utterly unrealistic. It is no exaggeration to describe it not as theory but as fantasy' (Reade, 1981, p. 6). The substantive/procedural dichotomy 'has served to muddy the waters' (Cooke and Rees, 1977).

The Marxist critique of procedural theory brought forth rejoinders by Harris (1978) and Taylor (1984). But perhaps Cooke and Rees were right, for there was too much mud stirred up to be able to see clearly a central point of Faludi's argument, namely, that the connection between planning and spatial development is *not* the only one, or perhaps even the main one, with which planning theorists ought to be concerned. Indeed, as I shall argue, the needs of practice cry out for a different connection to be made, the connection between planning practice and *political theory* (see also Taylor, 1980).

Aims, structure and ideological position

Political theory does not, and has never, provided uncontested answers to political questions, however much its users and inventors would like to persuade us otherwise in pursuit of their partisan ends. In that sense political knowledge is not in the least like scientific knowledge. Yet, as will be argued in chapter 3, political theory makes its own claim to truth. Political theory is inherently dialectical, pointing out this or that dimension of human action. If liberal theory contains contradictions, so too does class theory. Liberal theory does not deal adequately with the question of economic power, nor does democracy sit easily alongside the principles of hierarchy and management by which both the state and the business world are organized. Equally, however, the Marxist conception of politics as class struggle does not admit of simple answers to the political questions it raises: what are classes, how is democracy to be realized?

This book provides, for the planner, some theoretical foundations that cut across the main lines of political debate in the twentieth century. The aim is to put planning into political perspective. In doing so, a vast theoretical field has to be treated with great selectivity. It is not possible in this one volume to deal substantially with the antecedents of the theories in earlier centuries. The works of Hobbes, Locke, Rousseau, Madison, Mill, Bentham, Marx and Engels are arguably not much less relevant today than they were in their own period. The reader should also keep constantly in mind that political theory is not just a product of individual minds working *in vacuo*, but of individuals with particular histories in the midst of particular societies, which they react to or conform to as well as sometimes transcend. Nor is it possible to deal adequately with the most interesting theoretical developments emerging today. The aim is rather to provide a foundation for a better understanding of the present day literature relevant to planning and the state.

Another sort of compromise that will have to be made is between the need to explore the work of particular theorists in sufficient depth to understand what they are really trying to say – including their inconsistencies, variable foci and changes of mind – and the need to deal with the wider field of ideas, schools of thought, to which they belong and to which they contribute. A number of books were published in the 1980s, which cover political 'schools of thought' quite exhaustively. Held and his colleagues (1983) work through a range of interpretations of the modern state and its place in society. They introduce short extracts from the classic texts as appetizers. They cover different types of state in space and time, different aspects of the problematic of the state (citizenship, the economy, legitimacy, the world context), and prescriptions for future states and politics from different political perspectives. In a companion volume of essays (McLennan, Held and Hall, 1984), Held begins to explore his own conception of post-liberal democracy, which he has followed up with a book (1987) setting out in full the dimensions of his theoretical schema. Alford and Friedland (1985) examine three schools of thought: the pluralist, the managerialist and the 'class' perspectives of the state, and work out a synthesis, which suggests that different perspectives grasp different dimensions of the polity. Thus, the three perspectives respectively address situational power plays in the game, the rules of the game and the game itself. Self (1985) tackles a range of theories of the state with the purpose of responding to criticisms of the performance of government in the 1980s: 'government is viewed in turn through the lenses of economists concerned with the behaviour of rational individuals in political situations; of pluralist thinkers who see government as divided into numerous groups and organizations both private and public; of the new theorists of corporatism who deal with the growing integration of public and private interests; and of modern theorists of bureaucracy.' (ibid., p. xi). Self's aim is find ways of reforming existing political institutions so as to reach a new accommodation between the individualist tradition and social needs and responsibilities. Dunleavy and O'Leary (1987) explore the common themes and key dimensions of pluralism, the 'new right', elite theory, Marxism and neo-pluralism. In doing so, they assess the values contained in the theory, its methodological foundations and the way the theory handles the empirical collection and testing of evidence.

None of these books deals directly with planning, linking urban planning with theories of politics and the state. Those that have made this connection (e.g. Blowers, 1980; Saunders, 1980; Cooke, 1983; Mollenkopf, 1983; Catanese, 1978, 1984; Clark and Dear, 1984; Gottdiener, 1987) have done so from within a single perspective – Blowers, Mollenkopf and Catanese from different liberal viewpoints, Cooke, Clark and Dear and Gottdiener from varying Marxian viewpoints, and Saunders from a Weberian viewpoint. The intention of these writers is to interpret urban politics and planning and to reflect upon the particular theory in which their interpretations are embedded. The present book differs from both politics-centred and urban-planning-centred texts in looking at the way in which different perspectives of politics throw light on planning.

The book is divided into two main sections plus a concluding chapter. The first section deals with the political character of planning practice (chapter 2) and the way in which political theory is relevant to planning practice (chapter 3). The second section, which forms the main body of the book, is itself divided into two, the first part dealing with theory resting on an underlying position of assent to capitalist democracy, the second with dissenting theory. These terms are used in preference to more familiar labels such as 'liberal' or 'pluralist', 'critical' or 'class theory', both to denote the fundamental division in political theory and in order to free the latter labels for more specific uses.

The section on assenting theory begins with that body of theory that is most supportive of and closest to the idea of planning: the theory of the 'rational state' in the work of Max Weber (chapter 4). Rationality, the use of expertise for social ends and bureaucracy are themes developed by Weber that are central to the theory and practice of planning. But, as Weber explains, the concept of rationality embraces powerful tensions. Weber developed his own version of class theory, but, though critical, ultimately gave his assent to capitalism.

The theories of pluralism (chapter 5) were influenced by Weberian thought, but were grounded in the older liberal tradition of Madison, Locke and Tocqueville with its fear of concentrated state power. Anglo-American rather than continental European society formed the social context of these ideas. Here, the term 'pluralism' is used not to describe a large part of modern liberal political discourse (as in Alford and Friedland, 1985) but to define a theory of politics associated with the weak and disjointed state merging into a society comprised of multiple, dispersed interest groups, and dominated by open and competing elites. The primary focus of pluralism is political action, 'manifest influence', but pluralist discussions of the political game have led inevitably to a concern with its rules. These rules have generally been assumed to be fair or, at least, benign, though both Dahl and Lindblom have challenged that assumption with growing insistence. The theory of pluralism, within assenting theory, provides the basis for a critique of the rational state and defines new roles for the planner emphasizing policy process over policy content: the roles of advocate, negotiator, mediator, reticulist (networker – see p. 166) and innovator.

Completing the section on assenting theory are two theoretical positions that reaffirm the strong state: neo-corporatism (chapter 6) and neo-liberalism (chapter 7). Both, in different ways provide critiques of both pluralism and the rational state. Neo-corporatism has been appropriated by some Marxists (e.g. Panitch, 1979; Jessop, 1979) and therefore might seem to belong among *dissenting* theories. Yet the normative position of the theory itself, in so far as it has one, is accepting of capitalism and the function of the state in mediating between the two great power blocs of business and organized labour. Some versions of corporatism, stressing the incorporation of interest groups within the decision-making processes of the state, are little more than a European variant of pluralism (see Heisler and Kvavik, 1974; Heisler, 1979; Jordan, 1983). Neo-liberalism, though espousing a state with a restricted role, nevertheless demands a strong and coherent state to enforce the rule of law. (See, in particular, the work of Hayek, 1944, and Buchanan and Tullock, 1965). Whereas the planning role ascribed by corporatism is that of mediator, the neo-liberal role for the planner is that of umpire, and perhaps policeman, presiding over and enforcing a clearly articulated and universally applicable set of rules.

The part of the book dealing with dissenting theory begins with a discussion of the politics of classic Marxian class theory (chapter 8). The theorist who developed the most sophisticated exposition of Marxian political theory was Antonio Gramsci, and chapter 8 includes a substantial exegesis of his work. Gramsci was criticized in his time for departing from Marxian orthodoxy and some Marxists continue to have doubts (see Anderson, 1976/77). But he has been influential in the recent development of a Marxian politics fitted to the conditions of late capitalism (e.g. Przeworski, 1980; Jessop, 1982). The book then moves to a discussion of a different stream within Marxist theory, that of the 'critical theory' of the Frankfurt School (chapter 9). Not only did Marcuse, Adorno, Horkheimer and other leading members of the school make a distinctive contribution of their own, they also laid the foundation for the later development of critical theory by Jürgen Habermas and his colleagues. Habermas developed a theory of crisis that has been influential both in America (O'Connor, 1973) and in Europe (Offe, 1984, 1985). His more recent work returns to a theme with which the book started, that of rationality and the role of the subject. In this respect Habermas conducts a critical dialogue with Weber as well as with Marx.

The focus of dissenting theory is critical analysis of the rules of capitalist society stemming from the power relations inherent in the capitalist mode of production. The 'planner' roles that dissenting theory describes are mainly viewed as part of the problem rather than as part of the solution. In this respect, however, it is important to recognize what dissenting theory dissents from. The dissent is not from the day-to-day activities of political actors (such as planners) but from the contextual system within which they act and which shapes their roles. Dissenting theory does not tell planners how to act but what they are acting in and on. Nevertheless, both Gramsci and his successors and Habermas are concerned to indicate appropriate political action, and some conclusions can be drawn about the approach to planning prescribed by dissenting theory.

Like any other text, this book has its ideological bias and it is as well to state the position at the outset. This position is epitomized in the precept that justice is a matter of fair outcomes as well as fair process. The principle of individual dignity and freedom that underlies all democratic theory (even that of Marx) is threatened, and freedom remains a hollow abstraction unless it is accompanied by the material capacity to exercise free choice. We cannot honestly say that people living in great poverty are free, whatever legal rights they may have. The existence of grossly unequal wealth and power flies in the face of democracy and, what is more, inhibits and deforms the operation of the two social institutions that liberal democracy rightly claims as its greatest achievement: the market and open, democratic politics. Market systems can certainly work to satisfy the real preferences of a population. But, as Weber pointed out, they also reflect the power structure in society that takes the form of wealth. The more unequally economic power is distributed, the more will markets reflect a set of preferences distorted by that inequality. Likewise, openly contested pluralist politics will work to reflect the balance of political preferences in a society only when the participants have a broadly equal opportunity and capacity to participate. The state in a democratic society should guarantee not only freedom but equality. Held (1984, pp. 230, 231) puts the matter thus:

> What I want to argue . . . is that liberalism and Marxism share in common a set of aspirations which can be stated in the form of a central principle: [that] individuals should be free and equal in the determination of the rules bby which they live; that is, they should enjoy equal rights (and, accordingly, equal obligations) in the specification of the framework which generates and limits the opportunities available to them throughout their lives.

This is an ideological position based on selective and critical appropriation of ideas generated in the course of theoretical debates from about the seventeenth century to the present day.

Conclusion

Bridges need to be built between planning practice and political theory. This can be done only by breaching the convention that planning theory has to be associated with spatial theory. Since politics is a process we must again reconsider planning as a process, but from a wider and more explicit political perspective than that of 'procedural' theory. In this book the main form of the theoretical debate will be outlined by exploring in some depth the work of key theorists. It has been asserted that planners need political theory, but this has to be argued. Before turning to the main content of the book, then, two questions have to be addressed:

1   In what way does planning practice demonstrate a need for political theory?
2   In what way is political theory relevant to planning practice?

In order to answer the first question we shall have to be more clear about the development of the practice of urban and regional planning and what that practice entails today. In particular, we shall need to explore the relationship between politics and professionalism. The second question demands some consideration of what constitutes political knowledge. We shall argue that the key concepts that link political knowledge with the practice of planning are those of 'role' and 'rules', which suggest both action and social context. These questions are the subject of the next two chapters and it is to the first of them that we now turn.

Part 1

Planning practice and political theory

2 Planning practice

Planners face an uneasy tension between the world of politics, in which they increasingly have to see themselves playing a direct part, and planning as a profession. On the one hand, no practising planner can fail to be aware of the political dimension of that practice. On the other hand, practice continues to demand a professional approach, which we can sum up broadly here as the application of expert judgement during the process in which decisions are made and implemented (see Marcuse 1976; Blowers 1980; Howe, 1980; Reade, 1982a; Roweis, 1983; Shirvani, 1985; Healey, 1985; Beauregard, 1986). If we are to answer the first question posed at the end of chapter 1, that of the relevance of political theory to planning practice, we will have to sort out the relationship between professionalism and politics.

We need to show not merely *that* planning is a political activity but *how* modern urban planning has emerged through a combination of political and professional action and how professionalization became a solution to a political problem. In order to do this we will first have to look at the history of modern urban planning. We will confine the discussion to planning in Britain and the United States, although, as Sutcliffe (1981), points out, the movement towards urban planning was international in scope, with considerable diffusion of ideas and techniques between the nations of Europe and the United States. Today urban planning is a very widespread if not universal practice, with different forms developing in different countries. When we have seen how urban planning and politics have been interwoven historically we shall then be in a position to discuss in more general terms the relationship between the professional and political aspects of planning practice today and the uses of political theory to the practitioner.

Planning professionalized

For the most part, in earlier centuries the designed aspects of cities were those of special concern to the ruling class: the physical environment in which its members dwelt; the society's permanent cultural symbols for which they were responsible: churches and places of assembly, forums, palaces, great open spaces and military artefacts, including those whose main purpose was to control the urban population. Commenting on the admired symbols of European urban culture which 'fill the imagination' of the planning student, Eversley (1973, p. 39) acidly observed: 'The history of architecture and planning is built on inequality, on slavery, and on the exploitation of the mass of peasants, serfs and slaves.' The feudal city with its semi-autonomous guilds and often far from quiescent crowds always posed a political problem for the ruling class but, with the growth of industrial capitalism, new dimensions were added both to the problems and the opportunities of cities.

The industrial city of the mid-nineteenth century expressed in stark terms the contradiction between the economic growth and profit to be had from concentrated urban development and the political protest of organized masses of workers living in appalling conditions in close proximity to one another. Urban improvement in Europe has to be seen against the background of the political turmoil of the 1830s and 1840s as well as the threat of disease. Hobsbawm (1969, p. 158) writes of urban Britain in the second half of the century:

> The cities which now constituted the real Britain were no longer the totally abandoned and neglected money-making deserts of the first half of the century. The horrors of that period, dramatized in the growing epidemics which did not even spare the middle class, led to systematic sanitary reform from the 1850s (drainage, water supply, street cleaning, and so on); affluence produced municipal building and, combined with radical agitation, even managed to save some open spaces for the public in those fortunate areas where they had not already been built up.

A recurring issue in the nineteenth century, then, was the need to secure legitimacy for a system which produced both organization and protest, affluence and squalor. The design and regulation of towns evolved with the gradual consolidation of liberal capitalism. The state was implicated in different ways in different nations, depending on the prevailing political and economic conditions: the political stance of those in authority, the nature of the interests pressing for or resisting change and the urban conditions produced (see Benevolo, 1967).

Comparing the British with the continental experience of planning, Sutcliffe (1981, p. 48) writes: 'Britain's advantage lay in its prolific town-building process, which had secured the single-family house as the norm not only for the middle class but also for the majority of workers. Supplemented by slowly expanding public provision of services, and moderated by rudimentary regulation of the use of private land, this process produced an environment which in the later decades of the nineteenth century was not fundamentally questioned in Britain'. Pockets of terrible squalor nevertheless existed, largely out of sight of the respectable classes (as Engels reported in 1844). When these 'slums' began to be noticed by the authorities, who were already concerned about the spread of disease, comprehensive powers were eventually granted to municipalities to acquire, clear and redevelop slum housing (Sutcliffe, 1981, p. 53).

In France and Germany extremely bad urban conditions were more widespread and the state assumed much earlier a more directly interventive role in planned urban extension and reconstruction. In Berlin town planning was a traditional function of the police of the Prussian state, and in the 1850s laws were passed to permit the police to engage in comprehensive design of town extensions. These powers were eventually passed to municipalities, but only after the state had reorganized and 'strengthened' local government in such a way as to guarantee its domination by the capitalist class (Sutcliffe, 1981, p. 17).

Sutcliffe (1981, p. 132) notes the variety of economic and political purposes behind the remodelling of Paris following the installation of Napoleon III in 1852:

The immediate stimulus to the building of new streets was the need to provide access to the new railway stations, but there were such important related advantages that it amounted almost to an urban panacea. New sewerage and water distribution systems could be built more cheaply in association with street improvements. Some of the worst slum districts could be decimated to the advantage of both public health and public order. Visual order too could be imposed on districts old and new in accordance with the royal and imperial traditions of even the most republican of Frenchmen. Above all, the authorities recognised that urban public works directly stimulated the building industry, and so reduced unemployment more effectively than any other form of contrived stimulus.

Benevolo (1967) argued that town planning in Europe in the latter half of the nineteenth century became more technically oriented and separated from radical politics. This is probably most true of France, where the thought of Saint-Simon, Fourier and Cabet had linked political change with the planning of new communities. Now town planning was rejected as utopian by the Marxist Left and became absorbed into the state in the work of construction and reconstruction: boulevards and parks, drainage and sewerage schemes, roads and public transport; the work of 'a new class of planners and civil servants, scientific, competent and satisfied with their various departmental responsibilities' (Benevolo, 1967, p. 110).

In the United States the promoters of town planning at the end of the century could look back to a colonial past of 'town planting' governed by collectivist aspects of Puritan culture, and to the efforts of colonial landowners such as Penn in Philadelphia and representatives of the British crown such as Oglethorpe in Savannah to design new cities on virgin sites (Foglesong, 1986, ch 2). However, by the middle of the nineteenth century burgeoning growth of the cities, coupled with the establishment of the capitalist form of land tenure, created similar urban problems to those experienced in Europe: squalid working-class housing; inadequate sanitation, waste removal and water supply; lack of public open space; and poorly laid out and maintained streets. The flow of immigrants into the American cities was the lifeblood of capitalist expansion and: 'the concentration of immigrants in cities also tended to push up land values, stimulate the construction industry, and increase the value of private real estate holdings' (Fogelsong, 1986, p. 61). The resulting conditions triggered responses by state officals and charitable organizations which Foglesong (1986, p. 57) argues were a product of capital's need to maintain social control and some semblance of legitimacy for the system of production. Boyer (1983, p. 31) concludes that: 'Supervised play areas, friendly visitors, charity organization societies, settlement houses and tenement regulations were tactics designed to create a disciplined urban society. A discontinuous series of discourses, professional knowledge, institutions, architectural forms and legal regulations reached out to reorder the space of the American city.'

The problem of legitimacy was salient. However what is striking in all these cases is the variety of political and economic interests ranged behind increased state action for the design, reconstruction, management and regulation of cities and towns. The people who are now regarded as the founders of modern urban planning were not professionals but religious philanthopists, social reformers, political campaigners, state functionaries, industrial entrepreneurs and great landowners.

Socialism under the tutelage of Marx had embraced economic planning and inspired a fundamental critique of the causes of urban degradation. But the prospect of revolutionary seizure of power in Europe had receded by the 1880s and political change through trade unionism and democratic control of the state looked a more likely possibility. Even Engels was unsure (by 1884) about how the transition to socialism would be accomplished (Engels, [1884] 1962, p. 322).

Among British reformers Ebenezer Howard put forward the most comprehensive and radical solution to the urban problem. Howard figures centrally in histories of urban planning and his work poses something of a problem, for it was both revolutionary and popular with the middle classes. His solution was not based on a comprehensive critique of capitalism and he denied sympathy with communism and socialism, but his proposals for clusters of municipally owned garden cities were nevertheless designed to change the whole basis of capitalist urbanization.

He argued that the overcrowded cities were the product of a system based on 'selfishness' and 'rapacity' (individualism) and predicted that in the coming century 'the social side of our nature', the 'fraternal spirit' (collectivism) would demand increased expression (Howard, 1946, [1902] p. 146). He showed how new settlements built on cheap agricultural land would become increasingly attractive for industry, commerce and residential development. In the existing cities, by contrast, increasing congestion combined with the new opportunities for development outside them, would result in declining property values and rents. Thus by devoting their rising income from rents and land taxes to the provision of public services and welfare, the municipalities of the garden cities would gradually bring about a massive transfer of wealth from the landlord class to their residents (see Reade, 1982a).

The movement for 'garden cities' attracted the support of a variety of capitalist backers. Fishman (1977) thought that these capitalists saw in the movement the opportunity to defuse the threat of insurrection posed by large concentrations of the working class. However, Sutcliffe (1981, p. 65) points to a more prosaic, financial motive: increasing urban land rents and the corresponding declining popularity of the landowners who, following the agricultural depression at the end of the nineteenth century in Britain, were looking to their urban estates for 'financial salvation'. It must be remembered that, at the time, owner occupation was exceptional among the middle class. The interests of landowners were by no means congruent with those of industrial capitalists. Furthermore it is easy to see that the idea of developing new cities on cheap land is one that would appeal to private entrepreneurs with access to sufficient capital. The garden city form itself did not necessarily entail collective ownership and redistribution of wealth. Rather, it foreshadowed the inevitable private suburban expansion into the peripheral countryside made possible by new modes of transport.

The first garden city experiment at Letchworth in Hertfordshire employed private capital and was organized by businessmen in the interests of stockholders. But as a capitalist venture it was not a success. Much more successful was the 'garden suburb' founded by Henrietta Barnett at Hampstead in North-West London. Hampstead Garden Suburb was also financed by private capital, although with widespread ownership and control via co-partnership companies, and with special legislative support (the Act of 1906). The success of the suburb provided valuable support for those who preferred the 'gradual improvement of existing cities through planned extensions, but without massive construction of public housing' (Sutcliffe, 1981, p. 76).

Some of Howard's ideas about land reform can be traced to American sources: Edward Bellamy's plans for Boston and Henry George's land taxation proposals as well as Howard's own experience in the United States. His idea of the garden city recrossed the Atlantic. The Garden Cities Association of America was founded in 1906. But municipalization and redistribution of the unearned increment did not take root there any more than it did in Britain.

The growing movement in America at the turn of the century was looking to an older European tradition. The 'city beautiful' movement originated from small town, village and civic improvement, a 'pattern of activity sustained by thousands of civic groups across the nation' (Peterson, 1983, p. 53). It became a movement of professionals in alliance with 'progressive' businessmen and politicians, who saw in civic design a way of promoting tourism and investment and of inspiring respect for authority in the citizens of the overcrowded cities. The Chicago World's Fair of 1893 provided the occasion for architects, artists and businessmen to demonstrate, in their 'white city', the order and beauty which actual American cities lacked. The city beautiful movement recalls the earlier city building of the civic designers and businessmen of Victorian England (see Briggs, 1963). But whereas the works of the latter were mainly confined to city centres, with a few exceptions such as Cadbury's Bournville and Lever's Port Sunlight, the city beautiful movement extended to the planning of whole cities: Washington, Cleveland, San Francisco and Chicago. Because these designs depended upon local political will and voluntary compliance, both of which were in short supply, their implementation was very limited. For the most perfect example of the implementation of city beautiful planning we must look not to America but to Australia, where the capital, Canberra, was designed by an American architect and constructed under the direction of an authority modelled on Washington's National Capital Planning Commission but with powers comparable with those of a British new town development corporation. Thus the authority, which still exists, is called the National Capital *Development* Commission.

The idea of a city planning commission originated in America with the appointment of groups of arts professionals to advise on city design. It was an early administrative expression of the principle that a source of authority is needed to cope with the long-term problems entrenched in the concrete form of the city by the process of capitalist urbanization. Depoliticizing urban planning was necessary if longer-term and wider interests were to prevail over the short-term interests of landowners, developers and speculators without changing the economic system and power structure. Awareness of this longer-term interest grew more widespread with the campaign for planning, which drew active support from many different quarters. Foglesong (1986, pp. 177, 178) makes the interesting point (against orthodox Marxists) that the reduction of urban population congestion through judicious planning for suburban expansion served the interests of both workers and industrialists against owners of and speculators in peripheral land. Further, even landed interests were divided between those who might benefit from the protection of existing land values by zoning and those who saw planning as a threat to speculative profits. Thus 'the attack on congestion had at least potentially, a multi-class basis' (Foglesong, 1986, p. 178). But it was politically disadvantageous to define the problem around the interests of workers, and American reformers such as Benjamin Marsh who tried to do so faced immense opposition.

The aesthetic approach of the 'city beautiful' gave way to an approach that viewed the city as a socio-economic system: the 'city practical' (Moody, 1919) or 'city scientific' (Ford, 1913). The transition from 'city beautiful' to 'city practical' planning in America is a crucial one. A variety of interests converged in harmony with a nexus of ideas. In extending the idea of planning to the whole city, the limitations of the aesthetic approach rapidly became clear even to its exponents. Many participants in the Chicago conference on urban planning in 1909 spoke out against such an approach, arguing instead for the adoption of the German technique of zoning, for more economical and efficient organization of land use and transportation and for the relief of congestion by planned urban expansion. At the same time the application of engineering and science to the solution of urban problems was gaining ground, drawing on Taylor's social engineering concept of 'scientific management' and, later, Geddes's passionate advocacy of the application of science and social survey in order to understand how the city 'works' (see Meller, 1980). Geddes was a biologist, but his science was shaped in the mechanistic mould of the nineteenth century. The city was ultimately observable by the detached scientist and, at least statistically, predictable.

Ranged behind 'city practical' planning were property interests anxious to protect the value of developed land against encroachment by undesirable uses, industrialists seeking more efficient transport and means of communication and exchange for commercial enterprises, and those who still saw the overcrowded cities as a threat to the civil order. Both Boyer (1983) and Foglesong (1986) quote extensively from writings of this period and, to gain a more vivid picture of what was being said, it is worth repeating two such quotations:

If the task of planning is approached scientifically, carefully analyzing local conditions and ranking needed actions in terms of their urgency, one soon discovered that in almost every case there is one and only one, logical, convincing solution of the problems involved (Ford, G. B., 1913, quoted in Foglesong, 1986, p. 213).

City planning treats the city as a unit, as an organic whole . . . [it] anticipates the future with the foresightedness of an army commander so as to secure the orderly, harmonious and symmetrical development of the community . . . [it] makes provision for people as well as industry . . . [and it] involves a new vision of the city. It means a city built by experts, in architecture, landscape gardening, in engineering and in housing, by students of health, transportation, sanitation, water, gas, and electricity, by a new type of municipal officers who visualize the complex life of a million people (Howe F. C., 1913, quoted in Boyer, 1983, p. 78).

In America housing reformers, disillusioned by the dominance of city planning by business interests, separated themselves from the planning movement. In Britain the housing improvement lobby moved closer to 'town planning.' The main mouthpiece of housing reform, the National Housing Reform Council changed its name to the National Housing and Town Planning Council. But the working class arm of the housing movement also separated itself from the town planners, allying itself with the newly formed Labour Party in pressing for direct subsidies for housing (Sutcliffe, 1981, p. 81).

Institutionally it also became clear that the authority of the state was needed for planning to be effective. In America the independent city planning commission was an intermediate step towards governmental involvement. Boyer (1983, p. 128) comments that the commission 'evolved as an organisation distinct from administrative departments, acting as a check against governmental abuses, in a position to give both expert endorsement where warranted to city authorities and promotional support behind recommended petitions . . . It lay between city authorities on the one hand and the public on the other, between expert and normative service and the capitalist logic of productivity and profitability' (Boyer, 1983, p. 128). The commission was not a responsive democratic institution; rather it constituted a separate professional voice between local government and public pressure groups. These commissions were more effective in making and publicizing plans than in putting them into effect for, as Foglesong (1986, p. 226) observes, 'local officials were reluctant to grant broad powers to plan commissions or give much heed to planning that remained outside their control.'

Planning could not remain permanently detached from the purposes of the state. In Britain semi-autonomous professionally based 'corporations' were used (from 1946) for the construction of new towns.

But these were instruments of central government policy. The normal regulation of urban development was gradually acquired by local government from 1901 onwards through a series of Acts. Planning powers were firmly entrenched at municipal level by the 1947 Town and Country Planning Act. In America also land-use control became a function of municipalities and other Federal and State government agencies, bringing with it a variety of new functions and responsibilities. 'Urban renewal, neighbourhood community development, section 8 housing, business loan, environmental permit, and a range of other governmental programs required administrators trained in the technicalities of implementation. Individuals were needed for assessment and monitoring. Planners returned to implementation, but now as technocrats rather than designers' (Beauregard, 1986, p. 174).

Healey (1985) has argued that in Britain the municipal absorption of urban planning and the vastly increased demand for planners created by the Town and Country Planning Acts had a profound effect on the development of the profession. Whereas, in the early years, the interest in town planning had been shared among a number of professions, the creation of a large body of people in local government whose first and only professional training was in town planning greatly added to the pressure on the Town Planning Institute to think of itself as a single professional body. This had a number of consequences:

> It has encouraged the idea of the 'generalist' planner who possessed all the expertise necessary for local planning authority work, rather than recognising the need for a mixture of specialists. It has reduced the capacity for client-sensitivity, since clients' needs and values were channelled through the local government machinery of representative democracy and the accountability of officials. (Healey, 1985, pp. 502–3).

Boyer (1983, p. 127) comments in similar vein on the effect of municipalised planning in America: 'Expanding the role of the technical expert within municipal administrations meant concomitantly producing a depoliticized public, shut off from understanding the technical and organisational necessities of an urban society.'

Planning and professional public administration

The rise of technical expertise in public administration coincided with, and was no doubt greatly assisted by, the rise of the idea after the Second World War that governments should plan policies and programmes. Various factors converged to advance this idea.

The Depression had administered a severe shock to the conventional faith in the self-regulating and self-adjusting market. The Fascist and Communist nations had demonstrated what immense power could be forged through state planning. The Second World War had brought with it both the need to plan the war effort and the need to promise the fighting populations something better than a return to prewar conditions (see Partridge, 1941, p. 236).

The movement towards academic integration of the social sciences in the interests of policy analysis and planning had made progress in America in the 1920s and 1930s under the leadership of scholars such as Merriam, Barnes, Lynd and Lasswell. C. E. Rothwell, introducing a collection of essays edited by Lerner and Lasswell (1951), was able to claim that, despite their methodological disagreements:

> Social scientists are in accord that the problems of human relations can be made to yield to inquiry guided by scientific standards. They agree further that as the regularities of human behaviour become more apparent, the possibilities of reliable social planning on a local or global scale become greater. Planning suggests a systematic attempt to shape the future. When such planning becomes a prelude to action, it is policy-making. For policy, broadly speaking, is a body of principle to guide action. The application of policy is a calculated choice – a decision to pursue specific goals by doing specific things.

In Britain the notion of social and economic planning was promoted by a chorus of voices who formulated a persuasive ideological basis for planning (Mannheim, 1940; Cole, 1935; Wootton, 1934, 1945; Zweig, 1942). Leading political theorists of the 1940s framed their arguments in terms which suggested an acceptance that, in future, capitalism would yield to some form of 'planned society' (Mannheim, 1940; Schumpeter, 1943; Hayek, 1944).

Urban planning was swept forward by this current of thought but without being prepared for the tasks set for it or the dilemmas posed. Hebbert (1983) has described the dismay with which social scientists in Britain observed how unprepared urban planning professionals were to face the social, economic and political consequences of the passing of legislation (in 1947) which provided all the powers over urbanization demanded by the planning movement. The undertaking of urban planning in the form of applied *social* science immediately brings to light the dilemma with which political theorists have grappled for three centuries (at least). That is the contradiction between social decision-making, which is the basis of rational planning, and individualistic decision-making, which forms the basis of the politics of market society. Different political theorists have sought to resolve this contradiction in different ways, and it is the purpose of this book to explore some of them.

As urban planning became absorbed into administrative systems so also its theory converged with that of rational public administration. Planners became familiar with techniques of policy-making, evaluation and management: cost–benefit analysis, corporate planning, programme budgeting and management by objective (Hambleton, 1978). Other perspectives have depicted the planner as engaged in 'strategic choice' (Friend and Jessop, 1969), construction and manipulation of networks of influence (Friend, Power and Yewlett, 1974) or, most recently, a type of 'strategic planning' which adapts the experience of planning in the corporate sector for use by government agencies (see Bryson and Roering, 1987). But the dilemma remains. The deployment of managerial technique in the 1960s and 1970s did not isolate the planner from controversy. Resistance to planning came from those who had to suffer the cost of decisions arrived at 'rationally' and from those who felt themselves powerless in the face of centrally directed social planning by the state. They were supported by a number of writers who attacked the means–end rationality of planning methods and urged local mobilization for social action (Alinsky, 1946, 1971; Goodman, 1972). A people's organization, wrote Alinsky in 1946 (1969 edn, p. 135):

> lives in a world of hard reality. It lives in the midst of smashing forces, clashing struggles, sweeping cross-currents, ripping passions, conflict, confusion, seeming chaos, the hot and the cold, the squalor and the drama which people prosaically refer to as life and students describe as 'society'.

In such a hard world the rationality of efficiency, satisfaction maximization, indifference curves and marginal trade-offs is not appreciated by the losers in political decisions. The techniques of policy analysis, in focusing on optimal end results of distributions of value, failed to take account of the process of deciding and resolving conflicts. Tribe (1972) wrote:

> if an agency asks 'where should we build this highway?' the best answer would often be 'don't ask me that; ask me to help you design a procedure for consultation and bargaining to help decide where'.

The public policy movement produced a variety of works arguing for public participation, community consultation and decentralization of decision-making (see, for example, Ministry of Housing and Local Government, 1969; Altshuler, 1970; Warren, 1972; Burke, 1979).

Contemporaneously there developed a literature highly critical of the efforts to introduce 'public participation' (for example: Arnstein, 1969; Dennis, 1970, 1972; NCDP, 1977). These writers argued that the publicly acclaimed goals of public participation concealed a hidden agenda to curtail the power of the leaders of protest and to re-establish the authority of the state.

The dilemma posed by the professionalization of planning was particularly clearly stated by Rittel and Webber (1973). The social professions, they said, had come under attack from lay publics because the cognitive and operational style of the professions, 'mimicking' the style of science and engineering, had not worked to solve the problems they claimed to be able to solve. These were 'wicked problems' whose very definition was the proper subject of political controversy, as were the methods of analysis and the rationales leading to solutions. Marxists trace the source of these wicked problems to the contradictions of capitalism: between the socialized control of urban space (planning) and private ownership of property, and between such socialized control and democracy (e.g. Roweis and Scott, 1981; Harvey, 1985). Whether such contradictions, particularly the last-mentioned, are specific to capitalism is, however, debatable.

Two important consequences have flowed from the political-versus-professional dilemma. First, a great deal of planning theory has been written around what has been called the 'rational paradigm': 'a view of planning based on scientifically inferrable knowledge of the public interest, centrally controlled co-ordination of implementing agencies, and a rational foundation to planning and public management' (Alexander, 1984, p. 62). There can be little doubt of the prevalence of this view in practice, but the theoretical literature has been marked not by consensus over its utility but by controversy. In fact, many of the key texts set up the rational paradigm only to dispute it. Several writers have announced its dissolution and supersedence (e.g. Beauregard, 1980; Alexander, 1984), but was 'rationality' really ever a 'paradigm'? Even to speak in the Kuhnian terms of a 'theoretical paradigm' is to suggest that planning is a science. Simon, writing in 1945, argued that it was not rationality but its limits that posed the theoretical and practical challenge for the science of public administration (Simon, [1945] 1976, p. 240).

Secondly, the contrast between the political and the technical or professional dimensions of the role of the planner has repeatedly emerged from studies of American practice (Dyckman, 1961; Rabinowitz, 1969; Vasu, 1979; Howe, 1980; Shirvani, 1985). The situation in Britain seems somewhat different, although observers have often noted the political nature of planning practice (Simmie, 1974; Elkin, 1974; Blowers, 1980; Reade, 1982a; Cherry, 1982). In Britain the technical–professional dimension has been dominant. A recent survey of the attitudes to planning education of chief planning officers revealed a strong emphasis on knowledge of the techniques of development control, design and managerial skills (Collins, 1985). Some comments of planners surveyed by Collins showed an appreciation of the political dimension of planning practice but in terms of practical skills rather than theoretical knowledge, skills learned on the job and 'good political nous'. A rather similar conclusion was reached by Shirvani (1985, p. 493) in a survey of American planners. Of the participants, a small sample of senior planners from different places and situations, he writes: 'these planners have become political animals; they know how to try to expand their roles, yet they recognise the built-in limitations they face. They have learned through experience how to be of influence.' Howe (1980), in a national sample survey of 614 members of the American Planning Association, also found the political and technical dimensions of planning practice, which she describes in the following terms. Planners who favoured the political role thought that:

> planners should be open participants in the planning process, allowing their values to influence their work and openly advo-cating particular positions. They wanted planning to be placed in the governmental structure so that it would be involved in controversies related to planning. They also thought that planners should organize and use support groups, should try to neutralize opposition to their plans, and should actively lobby to defeat proposals they thought were bad.

Technically oriented planners, on the other hand thought that:

> planners should be objective, both in the sense of keeping their policy views to themselves, and in the sense that their primary source of effectiveness is based on their reputation for doing objective and accurate analysis. They believed that planning is rational and should be long-range, and that planners should be trained to develop technically correct solutions to planning problems. In terms of implementation, they thought that plans should stand or fall on their technical quality and internal logic, and that the planner should try to influence decisions primarily by disseminating and facilitating the use of technical information (Howe, 1980, p. 400).

Howe found, however, that the two dimensions, political and tech-nical, could not be represented as poles of a single continuum, for by far the largest group of planners (51 per cent) fell in the 'high political' as well as the 'high technical' brackets. She concludes that 'the choice of a role should not be thought of as a choice between two conflicting ideologies of planning. Rather there are several dimensions of role which can be used separately or in combination, depending on a planner's personality, skills and the contingencies of the work setting' (Howe, 1980, p. 408).

In the history of urban planning, then, various forms of professionalism have been closely intertwined with political decision-making. We have seen that modern urban planning became established because people with different purposes, some of whom were professionals, struggled to initiate and institutionalize it. Subsequently, planning became absorbed into government as an activity of public administration, offering to the practitioner participation in a contradictory mixture of professional and political decision making. The form planning has taken in different countries has been shaped both by the nature of the political struggle to implement it and the limitations under which this struggle has been waged: limitations of the power, interest and knowledge of the participants, and of the rule structures and social norms already established. In order to clarify the relationship between professionalism and politics we need now to consider the nature of these two dimensions of the planner's role in more abstract and general terms.

Professionalism and politics

Planning practice today includes a wide range of tasks. In the 1960s Dennis O'Harrow, Director of the American Society of Planning Officials and campaigner on behalf of planning in America, said that the *single* most important planning task was the administration of land-use control ordinances (Berger, 1981, p. 291). The power to regulate development is still the primary implementation tool and bargaining chip of the professional planner in both America and Britain, but there is a wide range of activities connected with preparing for the use of this tool and playing the game in which it is used. These activities include drawing up sets of policies for the longer-range future of all sorts of sites, localities and territories, undertaking the necessary research to justify these policies, promoting development, particularly employment-producing development, making sure that day-to-day controls reflect long-range plans, and negotiating with residents, developers and other consumers of policy on implementation. Much of the work may involve negotiation with other government agencies at the same or at a different jurisdictional level, and work may also be generated by funding from one level to another and by the need to link land use programmes with capital works budgets (see Shirvani, 1985; Collins, 1985). American observers have noted the great diversity of administrative tasks taken on by planning practitioners (De Neufville, 1983; Checkoway, 1983). On the British scene Healey (1985, p. 501) has pointed out that the economic recession has produced new tasks for land use and development management: 'Despite political rhetoric, no government can dismantle the planning system without devising an alternative mechanism to manage the coordination of spatial externality effects and the mediation of conflicts over land use change and development'. The claim of urban planning is to be able to define and solve or avert urban problems by means of the application of specialist technical knowledge: the problem-solving stance of the professional.

But what constitutes professionalism? Sociologists have tried to construct models of professionalism. Some have drawn up lists of traits of a typical profession (Carr-Saunders and Wilson, 1933; Cogan, 1953; Greenwood, 1965; Elliott, 1972). Others have tried to isolate key factors in the development of forms of professionalism in different social contexts (Freidson, 1970a, 1970b; Halmos, 1973; Wilding, 1982). The common experience has been that no generalization is able to cover all the relevant phenomena at different periods and in different places. This is certainly the case with urban planning where 'traits' and 'key elements' vary considerably with time and location.

It seems most likely that different sets of traits and different key factors have emerged as particularly salient to the professionalization of different occupations. Occupations differentiate and subdivide as new problem foci emerge and as new groups spring up to vie for and then defend occupational territory. Freidson (1970b), writing with the medical profession in mind, contends that a profession is merely 'an occupation that has assumed a dominant position in a division of labour so that it gains control over the substance of its own work.'

Nevertheless, those who have studied the professions remain convinced that professionalism is a distinctive form of practice. Prest (1987, p. 17) states:

Even if sociologists themselves have largely ceased compiling checklists of traits associated with professionalism, it can be quite useful to bear in mind that, for example, monopoly rights of practice, formalised training and certification, and a corporate ideology have all been identified at various times as key elements in the process of professional formation.

Particularly relevant for our present purpose is the observation that the professions have a distinctive relationship with the state. At some point, most professions have wanted to claim the backing of state sanction for their monopoly. The state, on the other hand, has been willing to hand over a certain domain of decision-making to the profession. Thus 'what produces the privileges of professional status is a profession–state alliance' (Wilding, 1982, p. 17). The profession needs the authority of state sanction, and the state 'needs professions to fulfil the responsibilities which modern governments assume, to legitimate state power, to make available expertise, to deal with the common situations of industrial society'.

Johnson (1972, p. 51) argues that professionalism arises where the tensions in the producer–consumer relationship are mediated by means of an institutional framework based upon occupational authority. This formula does not capture the elusive 'essence' of professionalism more than any other, but it does point to an aspect of professionalism of particular importance for planning. Expertise assumes a role in the wider framework of social control, order and decision-making. It is worth noting here that the political dimension of other professions concerned with social order, such as medicine and education, has been exploored by writers such as Illich (1974) and Laing (1982). The particular form of mediation accomplished by professionalized urban planning is between the producers and the consumers of the built environment; and presumably among different groups or classes of consumers (see Roweis, 1983; Harvey, 1985, for the Marxian version of this 'mediation').

Even though it is clear that planning is, in this wider sense, a political activity, it is in the interests of all concerned to portray it as a technical one. This is not a deliberate deception. Rather, professionalization has been the traditional way of integrating technical knowledge with political decision-making. And, in fact, the tasks of planning can be carried out without recourse to political theory. To imagine that the planner needs Marx, Weber, Bentley or Schumpeter to administer zoning ordinances is plainly absurd. Indeed, on the face of it, political theory may actually be regarded as a hindrance because many political theories cast doubt on the social usefulness of planning by the state.

But such a view rests on a number of incorrect assumptions. The first is that all the rules and tasks associated with urban planning are fixed and unchanging. There is no need for political theory, because this theory throws no light on the implementation of these rules and the carrying out of these tasks. Political theory can be used to reflect on the *nature* of the rules and tasks, what is being done, to whom and by whom, but it is of no immediate use to the actor engaged in a practice. Political theory is comparable to anthropological theories of practice, which as Bourdieu ([1972] 1977) has observed have a timeless quality about them. An action is always seen in a constructed context together with the total sequence of ramifying effects down the line. The actors do not see these effects and the practice would have a different meaning if they did. Political theory is like this. It is a reflection on practice. The intention is precisely to change practices. If the practice of urban planning is unchanging and the intention is to keep it so, then the practitioner has no use for political theory. But if it is changing and new elements are constantly being introduced while others are dropped, if this change is something to be struggled over, and if the direction of change is subject to influence by the actors, then political theory is indispensable. It supplies the means to judge whether a change is for the better or not. The evidence we have reviewed suggests that the rules and tasks of planning are by no means fixed.

The second assumption is that planners have no part in changing planning practice. They merely carry out what is prescribed by others. If planners themselves cannot affect the direction of change of their own practice, then political theory is of purely academic interest. It is true that many planners in the junior echelons of their profession do not have the opportunity to change anything. Their hold on their jobs depends on their doing competently what others expect of them. But this is not so of all planners. Junior planners become senior planners, and senior planners both inside and outside the state have some degree of power. They cannot change the structure of society, but they can choose whether or not to add their weight to movements for change, movements which are no more than many people pushing in the same direction. They can choose to help or hinder other people with power: politicians, business people, trade unionists, community activists. They can join with others to diminish or add to the power of those who have little. The latter became the goal of the Cleveland City Planning Commission in the 1970s (see Krumholz, Cogger and Linner, 1975; Krumholz, 1982). Other planners have taken the initiative with different political and economic ends in view. It should not be thought that inaction is politically neutral, for distributive consequences follow as much from not disturbing the status quo as from disturbing it. Political theory helps in this kind of choice and in understanding the basis of power in society.

A third assumption is that planners' knowledge is politically neutral. Roweis (1983, p. 151) has dealt with this assumption in a paper exploring the mediation role of planning professionals:

> Public policy professionals do much more than 'analyze' and 'solve' problems. They codify phenomena and inter-relationships between phenomena; develop 'languages' through which these can be observed and discussed; assign differential explanatory significances to various events, observations or facts; introduce methods and criteria for judging the plausibility of rival interpretations of situations; influence, as a result, conceptions of what aspects of existing realities can and cannot be changed;

comment, directly or indirectly, on the feasibility, importance, and/or legitimacy of competing political demands and advocacies . . . Once injected into the bloodstream of politics, these knowledges produce effects that go far beyond those we usually associate with 'analysis' and recommendations. These knowledges can aid or obstruct clarity of vision on the part of various political actors; reinforce or put in doubt their preconceptions; trigger or put to rest their concerns and apprehensions, influence the formation of alliances and cleavages amongst them, shape their conceptions of what is feasible and what is desirable.

Even if facts are logically different from values, in practice it is not possible to separate them and even more naive to suppose that value judgements can be kept in the political domain, while facts are the preserve of the professional. We will have more to say about this in the next chapter.

A fourth assumption typically connected with professionalism is that there is a single client to whom the professional acts as adviser or consultant. In a professional relationship, even if some of the decisions about what is 'for the best' are made by the adviser, the client expects (at least) to be better off as a result of the consultation. In planning there is almost always more than one interest at stake. Certainly the political boss can sometimes be regarded as the client, but often this person or committee expects the planner to help decide among conflicting interests. A wider view of the profession suggests that it is precisely the planner's role to attempt to resolve conflicts among different stake-holders in land. The planner is here acting not as an advocate or adviser but as a judge employing not only facts but also political values.

Finally, a possibility suggested by the work of Lindblom and Cohen (1979) is that the distinction between professionalism and politics may have been somewhat exaggerated. The authors examine the relationship between what they call 'professional social inquiry' (PSI) and other forms of 'social problem-solving': the use of markets, voting, bargaining, delegation and all forms of political action, which in this broad sense they term 'social interaction'. Some readers may balk at the reduction of what they see as a power struggle to 'social problem solving'. But it does not greatly alter the validity of Lindblom's and Cohen's argument to include struggle, or simply the deployment of power, among the means by which decisions are arrived at in society. The authors' critique is directed at the positivist view of social science and its use, embodied in the arguments of people such as Ford, Geddes and Rothwell quoted above, and the vision of the 'city scientific', which still apparently holds sway in urban studies journals and among many planning academics to this day.

Lindblom and Cohen suggest that some forms of social problem-solving, which are actually interactive, (that is, political), masquerade as analytical. Thus (in the authors' example) a group of people, having decided to dine together, may delegate the choice of a restaurant to one member. This is a way of arriving at a decision. The person delegated can make a choice impulsively or resort to exhaustive analysis to work out which restaurant to go to. In such a case, the group actually makes the choice interactively by the act of delegation. Likewise, society delegates certain classes of decision to public officials who may often handle these decisions by a process of analysis. Urban planning falls into this category. 'Some people mistakenly assume that the delegation is no more than an assigning of responsibility to specified officials to undertake analytical problem-solving' (Lindblom and Cohen, 1979, p. 23). In practice, urban planning is a disguised form of political decision-making involving delegation to 'expert' officials. This places the planner in a difficult and politically responsible role. Returning to Lindblom's and Cohen's example, the unfortunate person delegated to decide on a restaurant has much apparent power, which is nevertheless circumscribed by the powers (wealth, argumentativeness) and preferences of the other diners. He or she is expected to make a choice that will satisfy the rest. The reader can speculate what will happen if the delegate makes a 'wrong' choice. Planners find themselves in a similar position, being expected to offer decisions that will satisfy a number of contending parties potentially or actually disputing the use of land.

Political theory may but does not always address the needs of the 'delegate' for a basis for choice. Most frequently it reflects on the wider social context in which delegation and the accompanying social analysis occurs. It also postulates alternative means of decision-making. It can suggest to the planner what kinds of decision ought to be handled 'analytically' by 'delegates' and what might be made in other ways, by markets, for example, or through political struggle.

Consider the following activities in which planners are typically involved today: promoting and regulating industrial and commercial development; facilitating the development of public services such as freeways, roads, rail systems, power lines, hospitals and so forth in existing urban areas; redevelopment of existing residential areas; 'slum clearance', 'comprehensive development', 'gentrification'; converting rural land to urban use and, in so doing, placing density controls and other restrictions on the use of land; encouraging public participation in the formulation of public policy; conserving historic buildings and urban areas, and rural and natural landscapes; enforcing compliance with planning regulations.

In these and many other activities planners face political questions. Knowing that other localities are competing for the same job-providing industry, how far should regulations be modified or waived to allow development to proceed? How much time, effort and money should be spent in encouraging development instead of finding out about and dealing with other concerns of citizens? Should the planner wait for the citizens themselves to articulate issues through the formation of pressure groups, or attempt through survey and analysis (or by taking thought) to identify problems for which no vocal pressure group exists? Today almost every major industrial development tends to be regarded as suspect by those who may have to live near it, but in earlier times few people were aware of the insidious and dangerous effects of pollution. Even if resistance is actively organized, behind which group should planners throw their weight? Should they try to be neutral? Or simply do what they are told?

Some issues do not emerge because the people affected typically do not participate in the political process, or because the rules of debate keep certain issues off the political agenda. A special case of the non-vocal population is the future population. Meeting the needs of future generations may mean taking action now, which runs counter to shorter-run existing interests. Environmental and historic conservation is a case in point. Further, existing residents of a peripheral urban area may be extremely active in resisting any development that reduces the value of their property. But people at present living in overcrowded and otherwise unsatisfactory conditions elsewhere in the city will undoubtedly welcome reduced land values and will want schools, health facilities, roads, commercial centres and jobs. These people typically have no voice in the places where land is available. Should the use of the land, then, be determined by the market? Planning was introduced both because the market failed to take account of longer-term issues and the interests of large constituencies (all who have an interest in the efficient functioning of the city), and because many people had insufficient market power to command satisfaction of their needs. It would be convenient if practising planners could either rely on political processes external to their own professional practice or turn to a professional code of ethics to resolve questions such as these. But, for reasons discussed above, planning is itself part and parcel of the political process. The very belief that political questions can be separated out and left to designated people such as politicians and lawyers is itself a political belief. And political questions cannot be resolved by codes of professional ethics because such codes are themselves disputable, as Marcuse (1976) has shown: 'A clear statement of how planners should conduct themselves requires looking beyond professional ethics to the functions the profession serves, the tasks it is assigned. If a given task is harmful, executing it professionally is undesirable.' Beyond professional ethics lie political ethics.

Planners cannot and must not be allowed to avoid taking a measure of personal responsibility for what they do. They need to be able to make choices about their role and, in order to make those choices, they need to be aware of the different ways in which contending schools of political thought view that role.

3 Political theory

We have seen in the last chapter that knowledge and its use is a central issue in planning practice. The positivist view of knowledge, at the core of which stands the assumption of the detached observer, has in the past legitimized the apparent detachment and political neutrality of the professional planner. The idea that 'problems of human relations can be made to yield to inquiry guided by scientific standards' captures the hope that planners would magically absorb and resolve human conflict. In the second half of the twentieth century this hope gradually evaporated, stripping planners of their most fundamental claim to legitimacy, the legitimacy of scientific expertise. Planning today, therefore, has to be justified as a political activity in its own right without the flattering and mystifying veil of 'science'. Political theory is relevant, and indeed essential, to planning as the basis for the legitimacy of its practice.

To say this, of course, does not mean that science is of no use to planners. On the contrary 'planning', more or less by definition, means adapting ideas and concepts developed in the natural sciences for use in the political world. But these ideas and their 'scientific' origin do not by themselves justify planning. Equally, the knowledge of 'political things' is in no way an inferior branch of knowledge to that of natural science. What we have to do is rethink the relationship between science and politics as branches of knowledge. This chapter, then, has two main tasks: first, to argue that political knowledge, while different from scientific knowledge, is not inferior to it and can therefore perform a legitimating function; second, to show how the two branches of knowledge are related. We shall then be able to see more clearly what political theory has to offer the planner.

Urban problems, science and politics

The professional planner is a goal-seeker and problem-solver. In the early days of modern urban planning, social survey, medical biology and government regulation were combined to achieve a goal, public health, and eradicate a problem, water-borne disease. Neither the goal, nor the problem, nor the means to the end seems in hindsight to be in the least debatable: the goal was good, the problem was bad and the means to the end were correct. Whether they were seen to be so at the time need not concern us here, for the whole undertaking proved quite quickly to be a success. But this success was not generalizable. In the case of cholera the problem turned out to involve an external agent, a bacillus, and the cost of inaction was perceived by those with power to be greatly in excess of the cost of action. The greatest difficulty for positivist science arises where the causes of the problem are mainly what people themselves do to one another. Thanks to positivist science, we know what causes pollution of the ambient environment and what its effects are. The problem is to stop people polluting. And pollution is in some ways a straightforward political problem compared with problems like poverty, hunger, inadequate housing, the siting of public facilities, and the conversion of rural to urban land, which urban planners typically have to deal with. In order to describe meaningfully what people do to one another an interpretation must be applied that views some actions as problematic and others not. There has to be a filtering process whereby judgements are made about the criteria to be used in the definition of the problem. Rittel and Webber (1973, p. 161) touched on this difficulty:

> Consider, for example what would be necessary in identifying the nature of the poverty problem. Does poverty mean low income? Yes, in part. But what are the determinants of low income? Is it deficiency of the national and regional economies, or is it deficiencies of cognitive and occupational skills within the labor force? If the latter, the problem statement and the problem 'solution' must encompass the educational process. But, then, where within the educational system does the real problem lie? What then might it mean to improve the education system? Or does the poverty problem reside in deficient physical and mental health? If so, we must add those etiologies to our information package and search inside the health services. Does it include cultural deprivation? spatial dislocation? problems of ego identity? deficient political and social skills? – and so on. If we can formulate the problem by tracing it to some sorts of sources – such that we can say, 'Aha! That's the locus of the difficulty,' i.e. those are the root causes of the differences between the 'is' and the 'ought to be' conditions – then we have thereby also formulated a solution. To find the problem is thus the same thing as finding the solution; the problem can't be defined until the solution has been found.

But, of course, different solutions have different implications for the values, beliefs and interests of people and groups in society. Different people are affected by proposed actions in different ways and they will fight for their values and interests and the problem definition with which these values and interests are connected. They may even turn around and point to the planner and say, 'You are the problem'.

So science does not by itself solve political problems. But, at the same time political theory does something that professionals may find disturbing and that is rather foreign to the professional attitude of mind, something very different from positivist 'science'. It demands self-reflection. Where science offers the safety of an instrument such as a microscope or telescope between the observer (planner) and the observed (planned), political theory hands the planner a mirror. Rather than the city, planners looking into political theory will find themselves and their practice the object of inquiry.

Political theory asks questions like, 'What is planning?' and 'What are we *doing* by planning?' But such questions are uncomfortable to answer. As Miller (1977, p. 329) observes:

> Sound practice needs the clarity of understanding that theory can provide and it cannot take advantage of theory unless it concedes its own insufficiency. Yet the 'what is' questions that reveal this insufficiency are more likely to provoke anger with the questioner than a receptiveness to instruction, given the human tendency to find fault with those who make us aware of our ignorance rather than fault with ourselves.

One way of rejecting the reflective critique offered by political theory is to label it 'opinion'. In our individualist culture one person's opinions are usually held to be as good as another's. The question then is whether political theory can provide the planner with something better than opinion. In giving political knowledge the status of *theory* we are saying that it can. Political theory does more than provide an opinion, it claims to give access to *truth*.

Knowledge and values

In order to consider how political theory can be 'true' we need to consider the relationship between knowledge and values: 'being right' and 'doing good'. In order to take political action we need to believe that what we are doing is not just good for *us* but universally good, that is 'right' or 'true'. Hoch (1984a) claims that American planning theories have sought to link 'being right' with 'doing good' by means of a pragmatic theory of society, particularly that articulated by John Dewey.

Dewey felt that truth emerged from a particular kind of conduct. He wrote at the end of his life: 'If I ever get the needed strength, I want to write on *knowing* as the way of behaving in which linguistic artifacts transact business with physical artifacts, tools, implements, apparatus, both kinds being planned for the purpose and rendering *inquiry* of necessity an *experimental* transaction'. (Last letter from Dewey to Arthur Bentley, quoted by Sleeper, 1986, p. 16). In Dewey's view rules of inquiry which constitute the basis of true knowledge arise from a certain kind of human practice, a process in which people experiment with and interrogate their environment. Thus the most central condition for the development of true knowledge is the process itself of free inquiry and experiment. This normative position underwrites both scientific and political theory.

Dewey was searching for a basis for critique of society that would give political theory the same theoretical status as science which dealt with 'facts' about things. Mills (1966, p. 399) quotes Hans Reichenbach:

What he intends . . . is establishing the sphere of values, of human desires and aims, on the same basis and in an analogous form as the system of knowledge [science]. If concrete things as immediately experienced are the truly real world, if the scientific thing is nothing but an auxiliary logical construction for better handling of real things, then ethical and esthetical valuations are real properties of things as well as purely cognitive properties, and it is erroneous to separate valuations as subjective from cognitive properties as objective.

As Mills points out, this is a Socratic undertaking. Aristotle takes a comparable position, separating the art of persuasive speech in the *Rhetoric* from the theory of the regime – how we should be governed – which he deals with in the *Politics*. The *Politics* seeks to establish the truth and not just opinion on matters of justice, happiness and the public good. It makes a claim to be regarded as theory, involving a different sort of practice from the cut and thrust of everyday politics, a reflective and critical practice capable of detaching itself from daily conflict and observing it. Miller (1977, p. 316) writes of this practice: 'As inquiry inspired by the love of truth, it searches for answers to the primary political questions that can withstand the test of criticism'.

Dewey thought he had found in his own society the kind of practice from which such theoretical critique might spring. The characters who engage in this practice are his modern equivalent of Socrates: teachers and school administrators, scientists in laboratories, 'men in occupations in which they contact nature and handle tools e.g. farmers and hunters', professionals but 'not so much those who handle paper e.g. lawyers, as those who handle things, perhaps technically skilled groups, e.g. doctors' (Mills, 1966, p. 392).

Of course, this sort of practice can be criticized. The loss of faith in positivist science as noted above has produced a loss of faith in professional inquiry of the sort Dewey admired. Hoch (1984a, p. 341) berates Dewey for refusing to permit his politics to engage with the specifics of political debate. It can hardly be said that Dewey failed to take part in political debates. But it is true that he did not regard political practice as coterminous with political reflection. In fact, he wanted to maintain a certain philosophical distance between 'rhetoric' (in the Aristotelian sense) and 'politics'. Miller (1977, p. 329) suggests that the step from debate (or, in class terms, struggle) to politics might involve Socratic dialectic, building a picture of a political 'object' (justice, the state, planning) through criticism: 'Any particular view of the object will be perspectival and partial, so the visible form in its wholeness must somehow be perceived noetically, within and through perspectives.'

The question remains, however, whether the conditions for critique really exist within the confines of a single culture. Several planning theorists in the United States have confronted the implications of the critique of positivism. De Neufville (1987), for instance, proposes phenomenology as the basis for reconnecting knowledge and action, and there is a good practical message in what she says: understand the interpretations of the world through which actors make use of knowledge; find out what knowledge actors use and need in the pursuit of these interpretations. But her hope that phenomenology will provide a strategy 'to guard against framing issues in terms of largely personal values or values implicit in pre-existing social and political structures' is surely ill-conceived.

Habermas ([1968] 1978, pp. 306–7) has warned that phenomenology merely seeks to reconstitute value neutrality by claiming that the study of interpretations frees the observer from interest or partiality. In recommending 'community dialogue over definitions of reality' as a 'practical check against bias', De Neufville wishes to bring phenomenology to the service of pluralism much as Dewey brought in science for that purpose. Pluralism implies acceptance that the process of political conflict, as currently constituted in the present regime, can accomplish the task of social improvement and progress. But improvement for whom? Progress to what purpose? The phenomenologist's lack of 'bias' prevents an answer to these questions from emerging, except in purely subjective terms, just as surely as the scientist's. Yet these very processes of conflict, in this society, constituting this particular range of perspectives may be faulty and, indeed, may produce the observed problems.

Clark and Dear (1984), drawing on Edelman's work (1977), follow the Aristotelian strategy of radically separating rhetoric and political philosophy. Of course, there can be no doubt that political actors employ language (whole networks of concepts) for their own interests, particularly as these underwrite their status and legitimacy. But these authors' own political philosophy is not simply reflective in intent but active. They seek to reconstrue the terms of political discourse, to advance a different (Marxist) political language out of which they develop a radical state-centred programme of political action. Characteristically they refer to Wittgenstein's *early* view of language as a cage, forgetting his later conception of language as a tool. Rodgers (1987, p. 10) provides a contrasting view to that which regards political language as simply legitimating the state apparatus. He argues:

> When we dismiss the verbal guff of politics as 'mere rhetoric', a veil drawn over the hidden games of politics, we are clearly on to an important truth. But clearly political words do more than mystify; they inspire, persuade, enrage, mobilize. With words minds are changed, votes acquired, enemies labeled, alliances secured, unpopular programs made palatable, the status quo suddenly unveiled as unjust and intolerable.

The claim to 'truth' cannot be based on a clear demarcation between political rhetoric and philosophical reflection. Political philosophers have their active agendas and rhetoric is by no means always directed at short-term and ignoble ends. How then is political 'truth' possible?

Habermas finds the basis of political truth in the historical tendency in modern society towards emancipation of the individual, which is immanent in human praxis as he interprets it, a praxis that includes both the material transformation of nature (work) and the communicative work of speech and language whereby we define, reproduce and transform our relations with one another.

Although Hoch (1984a) criticises Dewey for failing to take account of the role of the power structure, 'state bureaucracies, political parties, corporations, trade unions', today's radical pragmatists (Forester, 1980; Hoch, 1984a, 1984b) are in the Dewey mould of American radical liberalism. They look to the practice of the self-aware planner much as Dewey looked to the teacher and scientist as the basis of progress and emancipation. Dewey also sought a political theory, a 'politics' in the Aristotelian sense from which to mount a critique of society, a politics moreover which had a profound effect on American society right up until the late 1970s. 'Nowhere in the world', wrote Dewey and Tufts ([1908] 1932, pp. 387–8), 'are those institutions which in fact operate equally to secure the full development of each individual and assure to all individuals a share in both the values they contribute and those they receive'. He believed that pluralist democracy in fact supplied an 'experimental' politics with the power to transform itself. We are entitled to ask, however, whether it is ever possible, through a particular political praxis, to see fully the conditions imposed on it by the culture in which it is embedded.

Here we are surely up against the limits of communicative practice as a means for approaching truth. We can perhaps extend the limits somewhat by allowing ideas that have arisen in other cultural contexts to play critically on those of our own culture, but we cannot abolish the limits. Nevertheless, critical pragmatism offers a way of understanding political theory that restores to it a status comparable with that of science, yet enables theory – the practice of observation – to be reconnected with action. In this respect it is suggested that Wittgenstein's later philosophy can be helpful in resolving some of the difficulties inherent in the search for political truth.

A critical pragmatic view of political knowledge

Political knowledge, which generates concepts such as 'the state', 'public policy' and 'planning', includes an object domain of facts, systems, processes and mechanisms that make a claim to existence in the external world, and a subject domain of values, decisions and judgements. These domains work together to produce knowledge. The philosophy of pragmatism reconceptualizes the relationship between subject and object domains by arguing that, although science and politics differ as activities, as realms of discourse or 'language regions', they do not differ fundamentally in the way they generate knowledge. Here pragmatism draws on the work of 'ordinary language' philosophers such as Searle, Austin and Ryle, and the later Wittgenstein (e.g. 1968) after he had disavowed logical positivism.

We shall look first at the question of how values work within and between the two branches of knowledge called 'science' and 'politics'. We shall then touch on the question of levels of knowledge (structure), before returning to the central thesis of pragmatism: that knowledge stems from action.

Central to positivism is the preconception that science deals with facts and politics deals with values. Facts are external, objective and verifiable; values are internal, subjective and inaccessible to analysis. Planners will be familiar with statements like 'our analysis suggests such and such options, but the choice must be a political decision', or, usually dismissively, 'that is a value judgement'. The question remains, however, what is the basis of a good political decision or judgement?

It has been repeatedly stressed by positivist sociologists that the criteria of validity of scientific theories are logically independent of moral or political commitments and that such commitments cannot be established solely by reference to scientific knowledge (see Keat, 1981,

p. 38). But 'moral and political commitments' are not the only sort of values. 'Criteria of validity' are also values. They indicate which conduct is best. Values enter into all choices made by human beings, including the choices involved in the practice of science. Polanyi (1958, ch.6) is particularly insistent that science is guided by passions every bit as much as by politics.

Values enter into science in various interrelated ways. Criteria such as accuracy, consistency, scope, simplicity and fruitfulness (Kuhn, 1977) are applied in the conduct of experiments and theory building. Some pragmatists argue that the noun 'value' is misleading and that it is more helpful to think of 'valuing' as a verb (see Neale, 1982). People value accurate, impartial experiments and logical, consistent theories by repeating the experiments, publishing books and papers; sometimes by praising and rewarding the scientists who engage in this behaviour but more often by talking about, writing about and criticizing their work and using it for practical purposes. But values are also anticipations of the reactions of others to the self, anticipations that have become fully internalized as belonging to and emotionally attached to the self ('What will they think of me if . . . ?'). These internalized values provide guidance for the construction of interpretive schemes that make sense of the world and, in turn, provide the direction of questioning and experiment, the strategy to be used in the interrogation of nature. Philosophers of science then codify these values as the criteria of scientific practice. In doing so, they have revealed quite fundamental disagreements on criteria (see Harré, 1972).

Moreover, linked to these criteria is a whole range of more or less tacit values (of communities of scientists) relating to what is significant and worth exploring and what is not. Polanyi (1985, p. 138) writes:

> It is the normal practice of scientists to ignore evidence which appears incompatible with the accepted system of scientific knowlege, in the hope that it will prove false or irrelevant. The wise neglect of such evidence prevents scientific laboratories from being plunged forever into a turmoil of incoherent and futile efforts to verify false allegations.

Or, as Popper might say, to falsify assertions alleged to be true. However, while the current system of ideas about how nature works acts as the normal means of focusing attention, science also progresses by insights that cut across and challenge existing systems. These insights are individual intuitions powered by the passionate conviction of the significance of certain events, phenomena or ideas. They may be ignored and fade out entirely, perhaps to be rediscovered years later. Or they may immediately lead to great scientific controversies, which culminate either in the destruction and suppression of their proponent or in fundamental change in the accepted system of ideas.

At a more fundamental level there is the value position that distinguishes *things* and *animals* from *people*. This value position provides the context for debates about 'reification', the tendency to view human relationships as things, separate from and outside human control. The distinction between things and people may seem self-evident but it is none the less a valuation that is crucial to the distinction between science and politics. The whole of natural science is predicated on the long-standing consensus that things and animals exist primarily to serve people and, therefore, have no rights of their own. It is true that in social science this distinction is sometimes legitimately suspended. When social scientists study the behaviour of populations, markets or traffic flows, for example, they treat their object of study as 'thinglike' without wishing to lose sight of its human character. They follow Durkheim's famous dictum: 'Treat social facts as things'. Such reification is often quite fruitful; like the objects of natural science, human behaviour is somewhat predictable, although the fact that people can sometimes change the 'laws' of their own behaviour is easily overlooked. But it is politically dangerous if the distinction between people and things becomes permanently suspended or forgotten: for example, when 'capital' and 'labour' are treated as equivalent 'factors of production', forgetting that labour is people and capital is things.

The power and status of science in the modern world has meant that questions of political validity have been overshadowed by the supposed objectivity of the science of things. Pitkin (1972, p. 236), however, reminds us:

> One must ask what is the measure of 'standards' or of 'objectivity' here. By what measure is science or mathematics found to be 'objective' while ethics or esthetics or politics is 'subjective' or normative? Standards, objectivity, rationality, work differently in different realms of discourse. The fact that we speak differently about art than about physical events is not proof that esthetic discourse is less objective than scientific discourse. On the contrary, we need to look and see how objectivity functions, what it is like, in different realms. Only then will we understand what rationality in ethics looks like, and how it differs from rationality in science.

The value position of human dominance over matter is today very slowly beginning to give way to less anthropocentric values. The worldwide conservation movement, the 'Green' movement, presents a new perspective of the impact of human activity on a finely balanced planetary ecosystem. This vision has a long way to go before it is established as a new consensus, but science itself is moving in the same direction. As the role of the scientist as actor rather than just observer is recognized, as the part played by values and interpretive choices in science is understood and as science develops tools for understanding complex systems as wholes, so the old clear distinction between people and things begins to break down: not, however, by reducing people to things but by elevating things to the status accorded to people. Thus physicists Prigogine (Nobel Laureate) and Stengers (1984, p. 312) conclude: 'We can no longer accept the old *a priori* distinction between scientific and ethical values.'

Traditionally, however, science has dealt with things, while politics, in the sense of political knowledge, has been an inquiry into people, their relationships, what they do to one another and how what they do to the world affects others. The value–laden meaning of human behaviour and relationships, captured in words like freedom and justice, shapes criteria for action and theories of what exists. Political theories are 'descriptive, prescriptive and justificatory'. 'Theories of the state have sought both to explain what the actual state was, and to show either that it was justified or necessary or that it ought to be and could be replaced by something else' (MacPherson, 1977, p. 224). MacPherson says that the theory of the state deals with questions of human nature: 'supposed essentially human purposes and capacities'. But, as he argues later in his paper (p. 230), this is not all that a theory of the state must deal with: 'A grand theory of the state . . . has to take account of the underlying nature of the society in which that state operates.' And 'society', and everything that constitutes it, can be observed and theorized.

The terms 'political science' and 'social science' signal claims that these fields deal not only with values but with facts. The enduring contribution of the positivist tradition in the political field is its striving to establish in that field a degree of objectivity with regard to observed phenomena comparable with that of the natural sciences. But since, as we have argued, values are always present in natural science, so too are they irreducibly present in social and political science. The choice of focus, of concepts, is guided by the values of the inquirer, just as in natural science. For example, when Marx and Engels centred their theory of capitalist society on the concept of class, that choice was predicated on values concerning human freedom and their reaction to the crushed and alienated condition of workers in their time. Because Marx's value position appears most clearly in his earlier works does not mean that he changed his mind about those values in his later work. They simply did not need to be constantly restated. Weber's focus on the rationality of society was likewise shaped by his account of the importance of the bourgeois virtues for progressive social change in Germany (Beetham, [1974] 1985, p. 269–76). Opposing versions of liberal democracy – institutional pluralism and neo-liberalism – are each focused by perspectives that place different normative emphases on the accountable hierarchy and on the market, both structures that are present in the political practice of modern capitalist society.

Turning now to the *structure* of knowledge, we can say that science and politics each has three levels: epistemology, theory and action. Each level has its own type of practice. There is an epistemology of politics, as there is in science, in which debates take place about what counts as truth, what is valid, what is theory, what constitutes agreement, what is the significance of disagreement, what counts as a fact, as a value, in short what counts as knowledge and how it is produced. This level of knowledge arises from contemplating and trying to sum up and classify the practice of theorizing. This latter practice (theory) constitutes a second level in the structure of knowledge in both science and politics: the construction of coherent systems of ideas based consistently upon axioms about the nature of the object of study – in the case of natural science, matter, in the case of politics, humanity. There are definite parallels between axioms in natural science and in political theory: for example, matter viewed as an aggregate of atoms, society viewed as an aggregate of individuals; matter viewed as a time-governed system, society viewed as a historically and geographically situated social system. At the theoretical level concepts from natural science are mapped on to politics (e.g. evolution, natural selection) and vice versa (equilibrium, hierarchy).

The level of theory is the contemplative practice of generalizing and making sense of a third level of knowledge and experience, that of action. In natural science, action typically includes both experiment and material production, which together enable the transformation of the material world. In politics, action includes both experiment and a variety of forms of social interaction in which people vote, buy, sell, debate, make, break or act out rules, conflict, dominate, enforce, make alliances, bargain, reach agreement, and so on. Dewey drew the parallel between an experimental science and experimental politics. Marx and Engels, although also 'pragmatic' in their philosophy, drew a contrasting link between the praxis of production and politics (see Marx and Engels, [1846] 1976, p. 31). For them bourgeois political theories and the whole 'superstructure' of norms, values, rules and institutions of capitalist society arose out of the particular capitalist mode of production. But the relation between praxis and theory cannot be a unidirectional one – theory following from practice. If it were, no realistic account could be given of the origin of Marx's own theory. For Marx's theory did not simply 'arise' from the revolutionary praxis of the proletariat. Neither Marx nor Engels were proletarians and their theory shaped at least as much as was shaped by proletarian consciousness.

Here we come to the central thesis of pragmatism: the claim that activity (action, work, 'praxis') provides the stimulus for the development and refinement of values and the formation of concepts. Values and concepts are part of the tool kit by which we operate on and shape the material world. As Waddington (1977, p. 27) has observed: 'Science involves thinking but does not arise from it; the groundwork of science is observation and experiment.' When people learn science they do not learn it from philosophers of science who tell them what science is and by what rules they should proceed. They learn science by doing things such as looking down microscopes, weighing materials, gathering social data and being told how to look for certain results and how to see things in a particular way. The derivation of criteria in the activity of observation and experiment is the 'pragmatic criterion' of science (Hesse, 1980). Turner (1981, p. 85) commenting on Horkheimer's critical philosophy, observes: 'systematization, quantification and verification in natural science were theoretical results which flowed from the application of science to pragmatic goals', which included the manipulation of both nature and society.

Rubinstein (1981, p. 163) has explored the pragmatic connection between Marx's and Wittgenstein's philosophy:

> Marx believes that language, or 'practical consciousness', arises from the 'necessity' of intercourse with other men. In a similar vein, Wittgenstein insists that linguistic skill, and the intellectual capacities that come with it, is necessarily an outcome of interaction with other human beings.

Different fields of knowledge as well as different levels of knowledge arise from different socially organized practices. Each field and level of knowledge overlaps and interacts with others in complex and varied ways. Wittgenstein's insight was that, in the act of trying to categorize and pin down exactly what these structures of knowledge are, in the act of trying to arrive at transcendental definitions of key concepts such as truth, we run up against paradoxes. These occur because the act of theorizing and categorizing, which is a contemplative activity, is not compatible with the use of language in other ways, for other purposes and in other contexts – in other 'language games'. The word 'game' here neither implies something frivolous nor, necessarily, the sort of competitive exchange associated with game theory. It is simply an analogue for the use of language in human activity.

In *Philosophical Investigations* (para. 18) Wittgenstein uses the image of 'regions' of a city to capture the complex subdivisions in language: 'the specialized technical subdivisions of language such as the symbolism of chemistry or the notation of calculus are "so to speak suburbs of our language", neat, clearly laid out, unmistakably separate. But in the old city, regions will be more difficult to distinguish or delineate precisely' (Pitkin, 1972, p. 140). With the aid of Wittgenstein's student Friedrich Waismann (1965), the ordinary language philosopher Gilbert Ryle (1965, 1966) and the political philosopher Michael Oakeshott (1962), Pitkin develops the idea of language regions to argue three points: that concepts are used differently in different regions, that language regions differ in the way that propositions within them are formulated and related to each other, and that the very nature of truth is different in different regions. Pitkin contrasts the truths of mathematics with the truths of history, politics, poetry, religious discourse and ordinary subjective experience ('I have a headache'). The concept of truth arises from people agreeing on what counts as truth, not just general agreement but agreement among an expert elite, the elite responsible for formulating the practices and procedures of their particular region.

> In mathematics – or at any rate in arithmetic – disputes arise only when someone is in error; there is no such thing as 'each man being entitled to his opinion'. Truth is established deductively, by proof. Contrast this with, say, truths of specific historical fact, where 'in case of dispute, only other witnesses but no third and higher instance can be invoked' (Arendt, 1967, p. 116). Where witnesses disagree, we are forced to adopt the majority account, or to estimate reliability, or to leave the conflict unresolved. Disagreement in political opinion, disagreement among literary critics, disagreement in moral judgement, each will have different significance and possible modes of resolution. (Pitkin, 1972, p. 145).

Thus 'truth' in political theory can be open to dispute without losing its meaning. Truth is, in fact, a product of dispute. The criteria for settling disputes in political theory are partly deductive, arguing from certain axioms about human nature and human society, and partly empirical, based on what theorists see and hear happening around them. The production of truth, as in science, is a social process.

The pragmatic perspective draws attention to this social process and context in which knowledge is produced. Scientists do not create theories by acting on their own in isolation. Rather science is 'an ongoing process of transformation of the fund of existing knowledge which has been built through the work of scientists'

(Bhaskar, [1975] 1978, p. 185). The process of transformation is one of dialogue, sometimes remote, sometimes personal, among members of an international and intergenerational community of scholars. The theoretical paradigm within which scientific work takes place is shaped by the 'social practices of the relevant scientific community' – the scientific 'polis' (Bernstein, 1983, pp. 54,55). There is a growing literature of the sociology of science, which deals with the nature of the scientific community, its practices and its 'tactics of criticism, persuasion and justification' (Kemp, 1977), in short its patterns of social interaction. Science, therefore, also has its politics.

If the production of knowledge is a social process, then choices about what to accept as real and how to act are embedded in a process through which knowledge is generated, appropriated and turned to action. Ideas emerge from the whole activity, the work, the praxis, the very being of their authors. Naturally this 'being' is conditioned by its historical, social and geographical circumstances. The notion of *practice* is that people work with and are influenced by others both immediately and indirectly. People are not isolates but, first and foremost, social. Practices consist of accepted modes of action, rules of conduct and knowledge.

This line of argument, however, could propel us rapidly towards relativism on the one hand and historicism on the other, both leading away from action. Relativism postulates that all ideas emerge from and are conditioned by material practices and historical circumstances and, therefore, they can never provide the means to change those practices because there are no external criteria by which to judge them. Historicism, so often associated with economism, imputes to material practices some mysterious teleological dynamic of their own; people and their ideas are simply swept along or held in place by social or economic 'forces'. Such a conception introduces a kind of social 'ether' to explain change and paralyses human action. Giddens (1979) has pointed out that this was not at all what Marx had in mind and that a more probable explanation of social dynamics is that both social change and social stability are produced by what people themselves do and by what they have done in the past, which *conditions* what they do now. This concept of structuration itself owes something to Wittgenstein's insight that structures of language – rules, criteria, grammar – are a codification of speech.

But we are still left with the possibility of relativism. If values are no more than products of our socially conditioned activity, then how can we lay hold of the value system that provides the lever to 'move the world'? This is the problem which the Frankfurt critical theorists grappled with, and the answer arrived at by Adorno and Marcuse was a bleak one: only through practice that negated and denied the current social reality could such values emerge. But this denial of the social reality also robs the actor of the potent weapon of ideology with which to form the necessary coalitions and alliances and with which to struggle for change. Habermas resolves this paradox by working out criteria based on no particular society but on the principles inherent in the practice through which all political action takes place: communication.

At all events the efficacy of political theory depends ultimately on its capacity to appeal to a 'truth' more general and universal than opinion, preference or 'rhetoric'. Critical pragmatism argues that, through practices, people have the capacity to go beyond the given ideas mediated by their environment. The ideas they produce can sometimes tap something universal. Rochberg-Halton (1986, p. 15) suggests:

> And when we ask the question, truth for whom? the answer in my opinion is that if truth is to retain its meaning, the truths of our particular lives and our particular and localized communities must align themselves with that larger living truth which animates, and is discovered through, the unlimited critical community of all future inquiry.

Universal ideas relating to humanity rather than to any particular part of humanity – which we recognise in art and literature as well as philosophy – have a special power and fascination. This is perhaps because they demonstrate new ways in which we are like one another and associated with one another. Ideas that have this universal property give the illusion of being a 'third world' waiting to be discovered, distinct from that of internal subjective experience or the world of external objects (Popper, 1972). Against Popper, however, we are proposing here that all ideas are produced, not discovered.

No sooner than universal ideas are produced, they are selectively appropriated back into practices. Once ideas, having the commanding quality of universality, are selectively appropriated they become what is usually termed 'ideology': ideas serving specific groups, interests and practices. Here we make a distinction between material human groups and 'interests', which are conceptions of ends and means appropriated by a particular group. Again we make the assumption that ends and means, like choices, are always socially generated. This assumption must, however, be distinguished from the universal norm – also socially generated – that individual choice and autonomy is a supreme good.

We can postulate a continuous social process through which practices generate ideas with universal properties. These ideas are then selectively appropriated by social groups and interests. But ideologies also help to constitute groups and interests so that the structure of a society is always changing as new constitutive ideas are thrown up and appropriated. Ideologies feed back into practices to constitute and reconstitute what people do (see Figure 3.1)

This model is really no more than a restatement of Giddens' (1979, 1984) conception of 'structuration' which links the production of structure with the production of meaning in society. The process it depicts is not 'good' or 'bad', although we may speculate that in some societies – those that tolerate many ideas and many groups – the process may work faster to generate new meanings and structures. The model also begs the question of how to tell universal truths from mere serviceable ideologies. Habermas approaches an answer by grounding truth in the universal human practices of work and communication. But the answer must remain debatable. The point of this book is not to provide an answer – such an undertaking would be far beyond its scope – but to suggest that readers reach their own answer by becoming familiar with political theory. As political subjects how do they, how do *you* want to be treated?

With Giddens, the model acknowledges that human action is conditioned by the circumstances in which it takes place, circumstances created by all prior action in that particular place. So, although recognizing the pressure of 'history', it also gives due weight to political contingency and the absolute importance of practical political action. Gramsci (1971a, p. 365) argues that 'theory' becomes most necessary at the transitional moments of history when the forces of change are mobilized: 'for it is then that the practical forces unleashed really demand justification in order to become more efficient and expansive; and that theoretical programmes multiply in number, and demand in their turn to be realistically justified, to the extent that they prove themselves assimilable into practical movements, thereby making the latter yet more practical and real.'

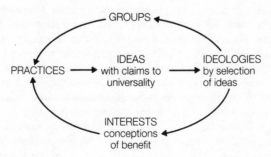

Figure 3.1 Ideas, practices, interests and ideologies

Political theory and the role of the planner

Political knowledge proceeds from the practices of social interaction and feeds back into those practices. The act of reflection that produces 'theory' is itself a form of social practice and can be reflected upon – and so on. Therefore, like natural science, political knowledge comes to have a hierarchical structure: action or praxis, theory, the theory of theorizing, etc. Political theory is the reflection on how a particular society is constituted, reflection powered and focused by the evaluation of how it ought to be constituted. This evaluation focuses attention on what can and cannot, should and should not be changed. Thus political theory indicates not only what is for the best (which may sometimes be embedded implicitly in the theory) but also what is. There can be no final answer to these questions. All that political theory does is extend the field of knowledge that provides the basis for good political judgement on the premiss of intrinsic human equality. But that is no less than what science has done on the premiss of human dominance over things.

Planning is a particular form of political practice, a particular form of what we might generally call governance. And to argue the relevance of political theory for people in governance, we turn to the same ethical premiss that has generated political theory itself, namely that every person is intrinsically of equal worth, that people are ends in themselves and require no justification for their existence or for the development to the maximum of their desires and capacities. From this, it follows that we should treat others as we would have others treat us, and that if what a person does affects another then she/he should act 'for the best', considering both her/his own interest with that of others.

The pursuit of self-interest can only be made consistent with 'acting for the best' by means of political institutions. Some would argue that the free market and pluralist democratic politics are sufficient institutions. If that is true, then planners have no need of political theory. They can simply pursue their own self-interest. But the seeming absurdity of such a proposition suggests that it is not true. Planning should not be defined merely as 'the interests of planners'. If planners are neither purely self-interested actors nor mere technicians obeying the orders of other people who decide things, then they have to consider the impact of their *own* actions on others. And because we do not yet have those institutions that always reconcile the pursuit of self-interest with the public good, the question of institutional failure and redesign remains on the political agenda. The very existence of planning and planners is symptomatic of the need to compensate for institutional failure and to engage in institutional design.

Political theory, particularly as grounded in social theory, is by no means optimistic on that score. The very idea of planning is bound up with a view of society as ultimately subject to human control and steering towards progressive improvement, a view that political theory frequently denies. Nevertheless, while such a gloomy view serves beneficially to remind planners of their own fallibility, it can also lead to cynicism, paralysis, even nihilism. If there is to be political action, that is, conduct endowed with meaning and purpose other than the short-term material gain of the actor, then there must be a sense in which that action can lead to social improvement. Planning is merely a logical extension of that proposition. Political theories provide the values necessary for inquiry and action, and describe and prescribe 'roles' for political actors, who happen in this case to be planners.

Here it must be noted that what planners do is not exhaustively described by the terms 'planning' and 'planner'. In fact, the attempt to define 'planning' has led to just the sort of paradoxical conclusions predicted by Wittgenstein (see, for example, the debate initiated by Wildavsky's provocatively titled paper, 'If planning is everything, maybe it's nothing'; see Wildavsky, 1973; Alexander, 1981, 1982; Reade, 1982b, 1983). We need to look at the social contexts and 'language games' in which 'plans' and 'planning' are used. Healey (1983) suggests they are many. In a later paper (Healey, 1985 p. 500) observes that planning academics, 'having contributed to the final demise of the underpinning ideologies which had sustained many practitioners and provided public support for planning, neglected to reconstruct new justifications for planning tasks and planning expertise.' (Healey, 1985, p. 500). Though not entirely the fault of planning academics, it is true that planners no longer have a clear conception of their role in society.

The concept of *role* links the working of the social order with the characteristics and conduct of the individuals who comprise it. Emmet ([1966] 1975, pp. 13, 14) says that 'a role is a capacity in which someone acts in relation to others, [it suggests] a way of acting in a social situation which takes account of the specific character of the relation'. For example, an early role of the planner, as noted in chapter 2, was that of the professional consultant whose expertise could be relied upon to solve problems, much in the way an architect solves a problem of accommodation for a client. In chapter 1, a variety of political roles was adumbrated and it was suggested that, because of its particular 'range of convenience', assenting political theory had more to say about active political roles than.had dissenting theory.

This is not the place for a lengthy discussion of role theory, but we must touch briefly on one question arising from the earlier discussion of structuration: to what extent can planners or any political actors choose their role or even be aware of the role they are playing? Role theorists do not necessarily regard political actors as mere functions in a social system, enacting set patterns of behaviour. Mead (1934) and Gerth and Mills (1953) connect the development of self-conciousness and individuation with the person's awareness of what he or she is in the eyes of others. Emmet ([1960] 1975, p. 157) observes:

> In 'reflexive' role-taking a person learns to see himself through the attitudes of others and to enter imaginatively into their roles. This may produce a 'What will they say?' kind of conscience; it may also go on to become something more objective – the notion of how one might appear to someone not directly involved in the situation, in fact Adam Smith's 'impartial spectator'. This clearly links up with the notion of Universalizability, the possibility of judging what one ought to do in a given situation by not making an exception in one's own favour to what one would judge anyone else similarly placed ought to do.

Unless we allow some possibility of choice in the matter of role we exclude both the possibility of personal, psychological growth and the participation of individuals in processes of social change, which in turn necessitates the reintroduction of external 'forces' to account for change.

Conclusion

In this chapter we have begun to answer the question 'how is political theory relevant to planning practice?' It was first argued that political knowledge is a necessary complement to science in understanding and approaching solutions to the sorts of practical problems that planners face, problems that involve human relations, power, interests, and values. The philosophy of pragmatism provides a resolution of the conceptual dualism of 'fact' and 'value', in which the latter is reduced to mere opinion. Therefore, political knowledge can provide access to truth and thus legitimacy, although the standards of truth in political theory are not the subject of such widespread consensus as those in science. More specifically, it was argued that political theory provides the basis for good political judgement and a choice of role for planners who wish to pursue ends rather than let their activities be determined by social custom and existing rules. This chapter is, however, only a beginning. In order to sustain the claim that political theory is useful and relevant to planning practice we must now turn to the theory itself.

Part 2

Assenting theory

4 Max Weber and the rational state

If planners have traditionally regarded themselves as outside politics, for the most part they are inside the state. Such is the role of the bureaucrat, a role most clearly and, many would argue, best defined by Max Weber. If politics is viewed as the overt daily struggle of individuals, groups and classes to pursue their legitimate interests, then the bureaucrat is either above politics – offering specialist expertise, continuity and, above all, rationality – or beneath politics, serving and aiding the people's representatives. Yet the bureaucrat is integrated within a structure of domination and authority. In the case of urban planners that structure is the state.

In America, Barr (1972) noted:

> The urban planner and his plans have become increasingly beholden to one master, the government. Either most planners work for the government or they are dependent on it. Far from serving many sectors of our society, planners serve one and are obligated to it. When you serve a particular entity exclusively you begin to assume its identity. Such is the prominence of government in this system that the planning we do is subordinated to and a part of the governing role.

Similar observations have been made by Beckman (1964), advocating the bureaucratic role in the interests of increased legitimacy for the planner (see also Rein, 1969), and by Wirt and Christovich (1984, pp. 99–100), who report on the systemic nature of professional powers 'which pervades the American urban system, whether in towns large or small, rimming or beyond the big city'. Writing of the British planning system, McAuslan (1980, p. 268) comments on a sprawling bureaucracy consisting of 'judges, senior legal practitioners, public servants both central and local, well established professions such as chartered surveyors, land agents and valuers, Ministers and leading local councillors, and planners'. These are people 'who have been appointed to their official positions, or who have arrived at their political or professional eminence because the overwhelming majority of them can be relied upon to maintain and uphold the governmental and societal status quo'. In the view of these writers the democratic state and the bureaucrat planner have a mutually supporting relationship: the former supplying legitimacy for the latter, the latter stability and continuity for the former.

We have described in chapter 2 how the alliance between the state and the planning profession was forged after the Second World War and how urban planning became a function of the state apparatus. We have also seen that the legitimacy of the planner's bureaucratic role hinges on the idea of rational technique. Catanese (1984, p. 59) argues that planners performing an 'apolitical–technical role' will try to perform their functions without invoking their political and social values; the best 'apolitical–technical planners will be quick to experiment with the new technology, especially such approaches as are contained in computer simulation, remote sensing, modelling and information systems'. Rational techniques were absorbed into planning faster in America than in Britain, though Britain may have caught up somewhat since Elkin (1974, p. 156) observed of London's planners 'while it is not clear precisely what talents planners were to have in order to interpret the planning principles, the emphasis would appear to have been on some quality of judgement which would come from experience rather than on technical skills'. This would suggest that competence in technical skills, while an important ingredient of the bureaucratic role, is not essential to it. What is essential is the capacity to exercise rational judgement, which is served by technical skill, experience and the detachment of the professional from day-to-day politics.

Both bureaucracy and rationality in planning have been the subject of constant and massive criticism. We will have more to say about this in later chapters. But in criticizing bureaucracy and rationality, it is easy to lose sight of the fact that, with all its defects, bureaucracy and rational method, not only in the state but in the business world, are an indispensable and characteristic part of modern society. Weber, while perhaps as yet unaware of the practical constraints on rational behaviour, brought out much more clearly than many later writers both the nature of the rationalism of modern society and its fundamental dilemma. In this chapter, we shall consider Weber's conception of rationality and the principal forms of rationalism, concluding with a discussion of the role of the bureaucrat planner in practice.

Rationality, rationalism and politics

The roots of Weber's analysis of society lie in his attempt to understand the nature of social action and the forms of order that make such action possible. 'Action' he understood as any human behaviour to which may be attached some meaning, either the subjective meaning ascribed to the behaviour by the actors themselves or the meaning placed upon it by the theoretical interpretations of an observer. Among the latter are those abstractions from complex actuality that Weber called ideal types. An ideal type is simply a concept or set of concepts that significantly enhances understanding of the object of study. An ideal type sets out to isolate certain key characteristics of the object, sieved out from the myriad of observed phenomena. The strategy of seizing on some dominant characteristic of society via an ideal type allows one to explain society meaningfully without necessarily claiming to have explained the *whole* of society. The sociologist Michael Mann (1986, p. 4) correctly observes that societies are much messier than our theories of them. 'In their more candid moments, systematizers such as Marx and Durkheim admitted this; whereas the greatest sociologist, Weber, devised a methodology (of "ideal types") to cope with messiness.'

Action is 'social' 'in so far as its subjective meaning takes account of the behaviour of others and is thereby oriented in its course' (Weber, [1924] 1968, p. 4). The implication here is of some *shared* meaning and, as we shall see, Weber gave a rather directional slant to 'meaning', so that social action tends to connote shared direction or purpose. Of even greater importance, however, is the implication of mutual influence. Social action encompassed both change and maintenance of the status quo, orientation to the past, present or future. 'Planning' is thus evidently a kind of social action in Weber's terms, one by definition oriented to the future. Planning is by no means a term reserved for action by the state, in fact planning is implicit in the widespread rationalization of modern society. Before dealing with Weber's theory of the state we shall first have to look at the part played by rationality in the meaning of action – the sense or point of action. We shall then examine two aspects of modern rationalism: that of the market (and its socialist counterpart) and that of bureaucracy. Both have to do with rules and shared assumptions about how people are to behave towards one another, which enable them to act in concert and which at the same time embody structures of domination (*Herrschaft*). He saw no way in which social co-operation, the co-ordination of individual activities to achieve a mutually beneficial outcome, could occur without domination.

Weber was, of course, deeply interested in and concerned to explain the historical development of the specific forms of order arising in or from mature capitalist societies, including socialist order. But he also wished to bear in mind the universal conditions of social action in so far as they could be determined from the study of human societies throughout history. Contrary to the more sanguine advocates of centralized collectivism such as Rousseau and Marx, Weber believed that the methods of rational organization and planning that were open to human beings imposed certain limits on future social action irrespective of tradition, culture, mode of production or other determining force. These limitations can be posed as a dilemma between means and ends.

The way people explain, organize, plan and guide action, (in short, behave rationally) was for Weber the key to understanding a society. He wrote in a climate of rationalism at the turn of the nineteenth and twentieth centuries and the analysis of rationality is part of his research apparatus, an *'idée maîtresse'*, as Brubaker (1984, p. 1) puts it, 'that links his empirical and methodological investigations with his political and moral reflections'. Different forms of social life throughout history carried with them different rationales and the task Weber set himself was to specify the particular way in which the industrial capitalism of his time was 'rationalized' in this sense.

Here we need to take account of a distinction crucial to the discussion that follows: Weber's distinction between formal and substantive rationality. The term 'rational' is a way of talking about the meaning we give to action, but it is not the only way. In fact, social action is given meaning in four ways. First, we can say that an action is meaningful if the means adopted result efficiently and effectively in the achievement of specified ends, no matter what the ends might be. This is formal rationality or *Zweckrationalität*. Second, an action may be said to be rational on account of a rationally argued system of ends. Here we are concerned to evaluate the ends themselves without really considering the means. Another way of expressing this is to say that an action is done for its own sake because it is arguably right, regardless of the consequences. This is substantive rationality or *Wertrationalität*. Third, an action may acquire meaning by being oriented to the emotions of the actor – an affectual orientation. And, finally, an action may be meaningful on account of its orientation to tradition 'through the habituation of long practice'.

Although the most significant and frequently drawn contrast is that between formal and substantive rationality, it is important also to note the distinction Weber made between substantive rationality and the affectual and traditional orientations of action. Substantive rationality cannot, in Weber's scheme of things, be reduced to emotions any more than to formal rationality. Substantive rationality is a measured, cognitive and *rational* judgement about ultimate ends, an ethical judgement that is quite separate from judgement on the basis of mere emotional whim or cultural tradition (see Weber, [1924] 1968, p. 25). Weber held that empirical science could never answer questions about what *ought* to be done, though it could reveal the logical connections between ends and means. Science could trace the consequences of an act and the values (which functioned like axioms in science) from which the act must logically be derived, or, conversely, the actions that would have to be taken if a certain end (or value) was to be achieved. This is precisely what the bureaucrat planner is supposed to do for the politician: reveal the logic of political decisions and choices, whether this logic is expressed in terms of the goals towards which day-to-day political acts lead, or in terms of the possible means of achieving political goals. However, action cannot escape from being based on judgement that is, by definition, subjective, so we can appeal to no higher or externally objective standard in order to choose between judgements about ends.

Weber's account of modern society was of a world dominated by formal functional rationality. In this he thought that socialist society, though less efficient, was not substantially different from capitalism (Shils, 1987 p. 557). In such a world, values are not absent but shrunken in stature, individualized and privatized to become no more than personal preferences or tastes. Weber's distinction between formal and substantive rationality reflected his desire to separate facts from values. A formally rational sequence of propositions, if . . . then . . . , could be determined factually. Whereas substantive rationality refers to the goodness or badness of ends or results (Brubaker, 1984, p. 36). In the terms explained in chapter 3, the former represents a different *use* of the term 'rational' from the latter. The Weberian scholar Arnold Brecht (1959, p. 225) explains Weber's position as follows:

> With all his insistence on the limitations of science, Max Weber never ceased personally to *believe* in ultimate values, nor did he ever underrate the importance of such belief for human person-ality and human dignity. He spoke of those aspects with great candour and warmth. We do regard those innermost elements of the personality, those highest and ultimate value judgements that determine our conduct and give meaning and significance to our life, as 'objectively' valuable, he said.

Yet there is a striking contradiction in Weber's thought between his acknowledgement of the need for action to be based on values that are grasped by the actor as objectively *true* and the value relativism towards which his uncompromising separation of fact and value leads: since we cannot judge rationally between ends, any end is as good (or bad) as any other. This contradiction has been much discussed by Weber's critics. Strauss (1953) argued that many of the categories of social science only come into view with the application of values, for, 'social science is necessarily the understanding of society from the point of view of the present' (p. 39). Runciman (1972, p. 38) holds that it does *not* follow that the concepts and hypotheses of the social must necessarily derive from the social scientist's values. But he acknowledges that the accounts which social scientists give of their subject matter are, in a sense, 'discretionary' (Runciman, 1972, p. 79). The view advanced in chapter 3 is that the knowledge of natural science and the knowledge of politics involve different criteria of truth; Weber's puzzlement stems from his failure to see this.

Dahrendorf (1987, p. 578) asks, 'why did Weber find it all but unbearable to live with his distinctions? Could it be that the distinctions are, at the same time, intellectually compelling and impossible to sustain in practice?' According to Marianne Weber (1975, p. 418) his constant struggle to keep separate the discussion of what exists from what ought to be did not follow from his underestimating the question of what ought to be. He said 'it is because I cannot bear it if problems of world shaking importance – in a sense the most exalted problems that can move a human heart – are here changed into a technical economic problem of production and made the subject of scholarly discussion'. In modern industrial society, questions of political and economic morality had simply retreated from the public sphere. Writing in the period leading up to the greatest mutual destruction in human history, Weber was pessimistic about the outlook for rationalism. But it was not Weber whose philosophy pointed towards nihilism and the formally rational solutions and bureaucracies of Hitler and Stalin, it was modern rationalist society (Eden, 1987; Shils, 1987).

Weber's view of rationality imbued his vision of politics. Politics in general was about the struggle for power and the active use of power; in particular, the leadership of a 'political association', the modern form of which was 'the state' (Weber, [1919] 1946, p. 77). He writes 'Politics for us means striving to share power or striving to influence the distribution of power, either among states or among groups within a state' (p. 78). When we say that a matter is decided by politics what is meant is that 'interests in the distribution, maintenance and transfer of power' decide the issue (p. 78). Because politics is the 'play of power' (Lindblom's term) it cannot be a functionally rational business in terms of society as a whole, or in any other terms than those of the particular interests of the participant. Yet interests were not to be interpreted only in the narrow sense of purely material gain. In *Politics as a Vocation* Weber set out his political ethics. Politics must serve a cause. This is the place Weber allocated in modern society for values. He contrasts the ethic of politics with that of the bureaucrat. The bureaucrat will administer his office dispassionately and without bias (*sine ira et studio*). But the politician must take a stand:

> His conduct is subject to quite a different, indeed, exactly the opposite, principle of responsibility from that of the civil servant. The honor of the civil servant is vested in his ability to execute conscientiously the order of the superior authorities, exactly as

if the order agreed with his own conviction. This holds even if the order appears wrong to him and if, despite the civil servant's remonstrances, the authority insists on the order. Without this moral discipline and self-denial, in the highest sense, the whole apparatus would fall to pieces. The honor of the political leader, of the leading statesman, however, lies precisely in an exclusive *personal* responsibility for what he does, a responsibility he cannot and must not reject or transfer (Weber, [1919] 1946, p. 95).

This 'ethic of responsibility' meant being personally responsible for both ends and means. Weber's distinction between facts and values did not allow him to regard the ends as the subject of rational debate. Taking a stand on values was a matter of following one's own particular 'god or demon'. But those who did not do so, who pursued power for its own sake – for 'the prestige feeling that power gives' – Weber regarded as poor politicians both because their personal lives would lack meaning, integrity and 'inner balance', and because they made no contribution to the meaning of life in a given society. Politicians, however, must also take personal responsibility for means. This immediately distinguished the politician from the saint, however noble the cause pursued, because, as Weber observed, 'the decisive means for politics is violence' (Weber, [1919] 1946, p. 121). The only way to attain a given end is by force, however much the means might be legitimized and sublimated. Yet moral ends usually did not include force and often explicitly excluded it. So the good politician must combine the pursuit of a good cause by the only means open to politics with the constant awareness of the immediate consequences of its pursuit. The personal responsibility for both ends and means, for values and the consequences of the power struggle, was a permanent dilemma confronting the politician and defining politics as a vocation. The functional rationality that characterized modern society was, however, embodied in two very different institutions from those of the political struggle: the market and bureaucracy.

Market rationalism

Modern capitalism was based on methods of formal rational calculation that permitted economic action: 'the peaceful use of the actor's control over resources which is rationally oriented, by deliberate planning, to economic ends' (Weber, [1924] 1968, p. 63). Rational economic action necessitated a system of market exchange and monetary calculation. Market exchange represented 'the archetype of all rational social action . . . a coexistence and sequence of rational consociations' (p. 635). Market transactions were formally rational in that people impersonally confronted one another as buyers or sellers of commodities with a view solely to the pursuit of self-interest by the most efficient means. Money was not merely the medium of exchange but also the basis of exact calculation. With the ability to assign money values to goods and services goes the ability accurately to evaluate economic success and to adjust action in the light of present and anticipated outcomes. In Weber's analysis modern industrial capitalism immensely extended monetary calculation into the realm of scientific planning by the organizations operating in the market. Modern industrial capitalism was, however, based not simply on monetary calculation but on 'a technically perfected form of capital accounting' (Brubaker, 1984, p. 12). This involved the comparison of the total value of the assets of an enterprise at the beginning of an accounting period with the value at the end, thus providing an accurate measure of profitability (Weber, [1924] 1968, p. 91). The 'calculability' of capitalism was based upon rigorous factory discipline and the precise control by the owners of all human and non-human means of production; upon a predictable legal system and the immense extension of labour productivity by modern technology (Brubaker, 1984, p. 12).

This formally rational system of impersonal calculation was based on certain substantive conditions that Weber dispassionately exposed. First of all, the market was a formal setting for a struggle among 'at least relatively autonomous' economic units. 'Money prices are the product of conflicts of interest and compromises; . . . they thus result from power constellations' (Weber, [1924] 1968, p. 108). One aspect of this power struggle was over the question of market freedom itself. Weber pointed out that as the market had been extended, the forms of regulation of the market had grown. Urban planning is obviously one such form of regulation. The highest degree of formal rationality embodied in capital accounting demanded the maximum market freedom (that is, autonomy of the participant enterprises in competing in any way they choose and in setting prices). But the development of market capitalism had seen a struggle between those various groups who had gained from the regulation of the market on specific occasions and those whose interests lay in the greatest possible extension and freedom of the market (see Weber, [1924] 1968, pp. 82–5). Modern urban planning is to some extent the product of a compromise between powerful interests in the protection of existing environments, land uses and values and those constituted by the normal capitalist thrust to profit by development and change.

Secondly, the 'free market' in mature capitalism was paralleled by a disciplined workforce organized in hierarchically ordered organizations. The formally rational process of production and exchange required that the means of production – workplace, tools, machinery, sources of power and raw materials – be concentrated in the hands of the entrepreneurial unit (the appropriation by the entrepreneur of the means of production). As a matter of history, Weber, like Marx, pointed out that, from the sixteenth century on, workers were increasingly dispossessed of their means of livelihood and made dependent upon the sale of their labour (Weber, [1924] 1968, p. 137). In this Weber acknowledged the significance of class struggle but, unlike Marx, he argued that this process was also part of a wider movement towards the rationalization and bureaucratization of society, in which individual labour of every kind became subsumed by the collective purpose of autonomous organizations. This movement was conditioned partly by the demands of modern technology and partly by the increased potential for output of imperatively co-ordinated organizations.

Finally, it was not the wants or needs of the people that regulated production by profit-making enterprises but 'effective demand for utilities'. What was to be produced was therefore determined by the preferences for goods and services (structure of marginal utilities) in the income group that had both the inclination and financial resources to purchase a given utility. Should inclination fail it may be guided and 'awakened' by advertising and the like. But it was possible to produce only for those consumers with enough income to make production worth while (Weber, [1924] 1968, p. 93).

Although Weber believed that market rationality was indispensable for the provision of goods and services for mass consumption, he also observed (following Sombart and Sismondi) that the criterion of profitability did not guarantee the optimum use of the available productive resources for the provision of consumers' goods for a population. The more the power struggle taking place in the market was unequal by virtue of the unequal distribution of wealth, the less would the market satisfy the real wants of a population. Indeed, in conditions of gross inequality, the opportunities of the powerless would come to be determined and administered by the powerful much as they would in a planned socialist economy, even though the participants were formally free. The unequal distribution of wealth, and particularly of capital goods, forces the non-owning group to comply with the authority of others in order to obtain any return at all for the utilities they can offer on the market. In a purely capitalist organization of production, this is the fate of the entire working class (Weber, [1924] 1968, pp. 109, 110). Thus, a market was a legally sanctioned expression of the struggle for the means of existence among groups with varying access to power. Money was not only an index of price and the key to formally rational accounting but also an important means by which power was concretized and wielded. So we may speak of groups having differential market power or market position as indicated by their possession of wealth.

For Weber, like Marx, 'property and the lack of property' were the basic categories of social class (Weber, 1946, pp. 181, 182). But Weber's focus of attention was the market (the process of exchange), rather than the production process. Thus it was when people with different powers over material property met in a market that their 'life chances' were determined. The market favoured those who had property and discriminated against those who did not. The non-owners were effectively prevented from competing for highly valued goods. And 'other things being equal, this mode of distribution monopolises the opportunities for profitable deals for all those who, provided with goods, do not necessarily have to exchange them.' (Weber, 1946, p. 181). In the labour market, price wars took place between the propertied classes and those who had only their labour to sell. But these two categories did not exhaust the concept of class. Within these categories there could be as many subdivisions as defined by categories of ownership and control of capital and types of labour.

The conditions supporting the market system were not, according to Weber's moral precepts, substantively rational. Ethical precepts such as justice (in the provision for need), loyalty, compassion, brotherhood, generosity of spirit and mutual concern were either explicitly excluded or simply absent. There was no ethical basis for the existing distribution of property. Stripped of its ideological trappings, the formally rational market system was, substantively speaking, fundamentally in conflict with any system of values that could reasonably be regarded as rational.

What then of an economic system that deliberately set out to embody just such rational substantive values, that of socialism? In order to translate, say, Marx's precept: 'from each according to their ability to each according to their need' into specific economic actions concerning the satisfaction of need in a population, it would be necessary to make a great many qualitative decisions about the economy. These decisions would ultimately necessitate 'calculations in kind'; that is to say calculations about who is to get what and how productive equipment is to be deployed, decisions that later became known as 'physical planning' (see Weber, [1924] 1968, pp. 101, 102). Urban planning, by definition, is a practice that works independently of the market as a means of allocating values and physical facilities, and therefore involves calculations in kind. Such calculations are typically made by bureaucratic decision, which we shall discuss in the next section.

Every capitalist enterprise concerned itself with such physical planning on its own behalf. But these calculations had to be evaluated in terms of profitability measured in money. It was, as a rule, possible for an enterprise to gauge how rationally its constituent parts were behaving with respect to profit, and immediately to pinpoint sources of irrationality. Profitability, therefore, functioned as a criterion which enabled the central administration of an enterprise to deploy its capital with maximum efficiency. But the criterion of efficiency, derived from competition among numerous autonomous enterprises, would be lacking in a centrally planned economy. Such an economy would also consist of many organizational units but without competition. In order to direct resources to these organizations with some semblance of rationality, 'a system of in-kind accounting would have to determine "value" indicators of some kind for the individual capital goods which could take over the role of the "prices" used in book valuation in modern business accounting' (Weber, [1924] 1968, p. 103).

When it came to weighing the relative value of the vast array of different wants arising in a society, Weber, foreshadowing Arrow (1951), concluded that the matter could only be determined by adherence to tradition or by dictatorial fiat. In both cases, obedience would be required of the population rather than freedom of choice. The same problem arose with the spatial location of industry, except in those cases where such location was determined by physical geography. Weber could conceive of no formally rational substitute for prices and profitability, and he believed the problem so fundamental that he concluded: 'we cannot speak of a *rational* "planned economy" so long as in this decisive respect we have no instrument for elaborating a rational plan' (Weber, [1924] 1968, p. 103). Equally he would have had to say that it is impossible to conceive of a rationally planned city other than one whose logic of development followed that of the market in land. In fact, Joseph Schumpeter (1943) showed that substitute mechanisms analogous to markets and prices were feasible in a planned economy. But such substitute mechanisms have not been followed up either in economic planning or in urban planning. Weber correctly foresaw that it was in the provision for mass demand by mass production that centrally planned economies would encounter the greatest difficulty.

The system of incentives that supplied the motivation for production in a market economy would be radically different in a planned economy. In a market economy the incentives to work productively varied according to one's station in life (see Weber, [1924] 1968, pp. 109, 110). The poor, people without substantial property, were motivated to sell their labour both by a belief in the virtue of work and by the threat of 'going without provision', in Weber's arid turn of phrase. Those with the privilege of wealth and education were stirred to work by the expectation of high income, 'ambition' (perhaps we might add: for power) and prestige arising from artistic, intellectual or technical mastery. Those involved in the fortunes of profit-seeking enterprises (owners or top management) combined a concern for the risk to which the capital of the enterprise was put in competitive markets, with the power and prestige of the 'calling' of business itself. The negative incentives of risk to both labour and capital would be lacking in a planned economy devoted to the satisfaction of need. If such *positive* incentives as could be supplied by appeal to altruistic values failed, the implication was that coercion by the authorities administering the economy would have to be instituted.

In the absence of coercion and dictatorial decision over the distribution of material goods, conflicts were bound to erupt over the distribution of rewards among the many individuals and groups participating in the economy. Just as in a capitalist economy there would be interest-group struggles and the strongest (for example, workers in essential services) would win (Weber, [1924] 1968, p. 203). Socialism, espousing a centrally planned economy, was thus deficient in formally rational mechanisms *for the very reason* that it embodied substantively rational goals for the organization of society and sought to translate them into economic action. Weber even considered that mass society, the maintenance of a certain density of population within a given area, might only be possible on the basis of the accurate calculation permitted by formally rational economic mechanisms (p. 104). The technical imperatives of providing for such a society demanded increasing rationalization of work in bureaucratically structured organizations. Under socialism, organizational units of production would be subject to a central plan and would be embedded in some hierarchy of command. But even within the formal freedom of market capitalism, work would be organized in hierarchical units within which most workers would spend their working lives.

Bureaucratic rationalism

The type of social order oriented to deliberate social action or 'planning' is, in Weber's terms, the organization (*Verband*). The 'rational planning', which was written about so extensively by procedural planning theorists in the 1960s and 1970s, embodies the bureaucratic principle that an organization can be designed to work towards a goal (or goals if they do not conflict with one another). However, Weber explores many more dimensions of bureaucratic rationality than just rational procedure: membership, leadership, domination and control, professionalism and expertise, the use of information, the application of rules within the organization, the question of political control of bureaucracy and the place of bureaucracy as an ideal type in modern society. Organizations are found in every sphere of society whenever there are people in a group 'whose action is concerned with carrying into effect the order governing the organization' (Weber, [1924] 1968, p. 48). By 'order' Weber evidently meant not just the rules governing relationships among official positions but also the purposes, goals or functions of the organization. In such an organization the actions of its individual members were, in certain respects, shaped by the organization within some structure of domination. There was a leader (or leadership function, which may be performed by a number of people) with the authority to direct action on behalf of the members of the organization. Membership was either closed or admission was limited by rules. The concept of organization was, in Weber's schema, unrestricted by size of membership or scope of action. It applied as much to a nation state as to the voluntary association (or 'task group') one may join for the benefits of group solidarity and for the collective performance of a task.

Organizations may be created by their own members (when they are 'autonomous') or by some outside agency ('heteronomous'). They may act purely on their own authority ('autocephalous') with their own ends in view, or under the authority of others contributing to ends directed by others ('heterocephalous'). They may be formed for 'corporate action', actively implementing the goals of the group (or society) or for the protection of members under the security provided by mutual regulation. The socialist state typically belonged to the former and the *laissez-faire* type of capitalist state belonged to the latter type of organization.

Clearly, the structure of different kinds of organization and their relationships in a given society form an immensely complex web. Georg Simmel ([1908] 1955) a colleague of Weber's, expanded upon this concept in his essay, *The Web of Group Affiliations*. Within this web the individual was enmeshed from birth. For example a person is born a citizen of a nation – also usually of some sub-national authority – and is immediately and compulsorily subject to its laws. The state is a compulsory association (*Anstalt*), however democratic the form of government, because the individual plays no part in its creation. Weber had no contractarian illusions. Majority rule, he noted, still means that the minority must submit. As citizens grow up they will go to school. The school may be part of the wider administrative order of a state education system subject to external control, or may be an autonomous and autocephalous unit in the education market. In the course of their induction into social life most people will, no doubt, voluntarily join a variety of groups for purposes of leisure, for the protection of their material interests (professional institutes or trades unions) or for the purposes of political action (political parties or pressure groups). In order to earn an income, most will have to join an organization playing a part in economic life and related in some way to material production.

Even if they are fortunate enough to earn their livelihood solely from the possession of capital, those funds will also be administered by an organization. Their birth, marriage, divorce and death will all be attended by the ministrations of other organizations – the church perhaps, the law certainly, the statistical office, the funeral parlour.

For all these types of organization above a certain size or level of functional complexity, the ideal type of rational administration is 'bureaucracy'. 'The development of modern forms of the organization in all fields is nothing less than identical with the development and continual spread of bureaucratic administration' (Weber, [1924] 1968, p. 223). 'Bureaucracy', as several commentators (Morstein Marx, 1957; Albrow, 1970) have pointed out, has various meanings, most of them pejorative. Weber's German cultural background, however, was one in which the word was 'drained of all satire' and 'the label of a system of superior accomplishment' (Morstein Marx, 1957, p. 22). Today bureaucracy, in the sense intended by Weber, is all-pervasive just as he foresaw. It might be said that the higher the expectations we have of administration, the more we notice its failures. And not all of these can be put down to bureaucracy. Many stem from imperfections such as human error or political waywardness. But the seeming obsession with standardized rules and procedures, the ignoring of individual concerns and interests, the red tape (which was used to bind 'the files'), the secrecy; all these result from the very quality of bureaucracy that makes it successful. This quality is the impersonal capacity to subordinate the individual to the single-minded pursuit of organizational functions and goals.

Weber's ideal model of bureaucracy is drawn in abstract terms and the main elements of the model are recognizable as the baseline, in practice, of rational administration in modern large-scale organizations. Although much of his description seems focused on government bureaucracies, it is clear he also meant the model to apply to large private-sector corporations (see Weber, 1946, p. 215). He described six key characteristics of bureaucracy.

1 The activities of the organization are ordered by fixed rules and these activities are parcelled out as the official duties of every specified 'post' in the organization, irrespective of who fills it. The authority to undertake these duties goes with the job description.
2 There is an 'office hierarchy' in which every level has responsibility for the supervision of a specified set of functions carried out by the level immediately beneath it. The point is to ensure that an order issued at any level is transmitted through the organization so that the action required by the order is taken (Morstein Marx, 1957, p. 22). The hierarchy is guided in the conduct of its business by certain procedural rules, which may be explicit or implicit:

a person in higher authority does not try to do the job of a subordinate; through training and supervision an official becomes an expert at doing a particular kind of job and does not need to be given detailed instructions on how to do it; if there is disagreement, decisions of lower authorities may be appealed against to higher levels; once established, a position tends to continue in existence after the office bearer has left it.

3 The management of the office is based on written records, 'the files', and there will be a member of staff whose job it is to see that the records are kept in order and up to date. The executive office (and its financial resources, records and transactions) is kept completely separate from the private household of the official.

4 Management requires special training above any specialized technical skills that the manager may possess.

5 Official activity demands the full working capacity of the official. Formerly, says Weber, official business was discharged by state officials as a secondary activity. He was thinking here of the official positions bestowed on members of privileged elites, who treated these jobs as secondary to the management of their own affairs and estates.

6 The conduct of official business is by stable and generally applicable rules, which can be learned by the officials as a form of special expertise. This provision prevents officials from bestowing patronage upon or discriminating against individuals.

For the official, office holding was a vocation involving training and qualifications. Although the status of the public service varied in different countries, the rank accompanying a position in a public bureaucracy guaranteed its holder a definite status and, in countries such as Britain and Germany, was rewarded with high public esteem and special honours. Acquisition of a post in a bureaucracy usually depended on appointment by a superior authority. The election of public officials (as in the USA), Weber said, modified the strictness of the hierarchical principle, for elected officials derive their authority from 'below' (the mass of voters) and thus had access to a separate source of power from that conferred on them by a superior. Furthermore, popular election of administrators, 'usually endangers the expert qualification of the official' since acceptability for office derived from personal popularity rather than strictly from technical competence (Weber, 1946, p. 201). In public bureaucracies, tenure of a post was usually for life. This security of employment guaranteed 'a strictly objective discharge of specific office duties free from all personal considerations' (p. 202). The occupants of positions in a bureaucracy changed as officials were promoted in a career structure from lower to higher paid and more responsible positions under specified conditions of promotion. They could also usually look forward to a generous pension on retirement. Although public officials were often not paid as well as their equivalents in the private sector, their security of salary meant that public service jobs were much sought after.

The formal rationality of the bureaucratic type of administration was, to Weber, incontestable. Indeed, he said, though there were plenty of examples of other types of organization, 'it would be sheer illusion to think for a moment that continuous administrative work can be carried out in any field except by means of officials working in offices. The whole pattern of everyday life is cut to fit this framework' (Weber, [1924] 1968, p. 223). The principle of hierarchy meant that a great deal of specialist skill and attention could be brought to bear on complex tasks without overloading any level of command. Very precise 'steering' of the organization could be achieved at the same time as depth of knowledge and experience. Compared with a bureaucratic hierarchy under a single directorship, collegiate forms (basically, control by committees) and honorific (amateur) forms of administration increased the probability of delay, indecisiveness and unresolved conflict. Bureaucracy offered the maximum potential for speed of corporate action and calculability of results.

These qualities of formal rationality were dependent upon certain substantive assumptions about the conduct of human beings in relation to the bureaucratic machinery. The very metaphor of the machine suggests something completely dehumanizing. Bureaucracy works calculably, precisely and quickly *only* in so far as every official behaves like a cog in a machine. In a machine a force applied by a 'big wheel' results in a completely predictable response from a smaller one. Given such operation it is easy to see why Weber thought that the increasing speed of communication made possible by technological development would have to be translated into speed of administrative reaction. So much the more, however, does the administrative apparatus strip the individual of humanity and freedom of action: 'the individual bureaucrat cannot squirm out of the apparatus in which he is harnessed. In contrast to the honorific or avocational "notable", the professional bureaucrat is chained to his activity by his entire material and ideal existence. In the great majority of cases he is only a cog in an ever-moving mechanism which prescribes to him an essentially fixed route of march' (Weber, 1946, p. 228). The spirit of bureaucracy was therefore for Weber one of formal rationality whose execution demanded the adoption of *values* which Weber regarded as inhuman (Weber, [1924] 1968, p. 975).

Bureaucracy was evident in the ancient civilizations of China, Egypt and Rome. But the modern form of bureaucracy developed with and immensely assisted industrial capitalism. Weber regarded bureaucracy, like market exchange, as an inevitable technical response to the demands of mass society rather than the product of a specific mode of production. However, on the one hand, capitalism created a need for stable, disciplined, intensive and calculable administration; on the other, capitalism provided the most rational economic climate for the growth of bureaucracy. The levelling of society, so that individuals were formally to be regarded as equals, provided the opportunity for the growth of new power structures better attuned to a capitalist system than were feudal structures with their normative rules of mutual obligation. Formal equality in the market place was paralleled by formal equality of opportunity to rise in a bureaucratic career structure on the basis of merit alone. In allocating to the urban planner a bureaucratic role, we tend to assume that the bureaucracy is controlled by elected politicians, parliaments or councils, and that this is sufficient to guarantee democracy. But, for Weber this was problematic and he stressed that bureaucracy, the rule of officials, was in fact opposed to democracy. To consider this question of democratic control we need now to turn to Weber's conception of the state and its legitimation.

The rational state

Whenever people are organized for purposes of action, *Herrschaft*, which may be translated as domination, authority or even rule, is to be found. Bureaucracy was the most efficient mode of domination in any large scale organization. Just as in the economic enterprise, so also in the political enterprise, bureaucracy efficiently concentrated power in the hands of a single leadership. Weber showed how, in European nations, state bureaucracies developed out of the power position and leadership needs of 'the prince' as traditional head of state. The prince could function most effectively only when he had gathered at his disposal an organization of technical experts dedicated to carrying out his commands with no material control over the means of administration: in short, who owned only their own labour and therefore represented no independent source of power.

The development of this structure, this state apparatus, was thus a separate matter from its control. The state apparatus, like the market, was a vehicle for the exercise of power, but the development of both involved technical questions of formal rationality and neither could be explained *simply* with reference to the struggle for power in the sphere of production. In global terms various forms of state were possible, depending on the way in which control of the state apparatus was legitimated and on the specific articulation between the state apparatus and its controllers.

As we have already noted, Weber concluded that all power rested ultimately on the use of force – literally, physical violence. The power structure in society was held in place or changed, both equally, through violence. But, of course, rule in the normal course of events could not be by the constant use of force. A society runs much more efficiently if people obey without being constantly coerced. People voluntarily obey because they subscribe to the legitimacy of the order of domination and conceive it in their interest to obey. Bureaucracy was not only an efficient means of organizing domination, it also contributed to the legitimation of domination. Weber identified three sources of legitimacy: custom or tradition; the extraordinary and personal 'gift of grace' – charisma – of the prince or leader ('the absolutely personal devotion and personal confidence in revelation, heroism or other qualities of individual leadership' (Weber, [1919] 1946, p. 79); and legal authority: 'the belief in the validity of legal statute and functional competence based on rationally created *rules*' (p. 79).

The legitimacy of the bureaucratic state apparatus depended partly on the legitimacy of the prince and partly on its own legal authority and technical rationality. With the growth of capitalism on the basis of formal freedom and legal equality of the individual, traditional values were called into question and the traditional legitimacy of the prince was swept away. The expropriator of the means of administration was finally expropriated, although frequently maintained at the public expense as a useful symbol of national unity. But the rational structure of administration formed under princely rule remained to play a crucial part in an integrated legal system of authority. In this system, legitimate control and rational administration were knitted together. Obedience to a body of law stood in place of obedience to a person. Ultimately, the making of this law rested on the electoral accountability of those who made it. The law was embodied in every official position in the bureaucracy that was empowered to put the law into effect: in the judicial system, the police, the armed forces and every service, productive and regulatory function of government. Where executive action was required, obedience was also to a legally established post and not to a person. Likewise the individual obeyed not as a person but as a member of an organization. This applied as much to a member of a functional organization as to a citizen of a territorial organization, e.g. a nation state. Hence the order had an impersonal, 'rule bound' quality, which ensured that its functionaries were both disinterested and objective in the performance of their duties. This technical competence was further guaranteed by the division of labour inherent in bureaucracy. Every post had a defined 'competence', in the legal sense of 'sphere of jurisdiction', and specified duties. And entry to bureaucracy was freely contracted, thus enabling candidates to be selected on the basis of their technical competence in the performance of a specified range of work. The bureaucracy, therefore, derived legitimacy not just from its funnction as a mechanism for transmitting commands but also from its capacity to supply impartial advice in the general interest.

The control of the state apparatus was determined by political struggle. Just as Weber switched Marx's focus from the mode of production to the mechanism of exchange (the market) so also did he switch the critical focus from the state as a structure *determined by* power relations embodied in the mode of production to the state as the *location of* a power struggle and the means of giving power concrete effect. If politics was essentially a power struggle, the questions then arose, as they did in the market, of who entered the struggle and what were the rules by which the struggle was to be conducted. The answers to these questions varied in different countries. The outcome was determined both by the historical distribution of power among classes and status groups and by the way in which control of the state apparatus was legitimated. For example, in nineteenth-century Britain, political power came to be shared by the aristocracy with the new rising class of industrialists. The former benefited as much as the latter from industrialization. There was no crisis of transition of power because the aristocracy had already adopted the rational habits of industrial capitalism. As Hobsbawn (1969, pp. 81, 82) points out, 'they did not have to stop being feudal for they had long since ceased to be so . . . The new business class found a firm pattern of life waiting for them.' Part of that pattern of life was the formal control of the state apparatus by Parliament. But although Parliament had formal sovereignty, the monocratic Ministerial and Cabinet system arose from the interest of the monarch and the inheritors of his power, the party leaders, *against* Parliament (see Weber, [1919] 1946, p. 90). This situation resulted in the emergence of 'a Caesarist plebiscitarian element' in democratic politics. The political struggle, culminating in electoral struggle, threw up a strong leader, 'the dictator of the battlefield of elections' who 'stands above Parliament' and 'brings the masses behind him by means of the [party] machine and the members of Parliament are, for him, merely political spokesmen enrolled in his following' (p. 107).

In the USA the way in which the executive (the office of the President) was separated from the legislature (Congress) tended to increase the dominance of the party leadership. The parties, Weber observed, were peopled by 'job hunters' whose primary aim was to win office in the electoral struggle. Indeed the political parties were 'fashioned' for the electoral campaigns that would deliver patronage: the campaigns for the presidency and the state governorships (Weber, [1919] 1946, p. 108). The autonomy of the professional bureaucracy in the USA has certainly grown since Weber's time, but the question of presidential control of the bureaucracy through political patronage remains an issue. Likewise, the domination of active politics by the wealthy (the 'tendency to plutocracy' that Weber observed) and the garnering of votes by the party bosses remain central features of American political life. The 'competitive struggle to win the favor of voters' was later elevated by Schumpeter into a new principle of democracy (see chapter 5).

In both Britain and the USA professional politicians still ruled the bureaucracy both formally and sometimes actually, given the emergence of strong leaders. From Weber's German perspective, England had been 'saved from bureaucratization' by the 'gentry', a 'patrician stratum of petty nobility and urban rentiers'. In the USA the structure of unprincipled parties and political bosses could, on occasion, help able men to attain the presidency. In Germany, by contrast, a highly autonomous and well esteemed bureaucracy was overwhelmingly dominant. The major parties tended to place little importance on the parliament as the arena of political struggle, and there was no compensating mechanism of control over the bureaucracy. As a result, political control was weak. From this point of view, even with nominally strong political control, it remained an open question for Weber whether the political leadership would be capable of controlling the state apparatus. On the one hand, Weber says that:

> the objective indispensability of the once-existing apparatus, with its peculiar, 'impersonal' character, means that the mechanism – in contrast to feudal orders based upon personal piety – is easily made to work for anybody who knows how to gain control over it. (Weber, 1946, p. 229).

On the other hand, the real controllers, those who 'know how to gain control', may not be the nominal controllers. A few pages later in the same text he notes:

> Under normal conditions the power position of a fully developed bureaucracy is always overtowering. The 'political master' finds himself in the position of the dilettante who stands opposite the 'expert', facing the trained official who stands within the management of administration (Weber, 1946, p. 232).

Thus bureaucratic interests themselves may stand against the political interests that are supposed by the demands of political legitimacy to control them. The bureaucracy, indeed, has its own source of legitimacy in the 'objectivity' of technical expertise and formal impartiality. And both the complexity of technical knowledge and the secrecy with which the bureaucracy guards the superiority of the professionally informed tend to diminish the capacity of the political leader to exercise control. Weber's qualification 'under normal conditions' is an important one, however, for as Morstein Marx (1957, p. 89) pointed out, the power of a civil service tends to evaporate before a political regime, however dilettante, that refuses to play by the rules.

Weber defines the state as 'a human community that (successfully) claims the monopoly of the legitimate use of force within a given territory' (Weber, [1919] 1946, p. 78). Engels had used territoriality as an identifying characteristic of a 'state', but Weber went somewhat further in teasing out its significance for the capitalist system. He drew a distinction between organizations producing goods for profit, and organizations that are 'in principle concerned with territorial validity' (*Gebietsgeltung*); that is, whose order extends beyond its immediate membership to all those related to a given territory by birth, residence or the performance of certain activities (e.g. work). This distinction has important consequences for the government of capitalism because, in the world market, nations are thrown into competition with one another. 'The rivalry among states', Weber wrote, 'created the largest opportunities for modern Western capitalism. The separate states had to compete for mobile capital which dictated to them the conditions under which it would assist them to augment their power. Out of this alliance of the state with capital, dictated by necessity, arose the national bourgeoisie in the modern sense of the word' (Andreski, 1983, p. 149). The nation state provided a congenial environment for the development of capitalism, not least because the interests that controlled it were those that controlled and benefited from capitalist enterprise. The democratic franchise was 'a later addition to a well-established liberal state, the mechanism of which was competitive non-democratic parties and the purpose of which was to provide the conditions for a competitive capitalist, market society' (Macpherson, 1966, p. 57). Eventually, however, the time would come when the organization of the enterprise would transcend national boundaries.

Finally we must remember that, for Weber, the state was a formally rational apparatus that was indispensable for social action. A socialist government could no more do without a bureaucratic apparatus than could a capitalist one. In fact, a socialist government endeavouring to translate its ideals into rational plans without relying on markets would increasingly have to depend on the technical expertise of bureaucracy. Moreover, under socialism, the private bureaucracies of capitalist enterprises would no longer provide a counterbalance to the public bureaucracy. Both would be merged into a single hierarchy (see Weber, [1924] 1968, p. 1402). The rational state was, therefore, confronted with the Scylla of the market and the Charybdis of bureaucracy. It seemed likely that the most rational state would set a course somewhere between the two.

The dilemma of rationality

Weber pointed out in the clearest terms what planners and social scientists have repeatedly rediscovered: that the requirements of formal and substantive rationality are fundamentally in conflict. Weber was a founder of empirical sociology. He sought to rest his analysis as much as possible on rational (that is, logical) argument based on fact. He believed that there was no place for political values in academic investigation, least of all when the subject of investigation was politics (Weber, 1946, p. 145). He was committed to objectivity in social understanding. Yet he also realized that the step from the accumulation of knowledge to its employment in social action required something other than science. Science, he said, does not give us the answer to the questions, 'what shall we do and how shall we live?' (Weber, 1946, p. 143).

Essentially the same dilemma was to be found in the sphere of social action. In those social structures characteristic of modern life and necessary to mass society, the market, bureaucracy, the nation state, Weber found a formal rationality unsupported by substantively rational values. This occurred not because people were dedicated to the pursuit of evil ends but rather because they were not dedicated to any substantive social ends. Society lacked an ethic. The ethics of the market and of bureaucracy were instrumental ethics, which looked only to the survival of those forms of association. 'Where the market is allowed to follow its own autonomous tendencies, its participants do not look toward the persons of each but only toward the commodity; there are no obligations of brotherliness or reverence, and none of those spontaneous human relations that are sustained by personal unions' (Weber, [1924] 1968, p. 636). The bureaucratic organization 'with its rules and hierarchical relations of authority' was the animate machine paralleling the inanimate machinery of production. Both, says Weber, are together 'fabricating the shell of bondage which men will perhaps be forced to inhabit some day' (p. 1402). However, he overstressed the machine-like quality of bureaucracy and failed to appreciate either that bureaucracy could itself become an arena of conflict for the various interests impinging on it or that the rules and discretionary action of officials might be far from neutral with respect to outside interests (Blau, 1963; Crozier, 1964; Downs, 1967).

Weber was devoted to rationality and his interest in exploring the rationalism of the modern world stemmed from that devotion. He was as much soaked in the value system that valued rational means as he was in the value system that valued objectivity in science. But, as a man of the Enlightenment, he saw the conflict between these means and the humanist values that he also held. There is an ambivalence in Weber's construct of formal versus substantive rationality, which has led some planning theorists to suppose that they can be reconciled rationally. Formal rationality involves an argument about what means lead to what ends. Viewed in this light, with a little stretching of the idea of planning, it is possible to have two different kinds of planning: one that is substantively rational and one that is formally or 'functionally' rational. This is the idea proposed by Friedmann (1967) and built into an ideal-typical model of 'modes' of planning by Faludi (1973b).

But, viewed in another way, substantive rationality cannot be reduced to any sort of formally rational scheme because the *value* of rational schemes confronts and opposes the *value* of substantive rationality (the discursive consideration of ends). They are opposing values in a *wertrational* debate. Brubaker (1984, p. 41) puts it thus:

> The antagonism between formal and substantive rationality may thus be interpreted as a tension between conflicting values: between calculability, efficiency and impersonality on the one hand and fraternity, equality and *caritas* on the other.

The dilemma Weber exposed was this. Society espouses a value system that includes such enlightened ends as freedom of the individual, brotherly love, personal growth and rational choice. There are various social means of implementing these values, which turn out to be extremely successful in achieving several goals that are plainly major steps on the way to society's highest values. Because of their success they are used more and more. But, says Weber, these means, in the very process of their being put into effect, absolutely militate against the highest values. In fact, the harder society tries to achieve its own highest values by (apparently) the most effective means at its disposal, the further it moves from the attainment of those values.

The nearest Weber came to a resolution was in his discussion of politics. In politics a certain kind of stoical compromise was necessary. Any striving either to produce or prevent social change involved the distribution of power in society, whether power be expressed in wealth, legal authority or naked coercion. All forms of functional rationality, the market, bureaucracy, the rational state – and therefore we must say urban planning – are modes for the expression of power. Any engagement with power was, at base, engagement with the use of violence. The ethical response to this situation was neither to forgo deliberate social action nor to deny the reality of violence. This reality should not be wrapped up in the pretence that such and such a violent act would be the last before eternal peace and harmony prevails: the war to end wars; the ultimate weapon to guarantee peace; the revolution to abolish class conflict. Therefore, the pretence that a society could do without a state was also no more than that: a pretence. The ethic of responsiblity that Weber commends is one that does not avoid political engagement but recognizes that politics involves violent means. We might also want to say that such an ethic recognizes that planning also involves violent and dehumanizing means. What is required is 'a trained relentlessness in viewing the realities of life' (Weber, 1946, p. 126) to face up to the limitations placed on the achievement of all ethical social ends by the available means.

Urban planning: a Weberian perspective

In Weberian perspective, urban planning is seen as part of the institutional fabric of modern 'market' society. Though Weberians might use the term 'capitalist' to describe such society, the term contains no implication of a workable alternative such as 'communist' or 'socialist' society. A plan is a system of rules for the control of urban development. The decision to institute urban planning sets in motion a sequence of events whose course is contingent on varying local political and market conditions. In the process of its development, urban planning defines new interests and pressure groups (for example, community pressure groups responding to initiatives in planning or urban development, and professional institutes), creates new bureaucratic organizations (committees, boards, ministries), lays down new rules for decision-making (land-use plans, appeal procedures), and creates new knowledge, which sets up public expectations of the state (expectations on the part of landowners to be able to influence the pattern of land use outside the parcel they own). As March and Olsen (1984, p. 738) observe, 'The bureaucratic agency, the legislative committee, and the appellate court are arenas for contending social forces, but they are also collections of standard operating procedures and structures that define and defend interests'. Although operating within the more general rules of property and exchange characterizing 'market' society, rule systems such as those controlling land-use will vary from time to time, from country to country and even from region to region within a country. The nature of such rule systems is contingent upon the array of local political actors and decision-making institutions. In order to understand a particular urban planning system, therefore, it is necessary to describe the particular characteristics of the rules, their interpretation, and the actors who constantly implement, use and change those rules in a particular time and place. Thus Elkin (1974) describes the differences between land-use politics in Britain and America; Healey (1983) writes of the variety of decision-making rules for the determination of planning issues in Britain.

While careful description is important in order to reach some understanding of urban planning, Weber's is more than a descriptive enterprise. The profound normative questions he poses should be of great concern to planners. Formal rationality, which legitimates the activity of planning by the state, the rationalism of the market and bureaucracy, also binds humanity to the working of a social machine and limits the achievement of those goals such as freedom, compassion and fellow-feeling, for which it is substantively rational to strive. Formal rationality is simply necessary in order to provide for the material well-being of society. But spiritual values are lost from the public domain, individualized and privatized. The market efficiently organizes the production and distribution of goods and the sharing of risk. But the market also transmits economic power and entrenches pre-existing inequality. The legitimacy of the planner is derived from contradictory sources: the expertise and objectivity of the professional administrator, and subordination to the elected officials. Bureaucratic legitimacy requires planners to accept the decisions of their political masters and to see that they are fully implemented. The bureaucrat role thus has a strong implication of a 'top-down' style of policy-making. But the bureaucratic role is not a passive one. Planners have goals and interests of their own and resources (e.g. knowledge of the city), which they may deploy to achieve their goals and serve their interests. Indeed, in performing the advice-giving function of the bureaucrat, planners cannot help but bring their own goals and resources into play.

Weber provides no way out of these dilemmas, which are inherent in the organization of any modern 'mass' society. All that can be said is that different societies struggle to find their own particular solutions to these antinomies. The Australian State of Victoria provides an interesting example of a changing bureaucracy. In Australia most of the functions of sub-national government are performed by the states. Until the 1970s the State of Victoria was governed by a plethora of powerful bureaucratic agencies only very loosely accountable to ministers and the State parliament. The relationship between the bureaucratic and political levels at that time was summed up quite accurately by the permanent head of the agency responsible for town and country planning: 'Once the planning authority [an independent Town and Country Planning Board] decides upon a certain policy, the Minister presents an outline to Cabinet, it is discussed there and then issued as a Cabinet Statement with the full authority of the government of the day' (Frazer, 1972, p. 139). Except for pet schemes of the premier and ministers, the policy initiative rested with the bureaucrats. This began to change in the 1970s, as the political executive sought to exert increasing control over policy (Low and Power, 1984; Painter, 1987). The change was greatly accelerated after 1982 when a Labour Government came to power after twenty seven years, a government whose explicit aim was to reshape the main programmes of the State rather than to make its political impact by adding new programmes at the margin. Almost the entire bureaucratic apparatus was restructured to give ministers and cabinet firm control. The Treasury was reconstructed as the 'Department of Management and Budget' in order to exercise an overall steering function on behalf of cabinet. Permanent heads of departments became less permanent, and a network of political advisers, linking ministers with party committees, was installed. The bureaucratic chiefs became more like 'bureaucratic politicians' in that political judgement and skills became important attributes of their role (Laffin, 1987). Here, there is a comparison with the American situation of which Catanese (1978, p. 184) observed 'The chief planner appears to be getting more and more involved in the political process, including partisan politics, because there is a widespread recognition that decision-makers take political factors into consideration at least as much as technical merits.' But the effort by the political executive to control the state apparatus from the top produces new strains and new bureaucratic outgrowths. Spann (1981, p. 19) suggested that the efficacy of management control systems designed to enforce the principle of accountability to the political level was more imagined than real: 'very large numbers of people have a vested interest in claiming that such systems exist, or are at least in gestation, even though the whole project may be, at least in part, a phantom'. Painter (1987) remarks on the growth of a new 'co-ordinating' bureaucracy with a new set of interests and perceptions.

Commenting on the nature of the bureaucratic role, Christensen (1985) argues that the role is limited by the degree to which goals (ends) are agreed and technologies (means) known. She mentions as examples water supply and sewerage sanitation, provision of roads, telecommunications and power supply, and inoculation against polio. The bureaucrat is a programmer, standardizer, rule-setter, regulator, scheduler, optimizer, analyst and administrator. The bureaucrat planner must assume a set of uncontradictory goals from which to derive or with which to justify programmes: 'a land use planner aiming at preserving a town's single family residential character, for example, would establish low density zoning' (Christensen, 1985, p. 66). Planners set up and then operate authoritative rules and procedures for deciding on land-uses and standards of building, car-parking and environmental quality. Other planners establish procedures for allocating funds for certain types of public service such as public housing. Planners may also be considered expert in scheduling tasks (e.g. with some form of critical path analysis), choosing the best option with the help of cost benefit or cost effectiveness techniques, or analyzing development costs. Planners may be called on to analyze trends in population or industrial location, using expert statistical techniques. Finally, planners have the task of the administration of their organization and of the set procedures and rules with which it works and which designate it as a legitimate function of government.

As Christensen observes, the bureaucratic role is both delineated and limited by the local political culture. At certain times and in certain places *debate* about goals comes to replace the implementation of accepted goals on the political agenda; change of rules, procedures and technologies become the most salient task. In these circumstances planners take on more political roles. They become advocates and politicians, in Weber's sense, on their own account and for their own values.

But there is a more general question, which an application of Weber's thought to planning must bring to mind. Underlying Weber's image of the modern state is the assumption of a boundary between two quite different spheres of decision-making: politics and hierarchical bureaucratic control. The location of this boundary and the relationship between the two spheres is problematic. To what extent does 'control' operate in the boundary layer and to what extent 'politics'? How do (or should) politicians control the bureaucracy through their relationship with its senior echelons? Further down the bureaucratic hierarchy, the classic rational image of the bureaucrat seems to prevail, but in the boundary layer something paradoxical can happen. The more that the politician seeks to control the bureaucracy, the more the senior bureaucrats have to take on political roles, that is if they do not resist the political boss. This is so simply because the bureaucrats have to start thinking like politicians in order to anticipate the requirements of their political superiors and respond to them effectively. This moves the boundary between political and bureaucratic decision-making further down the hierarchy. On the other hand, if bureaucratic control extends right up the organization, the politician will have less control over the bureaucracy, which will operate more according to bureaucratic and technical imperatives. The two spheres of political and bureaucratic decision-making do not fit neatly together like pieces of a jigsaw puzzle. They are more like oil and water, which can be mixed but never merge.

The contradictory requirements of control of the modern state have been explored by Campbell and Peters (1988). Campbell sets up two dimensions on which political leaders can vary: 'responsiveness' and 'institutionalization'. The first represents the Weberian virtue of the politician in responding to his or her values, to a 'cause' and to the constituency; the second represents the need to engage the bureaucratic apparatus in order to achieve political priorities and tasks: 'This enterprise requires the institutionalization of control and guidance mechanisms in the cores of departments and agencies, and the center of the entire executive branch' (Campbell and Peters, 1988, p. 370). This may be done in various ways: for example, by creating policy sections dominated by political appointees, by appointing sympathetic experts to key bureaucratic positions, by setting up controls along the lines of program budgeting, or by improving the machinery for processing the business of the executive – cabinet committees, premier's departments, departments of management and budget and the like. Campbell argues that the capacities for responsiveness and for institutionalization are both necessary for 'policy competence' and that they are not mutually exclusive. However he also postulates that political leaderships tend to fall into different styles depending on the degree of emphasis given to each capacity:

Under this framework, a *priorities and planning* style emerges when the political leadership encourages competing advice. It simultaneously entrusts central agencies with the task of developing overarching strategies and assuring that substantive decisions adhere to them. *Broker politics* results when countervailing views abound, but central agencies play only restrained roles in the integration of policies. *Administrative politics* develops when political leaders tend neither to encourage a variety of views nor rely heavily upon central agencies for guiding and controlling the rest of the executive branch. Finally, *survival politics* prevails when central agencies increasingly draw issues into their orbit and expressly seek to dampen competition between advisers (Campbell and Peters, 1988, p. 372).

Although the 'priorities and planning' style is regarded as the most desirable from the point of view of policy competence, it is neither easily achieved nor stable. External political or economic circumstances may push the leadership back towards one of the other styles or even into forms of incompetence. Institutional requirements for 'policies and planning' include the existence of strong 'policy-oriented shops' working directly to the chief executive (political) in order to ensure countervailing policy advice, a well structured system of standing cabinet committees to enable the executive to plan rather than just 'muddle through', a relatively unified cabinet rather than one in which many diverse interests are represented, and effective analytic and co-ordinating units in line departments to relate the activities of these organizations to those of the central agencies. Personnel-related factors include the integration of party political advice as a legitimate input to policy, a high degree of policy-oriented professionalism among political appointees, a tendency among policy advisers not to compromise too readily, and civil servants with strong policy analysis skills.

Bureaucratic 'rational' planning has been much criticized, and attempts to marry such planning with politics have often failed (the repeated trials and failures of program budgeting for example). But the need to do so remains, and is all the more necessary in an economic climate in which territorially based states are thrown into competition with one another by organizations that are less territorially bounded (i.e. competition for private investment). As Weber foresaw, functional rationality with all its profound contradictions is the defining characteristic of the modern age. Urban planning, however, with its potentially wide and somewhat diffuse range of concerns, can no longer be viewed as a self-contained professional/bureaucratic function. Rather, it will increasingly be subordinated to the more politically oriented strategies formulated at the centre of states. If we follow Weber, planners as bureaucrats cannot be complacent about their role in society. But the main danger to society is not when planners have doubts about their role and are aware of the difficulties posed by conflicting values. It occurs when planners become complacent, certain of the rightness of their technical methods, and display a closed mind to the demands of politics.

Conclusion

Weber's analysis assumes the existence of a strong, autonomous and formally rational state, whose form varies from nation to nation. The functions of this state would be performed through an accountable bureaucracy, but the reality of democratic control of bureaucracies is always problematic. For whole societies, or even portions of societies such as cities, only the market can provide an adequate mechanism for their rational co-ordination. However, both bureaucracy and markets merely express the power structure of society, a structure with no intrinsic moral justification but one which formal rationality clothes with legitimacy. Weber does not allow us to assume that moral ends of *universal* validity can ever be found to justify change in the power structure. Politics takes care of change. In the context of such a vision, we can see that the nature of urban planning has radically changed. What started as a political movement armed with an ideology that implied change in the distribution of power has become a bureaucratic function that must accept and work within the power structure. The best that the bureaucrat planner can do is to ensure that the demands of those who hold power are efficiently translated into physical outcomes. Bureaucrats, however, may sometimes find themselves in the midst of political struggles between, for example, the politically and the economically powerful, since the two sources of power do not necessarily coincide.

Weber's view of politics was coloured by his European outlook, in which states were relatively strong and organized. The climate of social reconstruction after the Second World War favoured the idea of planning by the state, particularly because substantive ends of social justice were once again on the political agenda (see Mannheim, 1940). In contrast to the Weberian conception of the strong rational state, pluralist theory with its roots in American political culture provides a view of politics in which the concept of the state is all but absent. Pluralist theory expounds a normative justification for that politics and puts forward a critique of even formally rational planning.

5 Pluralism, the game and the rules

The term 'pluralism' can be used to describe a very wide range of philosophical and political ideas. Dunleavy and O'Leary (1987, p. 13) begin their account of the theory with the statement, 'pluralism is the belief that there are, or ought to be, many things. It offers a defence of multiplicity in beliefs, institutions and societies and opposes 'monism' – the belief that there is, or ought to be, only one thing.' Alford and Friedland (1985) postulate a pluralist 'home domain' of theory, which spans a wide range of ideas broadly equated with methodological individualism and situational studies of power. For the purposes of this book, already wide-ranging enough, a narrower focus will be adopted. In this chapter we shall concentrate on a theoretical perspective that has been developed particularly in the context of American political practice but also has affinities with certain traditions of British political thought. Waste (1987, p. 3) describes this perspective as 'the view that public policy . . . is the result of a tug of war – often ending in a delicate balance or compromise between various interest groups'. Polsby (1980, pp. 153–7) writes of 'an intellectual tradition that has some strength in American political theory . . . showing some indebtedness to writers as varied as Madison, Tocqueville, Montesquieu and Locke'. We shall trace this intellectual tradition and the methodological questions surrounding it, focusing on the work of the 'analytical' pluralists, Bentley and Truman, the 'institutional' pluralists, Schumpeter, Lindblom and Dahl, and the critics of both schools. Here, attention is given mainly to American theory, although pluralist thought also developed strongly in Britain (see Nicholls, 1975).

Pluralist theory throws doubt on the traditional view of professional planning, which holds that a plan demands clear, unambiguous goals to be pursued consistently over a fairly long period of time; that planning demands right answers to problems; that the legitimacy of the planner depends on public accountability to a clearly identified source of authority; that the planner needs a defined 'client'; that success must be measured against known and agreed criteria. Pluralist theory asserts axiomatically that planners are one among many contending groups in the political arena. Just like the rest of society, planners have their own interests, and planning is the pursuit of those interests. The goals of public policy are liable to vary with the changing balance of group pressure; every group will have its own interpretation of 'the problem'; because democracy is constituted ultimately by the freedom of groups to interact, there is no single authoritative line of accountability to 'the public'; accordingly, planners have multiple clients; the plurality of goals and interpretations means that there are also multiple and possibly conflicting criteria of success.

Pluralism provided a critique of the strong unified state. Weber's image of the rational state and bureaucracy secured a legitimate role for expertise in the service of the state on the basis of functional rationality. But, as we have seen, this image contained its own dilemma. Modern society was trapped in the iron cage of its own rationality. Offering a softer, more humane and perhaps more complacent image of the modern polity, pluralist theory tends to make the state disappear, substituting for it 'the political process'. As a result, the boundaries both between governments and the public, and between politicians and bureaucrats are blurred. The legitimacy of the planner comes to depend not on the state but on the good political process. However, far from destroying the idea of planning, pluralist theory stimulated a massive reconstruction of planning theory and a reinterpretation of planning practice, defining a variety of new 'political' roles for the planner: advocate, negotiator, activist and organizer, entrepreneur, mediator. These roles raise questions about the rules that condition and shape them. Just as Dahl has moved from a concern with group interaction in society to a concern with 'the rules of the game', so, it will be argued, must planning theory and practice follow suit. The proper focus of planning which a consideration of the history of pluralist thought suggests is the structures of rules and meanings within which all attempts at problem-solving in society occur. In this chapter we shall first look briefly at the historical antecedents of pluralist theory. Then the work of the 'analytical' pluralists and their critics will be discussed. This work is important because it introduces the concept of group interaction, which remains a core idea of pluralist theory. There follows an extended discussion of the 'institutional pluralism' of Lindblom and Dahl and their concept of 'polyarchy'. This work raises questions about the institutional rules of democracy. Finally, we shall see how questions of roles and rules come together in pluralist analyses of urban planning.

The background to pluralism

From the sixteenth century, rationalist political theory attempted to reconcile two principles: that individuals should be regarded as autonomous and in possession of certain natural rights, and that a structure of rules was necessary in order for them to obtain a degree of security and the fruits of collective action. With the growth of capitalism, the explanation of a just human society crystallized around the notion of individual liberty. To have any reality, liberty required a material basis in property. Society was conceived in terms of stable, law-governed relations among free individual 'atoms'[1]. These social relations among individuals were to be maintained by the laws of property and of contract. Individualism, politics, private property and contract were part of a conceptual whole that embodied the very identity of the ascendant bourgeoisie. 'To assert private control of a piece of the world, to possess and be self-possessed' were the insignia of this vision of the world (Lustig, 1982, p. 50).

Such a perspective is the basis of liberalism but not necessarily of pluralism. It leads equally to the formulation of the neo-liberal perspective of the 'new right' (see chapter 7), which is antagonistic to pluralism. Pluralism emerges from normative concepts that approve of the division of authority and power in society. These concepts are to be found in the work of Locke, Montesquieu, Madison and Tocqueville. Locke ([1690] 1970) argued that government was based on consent and arose as a means of adjudicating civil conflict. He opposed Hobbes's absolutist conception of the state, proposing instead that the powers of government should be divided between the executive (the sovereign), the legislative (parliament) and the judiciary. Montesquieu was a student and admirer of the British constitution, and his concern that the power of the state should be dispersed among different sources of authority was reflected in *The Spirit of Laws* ([1746] 1900, pp. 151–2)):

> When the legislative and executive powers are united in the same person, or in the same body of magistrates, there can be no liberty; because apprehensions may arise, lest the same monarch or senate should enact tyrannical laws, to execute them in a tyrannical manner. Again there is no liberty, if the judiciary power be not separated from the legislative and executive. Were it joined with the legislative, the life and liberty of the subject would be exposed to arbitrary control; for the judge would then be the legislator. Were it joined to the executive power, the judge might behave with violence and oppression.

The writers of the American Constitution were influenced by both Locke and Montesquieu. Madison, who was concerned about the potential conflict between majoritarian democracy and 'liberty', comments at length in *Federalist No. 47* on the passage from Montesquieu

---

1 Atoms are the ultimate and indivisible components of a whole. The parallel here with the atomism of reductionist science is easy to see.

quoted above, observing, however, that neither in Britain nor in the constitutions of the American States were the legislative, executive and judiciary departments totally separate from each other. The essential point (as argued in *Federalist 48*) was rather that each department should have a degree of constitutional control over the others.

Here it should be noted that Locke, Montesquieu and Madison associated liberty with the security to enjoy one's rights. Some fifty years after the publication of the *Federalist Papers*, Tocqueville ([1835] 1945, p. 245) could observe: 'The government of a democracy brings the notion of political rights to the level of the humblest citizen, just as the dissemination of wealth brings the notion of property within the reach of all men . . . In America there are no paupers'. The freedoms that this widespread dissemination of wealth and political rights guaranteed seemed, however, to be threatened by majoritarian democracy. In *Federalist 10* Madison wrote that democracy required majority rule, but a united majority faction could 'sacrifice to its ruling passion or interest both the public good and the rights of other citizens'. Madison was thinking particularly of property rights, since the possession of property was the most prominent source of faction. Following the classical economists, he said that different interests in property divide a nation into different classes 'actuated by different sentiments and views' (Madison, [1787] 1888, p. 54). In majoritarian democracy any one of these interests could rule against the rights of the others. Madison's solution was for the maximum territorial extent of the sphere of national government (the Federal Republic) to bring together the maximum variety of interests, factions and parties. Thus, to the plurality of interests connected with property and the three departments of government was added the plurality of interests connected with place, providing a system of checks on every part, which would prevent the emergence of a majority united by common interest.

Tocqueville believed that three factors acted to contain the threat of majority tyranny in America: the territorially fragmented system for implementing central policy; the independent, conservative, anti-democratic nature of the legal profession, which mediated between the executive and the people; and trial by jury, which asserted the principle of popular sovereignty against the exercise of central power. Of dispersed implementation Tocqueville ([1835] 1945, p. 272) wrote:

When the central government which represents that majority has issued a decree it must entrust the execution of its will to agents over whom it frequently has no control and whom it cannot perpetually direct. The townships, municipal bodies and counties form so many concealed breakwaters which check or part the tide of popular determination.

What later came to be regarded as a problem of implementation of central policy was for Tocqueville a virtue. For example, large-scale comprehensive planning of the urban region in America is widely regarded as impossible because of the myriad of semi-autonomous public authorities involved (see Sharkansky, 1975; Rich, 1977, 1982). However, such planning on behalf of the majority of the electorate of a region would have been regarded by Tocqueville as politically threatening to the rights of minorities.

The demand for public participation in planning became a major issue in the 1960s following the destructive effects of urban redevelopment on minority interests. Tocqueville viewed participation (through, for example, the institution of jury trials) as a powerful way of educating the public in rights, laws and 'political good sense'. From a British perspective, John Stuart Mill placed even greater weight on participation, not only in the administration of justice but in government generally. He viewed participation as an instrument and, more broadly, a body of influence, which was capable of undermining the related evils of ignorance, indolence and class conflict (see Duncan, 1973, p. 250). Mill argued that, since the leadership of society would inevitably be in the hands of an elite, it was necessary to ensure that its members were educated in the broadest sense and deeply valued individual liberty and democracy. The individual would, therefore, learn the politics of democracy by participating in local institutions and associations. 'We do not learn to read or write, to ride or swim, by merely being told how to do it but by doing it, so it is only by practising popular government on a limited scale, that people will ever learn how to exercise it on a large scale' (Mill, [1835] 1973, p. 186). Local democracy was not just local representative government, although this was important, but participation in the organization and 'governance' of any kind of group that makes political demands and plays a political role.

Both Tocqueville ([1835] 1945, Vol. 2, p. 109) and, later, Weber (1946, p. 57 and p. 308) noticed the tendency of Americans to join groups. Tocqueville observed that, 'as soon as several of the inhabitants of the United States have taken up an opinion or a feeling which they wish to promote in the world, they look for mutual assistance; and as soon as they have found one another out, they combine'. Weber observed that American society was constituted not so much by 'a formless sand heap of individuals' (an image of Durkheim's) but by a multitude of organized groups. Individuals referred to groups – not only voluntary associations but families, schools, trade unions, ethnic and religious groups – for their political understanding. Class interests, in so far as they could be observed, worked through the agency of pressure groups, unions and political parties. Social action occurred not so much through the direct participation of individuals as through participation by individuals in active groups. Simmel ([1908] 1955) argued that intergroup conflict should not be regarded as socially destructive. What appeared destructive to relationships between individuals considered in isolation could play a positive role in consolidating the wider system of social relationships. Lewis Coser (1956) later found in Simmel's work sixteen propositions concerning the functions of social conflict, to which he added his own commentary and his own reformulated propositions. Group participation was thus viewed as a binding force in society and conflict and competition among interest groups was something to be valued.

By the beginning of this century, the ideas that formed the foundations for the modern theory of pluralism were already widely known and discussed. As we have seen there were three main strands of thought: the defence of individual liberty from state power and majority tyranny, the virtues of interest group membership in educating people, particularly elites, in democratic norms, and the capacity of interest groups to create solidarity in an individualistic and atomized society. We now turn to a more direct line of development of the pluralist ideal type, beginning with the work of Bentley and Truman.

The analytical pluralists and group activity

The starting point for modern pluralist theory is the significance in political life of active interest groups. There are two distinct, if related, streams in American pluralism, one which stressed the organic composition of society stemming from group membership (see Lustig, 1982) and one which remained more strongly under the influence of atomism and individualism. We shall refer to the former in the next chapter; here we focus on the latter stream. Olson (1965) used the term 'analytical pluralists' to describe those such as Bentley and Truman who postulated that politics was entirely derivative of group activity. Both these writers followed the principle of 'methodological individualism' (see Lukes, 1973), which holds that, to be meaningful, all statements about society must be reduced to statements about individuals. All collectivities (classes, groups, the state) are therefore to be regarded as aggregates of individuals. The group, however, became the means of expression of individuals and took the place of the individual as the 'social atom'. Odegard provides a comprehensive list of writers of this school, and those influenced directly by Bentley in particular, in his introduction to the 1963 Harvard University Press edition of Bentley's *The Process of Government*.

Following the lead of Weber's positivism and Marx's materialism,

Bentley sought to identify the basic practices from which all political ideas and moral sentiments flowed. He attacked what he regarded as specious rhetoric, which passed for political analysis at the turn of the century. The expression of such 'feelings and ideas' could not be separated from the real political activities and interests that generated them. Action, including all the political 'talk' as one variety of action, was for Bentley the raw material of political analysis (Bentley, [1908] 1935, p. 198).

Bentley wanted to emulate what he understood as the method of physics, which was to reduce the object of inquiry to its most basic components and measure their interactions. This most basic component of political society was the group. Individuals were only politically significant in their capacity to act socially, that is, in groups. It is interesting that Bentley considered the starting point for the group interpretation of society to be the work of Karl Marx (see, for example, Bentley, [1908] 1935, pp. 304, 305, 466, 467). But he did not, of course, conceive of class as Marx did, in terms of a wider economic theory of production and exploitation. Like Madison, he viewed class in political terms as a form of interest group. Marx and Engels were, in Bentley's view, political activists and the leaders of a group cause, that of the proletariat. In promoting this cause, Bentley argued, 'the group [the proletariat], was erected in talk into a class' (p. 466.). The specific group interest of Marx and Engels led them to create historical materialism as a theory of society that was not, in fact, capable of explaining the variety of politically significant group interests.

Political phenomena, government, interests, ideals, values, opinions and social structures were derived, in the first place, from the activity of groups pressing against one another. Having stated that the phenomena of government are 'from start to finish phenomena of force' Bentley immediately reinterpreted 'force' as 'pressure', since 'bringing pressure to bear' was what groups did to one another. Therefore: 'All phenomena of government are phenomena of groups pressing against one another, and pushing out new groups and group representatives to mediate the adjustments' (Bentley, [1908] 1935, p. 269). Later, we shall see that urban planners can be seen in this light, as mediators of interest group adjustment. This view of government is, of course, very different from that of Weber, who said that government was based on the legitimate use of *violence*.

Bentley defined his term, 'pressure' in very broad terms because he was aware of the need to account for things he could not directly observe. He writes: 'tendencies to activity are pressures as well as the more visible activities' (p. 259). He describes 'underlying groups' that are formed by biological factors (racial or ethnic), environmental conditions ('we have groups resting on mines, farms, cattle herds, city lots'; p. 462), the technical division of labour in industry, and the ownership of wealth. He did not regard territory as a strong influence on group formation and placed much more importance on the ownership of wealth 'because of their [wealth groups'] liability to fierce activity when thrown out of adjustment at any time, and further because of the direct and indirect technical advantages that the wealthier groups secure' (p. 462).

Government was defined in four ways: first, as any process of adjustment of interest groups in a society; secondly, in a narrow sense, as 'a differentiated, representative group or set of groups performing specified governing functions for the underlying groups in the population'. Thirdly, in an intermediate sense, government is a political process in which organized groups take part; in this sense, economic organizations, firms, when they make political demands, are part of the governing process as much as political parties or any pressure groups. The fourth sense of the term is the governance or administration of any organization. 'A corporation is government through and through. It is itself a balancing of interests, even though it presents itself in many of its activities as a unit' (Bentley, [1908] 1935, p. 268).

Bentley says he is not interested in the concept of the state, only in actual human processes. Dewey (1927, pp. 8–9), likewise, preferred terms like 'the public domain' or 'public sphere' or simply 'the public', arguing that theories of the state tended to obscure real differences among actual states, which could only be understood by looking at 'the facts' of human activity. Before dismissing the concept, however, Bentley makes an interesting point which, improbably perhaps, finds an echo in Gramsci's blurring of the boundary between civil and political power (see chapter 8). The state 'could probably be well defined as the sum of the activities comprised within the intermediate sense of the word "government". All those activities which together make up the whole process would correspond fairly well to "the politically organized society"' (Bentley, [1908] 1935, p. 263). Thus Bentley has no difficulty in including many of the activities of the 'private sector' within both government and the state. Indeed, he specifically denies a clear distinction between the private and public sectors: 'As for a very common mode of expression, which puts the state and the phenomena of government in general in a class all by themselves with sanctions peculiar and distinct from those of other forms of social organization, it is perhaps needless to add that we shall have no use for it here . . . The penalties the state inflicts are simply special forms of a great class of penalties imposed by all social organizations' (p. 264).

Finally, throughout his discussion Bentley is careful to avoid any sort of normative commitment and he scoffs at ideas and political talk.

Is there not nevertheless a normative theme to be found in Bentley's work? Rothman (1960) discerns two 'supernumerary propositions': first, that politics is group competition and, second, that group interaction produces stability. 'Stability' is plainly an evaluative term, which Bentley does not appear to have used. However, he did consider the possibility of a society being 'well adjusted', which might be said to amount to the same thing. If society is 'nothing other than the complex of groups that compose it', then government is the process whereby group pressures are 'adjusted'. If there has ever been 'a relatively perfect adjustment of any society', then it would have been a function of 'underlying group conditions, of situations and disturbances of situations due to factors far down beneath the political level, however reacted upon in special phases from the political level' (Rothman, 1960, p. 458).

David Truman ([1951] 1965) both popularized and extended Bentley's work. He divided interest groups into active pressure groups, always small minorities, and more widespread *potential* interest groups, which possess an attitude but do not interact. Since pressure groups frequently needed the support and approval of potential groups, the latter could be said to exercise real power. 'The unacknowledged power of such unorganized interests lies in the possibility that, if too flagrantly ignored, they may be stimulated to organize for aggressive counteraction' (Truman, [1951] 1965, p. 114).

Two main factors tended to produce cohesion and stability in society: overlapping group membership and 'the rules of the game'. Most people participated in many different activities and had a variety of interests and loyalties. These interests involved them in the network of group activities at many different points. For example, members of a local conservation group might variously belong to the ratepayers' association, the football club, a building workers' union, the chamber of commerce or the planning profession. When a conflict arose over a new development, a variety of views would then be heard within the conservation group itself, making some accommodation with the developer more likely. The power of potential interests effectively constituted the 'rules of the game'. These rules referred to the basic democratic freedoms (of speech, the press and assembly as contained in the Bill of Rights Amendments to the American Constitution), the protection of opportunities for mass participation in the selection of leaders and policies in all social groups, the rule of law, and 'semi-egalitarian notions of material welfare' (Truman, [1951] 1965, p. 513). In short, they are widely held democratic values whose violation would weaken the legitimacy of claims made by the violators.

The postulated existence of 'rules' embedded in widespread opinion perhaps accounts for the fairly common view that pluralism necessarily assumes an underlying consensus in society on political values (Alford and Friedland, 1985, pp. 59–82). However, there is no consensus among pluralists on this matter. Talcott Parsons and some others (e.g. Riesman, 1950; Parsons and Smelser, 1956; Almond and Verba, 1963) have undoubtedly stressed value consensus as the basis of social order. Dahl and Lindblom postulated a certain level of 'agreement' on democratic methods as one of the preconditions for polyarchy (see p. 101). But consensus certainly formed no part of Bentley's thinking, and Truman quite explicitly did not expect people to agree on underlying democratic values, because he understood that different interpretations of what constituted democracy could be in conflict. In his earlier work he believed these various interpretations to be widely held, but in an introduction to the 1971 second edition of *The Governmental Process* (Truman, [1951] 1965), he substantially revised his view of 'the rules of the game', admitting that the rules may have little basis in widespread opinion, let alone popular consensus. Rather, they are underpinned by assumptions by *competing elites* about what will be regarded as publicly acceptable.

Truman ([1951] 1965, pp. 506, 507) says that groups have varying 'access' to government decision-making. The degree to which they can exert influence depends on three somewhat overlapping factors: (1) the group's status or prestige in society, the standing it has with regard to the 'rules of the game' (the values of potential groups), the extent to which government officials (elected and appointed) are formally or informally members of the group, and the group's usefulness as a source of technical or political knowledge; (2) the internal organization of the group in terms of its cohesion and the effectiveness of its leadership, and its resources (membership numbers and money); (3) the operating structure of the government institutions, which may give certain groups or types of groups a particular advantage. The product of effective access – of groups contending for influence – is government decision. The interests that result in government decision need not be 'selfish', solidly unified or even represented by organized groups – potential groups also exert influence without actively pressing claims.

Truman ([1951] 1965, p. 522) considered two possible sources of instability in group interaction, both associated with social stratification. The first stemmed from the fact that participation in organized groups occurred to a greater degree in the 'higher than the lower reaches of the class structure'. People who did not normally participate in group interaction in the ordinary course of events would not learn the 'rules' of democratic pressure. When eventually stimulated by changing conditions to act, they might not do so by acceptable democratic means or be restrained by the norms of potential groups. 'Extensive unemployment and severe inflation', Truman wrote, 'bring such drastic changes, and the history of movements of the fascist type illustrate the destructive forms such situations can produce' (p. 522). Secondly, the alignment of group with class interests could possibly produce widely divergent interpretations of the public interest, which could possibly not be reconciled or result in a stable compromise.

Normatively, Truman is somewhat more forthcoming than Bentley. He proceeds from the assumption that a stable and acceptable form of democracy is operating in the United States. This 'going political system' is 'balanced', 'responsive', 'flexible' and 'stable'. He feels no need to restate at any length the basic democratic freedoms, because these are entrenched as rules not just in the Constitution but as public interests. Because society is composed of nothing but a plurality of interests, none of which has a privileged claim over any other (there is no way of judging 'fairness' other than from the point of view of a particular interest), a good polity will be a process that allows those interests to find expression and to influence government decisions.

For Bentley and Truman politics was derived from and explained by group interaction. All policy, including that which created structures of government, was the outcome of the *process* of groups acting separately or in coalition. Therefore, political structure did not have to be conceptualized separately as 'the state'. What appeared as the state was merely the outcome of the process. A stable and representative polity was the product of participation by individuals in group activity, of overlapping membership, of shared conceptions of what constitutes acceptable political behaviour enforced by larger and more widespread 'potential groups' – the many checking the power of the few.

Urban planners in practice have to take account of many interest groups in society, some of which bring formidable pressure to bear to make them alter their plans. What right have these groups to be heard and to exert influence? Bentley and Truman suggested some answers. Accountability in a pluralist democracy does not flow from elected office alone but from the political process. Elections, which enable large unorganized 'potential' interest groups to exert influence through their elected representatives in government, are just one part of this process. But the process itself is based on free interaction among many *minority* interest groups. The job of people in government, like planners, is to 'mediate the adjustments' among all interest groups (both pressure groups and potential groups). Urban plans, like all government policies, must encompass the many minority interests in society; so, of course, interest groups have a right to exert influence. Planners must recognize that right by looking after those interests in the plans they make. Above all, planners must respect the 'rules of the game' in a pluralist democracy that allow for political decisions to be made through group competition. Planners play significant roles in this game (see p. 117) but they have no special privilege that makes their value judgements superior to those of any other players.

Criticisms of analytical pluralism

The work of political scientists and sociologists challenged two central aspects of analytical pluralism: the theory's assumptions about interest groups, and the consequences of interest-group activity for society and its political organization (see Waste, 1987 pp. 13, 14). Analytical pluralism was modelled on a certain conception of a purposeful and politically active group pressing demands. Individuals joined or formed groups to pursue their interests. Structures of interest and mutual influence in society were understood in terms of this conception. But when examined at the interpersonal level, influence within groups was found to be far from purposeful. Lazarsfeld, Berelson and Gaudet (1944, p. 138) turned the matter the other way around: people join 'interest groups' that tend to confirm their viewpoint, which has already been determined by primary factors (for example, family and personal contacts of similar socio-economic status, religion and place of residence). Further, groups tend to shape the opinions of individuals (Festinger, Schachter and Back, 1950, p. 168).

As Sidney Verba (1961, p. 18) put it, the 'primary group' was rediscovered: 'it is to the face-to-face group that one must look if one is to find the locus of decision-making in political systems' (p. 19). The study of social psychology by scholars as varied as Whyte (1947), Lewin (1948), Homans (1951) and Moreno (1947) showed that group membership performed a variety of psychological and emotional functions for the individual, that power structures within the group often determined its decisions, and that the pursuit of the task of representing the interests of its members was subject to dynamics of which its members were unlikely to be aware.

From a quite different perspective, Michels ([1915] 1968) had argued that the interests of leaders of organizations invariably come to differ from those of the rank and file members; this 'iron law of oligarchy' called into question the representativeness of pressure groups. Furthermore, from empirical studies of group membership it was found that joining interest groups was by no means a universal phenomenon in America but was linked to class and status (Dotson, 1951; Scott, 1957; Hausknecht, 1962). Olson (1965), in an argument from utility theory, demonstrated why the ties that hold together the membership of large voluntary associations must be quite different from those that bind small family and kinship groups. He concluded that the larger the group, the less it will be able to further its common interests (Olson,

1965, p. 36). This is because, for the individual the opportunity costs of actively organizing to obtain a *collective* benefit are always greater than the benefit received, which must be shared among all members of the group. The economically attractive alternative (opportunity) is to be a 'free rider' – to share in the public goods provided without being actively involved oneself. In order to hold members, then, a large association must offer inducements (either negative in the form of coercion or exclusiveness, or positive in the form of fringe benefits) other than those associated directly with the pursuit of the collective interests of its members. However, Olson's view of the self-interested rationality of the individual may be too narrow. In support of his argument he writes: 'There are multitudes with an interest in peace, but they have no lobby to match those of the special interests that may on occasion have an interest in war' (Olson, 1965, p. 166). But a peace lobby did emerge against the Vietnam War. How are the Women's Movement or the Environment Movement to be explained, or the workers' movements in nineteenth century Europe? (see Colby, 1982).

The work of Eckstein (1960), Olson (1965, pp. 148–53) and McConnell (1967) all pointed to the fact that the relationship between interest groups and the state was not simply one of demand and supply but rather of interpenetration. McConnell found that regulatory agencies were frequently 'captured' by those they were supposed to regulate. The major conflicts in the field of land and water policy in the USA, for example, took the form of conflicts about jurisdictional demarcation and spheres of influence among rival agencies. These disputes were typically settled by 'log rolling' in which substantial parts of the population and important interests were simply excluded (McConnell, 1967, p. 244). Decentralization of control enhanced the power of local elites and prevented broader constituencies – those, for instance, with an interest in the abolition of rural poverty – from being represented. Similar observations have been made about the effect of government intervention and government structures on urban land-use politics and the provision of social services (see Hill, 1974; Rich, 1982; Mollenkopf, 1983; Badcock, 1984). Mollenkopf (1983, p. 14) points out that Federal government intervention shaped by national party elites 'accelerated and directed the second [post-industrial] transformation of American cities'. But, as Badcock observes, any government action in the USA has to be viewed in the context of a system that is 'a hotch-potch of myriad overlapping jurisdictions in which the underlying purpose seems to be to restrict delivery [of services] to a group of ratepayers hand picked by the housing market, and to avoid the issues and costs of redistribution'. We could go further (with Zeigler, 1980, p. 16) and turn upside down the analytical pluralists' view of the role of interest groups *vis-à-vis* the state. The activity of groups does not create the state; rather, public policy decisions bring interest groups into existence, and the structure of the state shapes the form they will take.

Turning to the normative aspect of pluralism, the analytical pluralists had argued that the consequence of interest group activity was a stable equilibrium among multiple sources of power, all contending for dominance. Rothman (1960, p. 21) asks why the present distribution of power should be regarded as any more stable than in the past. Mills (1956) had suggested that the 'romantic pluralism' of the 'balance of power theory' was convenient for the power elite, because it enabled those who wanted to change the power structure to be labelled 'disturbers of the peace and upsetters of the universal interests inherent in business–labor co-operation' (Mills, 1956, p. 246). He agreed that a multiplicity of groups with different interests and sources of power existed in the middle levels of American society, but he said that pluralism paid undue attention to the middle levels and obscured the structure of power as a whole, especially the top and the bottom. Lowi (1969) contended that there was nothing ideal about present-day group competition that excluded certain groups (blacks in particular) from most of the benefits of society, that the theory failed to account for oligopoly and imperfect competition and that the pluralist paradigm depended on an idealized and miscast conception of 'the group'. Lowi pointed out that in factional rivalry the most powerful faction wins. It was the business of government to rule in the public interest. 'Once sentimentality toward the group is destroyed', he writes, 'it will be possible to see how group interactions fall short of creating an ideal equilibrium.' McConnell (1967) insisted that a pluralist decentralized politics provided no guarantee that all significant interests in society would find representation. Although it was true that in 'public' government the presumption existed that nobody was excluded from the constituency of some unit and therefore everyone had some chance of exerting influence, no such presumption could be made about 'private' political organizations such as corporations and 'quasi-public functional units' (McConnell, 1967, p. 349).

The critics of analytical pluralism threw considerable doubt on the benign effect of interest group competition and on the role of the planner as mediator. In the perspective put forward by these critics, planners were likely to have a symbiotic relationship with the development industry. It could not be said that professional judgements on urban planning matters would necessarily produce just and right decisions. But nor could it be assumed that group competition would result in such decisions either. The criteria for just decisions 'in the public interest' in fact remained highly debatable. Both the analytical pluralists and their critics draw attention to the fact that 'governance' is not an exclusive function of 'governments' and extends to corporations in a 'sector' of public life we are accustomed to call 'private'.

Institutional Pluralism

The major stimulus to the further development of pluralism arguably did not come from theoretical critique but from political practice. As noted above, analytical pluralism had little to say about the leadership, organization or planning of the state. But, by the time of the Second World War, states in all countries of the industrialized world were playing an active and increasingly dominant role in the economy and society. The war further advanced the growth of the state and emphasized the need for political leadership and planning. Theorists from divergent normative perspectives considered the possibility that capitalism would be swept away, to be replaced by some form of 'planned society' organized by the state (Lippmann, 1937; Mannheim, 1940; Schumpeter, 1943; Hayek, 1944; Lorwin, 1945; Jay, 1947; Mises, [1949] 1963). Schumpeter, however much he regretted the passing of the liberal era, regarded the planned society (whether accomplished by state or corporate sector bureaucracies) as a natural and logical extension of mature capitalism. The question was how the elite could be controlled. His theory of 'competitive leadership' refocused pluralist thinking on the institutional context of group competition and foreshadowed Dahl's and Lindblom's concept of 'polyarchy' as 'control of leaders'.

Before discussing polyarchy, therefore, it is worth briefly considering Schumpeter's argument. First, he suggested that there could be no such thing as a uniquely determined 'common good', because to different individuals the 'common good' was bound to mean different things. Furthermore, even if a people could agree on some way of defining a common good – for example, with reference to the utilitarian conception of the aggregate of individual economic satisfactions – there would still be a great deal of irreducible conflict of opinion over the means of achieving it.

Secondly, the importance that classic democratic theory attached to the 'independence and rational quality' of the individual, he said, was wholly unrealistic. Everyone would have to know definitely what he stood for. And from each definite standpoint 'a clear and *prompt* conclusion as to particular issues would have to be derived according to the rules of logical inference – with so high a degree of general efficiency, moreover, that one man's opinion could be held, without glaring absurdity, to be roughly as good as every other man's' (Schumpeter, 1943, pp. 253–4). Further, even if such a condition realistically held good, it would not necessarily follow that, where there were many different, equally valid opinions, the outcome by majoritarian voting would conform to 'what people really want'. And not only may democratic decision-making *not* produce what people really want but non-democratic decision-making may produce it. Thirdly, human nature was such that rational argument was not, by a long way, the most important influence on human behaviour. There was every reason to suppose that people often behaved irrationally, especially when in large masses. Individually, too, people could be easily influenced by non-rational methods of persuasion. Where people did behave rationally, as in assessing the pecuniary effects of policies on them, they tended to take account only of their short-run benefit. Finally, echoing analytical pluralism, Schumpeter asserted that it was not the individual but the group that is the most significant unit in political organization. The activity of political groups (parties and pressure groups) 'fashion and within very wide limits even . . . create the will of the people' (Schumpeter, 1943, p. 264).

Schumpeter explained the persistence of democracy as a set of ideas in terms of its religious origins. Its values of equality and fraternity were to be found in the ethic of protestant dissent. Further, the forms and language of democracy were, for many nations, associated with historical events that were enthusiastically approved by large majorities. Politicians found that the symbolic language of democracy 'flatters the masses and offers an excellent opportunity not only for evading responsibility but also for crushing opponents in the name of the people' (Schumpeter, 1943, p. 268). The principal virtue of the present democratic system was that it enabled responsible and competent leaders to emerge. Therefore, Schumpeter redefined democracy as: 'That institutional arrangement for arriving at political decisions in which individuals acquire the power to decide by means of a competitive struggle for the people's vote.' Thus the core of the idea of democracy was seen not as popular representation but as elite competition.

Although taking a less jaundiced view of democratic ideas than Schumpeter, Dahl and Lindblom built political competition and the struggle for leadership into their concept of polyarchy, for only through political competition for votes could leaders be popularly controlled. *Politics, Economics and Welfare* (Dahl and Lindblom, 1953) is a response to the idea of 'the planned society'. As such it is a book about planning. The authors do not limit their analysis to governments and states but speak in terms of 'organizations'. They thus go beyond the ideological distinction between 'public' and 'private' sectors. In an analysis reminiscent of Mannheim (1940), Dahl and Lindblom postulate four 'politico-economic techniques' through which people are organized to attack social problems and pursue goals. These are techniques of social control without which any social action is impossible. The four techniques are the price system (control of and by leaders), hierarchy (control by leaders), bargaining (control among leaders) and polyarchy (control of leaders by non-leaders). In modern societies, according to the authors, all of these processes are necessary. Polyarchy, which is the newest and least developed of the four techniques, is about the institutionalized control of those who control the planners: the 'first problem of politics' – of 'how citizens can keep their rulers from becoming tyrants' (Dahl and Lindblom, 1953, p. 273).

As Waste (1987, pp. 17–19) has pointed out, 'polyarchy' is an ideal type derived from observation of modern capitalist democracies. It is descriptive of the politics of such societies, but it is also a normative concept in both an implicit and an explicit sense. In choosing existing modern Western capitalist society as a model, Dahl and Lindblom implicitly express an *assenting* value position. They also explicitly refine certain institutional characteristics of modern Western politics which act as a benchmark or which suggest patterns in which states may evolve as they strengthen democratic institutions and practices and which 'suggest the shape(s) that truly democratic government – government "at the limits of human realization" – might eventually take' (Waste, 1987, p. 18). It is the normative propositions of polyarchy that provide Dahl's and Lindblom's pluralism with its critical edge.

The characteristics of polyarchy (Dahl and Lindblom 1953 pp. 277–8) are those institutional arrangements for popular control of leadership that have evolved in varying shapes and forms in Western capitalist democracies:

1   Most adults in the organization have the opportunity to vote in elections with no significant rewards and penalties directly attached either to the act of voting or to the choices among candidates.
2   In elections the vote of each member has about the same weight.
3   Non-elected officials are subordinate to elected leaders in making organization policy. That is, when they so wish, elected leaders can have the last word on policy with non-elected officials.
4   Elected leaders in turn are subordinate to non-leaders, in the sense that those in office will be displaced by alternative leaders in a peaceful and relatively prompt manner whenever a greater number of voters cast their votes for alternative leaders than for those in office.
5   Adults in the organization have available to them several alternative sources of information, including some that are not under significant unilateral control by government leaders. 'Available'

in this context means only that members who wish to do so can utilize these sources without incurring penalties initiated by government leaders or their subordinates.

6 Members of the organization who accept these rules have an opportunity, either directly or through delegates to offer rival policies and candidates without severe penalties for their doing so.

Dahl uses the term 'polyarchy' to refer both to a set of criteria for an ideal or 'egalitarian' polyarchy, and to those societies that approximate to the ideal (see Waste, 1987, p. 26). The shift from description to prescription has given rise to criticism of Dahl, not all of it deserved. To qualify as a polyarchy a modern state must at least have a majoritarian form of rule and extend institutional guarantees to its members, which enable them: (i) to formulate their preferences; (ii) to signify their preferences to their fellow citizens and the government by individual and collective action; (iii) to have their preferences weighed equally in the conduct of government, that is, weighed with no discrimination because of the content or source of the preference (Dahl, 1971, p. 2). The ideal criteria of polyarchy, whose complete achievement would define a state as an 'egalitarian polyarchy', are those already put forth in *Politics, Economics and Welfare* (Dahl and Lindblom, 1953), but conceptually re-organized and with two additions. For clarity, it is worth giving Dahl's reworked version in full (Dahl, 1956, p. 84):

Polyarchy is defined loosely as a political system in which the following conditions exist to a relatively high degree:

During the voting period:
1 Every member of the organization performs the acts we assume to constitute an expression of preference among the scheduled alternatives, e.g., voting.
2 In tabulating these expressions (votes), the weight assigned to the choice of each individual is identical.
3 The alternative with the greatest number of votes is declared the winning choice.

During the pre-voting period:
4 Any member who perceives a set of alternatives, at least one of which he regards as preferable to any of the alternatives presently scheduled, can insert his preferred alternative(s) among those scheduled for voting.
5 All individuals possess identical information about the alternatives.

During the post-voting period:
6   Alternatives (leaders or policies) with the greatest number of votes displace any alternatives (leaders or policies) with fewer votes.
7   The orders of elected officials are executed.

During the inter-election stage:
8.1   Either all interelection decisions are subordinate or executory to those arrived at during the election stage, i.e., elections are in a sense controlling.
8.2   Or new decisions during the interelection period are governed by the preceding seven conditions, operating, however, under rather different institutional circumstances.
8.3   Or both.

We now have a picture of an ideal state approximated but not achieved by Western democracies, as well as a list of necessary but not sufficient conditions which would allow a state to qualify as a polyarchy in a less restrictive sense of the term. Dahl and Lindblom (1953) and later Dahl (1956, 1971) also considered the 'socio-political' preconditions that would encourage the growth of such a state. What the authors evidently mean by 'preconditions' are the non-institutional aspects of the political organization of a given society. They are not 'prior' in any temporal sense but outside the formal institutional structure. Agreeing with Michels about the tendency to inequality of power in organizations, Dahl and Lindblom nevertheless argue that the 'iron law of oligarchy' is counteracted by a 'law' of reciprocity. Social control can very rarely be exercised by pure command. Because almost everyone in an organization has some power – over other people, information, perceptions, rewards and deprivations, the use of time, – social control, even in a hierarchy, requires bilateral or multilateral relationships 'in which two or more people are controlling one another through command or manipulation of fields, or both' (Dahl and Lindblom, 1953, p. 109). Reciprocity is assisted when leaders must win their control by competing with one another for the support of non-leaders and where non-leaders have the opportunity to switch their support away from the incumbent leaders to their rivals (p. 283). Here the authors are talking not about political institutions but the organization of groups, from street corner gangs to political parties. What is required is the existence of alternatives, so that non-leaders retain some power over who receives their allegiance. What then accounts for the existence of such alternatives?

There are, say the authors, six preconditions. First, all people have to be socialized in the tradition of democratic culture. Through myth and history, stories, ceremonials, parades, oratory, music, the schools, theatre, movies, books, magazines, newspapers and all the paraphernalia of ideology, people learn what is acceptable, what is approved and rewarded and what political behaviour is taboo: 'In these ways individuals are indoctrinated with an unreasoned inner conviction of the fitness and rightness – in a word, the legitimacy – of polyarchal systems' (Dahl and Lindblom, 1953, p. 289). Political leaders in particular are products of this process. Their own indoctrination in the value of polyarchy as well as their assumption that wrong behaviour will be punished prevents them from contemplating autocratic or unilateral control. The ideological system itself provides acceptable alternatives to violence for attacking opponents. Secondly, and following from the above, a certain level of consensus among the politically active on democratic methods is necessary. How much agreement and on what, the authors concede, is little understood. Although acknowledging that agreement on basic constitutional matters is essential, they argue both that rational planning does not *require* agreement on an overriding purpose and that the degree of agreement in most polyarchies is, in any case, sufficient to ensure the continuity of most major policies.

A third precondition for polyarchy is 'social pluralism': the existence in society of 'a number of different organizations through which control is exerted and over which no unified body of leaders exerts control' (Dahl and Lindblom, 1953, p. 302). Social pluralism provides citizens with the power to express their policy preferences with the weight of an organization behind them; it throws up rival leaders, it supplies leaders with the skills to negotiate and to consolidate alliances, thus welding society together. Social pluralism also 'increases the probability that one is simultaneously a member of more than one social organization; hence, action by a leader against what seems to be an enemy organization may in fact strike against his own alliance' (p. 305). These cross-cutting allegiances help further guarantee the solidarity of society. Social pluralism helps secure alternative sources of advice and information. While the mass of the people may not want to hear alternative views, as Lazarsfeld, Berelson and Gaudet (1944) suggested, 'those who specialize in criticism and communication *can* make use of alternative sources of information' (Dahl and Lindblom, 1953, p. 305).

The fourth and fifth preconditions of polyarchy are, respectively, a relatively high level of participation in the governmental process and the openness of political elites to new recruitment. Enough people must participate, so that political leaders compete for the support of a 'more or less representative cross-section of the population' (Dahl and Lindblom, 1953, p. 309). In practice, participation varies greatly both among polyarchies and on different issues within polyarchies. A variety of factors operates so that participation is unlikely to result in a specific policy decision reflecting the preferences of a majority of people:

> About the most that can be said for polyarchy is that, if opportunities for political action are kept open to a representative section of the adult population, specific policies will rarely violate highly ranked, intense, stable, and relatively broad preferences of the greater number for a longer period than about the interval between elections (Dahl and Lindblom, 1953, p. 314).

Polyarchy is thus a system which, in the long term and only in fits and starts, adjusts itself to the demands of a population. In a later formulation, Lindblom (1968) conceived of the political public in terms of a pyramid with a broad base of people who merely 'expose themselves to political stimuli' (40 to 70 per cent of citizens in the USA, according to Lindblom) and a very small apex who hold public and party office (less than 1 per cent). Lindblom admits: 'Most citizens are little interested in playing even a small policy-making role; fully a third of American citizens neither vote, join interest groups, do party work, communicate with their representatives, nor talk politics with their friends, except occasionally in a vague and uninformed way' (Lindblom, 1968, p. 44). However, Lindblom suggested that political parties tend both to seek out preferences and to shape them. 'The politician maintains a sensitive listening post; a small rustle among his constituents often makes a big noise in his office' (Dahl and Lindblom, 1953, p. 314) A democratic system is like a ladder in which simultaneously there is an upward flow of opinion and a downward flow of decisions on policies and programmes. While the upward flow starts with only vague and inchoate opinions, on the way up these views are given definite form by politically active groups interacting with and criticizing decisions flowing down, and formulating alternatives. Throughout the system there are many sources of information and advice competing for followings. Not only political leaders but also analysts and advisers seek to outperform their rivals in offering pertinent information (Lindblom, 1968, pp. 103–4).

The sixth precondition consists of a set of variables including psychological security, limited disparity of wealth, and widespread education. Dahl and Lindblom do not develop these variables which, they claim, are widely accepted. These six conditions, then, work together to support and reproduce polyarchy: 'social indoctrination facilitates political circulation, maintenance and toleration of social pluralism, agreement and political activity. Agreement facilitates social indoctrination and toleration of social pluralism. Political activity facilitates circulation and may facilitate social pluralism, agreement and social indoctrination. And so it goes' (Dahl and Lindblom, 1953, p. 319). This is, of course, comparable with what Marxists call 'overdetermination' (see chapter 8 p. 217) or even 'hegemony' (see chapter 8 pp. 204-6).

Dahl and Lindblom have always acknowledged the obvious fact that economic resources in the United States are extremely unequally distributed, a situation very different from the America Tocqueville observed. They also agree that economic power not only opens the way to political power but *is* itself a form of political power (see Dahl and Lindblom, 1953, p. 318). The question they pose is whether political power has many sources that compete with one another (pluralism), or whether most political power is concentrated in the hands of a single long-enduring if not permanent elite (elitism). The empirical studies of the power structure of local communities undertaken by Robert and Helen Lynd in Muncie, Indiana, and Floyd Hunter in Atlanta, Georgia, had supported the latter conclusion. Hunter (1963) conducted a survey of key people in the city and asked them to pick the most powerful ten people from a long list of the city's leaders. This list was compiled from a study of contemporary documentation on Atlanta and various authoritative sources. Hunter concluded that there were only a small number of people who held real power in Atlanta and most of them were leaders of the business community. Within this group there were different overlapping cliques who took the lead on different policy issues.

Dahl (1961) argued that the investigation of reputation might not be sufficient to reveal the answer to his question 'who really governs?' To answer this question one needed to investigate not only the perceptions of leaders but also actual governmental decisions. In his own community power study of New Haven, therefore, Dahl included a study of major decisions in four key areas: urban redevelopment, public schools, nominations for election to political office, and the decision on a new charter for the city. His conclusions on urban renewal, as well as being obviously relevant to the topic of this book, contain the essence of his findings on power.

The redevelopment of New Haven's urban core was 'the direct product of a small handful of leaders' (Dahl, 1961, p. 115). It was accomplished not by professional experts or by a power elite of the business class – only halting progress had been made before the mid-1950s – but through the entrepreneurship of a political leader. The Democrat politician who later became mayor, Richard Lee, saw in urban redevelopment an idea, made viable by Federal funds, around which to shape victory for his party and a successful political career for himself. Lee picked able professional supporters to devise and maintain the programme of redevelopment. And he surrounded this active hub with a wider circle of committees (totalling more than 400 people) representing New Haven's elites. This committee structure headed by the Citizens' Action Committee (CAC) included the leadership of all the politically salient interests in the community: for example, the heads of the large utility companies, manufacturing firms, banks, the leadership of Yale University, labour leaders and the black community.

Dahl's point, however, is not that power was widely dispersed – although it was not entirely concentrated either – but that the political leadership that really drove the whole enterprise was always attentive to, and dependent on the consensual support of both the elites and the voters. We can also infer that voter reaction depended on the political activity of the elites. 'In redevelopment as in other issue-areas the relation of leaders to constituents is reciprocal. The collective influence of the political stratum would have been sufficient to end redevelopment at any moment. Indeed if the political stratum had been sharply divided over redevelopment, the program could never have moved so rapidly or covered so much of the city's area' (Dahl, 1961, p. 137). It is noteworthy that the CAC committees, described by Lee as the 'muscles' of the community, were remarkably quiescent. Most of the committees rarely met; according to Dahl (p. 131) they never initiated, opposed, vetoed or substantially altered any proposal, and they accepted the information fed to them by Lee and his staff. Dahl says that the CAC was a mechanism not for *settling* disputes but for *avoiding* them altogether. Symbolic citizen participation was instituted to provide legitimacy for the decisions of the leaders and, as Dahl put it, to 'decapitate the opposition'.

In his conclusion to *Who Governs?* Dahl depicts a social structure consisting of an apex of a few political leaders, resting on a 'political stratum' of elites moved at least as much by the desire for mutual accommodation as by competition (see Dye and Zeigler, 1972, p. 353). This stratum was based on a large apolitical majority of voters. Unequal economic resources are acknowledged, but unequal *skills* and conflicting *preferences* and *weak* preferences all combined to maintain stability (Dye and Zeigler, 1972, p. 315). 'Power', says Dahl in a later text (1976), 'is manifest influence': people actively changing one another's actions or predispositions. There is a circular process of the growth of influence. Differences in personal endowments (knowledge, intelligence, wealth, etc.) and experience give rise to differences in political resources (whatever means can legitimately be mobilized to influence decisions) which, in turn, lead to differences in political influence. Differences of influence lead to differences in personal endowments and experience – and so on.

Dahl and Lindblom turned the attention of pluralist theory to the institutional rules under which activities of governments such as urban planning are carried out. The metaphor of the game is irresistible.

They concluded that the rules were, on the whole fair, though they nowhere reached an ideal state. Like the analytical pluralists they invited us to have faith in the political process. But they derived criteria from the claims made by existing democratic systems to mount a critique of the process. The message for planners is that, if they know the rules and respect them, something approximating to a just outcome will be ensured.

Institutional pluralism: criticisms and responses

The critique of Dahl's institutional pluralism (following Waste, 1987, pp. 35–9) can be divided into three broad categories: arguments that charge him specifically with failing to make a clear enough distinction between normative and descriptive analysis (a failure that tends to underwrite the status quo), those that accuse him of creating a revised and diluted normative version of democracy whose only achievement is to legitimate elite domination, and work that, within the 'broad church' of assenting (liberal democratic) theory, presents an alternative description of the social structure and politics of Western democracies and of the United States in particular.

First of all, Connolly (1969), Lowi (1969) and Ricci (1971) argue that, although polyarchy is a reasonable description of the politics of American society, this description does not provide an adequate basis for political inquiry. Such inquiry should include a clearly defined normative commitment or, as Connolly puts it, 'critical temper'. Pluralism is, according to Lowi (1969) a theory of the self-regulating 'automatic' society. Lowi claims that, in a few short steps, interest group pluralism and bargaining, which starts as a description, come to replace the theory of the market as the ideology of capitalism. Thus, he concludes, 'By definition, if the system is stable and peaceful it proves the self-regulative character of pluralism. It is therefore the way the system works and the way it ought to work' (Lowi, 1969, p. 46). Lowi accuses Dahl of failing to consider the underlying sanctions that ensure that the whole bargaining and adjustment process in society works. Following Weber, he draws attention to the inherently coercive nature of all governmental processes, both public and private. What appears in Dahl's schema to be 'peaceful adjustment' is in fact peaceful adjustment in the context of administered rules backed ultimately by the threat of force whose legitimacy has been fully internalized by all participants: 'The element of coercion may seem absent when in actuality the participants are conducting themselves in a certain way largely because they do not feel they have any choice' (Lowi, 1969, p. 52). Because Dahl fails to take account of this aspect of reality he also implicitly rules out action by a strong state to overcome problems arising from the current political status quo. In Lowi's model, urban planning, though taking account of minority interests, must be structured to be accountable to the whole population of a territory defined according to boundaries prescribed by the scope of the problem. If the problem is of metropolitan scale, then accountability must also be metropolitan.

As we have seen, Dahl explicitly claims to derive his normative concept of polyarchy from the study of actual societies described as democratic by Western liberal political scientists. This approach is probably in reality little different from that of any other exponent of liberal democratic theory, but in seeming to imply that it is, and in prevaricating about whether he is or is not evaluating the American system (in *A Preface to Democratic Theory 1956*), Dahl invites criticism. Thus Christian Bay ([1965] 1970) denounces Dahl's political science as 'pseudopolitics' because it fails to deal with questions of human need and the 'ought side of politics'.

The methodological criticism of Dahl's community power research is a fascinating maze of argument about what Dahl did or did not mean and what can and cannot be concluded from empirical studies of power. Waste (1987) provides an excellent guide to the maze, but we will not attempt to enter it here. The essential point is that the treatment of power as 'manifest influence' is, if it means what it says, impoverished. It is quite meaningful to say that power can be expressed in ways that are not manifest. As Bachrach and Baratz (1962) pointed out, Dahl's own work in New Haven leaves open the possibility, indeed probability, that certain causes of conflict in the community, which might have become political issues, did not because of the weight of ideology or the 'mobilization of bias', to use Schattschneider's term (1960). Further, the anticipation by political leaders of what will be acceptable or unacceptable to the powerful constitutes another way in which power is invisibly exercised ('anticipated reactions'). Finally, the powerful may conspire deliberately to keep certain conflicts from coming to a decision ('non-decision making'). Consensus extends beyond the 'democratic creed' to include *who* is acceptable, *what* it is acceptable to demand and what can be *changed* (see Lukes, 1974, 1986). Power in society does not necessarily imply power *over* someone. Power can be viewed simply as the force (albeit generated by the aggregate of human actions) that keeps a particular social structure in place.

Mann (1986), in his study of social power from a Weberian perspective, conceives of society *as* 'multiple overlapping and intersecting power networks'. He identifies four principal sources of social power: ideological, economic, military and political. These 'offer alternative organizational means of social control'. Here we are surely not far from some of the conceptions of social control that Dahl and Lindblom (1953) themselves began to develop in *Politics, Economics and Welfare*. Their concept of 'field control' seems designed to encompass a variety of types of power (see also Mannheim, 1940). 'Spontaneous field control', for example, is the term the authors give to what happens when one person influences another without intending to. This type of control is invisible: 'there are no commands, no articulated directives, no evident statutes or laws, no specified judicial systems, no prisons for violators' (Dahl and Lindblom, 1953, p. 101). Typically, such a system of control operates in a market governed by a price system. However, might not such control also operate in an ideological system? (See chapter 9: critical theory.) Consider the authors' comments on internalized rewards and penalties. 'Great social effort', they say, 'is invested in building into people some particular type of conscience'. A heavy investment in training the superegos of people in a social organization often pays rich dividends because of two vital functions carried on by the conscience: surrogate control which enables superiors to count on the co-operative behaviour of subordinates and therefore to 'grant them discretion'; and the legitimation of a social order which depends on internalized feelings of what is right and wrong (Dahl and Lindblom, 1953, pp. 112–5). Power that is not manifest cannot be researched in the same way as manifest influence. If we wish to understand the rules of the game we can certainly gain some impression of them by watching the play. Some of the players may, on occasion, break the rules and be penalized. But breach of rules does not tell us about rules which are not broken. To research these we must have some preconception of what moves might (or ought to) be allowed but are not. For such preconceptions we are dependent upon the normative concepts supplied by different political theorists.

Secondly, critics such as Walker (1966, 1970), Kariel (1961, 1970), Bay ([1965] 1970), and Pateman (1970) argued that the polyarchal revision of democratic theory leaves out the most central and most radical feature of the normative concept of pluralist democracy: citizen participation. Walker (1970, p. 240) pointed out that the revisionists have been too taken with Weber's (and Machiavelli's) image of the 'professional politician as hero', conflating politics with the activity of political leaders. Pateman (1970) says that Schumpeter and Dahl misunderstood the arguments of the 'classic' democratic theorists, particularly those of Rousseau and John Stuart Mill on the value of participation. According to Pateman, the revisionists made a virtue out of 'the non-participation of the ordinary man'. 'Apparently', she writes, 'it has not occurred to recent theorists to wonder why there should be a positive correlation between apathy and low feelings of political efficacy, and low socio-economic status' (Pateman, 1970, p. 104). A high level of political participation does not lead to instability, and stability may, in fact, be assisted by participation. Pateman suggests that participation is most needed where, at present, democracy is most conspicuously lacking, namely in the management of industry.

It is true that Dahl and Lindblom placed little emphasis on widespread political participation as a defining characteristic of pluralist democracy. But, equally, it is unfair to accuse them of making political apathy into a norm. They merely observed that a society could be regarded as democratic *without* a high level of participation. If it were not so, no existing societies could be regarded as democratic and democracy might come to be regarded as cloud-cuckoo-land. This is a point that would have appealed to Bentley.

A third element in the critique suggests that Dahl has misunderstood the nature of American society and that permanent socio-economic stratification has profound effects on the politics of capitalist democracy. Elite theory and ruling-class theory call attention to the domination of the economy and of politics by the upper echelons of society (see, for example, the work of Mills, 1956; Hunter, 1953, 1963, 1980; Keller, 1963; Domhoff, 1967, 1983). Mills (1956) in his historical analysis of the development of the top level of power in America, depicted a more or less exclusive clique at the intersection of three circles of power, the military, the political and the economic: 'The power elite', he says, 'has been shaped by the coincidence of interest between those who control the major means of production and those who control the newly enlarged means of violence' (Mills, 1956, p. 276). In a functionalist analysis that draws on the work of Talcott Parsons as well as Mills, Keller (1963) identifies a number of 'strategic elites' with distinctive functions which currently constitute a 'core group [in society] representing its unity and potentiality for common action' (Keller, 1963, p. 259). These are the political elite organizing the attainment of general social purposes; the economic, military, diplomatic and scientific elites 'developing the means to achieve these purposes' and the artistic and cultural elites 'promoting social solidarity and morale'.

Domhoff (1967) presented a less abstract account of the elite than did Keller, adding to Mills's conception the important distinction between 'power elite' and 'governing class'. A governing class 'owns a disproportionate amount of the country's wealth, receives a disproportionate amount of the country's yearly income, and contributes a disproportionate number of its members to positions of leadership' (Domhoff, 1967, p. 9). The power elite encompasses all those in command positions in institutions controlled by members of the governing class. 'Any given member of the power elite may or may not be a member of the upper class. The important thing is whether or not the institution he serves is controlled by members of the upper class' (p. 10).

For Domhoff, 'class' is a division in society signifying approximately equal status within it in terms of income, wealth and occupation, consolidated by intermarriage. The members of a class share similar values and interests and have a similar style of life. Domhoff endeavours to show that members of the American upper class control the key political institutions through privileged access provided by their wealth. He concluded that the business world is ultimately steered by the directorates of corporations, whose primary interest lies in the profitability of the enterprise. 'Interlocking directorates show beyond question that there is a national corporate economy that is run by the same group of several thousand men. *Social Register* listings, private school attendance, and club membership suggest that this group is very much part of the American upper class' (Domhoff, 1967, p. 57). The selection of candidates for political office is determined by the influence of wealth (p. 85). The 'now dominant' Federal executive is honeycombed to an overwhelming degree by members of the power elite (p. 152). The Federal judiciary is drawn mainly from 'the higher levels of society' (p. 111). Although at State and local levels the governing class does not have exclusive control it does have substantial means of influencing policy, through close relationships with the bureaucracy, indirect pressure exercised through control of the media and the direction of corporate investment. Domhoff points to the ever present threat, which need never be openly stated, that a firm will cut production or move elsewhere if it does not get what it wants from a government (p. 137). This power, Domhoff said in 1967, is almost unique to local government. With the growth of global corporate networks in the 1980s we can see that it has been extended to the national level.

Institutional pluralists argue that, however powerful, elites are restrained by the electoral process. Domhoff (1983, pp. 116–51) refutes this. There is ample evidence, he says, to show that politicians will not necessarily adopt the views of the majority in order to be elected, nor will political parties always select candidates who are likely to be popular with the electorate. Also, despite rhetoric to the contrary, parties sometimes collude rather than compete on policy matters. Indeed, one researcher, using a game theory argument, claims that it often makes sense for parties to compete more *with* the voters than *for* the voters or *with each other* (Wittman, 1973, p. 498). Frequently, the major issues of political campaigns involve no matters of substance and, increasingly, politicians are finding themselves free to say one thing in the campaign and to do another in office. As a result, the role of elections has become more and more symbolic, with real power being exercised via the 'special interest process' and the 'policy-making process', which provide many channels for the power elite, representing governing-class interests, to exert influence.

Elite theory is paralleled by what might be called 'exclusion theory'. Several studies have argued the existence of a more or less permanent minority underclass, who are excluded from any of the usual routes to political power (Harrington, 1964,1985; Ten Broek, 1966; Parenti, 1970; Cohen and Rogers, 1983; Wilson, 1985; Nathan, 1986). Harrington (1964, pp. 20–21) graphically described an 'economic underworld' which is literally to be found under the city: 'the kitchens and furnaces . . . the place where tens of thousands of hidden people labor at impossible wages'. These underworld workers were part of a second 'underdeveloped' nation within America, consisting of such marginal workers, the unemployed, the rejected workers of declining industry, the rural poor, the urban slum dwellers, the blacks everywhere and the aged without private wealth. This second nation was invisible to the affluent 'first nation' and entirely dependent on it. Above all, the fact of poverty itself prevented the poor from making political demands and frequently excluded them from the security of the welfare state: 'the mechanism of impoverishment is fundamentally the same in every part of the system. The vicious circle is a basic pattern. It takes different forms for the unskilled workers, for the aged, for the Negroes, for the agricultural workers, but in each case the principle is the same. There are people in the affluent society who are poor because they are poor; and who stay poor because they are poor' (Harrington, 1964, p. 160).

Nathan (1986) concluded that there is now quite a broad consensus among politicians and experts that the term 'underclass' accurately describes an important aspect of the structure of American society. Cohen and Rogers (1983) came to similar conclusions, arguing that the formal institutional guarantees of 'polyarchy', though necessary for democracy, are insufficient to prevent a large minority from being excluded from the political process. They extend the point made by Harrington and others into a general theoretical discussion of the relationship between economic equality and political freedom. In capitalist democracy, they say, inequality in the distribution of resources (wealth) systematically restricts the exercise of formal political rights and channels political demands in certain acceptable directions: 'It is clear that within capitalist democracies there are profound underlying structural inequalities that shape the normal course of politics. What is less clear is how that normal course is possible at all. How is it that politics in a capitalist democracy can proceed at all without the underlying inequalities themselves becoming a central object of political conflict? Why do people consent? This is a central question for anyone whose interest in understanding capitalist democracy is informed by a desire to transform it' (Cohen and Rogers, 1983, p. 51).

Plainly, normative questions and questions about what constitutes an accurate description of society are closely intertwined. Polyarchy may be a reasonable normative guide if society is structured in the way Lindblom and Dahl initially supposed it to be. Popular control of society's leaders, the elite, *is* an important democratic norm. If, however, such control does not occur to any substantial degree because of permanent socio-economic stratification, then it may be necessary to look for supplementary norms against which to measure democracy.

From the start of their collaboration Lindblom and Dahl were worried about the impact of economic power on democracy. They write about four processes of social control. A crucial question that must be posed is: what mixture of these processes of control is desirable? To be more specific, if business corporations are predominantly hierarchies whose relationships are organized by the price system, and governments are polyarchies, what does this tell us about the distribution of power in (and therefore the politics of) a society? This question emerges as a subordinate theme in the early pluralism of Dahl and Lindblom to be taken up as the dominant theme of Dahl's later work (1982, 1985) and by Lindblom (1977) in *Politics and Markets*.

Dahl and Lindblom (1953, p. 371) observed that large enterprises 'must' be organized as hierarchies, that: 'internally hierarchies typically produce inequality of control, status and income. Therefore they endanger both subjective equality and political equality' (Dahl and Lindblom, 1953, p. 255). Although polyarchy and hierarchy 'check and balance' each other, and although polyarchy actually requires hierarchy to ensure accountability of the bureaucracy, hierarchies impose limits on the extent to which political equality is attainable (p. 257). Property is a source of inequality and (citing with approval contemporary Fabian socialism) the private corporation is a major obstacle to income equality (p. 442). In a section on the legitimacy of control in business organizations, the authors, citing Jefferson and Andrew Jackson, express concern about the growth of massive business power in America. Big business is 'the' representative institution of American society, 'yet from the Jeffersonian point of view, the power of corporate managers and owners remains illegitimate, for it is not arrived at through the process of polyarchy that alone can give it the stamp of legitimacy' (p. 481). The point that business organizations must be considered just as much part of the public political domain as governments was later echoed by Bachrach (1967, p. 96) and Pateman (1970).

With *Dilemmas of Pluralist Democracy* (1982) Dahl begins a complete reappraisal of democracy in capitalism. As in *Politics, Economics and Welfare*, he turns the pluralist discussion of 'groups' into a discussion of organizations. Whereas 'group' has no particular stuctural connotation, 'organization' has a quite intended connotation of oligarchy and hierarchy. He redefines the 'central problem of politics', which was stated in *Politics, Economics and Welfare*, as 'the control of leaders'. Independent organizations, he says, exist in all democratic countries, and, for a variety of reasons, should exist (Dahl, 1982, p. 4). The problem is to control them.

Acknowledging many of the criticisms of polyarchy, Dahl lists four potential defects of pluralist democratic systems that the institutions of polyarchy cannot remedy. These defects arise from the fact that such systems necessarily permit the existence of independent organizations. First, the existence of independent organizations may help to stabilize injustices. Typically the balance of interests in a polyarchy crystallizes around a given configuration of organizations. In this case, 'each of the major organized forces in a country prevents the others from making changes that might seriously damage its perceived interests'. A kind of equilibrium is reached, but it is one in which substantial social injustice remains. Secondly, organizational autonomy tends to exaggerate the fragmentation of interests. In order to gain and retain members and influence governmental decisions, organizations emphasize their own particularity and solidarity. Absence of a widely shared set of interests, a 'public interest', becomes a self-fulfilling prophecy. Thirdly, the pursuit by organizations of their particular interests may lead to some items of more general interest being excluded from the governmental agenda. Furthermore, the unequal resources that enable some organizations to stabilize injustice also allow them to exercise unequal influence in determining what alternatives are considered. Fourthly, although some degree of organizational autonomy is a requirement of democracy, so too is 'final control' by the people's representatives. Organizations may sometimes become powerful enough to alienate this final control. Dahl cites the organized power of business corporations and trades unions, and the sheer difficulty of steering an extremely complex political system.

Different countries vary greatly not only in the structure and processes of organizational pluralism but also 'in the shape and importance of the problem of democratic pluralism itself' (Dahl, 1982, p. 75). Therefore, it is difficult to separate what are real defects of pluralism in general from those that are contingent on the specific conditions prevailing in a particular country. However, Dahl concludes that the problems posed above point to the existence of certain normative 'dilemmas' or antinomies, which are fundamental to all democratic societies: the good of the whole (utility) versus the rights of individuals; the choice of who is to be included in the 'demos' (where to draw the social and spatial boundary defining a people); the votes of individuals versus the autonomy of organizations; the right of individuals and groups to be different (diversity) versus the right of groups to enforce internal conformity (and the need for a society to conform to democratic norms such as equality); centralized control, which gives power to the demos, versus decentralized control, which maximizes diversity; and its corollary, the concentration versus dispersion of political power.

In what marks both a return to the unresolved questions of *Politics, Economics and Welfare* and a decisive break with the tradition of pluralist inquiry dominating the previous thirty years, Dahl then turns to the question that underlies much of the criticism of pluralism, that of the *political* organization of *economic* production. Dahl (1982, p. 110) observes: 'Whatever may have been the reality in the nineteenth century, the twentieth saw the emergence of giant corporations whose governments in both their internal and their external relations took on many of the characteristics of the governments of states. The giant corporation thus became, *de facto*, if not *de jure*, both a *public* enterprise and a *political* system'. He argues both that political pluralism is consistent with *social* control of enterprises and that *decentralized* control of enterprises, as occurs in most capitalist countries, is *not* a sufficient condition for political pluralism. In his next book (1985) Dahl explored what he now takes to be the new normative challenge for democracy, the creation of a democratically controlled system of decentralized economic power, a system of self-governing enterprises.

The book is not for the most part concerned with the mechanics of industrial democracy but with its political justification. Dahl now explicitly rejects a position which, he says, he came 'perilously close' to upholding in his previous work, that the only way of determining a just outcome is by virtue of its being arrived at by a just process (Dahl, 1985, p. 16, fn.). Referring to Tocqueville and Madison, Dahl argues that majoritarian democracy entails equality of political control. However, the threat of majority tyranny, he says, is no longer a salient issue. No political constitution is immune from turning into tyranny, but democracy is less prone to this danger than most. This is not only a matter of empirical observation but of internal logic. It cannot be true that a given aggregate of persons ought to govern themselves by democratic processes and also that a majority of those persons may properly strip a minority of their primary democratic rights. For, in doing so, the majority would be affirming that the aggregate ought *not* to govern itself by democratic processes. Dahl then returns to the dilemma introduced earlier between organizational autonomy and democratic control. The dilemma is now restated in more general terms as between *liberty* and *equality*. If Tocqueville in his time was concerned about the conditions that would enable liberty to survive when equality seemed assured, Dahl is now concerned about the conditions that would enable equality to survive when liberty (viewed as the autonomy of economic enterprises) is assured:

The problem we face, and all modern democracies face, is therefore even more difficult than the one Tocqueville posed. For not only must we identify and create the conditions that reduce the possible adverse effects of equality on liberty but also we must strive to reduce the adverse effects on democracy and political equality that result when economic liberty produces great inequality in the distribution of resources and thus, directly or indirectly, of power (Dahl, 1985, p. 50).

The basis of the original American concept of economic liberty lies in a past agrarian and rather egalitarian structure of property ownership. Locke, writing in the context of a much less egalitarian structure of property ownership, was well aware of the problem and included quite stringent restrictions on property ownership in his normative scheme. Nevertheless, the ideology of this period has today been selectively mobilized to serve the need for legitimacy of corporate enterprises (Dahl, 1985, p. 55). Consider, Dahl says, the logical steps necessary to justify the right to private ownership and control of corporate enterprises:

1 Everyone has a right to economic liberty.
2 The right to economic liberty justifies a right to private property.
3 The right to private property justifies a right to private ownership of economic enterprises.
4 The right to privately owned economic enterprises justifies privately owned corporations of great size.
5 The right to private ownership of corporate enterprises cannot properly be curtailed by the democratic process.

Dahl then shows that none of these steps in reasoning follows logically from the previous one or from the first axiom. Consequently, the polity (the demos and its representatives) is entitled to decide by means of the democratic process how economic enterprises should be owned and controlled in order to achieve values such as 'democracy, fairness, efficiency, the cultivation of desirable human qualities, and an entitlement to such minimal personal resources as may be necessary to a good life'. In short, in a democracy the same criteria must be applied to the government of economic enterprises as are applied to the government of the state. According to Dahl, the arguments in favour of a system of decentralized economic power are overwhelming. He says, 'I assume that after contemplating the large body of historical experience with bureaucratic socialism in this century, we would judge it to be fundamentally inconsistent with our goals' (Dahl, 1985, p. 89).

All of the above is preparation for Dahl's exposition of the idea of a self-regulating, egalitarian system, 'a system of economic enterprises collectively owned and democratically governed by all the people who work in them' (Dahl, 1985, p. 89). Here, it should be noted that the question of separation of ownership from control, which Dahl regarded as politically important in 1982, was viewed in 1985 as something of a red herring. Dahl now regards co-ownership by the workers of an enterprise as a necessary ingredient of economic democracy. Dahl argues that, although the evidence is so far inconclusive, there is reason to believe that economic democracy would foster in citizens qualities of public concern, co-operativeness, respect for democracy and moral responsibility. Such a system would help to connect the citizens of an enterprise more closely to the results of their economic decisions and actions (to work hard or not, to strike or not, to invest or not, to consume or save, etc.), learning from experience about public demands would be enhanced and the system would greatly increase economic equality within the enterprise. The conflictive relations inherent in the organization of 'private enterprise', which spill over into the politics of the state, would be considerably reduced.[2]

Dahl then considers the rational objections to a state introducing laws requiring economic democracy. He has already dealt with the objection that a system of self-governing enterprises would violate a prior right to property. But it could be said that decisions in economic enterprises are not binding upon their citizens in the same way as decisions made and enforced by states. Dahl proposes that there are more similarities between states and firms than the classical liberal position allows for. Especially interesting is his discussion of the right of 'exit'. If you are a member of a state or a firm you obey its laws; if you do not wish to do so you have the right to leave. But the costs of exercising the right of exit constitute the real basis of the sanctions available to both states and firms. In the case of *local* government the sanction is less severe in the state sector than in the corporate sector for, while a citizen who leaves one municipality has an automatic right to take up citizenship in another, a citizen who leaves a firm has no right to employment in another firm.

2 In Australia it has been reported that the chairman of the TNT corporation which controls Australia's only major privately owned domestic airline commanded a salary of AUS$4.75 million (Colebatch, 1989). This is more than two hundred times the average wage and some fifty times the salary of domestic airline pilots. Knowledge of this and similar salary differentials almost certainly played a substantial role in the prolonged and economically damaging strike of domestic pilots in 1989, in which the Australian Federal Government was deeply implicated.

It might also be argued that workers in economic enterprises are not qualified to govern a company. Dahl acknowledges the 'weight of existing institutions and ideologies' that uphold the principle of 'guardianship': managers are selected by officials who are in turn accountable to a population of either shareholders or voters. Dahl, however, refers to what he calls the 'strong principle of equality', which holds that citizens are 'competent to decide whether they are themselves sufficiently qualified to make the decisions collectively through the democratic process'. On matters they do not feel competent to decide for themselves, Dahl argues, they must be regarded as qualified to set the terms on which they will delegate the decisions to others (Dahl, 1985, p. 118).

Against the criticism that workers would be more tempted than managerial guardians to maximize their short-term income over the long-term benefits of investment, Dahl refers to experiences in America, Scandinavia, Yugoslavia and Spain to show that, in practice, this seems not to occur. Indeed, linked to an appropriate scheme for channelling investment (there are many possibilities, more and less centralized) there is no reason why a self-governed system should not be more efficient than the present one. He points out, however, that any self-governed system would have to invest heavily in training management in the principles of co-operative enterprise. Here, the experience of the Mondragon co-operative system in Spain is instructive (see Thomas and Logan, 1982). The reduction of conflict between workers and management in the firm would help enterprises to respond flexibly to market pressures. But, given a principle that every worker has an equal chance of being declared redundant, this response would be in the direction of reduction of wages rather than laying off workers. Finally, it might be argued that power is so deeply entrenched that any attempt to introduce industrial democracy would be a sham. In this respect Dahl admits that many co-operative enterprises have failed, but he says that such failures have often occurred in highly adverse circumstances and where co-operatives have been tried as a last resort. Even in these circumstances there have been successes.

Having established that a system of self-governing enterprises is both desirable and feasible, Dahl turns to the question of how it might be achieved. Dealing cursorily with the role of the state in ensuring fairness among enterprises and somewhat more fully with types of co-ownership, Dahl never really gets round to exploring the practicalities of transition from corporate capitalism to economic democracy. Who is to struggle against enormously powerful vested interests for this new extension of democracy? How will the struggle be conducted? Beyond espousing a piecemeal and gradualist approach, Dahl does not tell us. Unlike polyarchy, industrial democracy cannot be said to be a 'going concern' and the practical question of its achievement demands that attention be paid to the role and form of political struggle in bringing about real social change. As Cohen and Rogers (1983, p. 146) point out, 'the choice for an alternative set of rules is a choice against capitalist democracy'. This is a choice against the institutional structure of the social order. It is questionable whether change of that magnitude can be accomplished within the rules of the social order.

Pluralism develops the polar opposite to a world view focused on the instrumental state, a state capable of strong rational action on behalf of society or any set of interests in society. Pluralist theory draws our attention away from the idea of a society held together by 'domination'. As we have seen in the last chapter, the idea of technical rationality is closely connected with domination. Once the rational decision is made, the rational plan decided upon, it is imposed. The 'plan' is both an instrument and a cage. In the Weberian schema the planner is considered to be either outside politics or integrated within some hierarchy. Pluralism started from a different viewpoint, that societies are structured by groups forming and adjusting to one another. The planner's role is to be found within that political process. Whereas Weber viewed politics within the context of society, pluralist theory views society within the context of politics. Value conflict was simply part and parcel of the political process. Certainly, there remains the question of what constitutes a 'good' political process, but pluralist theory assumes that the basis for a normative model can be found in existing Western-style democracies. Something analogous to the concept of domination reappears in pluralist theory in the form of rules, or widely supported institutions, within which group interaction occurs. Pluralists have tended to portray the 'rules of the game' in terms of values rather than coercively imposed norms, though whether these values are in fact widely shared is a matter of dispute among pluralists. But the importance of group organization, group structure and groups bearing on one another remains central to pluralism, as is the notion of reciprocity in power relationships, however unequal these relationships may be. Democratic institutions force groups to interact with one another and heed each others' needs and demands. Dahl, in his new analysis of the rules of the game, is looking beyond the axioms that have, hitherto, defined pluralist thought.

Pluralism: roles, rules and urban planning

It is important to distinguish between what pluralist theory has to say about the politics of social interaction and about the ground rules that govern and shape this social interaction. In the course of interaction, groups and group interests inevitably come into conflict and various political roles emerge. Pluralist theory suggests that to be politically effective planners must adapt themselves to these roles. That is, if they want to see their ideas implemented, they must either play political roles or make themselves useful to those who are already playing them: career politicians and political activists. But the very concept of 'role' also invokes that of 'rule'. Politics as social interaction is played out within a structured environment consisting of institutions, laws, boundaries, norms and conventions, in short, rules. The rules of the game interact with political roles in various ways. They may shape the role, or determine who is to play what role on behalf of whom; they allocate authority to political actors, distribute legitimacy and forge links of accountability. Pluralism makes a seemingly obvious proposition: that social change occurs as a result of political action. But what happens if the problems that are the focus of action arise not from inaction or wrong action but from the rules structuring and governing action? Before considering this question we shall look first at some of the politically active roles that pluralism delineates. There are four closely related clusters of roles, centring on the advocate, the negotiator, the activist, and the mediator.

The case of 'advocacy planning' demonstrates the relationship between roles and rules. Believing that different interest groups had different political values and that different values would result in different plans, Davidoff (1965) proposed a system in which groups would hire a planner to act as advocate for the plan most favouring the group's values and interests. The planner would act for a client within a framework of rules comparable with those governing the administration of justice, and would prepare a plan much as a lawyer prepares a brief. There would be many plans: 'a Republican and Democratic way of viewing city development . . . conservative and liberal plans, plans to support the private market and plans to support greater government control' (Davidoff, 1965, p. 335). However Davidoff had in mind particularly the representation by planners of interests that frequently went unrepresented in urban redevelopment, those of the poor and underprivileged. He also wished to attack the concealment of value choices in technically rational plans, choices that in a pluralist democratic process should be explicit (Davidoff and Reiner, 1962).

When the effects of urban redevelopment on poor neighbourhoods began to be felt, advocacy planning was put into practice. Peattie (1968) described her experience as an advocate planner working for a group representing the poor in Cambridge, Massachusetts. She found many problems. Planners, like lawyers, expect to earn a living from their work, but the poor do not have the means to pay. Advocacy for the poor is either dependent on government funding or on charitable organizations or on volunteer labour. If planners were prepared to act as advocates for the poor, it was not at all easy to define 'the client'. Peattie (1968, p. 241) says, 'the urban slum lacks institutions by which it might represent itself as a community'. Marris (1963) also observed that the slum 'has no leaders, few community associations, no means of asserting a common purpose'. In Davidoff's thesis we find the pluralist assumption that every interest has its group. In fact, the neighbourhood proved nebulous and heterogeneous. The planners found themselves acting as community organizers, drawing residents into their organization's activities. But they could never claim to *represent* the 'neighbourhood' or 'community' and they lacked legitimacy. They set out to represent a single point of view and ended up trying to do what planners traditionally do, namely, reconcile conflicting interests in a single plan. Middle-class residents were the most vocal and politically active; and the more effective the community planning, the more likely it was to represent middle-class interests. In one neighbourhood in Boston the local people were able to mobilize against any further low-income housing being located there. 'The community is organized against it, and from these experiences one might suggest that a consequence of giving every neighbourhood in a city its advocate planner might be a general closing-up of the city against the poor' (Peattie 1968, p. 243).

In practice, planners are far more likely to be able to act as advocates for those who are already politically organized than for the poor who, without external intervention, are usually not. Gottdiener (1987) has recently observed that quiescence is the norm among the poor. Conversely, those who are capable of political organization have never had any trouble using planners and land-use controls to protect their interests. Hall *et al.* (1973) in Britain and Danielson and Doig (1982) in America have shown how certain coalitions of local interests have been able to protect the value of their property by excluding undesirable people, dirty industry and road traffic and by preserving environmental externalities such as open space and high quality (expensive) dwellings arranged in low densities.

Being an advocate means advancing a proposal within certain institutional rules that define the procedures to be followed and to whom the advocate is accountable. In a broad sense the role of advocate for a particular policy is one every planner can expect to perform. The skill of the advocate lies in developing a persuasive case and then presenting it for decision. The effective advocate will therefore marshal a great deal of evidential information. However, a commanding knowledge of the rules by which decisions are made is also a central part of the skill of advocacy. The advocate must know what information will be persuasive and use *that* knowledge to select what information to obtain and develop. The irony of advocacy planning as it was conceived in the 1960s is that it contradicted the existing institutional rules and procedures without substituting new ones. Sherry Arnstein (1969) made this clear in her analysis of public participation, which portrayed a continuum from placation and tokenism to 'citizen control'. The demand for citizen control is plainly a demand for new institutional rules (see also Coit, 1978).

The role of advocate rapidly becomes that of negotiator once it is recognized that a compromise has to be reached between competing interests and alternative plans. Both advocacy and bargaining, or negotiation, are applicable inside the state and outside it, between governmental and non-government units, and between levels of government. Although it is not true that every interest has its group, every group, once formed, has its interest. Pluralism holds that group interests exist and are entitled to assert themselves wherever it is possible to delineate the boundaries of an active group. While this is obviously an expectation of pluralist theory in the political world outside the state, it is less obvious that the same is held to apply within government. However, Lindblom's well known formulae of 'disjointed incrementalism', 'partisan mutual adjustment' and the 'play of power' assert just that. Within governmental circles 'specialists' offer competing advice. The test of a good policy is whether the specialists agree on it. Of course, to reach that state of agreement they must negotiate over the policy and come to some sort of compromise.

The point was later reinforced by the studies of policy implementation of Pressman and Wildavsky (1973) and Bardach (1977). Pressman and Wildavsky note that the more steps there are in the process from origin to execution of a policy and the more agencies are involved, the more scope there is for bargaining. Since bureaucrats in different agencies could rarely be coerced, the frequently heard demand for 'co-ordination' became an invitation to negotiate. Consequently, 'implementation should not be divorced from policy . . . The great problem as we understand it, is to make the difficulties of implementation a part of the initial formulation of policy' (Pressman and Wildavsky, 1973, p. 143). Bardach characterized the implementation process as one of 'assembling' the components for the delivery of a programme, during which many semi-autonomous players negotiate with one another the terms under which they will co-operate in supplying the components to be assembled.

With his metaphor of the 'implementation game', Bardach (1977) drew attention to the rules under which the game is to be played (the 'rules of play' and the 'rules of fair play'; p. 36). But he has much more to say about the problems of negotiation and the strategies of the players than about the rules, particularly those of the structure of government, and the limitations on policy outcomes that those rules impose. He is complacent about the nature of the social problems that governments try to solve. For Bardach, failure to find an efficient solution is due to the immense complexity and difficulty of the *problems* rather than to the politico-economic rules under which solutions are constructed. 'Clearly', he says, 'we would all be better off if government simply stayed away from problems it could not solve. Alas, if only we could know, before trying and failing what they were' (Bardach, 1977, p. 251). 'Government' is a given and, in keeping with the pluralist normative tradition, Bardach applauds the competitive game-playing among multiple competing agencies that attends the policy process in the United States (see Bardach, 1977, p. 151).

American pluralist insights into the implementation process were melded with European conceptions and transplanted on to British soil in a series of case studies edited by Barrett and Fudge (1981). These authors challenge the conventional distinction between politics and administration and the typically European assumption that a mandated government can be expected to implement policy from the top down. Throughout their analysis much stress is placed on the subtleties of reciprocal power relationships among multiple agencies and the 'discretion' of the bureaucratic and other actors in the system. One way of looking at policy is to regard it as 'property'. With the sense of ownership of policy comes increased motivation on the part of implementing agencies to make the policy work . But there is likely to be something of a trade-off between conformance and performance. Only when an implementing agency feels a sense of policy ownership will it be prepared to perform effectively. But this enhanced performance will be at the expense of conformity with requirements imposed from above (Barrett and Fudge, 1981, p. 271). Here we may recall Toqueville's 'concealed breakwaters which check or part the tide of popular determination'.

Rhodes (1988) uses the concept of 'policy networks' to describe the complex reality of what he calls 'the differentiated polity' of sub-central government in Britain. Rhodes's main point is that central governments have to understand the differentiated polity in order to be able to work with it competently. Rhodes castigates the Thatcher government for failing to understand it, for using simplistic bureaucratic methods for dealing with it and, as a result, for producing a 'policy mess'. He describes five different types of network and several different types of interaction taking place within them. He also attempts a far-reaching evaluation of the central government's attempts to come to grips with the networks on the basis of criteria of 'stability', 'effectiveness', 'complexity', 'equity' and 'accountability'.

His message is not an optimistic one for Britain, and he points to the multiple 'contradictions of the centreless society' which has the misfortune to have inherited a unitary state and a differentiated polity. Rhodes's 'test cases' demonstrate that a low degree of integration generates many problems for effective government action:

> They also point to a conundrum. Effective action presupposes means for involving the interdependent parties. Without such means – the policy network – central intervention is ad hoc and ineffective. But creating policy networks imposes a range of constraints on the centre whereby unilateral central action within a network also renders policy ineffective. Helpless with, and hopeless without policy networks, the centre seeks to avoid being a stranger in a strange land without becoming a prisoner of the very means of assimilation (Rhodes, 1988, p. 370).

Christensen (1985) suggests that advocacy and bargaining are appropriate in conditions where goals are not agreed but the 'technology' is known; by technology she refers to the *means* of solving a problem. Here, however, it is proposed that the significant factor is the *rules* of the game, in particular the rules for decision-making. Advocacy and bargaining both depend on known and agreed rules. Rhodes's (1986, pp. 391–2) analysis of the 'rules of the game' in the context of British sub-national government makes worthwhile reading.

A quite different political strategy is required where the rules are unknown or not agreed. This is the activist strategy. Mollenkopf (1983) describes how, in the United States, the political coalition favouring urban redevelopment forged by New Deal Democrats fell apart in the 1960s and 1970s largely as a result of its own success in restructuring the city and the political terrain. The dissolution of the old conflicts of the industrial city through residential and industrial suburbanization and the remodelling of the urban core for use as the hub of the service economy produced a spatial redistribution of the 'liberal' constituency and new conflicts in central city neighbourhoods. The New Deal and Great Society programmes failed to produce real economic gains for minority groups left behind in the central cities. The Democratic urban programmes designed to improve urban life sacrificed central city minority communities in favour of 'dominant institutions' (Mollenkopf, 1983, p. 295). Neighbourhoods were torn down, the supply of low price housing reduced and poor minority groups forced into the secondary labour market offering 'opportunities in small, low-wage, service and manufacturing firms lacking market power and strong unions' (p. 262). Mollenkopf's case studies of urban redevelopment in Boston and San Francisco demonstrate the same pattern of 'progrowth coalition' in the postwar years that Dahl found in New Haven. But Mollenkopf goes on to describe its aftermath. The destructive impact of 'renewal' programmes on urban neighbourhoods and local communities threw up new 'neighbourhood activists', who sought to challenge the old neighbourhood leaders who had co-operated with redevelopment agencies, to mobilize the local resident populations and to gain control of the programmes. Some of these activists came from a new stratum of young professionals (including advocate planners working for agencies similar to that described by Peattie above) who had begun to move back into central city areas as a result of the post-industrial development of the city centre as an administrative and service core.

The most explicit statements of the activist role came from Saul Alinsky ([1946] 1969, 1971), who was influential in shaping the demands and strategies of the neighbourhood movements in the United States. Alinsky's attitude to the (liberal pluralist) rules of the game is ambivalent and might be described as 'breaking the rules – within the rules'. On the one hand, he displays a constant faith in the political process. Of the student protests of 1968 he says, 'It hurt me to see the American army with drawn bayonets advancing on American boys and girls. But the answer I gave the young radicals seemed to me the only realistic one: "Do one of three things. One, go find a wailing wall and feel sorry for yourselves. Two, go psycho and start bombing – but this will only swing people to the right. Three, learn a lesson. Go home, organize, build power and at the next [Democratic Party] convention, *you be the delegates*"' (Alinsky, 1971, p. xxiii). On the other hand, in the same book, Alinsky spells out his attitude to the ends of democratic society, which is that, broadly speaking, political ethics are the luxury of the powerful and the battle standard of the radical. Ethics are determined by the tactical requirements of each particular situation of conflict. The prescribed tactics are to ignore the rules yourself but use them against the enemy. The only values that count are those you are fighting for, which are those of your immediate interest group. As Colby (1982) points out, 'interest' need not always mean 'interest in short-term material gain'. There are 'public interest' groups seeking 'purposive goals through expressive action' (e.g consumerism, the environment movement). Colby argues that broad public interest movements become organized through the entrepreneurial activity of charismatic leaders or small groups. Others such as Morris and Hess (1975), Bookchin (1974), Perlman (1979) and Boyte (1980) have outlined a programme for urban social change and reform based on local action, aiming at a more egalitarian redistribution of resources and a return to localized association and control of the environment.

A dispassionate and scholarly account of the literature useful to the professional community worker or 'change agent' was prepared by

Rothman (1974). Rothman explored the activist role in depth, dealing
with dimensions of the role, the organizational framework of social
change, the community setting, citizen participation, and the diffusion
and adoption of innovation. Rothman's survey was designed to link
the appraisal of a huge volume of social science literature to specific
prescriptions for action via a series of 'generalizations'. As such it is
a useful practical manual for the activist planner. Rothman's observations are almost as applicable to the 'policy entrepreneur' within
government agencies as to the activist outside them, particularly his
prescriptions for innovation (drawing on the seminal work of Everett
Rogers, 1962), for the planner wishing to introduce a new policy is
of course an innovator (see Barrett and Fudge, p. 271).

A more explicit treatment of policy entrepreneurship was provided
by Friend, Power and Yewlett (1974), who placed more emphasis
on the networking or 'reticulist' abilities of the successful planner.
They say: 'The basic problem facing the would-be reticulist can
be seen as that of initiating and cultivating a network of human
relationships, in such a way as to maintain access to information about
changing problem situations' (p. 365). Their case studies described the
inter-organizational networks and strategies of policy entrepreneurs in
urban development in the West Midlands in Britain in the 1960s and
1970s. A less optimistic account of the activist in the government
agency was supplied by the Needlemans (1974), who confronted
the dilemmas faced by state employees of the 'Great Society' programmes of citizen participation in the United States. 'Community
planning', they say, was 'intended to serve the planning department
symbolically, through its existence rather than its operation' (p.
323). But, once instituted, it created a new breed of 'guerrillas in
the bureaucracy', dissatisfied with existing programmes and with
the available instruments for the performance of their task, and
dedicated to the service of the local communities rather than their
political masters.

Activists outside the state or policy entrepreneurs inside it take a
different attitude to the rules of the game from that of advocates or
negotiators. Activists and entrepreneurs depend for guidance on their
own existential values (e.g. with regard to poverty [Alinsky], or the
environment [Bookchin]). They aim to achieve their goals and pursue
their values irrespective of the rules or in spite of them. This does
not mean that activists necessarily work to overturn the rules, though
some may try to do so. More recently, and faced with the failure
of accepted methods to achieve real material improvement in the
conditions of the poor, followed by regressive measures of the Nixon
and Reagan administrations and the threat to pluralist values from
further corporate consolidation, pluralists have begun to question the
rules. Friedmann (1987) is critical of Alinsky's acceptance of capitalist

values and proposes a new version of 'radical planning' that looks back to the revolutionary traditions of Luxemburg and Gramsci (see chapter 8, pp. 203–11). 'Radical planning', writes Friedmann, 'begins with a critique of the present situation' (p. 303). Friedmann means that radicals must understand the structural rules and provide a critical account of the situation to be changed. The strategies to be adopted, however, are those of activist pluralism. Political values are determined at the level of the individual but action begins at the level of the group. 'Even transformative social movements . . . whose contact networks may circle the entire globe, have their true strength in the practice of local action groups' (p. 396). Planners must learn to enable the group to decide its own destiny. They must have skills in group dynamics, networking and coalition building. But they must also provide a new transcendental ideology that makes sense of local group struggles in terms of a wider conception of society, informed by a utopian vision of 'political community' embodying reform of social practices at the level of the household.

The experience of activist pluralism in the United States in the 1960s and 1970s revealed both its strengths and its limitations. A plethora of new grassroots networks and organizations grew rapidly among the poor in response to the activities of the state, first in promoting urban redevelopment and then in funding local initiatives. 'The 'neighborhood movement', writes Mollenkopf (1983, p. 294), 'established a political rhetoric of citizen participation, participatory planning, and community review which challenges the prevailing ideologies of progrowth politics, whether of the liberal or conservative variety.' No longer can government so easily engage in regressive social engineering. Community organizations and agencies 'provide the organizational infrastructure through which citizens at the grass roots participate in political life on a daily basis' (Mollenkopf, 1983). The new neighbourhood structures, however, reproduced exactly the conditions expected by pluralist theory: the splintering of interests into *interest groups*, the diffusing of united political action by multiple cross-cutting allegiances, the diversion of power struggles into internal conflict and the absorbtion of political leadership into channels regulated by the state and 'normal' politics. Piven and Cloward ([1977] 1982) point out that the 'lower classes' are usually in a weak position to use tactics of institutional disruption to get what they want from society (see also Gottdiener, 1986). Their co-operation is not crucial to the working of the capitalist economy or the state; they are often exploited directly by those just a little higher up the scale who have little to give (e.g. slumlords and marginal small enterprises); and they are vulnerable to reprisals through loss of home, job or welfare support. Political mobilization is limited by the ability of governments to co-opt movement leaders and buy off widespread popular support by token gestures and rhetoric. Such, in the authors' view, was the case with the Great Society programs and the much trumpeted 'War on Poverty'.

Castells (1983, p. 124), in his case study of the social movements in San Francisco's Mission District, concluded that the American experience of social mobilization was generally characterized by two features. First, action was directed towards improvement of immediate conditions rather than towards change of the system that produced these conditions. Secondly (and correspondingly), each group would try to pursue objectives specific to itself as an interest group, without considering the wider structures of interest to which the group belonged (city, class, race). A temporary coalition of immediate interests might be established to fight a common enemy, such as the San Francisco Redevelopment Authority, but as soon as the battle *against* an enemy was turned by external (Federal) political action into a battle *for* resources, internal conflict erupted, which destroyed the coalition. At a deeper level, the rules for allocating resources in society remained unchallenged. In Castells's view the discrimination by society against a particular group will invoke a reaction of the kind described above. The group will eventually develop its own internal solidarity, it will become an 'interest group'. 'Once people are institutionally segmented in different interest groups, it is impossible to reconcile the different demands competing for the distribution of increasingly scarce resources' (Castells, 1983, p. 128), a point already made by Dahl (1982). However it is still too early to judge the long-term effects of the establishment of new community structures and networks and their associated ideologies on the politics of capitalist societies. Castells (1983), Friedmann (1987) and political theorists such as Cohen and Rogers (1983) and Bowles and Gintis (1986) make important links between pluralism and the dissenting tradition of political theory influenced by Marx, and we will have more to say about these links in chapter 8.

The role of a profession in mediating political struggles was discussed in chapter 2. Tocqueville observed that a conservative legal profession mediated between the executive and the people. Bentley argued that a primary function of government was to 'mediate the adjustments' among pressure groups. In New Haven, Dahl found in 'the plan' for urban redevelopment a formula for mediating among the various groups with an interest in redevelopment. Dahl claims that the plan succeeded largely by anticipating the demands that would be made. Accordingly, the groups co-opted into the planning process were quiescent. What happened subsequently in urban redevelopment across America, as described by Mollenkopf and others, testifies to the fact that pressure groups are often brought into existence by the execution of government policy. It is not enough to assume that the interests it will be necessary to mediate among are already articulated.

However, the role of 'mediator' or 'broker' is one that pluralist theory clearly delineates for the urban planner. It is also one which is consistent both with the tradition of professionalism and with the pluralist view of the state. Mollenkopf (1983, pp. 295–9) points to the need to mediate a new 'progrowth' coalition in the United States. 'A new social contract', he says, 'must distribute economic opportunity more equally across urban constituencies.' But he acknowledges that this will require 'renewed political reform'. By this, he evidently means reform of the rules of the urban game; reform of the 'competitive framework that private institutions have exploited to undermine redistributive politics in the past'. But some quid pro quo must be offered to these institutions if 'massive debilitating conflict' is to be avoided. What such a quid pro quo might be and what the planning vehicle to bring it into effect might look like is the challenge that planners now confront. Forester (1987) argues that the strategies adopted in mediation and negotiation, if guided by ethical principles, can help to equalize gross power imbalances among the participants.

Healey, McNamara, Elson and Doak published in 1988 what is arguably the most important analysis of urban planning practice in Britain since that of Hall, Gracey, Drewett and Thomas (1973). Healey *et al.* centre their analysis on the ways in which the planning system mediates the conflict of interests in land. The urban planning system, they suggest, is not only a mediating device but also, like the market, an institution through which interests are realized. The biases in the criteria of access, discourse and decision-making are ways in which power is exercised. Their work begins by recognizing the plurality of actors on the urban scene (Healey *et al.*, p. 6) and ends with typically pluralist prescriptions for change (less centralization of power, more 'rights of challenge' to public sector decisions, variety in strategies and policies; p. 259). However, they seek to go beyond pluralism in their analysis. Their method is to unpack the structural interests that different actors (groups or individuals) reconcile and express in action – or in some cases inaction. These structural interests are found to be patterns embedded in 'social relations'. What the authors mean by social relations seems to be very close to what is meant by institutional pluralists when they talk about the 'rules of the game' (in fact the authors themselves sometimes use this term, e.g. p. 253). Social relations are not separate from the rules that embody them, in just the same way as a 'game' has no specific meaning outside the rules that constitute it. Healey *et al.* write extensively on the 'rules' that apply to land-use planning in Britain (pp. 167–8 and *passim*). Where they differ from mainstream pluralists, and also

where they share the direction in which Dahl and Lindblom seem
headed, is their emphasis on the political significance of the rules
related to the economic organization of capitalism. In this respect
they have been influenced by the Marxist thrust of urban studies
in the 1970s and 1980s. But they also seek to balance this emphasis
with the acknowledgement of a variety of equally important sources
of interest other than (economic) class: gender, ethnic affiliation,
locale, social status, etc. Unlike Marxists, they do not try to find
out which source of interest is superordinate. Unlike Dahl, in his
latest work, they do not seek to isolate a single 'most crucial' danger
to democracy. Instead they spell out the biases inherent in the rules
of land-use planning as evidenced in particular contexts.

It may be argued by mainstream pluralists that there is nothing
new in the recognition that individuals and groups reconcile multiple
conflicting interests. Pluralists have long noted how political parties
perform this function. Now the authors say that the planning system
also does this. But, by conceptually detaching interests from actors
and action, it becomes possible to conceive of interests in a community
that are neither expressed nor organized (cf. Bentley's 'tendencies to
activity' and 'underlying groups'). The normative implication of such
a view is that planners should construct arenas in which people affected
by plans can perceive their interests and take a planner's perspective
themselves: the wider scope, the longer term, the future. Only with a
deeper understanding of their interests will social mobilization around
interests be likely to produce a better outcome. This suggests a
putative activist/mediating role for the planner. If the assumption
is that people do not always perceive their best interests, such a view
might seem elitist. But the history of urban development in the United
States and Britain suggests compelling reasons for planners to take on
such a role. If Mollenkopf is right, the political entrepreneurs who
set in motion the restructuring of American cities in the 1950s did
not anticipate the new political forces that such restructuring would
generate. If they had, it is at least conceivable that much anguish could
have been avoided and the Democratic Party might have retained its
ascendancy.

We have seen that discussion of roles invokes questions about rules
(see also Strauss, 1978; Giddens, 1979, 1984; Benson, 1975, 1980;
Benson and Weitzel, 1985). Increasingly pluralists are questioning
the rules under which interest group activity takes place. In America
some urban analysts have become disenchanted with the rules of
urban development. Hartman (1984, p. 320), on planning in San
Francisco, concludes, 'As is to be expected, "the golden rule" often
explains the outcome – those who have the gold make the rules. In
an economic and political system which relies so centrally on private
market forces to initiate investment and create economic activity, the

large corporations and their plans appear as the only game in town: their decisions on whether and where to invest become the reference point. Their decisions create or destroy jobs and the city's tax base.' Rich (1977, 1982) has argued that unbridled competition between localities and bureaucracies in the American political system has caused gross inequities in the provision of urban public services. Sharkansky (1975) makes a similar observation about the difficulties the governmental structure creates for urban planning in America. Gottdiener (1987, p. 283) warns, 'No mechanisms currently exist that can aggregate neighbourhood mobilization of needs into a viable public discourse on the future state of the metropolis.' An attitude that characterizes urban problems as 'insoluble' or 'wicked' overlooks the deficiencies of the structures of rules within which the problem is expected to be solved. Some of these structures are popularly held assumptions generated and reproduced by the politically powerful who set agendas and 'massage' the public via the media; others are actual 'structures' of government, which determine bureaucratic resources, accountability and responsibility and delineate territorial boundaries. Several pluralists have argued in favour of new types of institutions, which 'mediate our social differences' (Berger and Neuhaus, 1977; Wilber and Jameson, 1981; Van Til, 1984). New structures are needed that will share out power more equitably and guard against the danger to democracy of the vast hierarchies of the industrial corporations and the state. Urban planners should be concerning themselves with what these new institutions might be like, for it is these mediating and decision-making structures that will come to define urban problems and their solution (see Friedmann, 1987).

A different focus for planning is required, not, as neo-liberal ideology has it, less planning. Marris (1982), commenting on the results of community action in Britain in the 1970s, writes: 'The lesson of this is not to reject planning in favour of political struggles, but to incorporate into those struggles a demand for effective, open, collective planning, as a crucial part of carrying out any practical ideal of social justice. Otherwise, the struggle does not lead towards any resolution except competitive bargaining between different kinds of interests, and that cannot protect the weaker and more vulnerable members of society' (p. 127). Planning, then, is a matter of gaining a wider and longer perspective about the *context* of problems as well as about the immediate problems themselves. Self (1985, p. 98) suggests that a 'planning' approach has two advantages: 'First it may enable policy problems to be redefined and resolved upon a scale which better matches their actual social complexity. Secondly, it may enable a more effective and balanced synthesis of interests to be achieved than would occur through organizational competition which is one-sided or mutually frustrating.'

Planners must, on occasion, play political roles but the real material of *planning* is the structures of rules and meanings, which infuse the attempt to solve problems and pursue opportunities. The key questions are not so much 'who gets what, when and how?' as 'who decides on behalf of whom?' Planning in this sense is indeed 'decision-centred' (see Faludi, 1987). But the decisions that now need to be made are far-reaching. We have not so far explored the implications for urban planning of pluralist critiques (of Dahl and others), which propose a change in the rules at a deep level. This exploration will be reserved for the last chapter, when such critiques can be considered in the light of corporatist, neo-liberal and dissenting theories.

Conclusion

Analytical pluralism emphasized 'social interaction'. In this view of things the state is a mere 'weathervane', a mechanism for indicating the resultant of all political forces in society. Current policies and structures simply reflect the *balance* of forces (Dunleavy and O'Leary, 1987). Such a model suggests for the planner the roles of the advocate, negotiator and activist. A different view of the state gained acceptance in the 1950s and 1960s, a more interventionist view derived from Weber and his successors. This view when integrated into political practice produced new dominant images, those of the 'neutral state' and the 'broker state'. The neutral state evokes the role of referee, someone who presides over a struggle and ensures that the rules of the game as customarily recognized are observed. A more interventionist version of the image is one in which the state actively seeks to promote substantive 'fairness', the welfare state. Dunleavy and O'Leary (1987, p. 45) say that 'there is little doubt that since the 1950s pluralists' normative ideal form for the state has been one which balances, re-weights and referees pressure group contests to protect unorganized or weakly organized groups "in the public interest"'. The broker state invokes the role of the 'mediator' standing between conflicting parties, but with distinctive interests of his/her own (Dunleavy and O'Leary, 1987, pp. 47–49). As we shall see in the next chapter, the role of 'mediator' was further developed within the framework of the 'strong state' in the theory of corporatism.

Dahl and Lindblom moved away from the perspective of analytical pluralism to focus on the institutional rules within which social interaction takes place. Their basic stance was one of acceptance of (capitalist) liberal democracy as established in the latter half of the twentieth century. However, their quest eventually led them to question and criticize 'the rules'. Pluralists found themselves on the defensive in the 1970s and 1980s against an agenda, set mainly by the right, with a model of a much more active and 'strong' state. In Britain and America, the right set to work with a vengeance on 'the rules' within which modest gains had been made in the empowerment of the poor. This was accomplished under the rhetoric of 'rolling back the state'. Deconstruction of the welfare state was, however, accomplished by and through reconstruction of the authoritarian state. Mollenkopf (1983, p. 282) quotes a Reagan supporter in Congress as saying 'We're going to de-fund the left'. The Thatcher government in Britain cut deeper into the rules than the Reagan administration in the United States, perhaps because there was more (from its viewpoint) that needed changing.

If action on the rules is required, two strategies are available: (i) change within the state by means of active political struggle, and (ii) capture of the state and its use as an instrument of change. The former is the favoured strategy of pluralists. The latter is the more traditional 'planning' strategy and assumes a different model of the state, a strong state legitimized by a unitary conception of the public interest. Such an image is associated with the theories to be discussed in the next two chapters, neo-corporatism and neo-liberalism.

6 Neo-corporatism and the organic state

The focus of pluralism is the game of politics and its rules. In so far as pluralist theory contains an image of the state it is an image of a weak, decentralized and fragmented state. It is true that postwar welfare states in Europe and America grew to control the allocation of vast expenditures. State bureaucracies sometimes took on the roles of 'honest broker' or 'referee', and sometimes this entailed intervention on behalf of the powerless (see Dunleavy and O'Leary, 1987, pp. 44–9). But pluralist theory did not find in this experience principles governing the relationship between society and the state that were substantially different from the earlier traditional conceptions of liberalism. Neo-corporatism re-introduced 'the active state' and construed the postwar experience in terms of the state's pivotal role in mediating between the politico-economic interests central to capitalist society. As we shall see, although some political scholars referred to corporatism to describe aspects of interest mediation in the United States, the concept developed on European soil and is more applicable to European politics.

In planning, corporatism has been invoked to explain 'a plan' as the outcome of class compromise. But this perspective works better with economic planning than with urban planning. In the latter field the term 'corporatist' is used to describe a form of 'interest intermediation' in which land-use decisions or decisions on the provision of services emerge either from secret negotiations between developers and agents of the state, or from committees broadly within the ambit of the state apparatus into which representatives of key organizational actors are incorporated.

The origins of corporatism

The idea of corporatism has its origins in the organic states of medieval Europe. In aristocratic societies the function of government was integrated within the society. Governance was a natural right possessed by the privileged minority and exercised by each privileged group within its own sphere (Poggi, 1972, p. 6; Bendix, 1964, pp. 33–48). Thus the French *droit* and the German *recht* both have the same meaning of right *and* law. The right of the feudal lord was also the law. Poggi (1978) and Bendix (1964, 1978) have traced the path of different societies from organic aristocratic government to the concentration of governmental powers and their displacement into a specialized public sphere, the modern state. We shall call this form of state 'ectopic' (displaced) in contrast to the 'organic' state. This movement was accompanied, enhanced and perhaps even caused by the gradual equalization of the legal status of individuals, who were then thrown into competition with each other. An intermediate stage in this process of modernization was the Ständesstaat: government through the 'estates'.[1] The estates were numerous, more or less autonomous spheres of government. Poggi (1972, p. 9) explains:

> The Ständesstaat was a unified, sovereign political entity whose governmental functions were performed not only by the ruler and his own administrative apparatus but also by many other groups with overlapping authority. The feudal lord, as head of a lineage, presided over his own landed estate and its villages, and also sat in a regional assembly of his peers. The craft and the trade guilds ruled their members and their members' families, and indirectly affected their customers. The Church held power over its own personnel, and over all people where certain relationships were concerned. A city's authority encompassed its own citizens, visitors to its market, and to some extent people living or travelling in the adjoining countryside. There were also independent regional and municipal courts and so on.

The Ständesstaat was an organic state. Linking the Ständesstaat with corporatism, Newman (1981, p. 4) observed that the estates were viewed as 'autonomous yet organically aligned, functionally segregated yet reciprocally interdependent, sovereign within their particular sphere of competence yet uniformly subordinate to central authority, all embracing in membership and co-ordinate in their purpose'. The Ständesstaat was succeeded by monarchies (sometimes absolutist as in France, sometimes parliamentary as in England), which were themselves eventually transformed, with the rise of capitalism, into liberal constitutions. But capitalism and legal equalization brought with them the fear of social breakdown, a fear which grew in proportion to the social dislocation caused by the industrial revolution. How could an atomistic society of individuals selfishly pursuing their own ends be held together by a state displaced from the body of society? The solution to this problem, as we know, was

1 The French word, *état*, has the dual meaning of estate (e.g. *les trois états*) and state.

the representative state legitimated by popular mandate and by its capacity to improve the social security and basic living standard of the population. We can trace the theoretical development of this solution in the ideas of the social contract, natural human rights, utilitarianism and representative democracy. This particular theoretical progression dominated British and American political thought. But the sub-theme of the 'organic state' survived more strongly in continental Europe. Two theorists in particular brought the idea of the organic state into their analysis of contemporary societies. They were G. W. F. Hegel and Emile Durkheim.

In common with the political economists of his time, Hegel portrayed a world in which production to meet human needs could only be driven by the competitive pursuit of self-interest, 'the war of all against all'. In the process, both the height of luxury and the depth of poverty were created. Hegel thought that extreme poverty was an inevitable concomitant of a system of production based on private property. Those without property were caught in a trap from which they could never escape of their own volition. Such a highly atomized and conflictual society could not be expected to hold together without a strong and institutionalized expression of the 'universal' interest of society as a whole. This principle of universality was embodied in organic structures of authority in civil society, structures that carried out some of the functions of government. The state was woven into civil society and there was no clearly demarcated boundary between the two spheres.

The legitimacy of Hegel's state (*Rechtsstaat*) depended not on the social contract, utilitarian accountability or representative democracy but upon the subjective identification of the individual with the whole of society: 'The principle of modern states has prodigious strength and depth because it allows the principle of subjectivity to progress to its culmination in the extreme of self-subsistent particularity, and yet at the same time brings it back to the substantive unity and so maintains this unity in the principle of subjectivity itself' (Hegel, [1821] 1967, para. 260).

Individuals were 'raised to universality' through their identification with the mediating institutions that make up the state: the monarchy, the bureaucracy and the estates (*Stände*) in assembly. Open access to the 'universal class' of state bureaucrats was an important feature of Hegel's system. The estates were formed out of the multiplicity of individual transactions that caused people to become conscious of their common interests and form interest groups. Basically, the three estates were those of agriculture, business and the bureaucracy but these were further subdivided into various fractions. In addition to the estates, Hegel also identified the public authority ('*polizei*' in German, but not just the police) and the corporations as bearing the principle of universality in civil society. The public authority not only maintained the legal basis of the system of production (the law governing property relations), but also undertook public works including street lighting, bridge building, the pricing of daily necessities, the care of public health, the provision of public charity and public education. The corporations were institutions close in conception to the medieval guilds. Their purpose was to protect their members' individual interests and, at the same time, to look after the general interest of the membership as a whole, who would otherwise only relate to one another as competitors. Thus the corporation provided both mutual security and group discipline. Hegel considered the corporation to be as important an institution as marriage for the integration of society. But he excluded wage earners, mere labourers in the factories, the proletariat, from the possibility of forming or joining corporations. Hegel thus modernized the idea of the organic state to fit the atomized market society that had developed at the beginning of the nineteenth century.

The concept of the corporation as an integrating and mediating institution was later taken up by Durkheim. Contrary to the classic political economists, Durkheim saw in the modern economy not competitive atomism, the anarchy of the market, but organic solidarity arising from the division of labour. However, in the preface to the second edition of *The Social Division of Labour*, Durkheim tells us that social solidarity is not fully explained by the division of labour. Like Hegel, he makes a connection between the family and the corporation as solidary structures. In fact, he says, 'the corporation has been in a sense the heir of the family' (Durkheim, [1902] 1949, p. 17). This was so because the corporation was a source of occupational ethics and law, just as the family was a source of domestic ethics and law. However, Durkheim acknowledged that the medieval corporations were defunct, and rightfully so, since in their medieval form they prevented the emergence of the new regime of market capitalism. Yet the human need to feel associated with others and not to be perpetually in competition remained. The satisfaction of this need demanded some form of corporative association, representing a moral order in which individual interest was subordinate to a wider interest.

Durkheim found the prospect of the ectopic state extremely worrying: 'A society composed of an infinite number of unorganized individuals that a hypertrophied State is forced to oppress and contain, constitutes a veritable sociological monstrosity. For collective activity is always too complex to be expressed through the single and unique organ of the State'. Since the market had expanded from local to national and international scale, Durkheim looked forward to the re-emergence of the corporations in modern society as non-territorial, occupationally bounded institutions, exacting discipline from their members but also morally responsible for them and electorally accountable to them. He viewed the corporation as fitting into a pattern of sovereign nations, but perhaps today, with the global market so firmly established, he would have rather countenanced global corporations. He writes: 'Society, instead of remaining what it is today, an aggregate of juxtaposed territorial districts, would become a vast system of national corporations . . . Does this not mean that the organized occupation or corporation should be the essential organ of public life?' (Durkheim, [1902] 1949, p. 27).

Durkheim's vision did not eventuate. The representative ectopic state became the predominant form. However, political events and ideas in Europe from the latter half of the nineteenth century up to the Second World War did show decidedly corporatist tendencies. What we have to look for is not just the strong state, the large (hypertrophic) state, or the welfare state – all much in evidence – but the state organically linked to society through semi-autonomous political structures, corporations. Newman (1981) finds evidence of these structures in Germany in the development of industrial cartels and political parties representing distinct estates (*Stände*) and in Italy in the 'ubiquitous' factory councils. Corporatist ideas formed part of the ideological baggage of Italian Fascism. The corporatist teachings of Othmar Spann were written into the post-1934 Austrian constitution; corporatist ideas legitimated authoritarian regimes in Vichy France and Salazar's Portugal, and were to be found in the Iron Guard of Romania, and, in Britain, in Mosleyite Fascism and the Guild Socialism of G. D. H. Cole.

With the defeat of the Axis powers corporatism disappeared as an ideology and, indeed, acquired a strongly pejorative connotation associated with authoritarianism. Yet the concept was later seen still to have explanatory power. Schmitter (1974, p. 86) observes: 'Undoubtedly the most difficult task is to strip the concept of its pejorative tone and implication.' But something of the pejorative tone remains in Schmitter's work and this tone serves the purpose of critique. It contrasts with the tone of approval reserved for 'pluralist' societies. So, unlike pluralism and earlier corporatist ideas, neo-corporatism provides no normative framework of its own. Such normative content as there is lies in its depiction of the absence of pluralism. Much neo-corporatist theory, in fact, shares a common intellectual foundation with pluralism. Both construe the desired relationship between the individual and society in the terms expressed by the classic theorists of the Enlightenment. In dealing with the problem of order in society, both place organized association among individuals and cohesion in the face of conflict centrally in their conceptual schemes. Both adopt an empiricist methodology. Let us now look at the ideal types of corporatism that neo-corporatist theorists developed to clarify the concept.

Ideal types of neo-corporatism

In a seminal article that set the scene for a substantial body of empirical research Schmitter (1974) explicitly set out to provide an alternative to 'the paradigm of interest politics which has heretofore completely dominated the discipline of North American political science: *pluralism*' (p. 95). Schmitter's theory is a theory of the formulation, representation and articulation of *interests*. Following Weber's method, Schmitter created four contrasting ideal types: monism, corporatism, pluralism and syndicalism. A monist society was one like that of Soviet Russia where there were, officially at least, no separate organized interests. All representation of interests was sanctioned by one organization (e.g. the Communist Party). Monist and corporatist societies shared the characteristic of having organizations that did not compete with one another for the representation of individual interests. If people wished their interests to count in politics and in the making of policy by the state they had to join, and submit to the discipline of, the organization that represented a particular functional sphere with which those interests were associated. The analogy was with the process of production and the craft organization of labour: 'if I am a boiler maker I join the Boilermakers' Union'. In every sphere of interest there was room for only one organization to act as a channel for the expression of interests: 'one interest group, or at least a closely integrated coalition of interest groups in each major social category' (Wilson, 1982, p. 220). Corporatist states, therefore, sought to limit the number of representative organizations and granted those they officially recognized a monopoly in the forums where policies were decided. Within the representative organizations, control had to be strictly hierarchical because interactions among representative organizations facilitated by the state had to produce decisions that were binding on their members.

In pluralist and syndicalist systems none of these characteristics were operative. People might form whatever associations they liked for whatever purposes they chose, and they could expect, through those associations, to get as much of a hearing in policy forums as any other organization. Membership was never compulsory and decisions of such organizations were not to be regarded as binding on their members. Furthermore, individuals were not expected to align their interests substantially with a single functional organization. Syndicalism differed radically from pluralism in its advocacy of participation and worker control in the economic sphere, though also through a system of decentralized groups. Syndicalism also differed from pluralism in not being set within an existing structure of political institutions, and in the utopian and loosely specified way in which syndicates of producers (for example, trades unions) came to resolve their differences in the absence of such institutions.

Schmitter (1974, p. 93) summarized these characteristics of corporatism in a well known specification:

> Corporatism can be defined as a system of interest representation in which the constituent units are organized into a limited number of singular, compulsory, noncompetitive, hierarchically ordered and functionally differentiated categories, recognized or licensed (if not created) by the state and granted a deliberate representational monopoly within their respective categories in exchange for observing certain controls on their selection of leaders and articulation of demands and supports.

Turning from this abstract formula to a consideration of societies in which corporatist tendencies are to found, Schmitter concluded that there was enough latitude in the above definition to allow for a further subdivision of the genus into what he called state corporatism and societal corporatism. This bifurcation of the corporatist idea, as Schmitter notes, can be found in the earlier work of Manoilesco (1936), Pinto (1955) and Cardoso (1958). Societal corporatism was a pattern of interest representation, in which the central features of corporatism were largely arrived at through voluntary adjustment, the gradual decay of pluralism and laissez-faire liberalism, and the emergence of a large and wide-ranging state apparatus. This development typically occurred against the background of a political system 'with relatively autonomous, multi-layered territorial units; open competitive electoral processes and party systems; ideologically varied, coalitionally based executive authorities – even with highly "layered" or "pillared" political subcultures' (Schmitter, 1974, p. 105).

In this model, corporatism became one pole of a continuum along which different countries had moved at different periods and at varying rates. Steps along the way were the assumption by the state of increasing responsibilities, particularly in the economic sphere (fostering full employment, promoting economic growth, preventing inflation, smoothing out business cycles, regulating working conditions, covering individual economic and social risks, and resolving labour conflicts: Schmitter, 1974, p. 112), the creation of semi-autonomous boards and commissions with closed membership for such purposes, and the concluding of agreements between the major interest groups, particularly peak employers' associations and organizations of trades unions.

State corporatism, on the other hand, tended to occur where nascent pluralism was suddenly brought to a halt by the intervention of authoritarian forces: 'strong leadership and repressive action, architectonic vision and inflated rhetoric' (Schmitter, 1974, p. 106). Such forces grasped the organs of legitimate violence to impose upon society 'by the stroke of the legislative baton' corporatist structural arrangements for the representation of interests and their articulation with those of the ruling group. Schmitter observed that the tendency towards both kinds of corporatism was a product of a particular turn in the development of capitalism. State corporatism arose from problems generated by retarded capitalist development in which hegemonic class relations were not yet established, and societal corporatism arose from the need of mature capitalism to maintain the momentum of accumulation, the legitimacy of the state and the reproduction of hegemonic class relations. (The concept of hegemony is discussed in chapter 8.)

A view that Schmitter resisted was of corporatism as a mode of production – distinct from capitalism and socialism. This was the perspective, however, that Winkler (1976) elaborated. He made the stimulating proposition that the tendency of political economists to view economic systems solely in terms of capitalism and socialism was nothing more than a reflection of the fact that 'the Axis powers lost the war' (Winkler, 1976, p. 103). The consequence of this historical fact was that we had also lost sight of an ideal type which would have enabled us better to understand what had happened to Western economies in the postwar world, particularly to Britain.

In Winkler's definition, 'corporatism is an economic system in which the state directs and controls predominantly privately-owned business according to four principles: unity, order, nationalism and success' (Winkler, 1976, p. 103). The crux of the definition is in the role of the state as the *director* of privately *owned* business. The defining characteristic of corporatism was that the state controlled the *internal* decisions of private firms. The state, through structures that engaged the authoritatively represented interests of capital, concluded agreements that prescribed or significantly limited the discretion of the capitalist owner and/or manager concerning, *inter alia*, what he produced, how he produced it, from what materials, to what standards, where he sold it, at what price, how much capital he employed and how many people he employed (p. 105).

Corporatism shared with socialism a view of competition as wasteful and dissipating of effort. Such a view immediately distinguished corporatism from pluralism. What was essential to a successful economy was consensus among the conflicting parties, particularly capital and labour; and the state provided the means to achieve it. But co-operation was more than just an attractive option, it was an obligation: 'workers have a duty to work, employers to provide work and both have an obligation to collaborate at work. This is expressed concretely in prohibitions on strikes and lock-outs and compulsory arbitration of disputes' (Winkler, 1976, p. 107). Co-operation, then, had to be backed by order, an order that was, in turn, backed by force and legitimated by the collective good of the nation (again a significant contrast with pluralism).

Finally, according to Winkler, corporatist governments evaluated themselves by their success in achieving concrete results in terms of the goals of the nation, arrived at collectively. Winkler said that the emphasis is on *effectiveness* rather than *efficiency* and on ends rather than means (p. 108). But the ends were plainly not the kind of ends entailed in democratic processes, for such processes 'may readily be put aside if they interfere with the achievement of results'.

Winkler emphasized the distinction between ownership and control of capital in the economic order. In both socialism and capitalism, ownership and control were unified, the former in the hands of the state, the latter in the hands of private capitalists (the shareholders, directors and managers of private firms). In capitalism, ownership involved an interlocking system of rights: to use the goods owned, to direct their use if one does not want to use them oneself, to appropriate the fruits of their use and to transfer the property to another owner (Winkler, 1976, p. 112). Although it could be said that the control vested in the management of a private firm was separated from the ownership of its capital, nevertheless the interests of the owners and managers, oriented as they were to profit, were not substantially divergent and remained in some measure overlapping. Senior managers, for example, frequently owned shares in the firm they worked for and the shareholders participated in control by selecting a governing board.

In corporatism, according to Winkler, ownership and control were radically separated. The state took over control of the investment and production process by chaining all private firms to the discipline of a national plan. This planning, said Winkler, is 'more than conventional state intervention, more than Keynesian demand management, indicative planning, technocracy or socially responsible capitalism. It is a planned, organized and controlled economic system, justified by its ability to achieve collective ends' (Winkler, 1976, p. 109).

Ownership, however, was left in the hands of private shareholders, who were reduced to mere rentiers. They drew their dividend from the productive activities of managers and workers, who were virtually integrated into the state bureaucracy. Such a dividend could hardly be called 'profit', because it had none of the functions of profit in directing investment or evaluating an enterprise. It was no more than a 'cash flow'. A corporatist system was not egalitarian or one in which the aim of state ownership was necessarily redistributive. But neither was it necessarily one that benefited capitalists. Instead, power was concentrated in the hands of the state and, therefore, the state bureaucracy, including the apparatus of legitimate control (the party), became in a sense a ruling class.

In drawing ideal-typical portraits of corporatism, Schmitter (in his earlier work) and Winkler set out to portray the corporatist form as a distinctive type of social organization. Other more recent analyses, however, tend to suggest that neo-corporatist theory is more in the nature of an assembly of real characteristics of capitalist societies, which are left out of the pluralist perspective. These are, in particular, characteristics of 'interest intermediation', that is, characteristics of the way in which private and public power is interwoven in the modern polity. Although it is difficult to see how the above ideal-typical portraits of corporatism apply to urban planning, their application becomes becomes more clear when we consider the question of interest intermediation.

Neo-corporatist intermediation and urban planning

Neo-corporatist theory recognizes the special significance of the cleavage between capital and labour, it draws attention to the groups that form around this cleavage, and its focus is the structures in which these interests come together to resolve their differences. We have seen that Dahl and Lindblom have acknowledged the importance of 'private' economic power, but traditionally, pluralist theory has promoted a view of group activity as somewhat anarchic and unstructured. Group power is seen as being more or less randomly distributed rather than traceable to the relationships inherent in the labour contract and the possession of wealth. Neo-corporatist analyses bring class relations, in the sense of the basic conflict of interest between capital and labour, more clearly into view. However, significant differences arise, depending on whether the analysis is more influenced by Marx or by Weber. Some writers view corporatism as consistent with a Marxist analysis (Cawson, 1978, 1982; Jessop, 1979; Panitch, 1979, 1980), others are critical of Marxism (Crouch, 1977, 1979; Simmie 1981). But, in neo-corporatist theory, the particular relationship between capital and labour is always present, if only in the background.

The theory insists on the particular importance of the structures through which the conflicting interests of capital and labour are brought together through the agency of the state: tripartite structures. These structures embrace a wide variety of boards, committees and agencies of varying autonomy and permanence, incorporating leading groups into the state's sphere of authority and seeking to bind the interests involved to the decisions arrived at through negotiation. Attention is focused on the secretive and exclusive way in which 'mediation' between the interests of capital and labour occurs so as to remove contentious issues from the political limelight. This violates the central pluralist norm of open contestation, substituting the corporatist norm of social harmony. Schmitter (1974, p. 111) claims that: 'this osmotic process whereby the modern state and modern interest associations seek each other out leads, on the one hand, to even further extensions of public guarantees and equilibrations, and, on the other, to even further concentration and hierarchic control within these private governments'.

Many examples of corporatist arrangements for mediating the social relations of production have been described in European politics (see, for example, Schmitter and Lehmbruch, 1979; S. Berger, 1981; Goldthorpe, 1984; Katzenstein, 1985). The concept of 'social partnership' in Austria described by Lehmbruch (1979, p. 55) is widely held up as the paradigm of modern corporatism. In the Austrian system, business, agricultural and labour interests are organized into four statutory public corporations with strong centralized power over their member groups. They are the 'chambers' of commerce, agriculture and labour and the Confederation of Trade Unions. Consent of the last-named is required before constituent unions put forward wage demands or go on strike. Employers abide by the recommended price decisions agreed by the relevant chamber. Centralized leadership is further strengthened by the influence of legal experts and economists linked institutionally with the interest groups. Co-operation between these groups has been thoroughly institutionalized through the Parity Commission for Price and Wage Regulation, but the whole system rests on the voluntary co-operation of the interest groups, each of whom could repudiate the agreement without incurring sanctions 'other than the disapprobation of public opinion'. These institutional arrangements strongly resemble Williamson's (1985, p. 78) model of 'consensual-licensed corporatism' both in respect of the existence of state-licensed intermediary bodies and the pre-existing consensus on a 'general interest', which it is the purpose of the institutional arrangements to find and uphold (cf. Weber's conception of the 'order' of an organization).

Pluralist theory tends to regard the state as neutral with respect to the interests mediated and to let the matter rest at that. Neo-corporatist theory sugggests that there is more to the state's neutrality. The state is able to maintain a neutral stance only because (and only if) the structural rules within which bargaining takes place are certain to keep the outcome within limits acceptable to the existing power structure. These rules exclude 'marginal' groups and issues from consideration and tend to direct political behaviour into certain channels constrained by the power relationship between the interests involved. We have seen that, in conceiving of politics as the playing out of a game, pluralist theory points to the existence of 'rules of the game'. Neo-corporatist theory likewise, and even more explicitly, conceives of power as operating at two levels: in the political behaviour of groups and in the structural rules within which this behaviour takes place (see Williamson, 1985, pp. 166–83). In contrast with pluralism, power in neo-corporatist theory centres on the role, structure and institutions of the state. The theory focuses attention on a particular power relationship between organized groups and the state within which bargaining occurs. The essence of this relationship is one of exchange and mutual dependence. The organized group acquires authority from the state, that is, a degree of legitimate coercive power over its members. In exchange, the state acquires the power to implement policy. The content of the policy cannot be pre-determined by the state although state bureaucrats and politicians may have a hand in shaping it. Policy is the outcome of the bargain between opposing interests; and the state's primary goal is to secure an agreement and to make sure it is implemented.

Leadership, in the neo-corporatist perspective, takes the form of effective planning and the building of the consensual support necessary to guarantee implementation of the plan. As Weber pointed out, the bureaucratization of society, particularly of the state, leads to the formation of organizations of experts with a professional and technical interest in the creation of formally rational policies within their spheres of action: *planned* policies. The perceived complexity of mass society, the increasingly vast and complex engineering projects undertaken by the state, the demand for state intervention in the economy and the very existence of organized expertise itself, all point to policy being construed as a *plan* rather than simply as a vector varying over time as the result of changing political pressures. The interest in planning leads to an interest in consensus among the leading actors, once the experts turn from making plans to implementing them. Planners find that if they wish their plans to be implemented consistently they must incorporate the interests of the leading actors. If they do not, these actors may apply pressure through political channels to subvert or destroy the plan.

From another angle, the political need to reduce conflict in society also leads to planning. If opposing forces are brought together for the purposes of resolving differences on policy, the result is a *promise* to behave in certain ways over a given period of time. This is, of course, a plan. Panitch (1979, pp. 131–40) showed how, in most Western industrial nations after the Second World War, pressure from increasingly powerful trades unions and a tide of mass opinion finally forced governments into a commitment to full employment.

The adoption of this policy in turn greatly increased the power of the unions to demand and obtain higher wages. Increased wages could only be met by increased inflation or a transfer of power in the form of wealth from capital to labour. What emerged was a new balance of powers and risks: the power of the unions to obtain higher wages from individual firms, the power of firms to pass on the costs in higher prices, the risk to 'international competitiveness' of an inflationary spiral and the risk to both labour and capital of the effective devaluation of incomes engendered by the necessary adjustments of the economy to the effects of inflation. Shonfield (1984, pp. 150, 151) asks: 'Does a corporatist setting make planning more acceptable and effective?' His answer is in the affirmative. He claims that the chief function of corporatist intermediation is in obtaining consensual support for incomes policy without which economic planning is doomed to fail. The continuing failure of Conservative and Labour Governments in Britain to induce a lasting pact between capital and labour no doubt contributed to the eventual election of a government committed to ending full employment and breaking the power of the unions (see Middlemas, 1979).

In the planning of cities and towns much the same imperatives prevail as in economic planning. In the urban planning literature the reduction of conflict as 'the spur to planning' has been a durable theme. Pluralists have viewed urban planning as mediating among conflicting claims for the use of land (Foley, 1960; Simmie, 1974). The Fainsteins (1979) write, from a Marxist perspective, of planners '*managing* the contradictions of capitalism manifested in urban form and spatial development' (emphasis added). We have already mentioned Roweis (1983), who characterizes urban planning as 'professional mediation of territorial politics'. Harvey (1985, p. 182) points out that in America in the 1960s many people on the left of politics placed much faith in urban planning to solve the problems of the cities. Also from a Marxist perspective, he observes that the urban riots of the 1960s in America posed a major problem for the state, which responded by 'repression, co-optation and integration' in which urban planning was deeply implicated. Through the ideology of planning: 'political questions could be translated into technical questions that the mass of the population found hard to understand'. According to these views, then, urban planners actively seek to manage their political environment, incorporate interests, limit and channel access to the decision-making forum, generate consensus and look to pillared, functionally differentiated structures of interest to implement bargained plans.

The British sociologist of urban planning, James Simmie, has moved from a pluralist (in 1974) to a neo-corporatist position (1981) and back again to something approaching 'corporate pluralism' (1985).

The concept of 'corporate pluralism' is discussed below. Simmie now contends that conflicts about land-use in Britain diverge from 'the pluralist and accountable paradigm' (1985, p. 174) and exhibit a mixture of pluralist and corporatist tendencies. He argues that land-use decisions, which, in important respects, impinge on the process of production and investment of large-scale capital, are made through deals arrived at in secret between private sector and government oligarchies. The greater the resources (of organization, capital or land) at the disposal of the private oligarchy, the more the bargaining relationship of that oligarchy with government will take on a 'corporatist' character. Simmie's point, which is supported by empirical evidence (Simmie, 1981), is that powerful organizations with control over production and investment gain regular and direct access to government decision-making, not only with respect to specific land-use proposals but also to the procedures and rules whereby decisions are to be arrived at: the 'rules of the game'. Large powerful interest groups tend to become incorporated into the decision-making process at an early stage. Further, 'the more contentious the land uses at stake, the higher the level of government at which oligarchical interactions take place' (Simmie, 1985, p. 177). By contrast, individuals and groups concerned primarily with the consumption of resources channelled through the state and small businesses have to play the game by the given rules. These actors are often in competition with one another, are not incorporated into the decision-making process and make demands on the state. The latter mode of interaction, Simmie thinks, is characteristically 'pluralist'.

Unfortunately, Simmie exaggerates the contrast between pluralism and corporatism by postulating a supposedly 'popular' image of pluralist politics, which is nowhere to be found in the serious pluralist literature: 'a political system in which all individuals may participate equally in political decision-making, irrespective of the distribution of knowledge, wealth, social position, access to officials or other sources' (Simmie, 1985, p. 176). Against this criterion very little government decision-making anywhere could be regarded as pluralist. Simmie admits that singular and non-competitive interest representation was not found in British urban planning and there was only 'limited devolution' of state power from government to enable the participating organizations to implement the bargains struck. The findings adduced in support of corporatism could as easily be dealt with under the rubric of pluralism, as discussed in chapter 5. Simmie's work does, however, highlight the fact that bargaining between governments and organized interests is conducted in different ways, depending on the nature of the interests concerned.

Healey, McNamara, Elson and Doak (1988) conduct a searching analysis of the rules governing interest mediation in British planning practice. They concede that corporatism describes some aspects of mediation in some cases in Britain: 'Bargaining practices may become consolidated into corporatist relations when the expectation of a regular stream of development proposals fosters the maintenance of good working relations over time. We encountered such relations between locally dominant property consultants and local authorities in our earlier research (Wood, 1982; McNamara, 1985)'. But they observe, 'We found few cases where there was sufficient stability in the projects or the parties involved to foster corporatist practices' (Healey *et al.* 1988, p. 239). The key point here is the authors' insistence that corporatist arrangements entail 'negotiation among representatives of groups mutually dependent over a *range of issues over time*' (authors' emphasis). In terms of the original concept of corporatism this is correct: organized groups participating in governance on a permanent basis. But this is not what Simmie, Saunders or Cawson (see below) mean by 'corporatist intermediation'. These writers stress the way in which certain interests are *incorporated* into the policy process, whether or not the particular groups representing these interests vary over time. They also stress the permanence of the mechanisms or structures for incorporation. What Healey *et al.* describe as 'bargaining' has much in common with the processes described by American writers on corporatism (McConnell, 1967; Lowi, 1969; Lustig, 1982) and may be described as 'corporate pluralism' or 'micro-corporatism' (in the terms used by Cawson, 1986). However, Healey *et al.* (1988, p. 238) argue that it is the *criteria* of access to the decision-making forum rather than structures or processes that are the crucial factor. 'The key criterion', they write, 'in determining who had access to bargaining processes and how these were played out was the way the mutual dependencies were balanced.' Different actors can use different political resources to gain access. Developers can exploit a local authority's need for investment, or the ability to influence national or local politicians. They may use experts to negotiate on their behalf (McNamara, 1984; Healey, Davis, Wood and Elson, 1982). Infrastructure agencies can use finance and planning gain as their bargaining counter. Local authority officials, usually planners, can draw on councillor attitudes, local politics, agreed policies (Healey *et al.*, p. 238). Here we are back in the pluralist world of negotiation and bargaining, 'manifest influence', and 'the play of power'.

An important model of the state–society relationship, with explicit application to urban planning, has been developed by Cawson and Saunders. This has become known as the 'dual state' model. In work paralleling Simmie's, Cawson argued in 1978 that a crucial transformation from pluralist to corporatist interest mediation occurs 'when interest groups change from being private protective associations

and move towards the establishment of regular and mutually supportive relationships with government' (Cawson, 1978, p. 191). He
hypothesized the existence of a corporate and a pluralist sector, the
first characterized by 'oligarchic groups with stable clienteles but with
little scope for autonomous action because of their need to conform
to co-operative norms of behaviour', the second by ill-organized less
permanent groups frequently espousing a participatory ideology, or
established and permanent groups representing interests peripheral to
the major economic concerns of the state. 'Producer groups will be
corporatized as a necessity while the expansion and activity of consumer groups will occur largely outside the purview of the state' (p.
192). Cawson and Saunders (1983) take this thesis further. Saunders'
summary of the 'dualistic theory of politics' contained in a 1983
working paper on the regional state cannot be bettered and is quoted
here in full:

> The core elements of this dualistic theory of politics relate to the
> social base which is mobilised, the way in which it mobilises,
> the level at which it mobilises and the values around which it
> mobilises. Thus, the politics of production (i.e. decisions about,
> administration of and organisation around policies designed to
> maintain private sector profitability through provision of invest-
> ment finance, physical infrastructure, raw materials and so on)
> tend to be associated with:
>
> • the mobilisation of class-based interests such as employers'
>   organisations and trade unions;
> • the development of a corporatist exclusionary strategy where-
>   by other potentially competing interests are kept out of the
>   policy-making and administrative process;
> • state agencies located at the centre; and
> • a dominant ideological concern with private property rights
>   in a market system.
>
> The politics of consumption (i.e. those political processes relating
> to the provision of social consumption resources such as housing,
> health and education), on the other hand, tend to be characterised
> by:
>
> • the mobilisation of sectoral interests such as owner-occupiers
>   and tenants or private and public patients which are based on
>   cleavages arising out of the process of consumption;
> • competitive struggles between a plurality of groups mobilising
>   through electoral and pressure group strategies;
> • local level state agencies (particularly local government); and

- a dominant ideological concern with the rights of citizenship in a wwelfare system.

The politics of production may best be approached through a theory of the state which stresses its subordination to the interests and demands of dominant economic interests (i.e. instrumentalist versions of Marxist theory), whereas the politics of consumption are more appropriately analysed through a theory which stresses the relative openness of public agencies to popular pressure and opinion (i.e. pluralist versions of liberal democratic theory) (Saunders, 1983, p. 22).

The implications of this perspective for urban planning, which spans consumption and production, are considerable. If it is true that the type of interest intermediation varies regularly according to either the level of government (national, regional, local) or the functional focus of policy (production, consumption), or both, then planners will encounter different pressures to conform to the politics of the situation and different problematic aspects of that politics. For instance, as we have seen in the last chapter, competitive, pluralist politics is likely to mean that a wide variety of points of view and interests is brought to bear on matters of urban development or urban service provision, although powerless and unorganized interests will be greatly under-represented. It will be difficult to decide on a plan that meets the demands of all groups and, once decided, the plan may be continually derailed by fluctuating pressures from different quarters. There will also be difficulty in upholding a wider conception of 'the public good' in the face of multiple versions of 'the public good' advanced by each vested interest group. On the other hand, corporatist politics is likely to increase the decisiveness of the planners and the chances of consistent implementation of the plan over a reasonably long period of time, but at the expense of openness and democratic input from the 'grass roots' level. Further, there is the possibility that the plan, ostensibly representing the wider public interest, actually only serves the interests of the elites. Sealed off from criticism, this may not readily become apparent.

An advantage of the dual state theory is that it presents a package that is empirically testable and refutable. The model was developed inductively from the British experience, and doubts have been expressed about whether it applies as a package in any other country (Paris, 1983). For example, in Australia, health services, public education, public housing (such as there is) and welfare services, all typical 'social consumption' activities, are provided by the regional (State) level of government (Low and Power, 1984). In America, local governments compete to provide services and infrastructure to businesses engaged in production (Bluestone and Harrison, 1982). However it is always possible to unpack a package. So Saunders (1985) goes on to ask which of the situational characteristics described in the model is *dominant*? Is it the level of government or the policy focus, or neither, that determines the mode of interest intermediation?

From the evidence of two case studies of urban planning in Australia and one of regional authorities in Britain, Saunders concludes that: 'it does seem that the major factor determining whether or not corporatist forms of mediation develop is the type of policy area and hence the type of interests most directly affected by the state's actions' (Saunders, 1985, p. 170). However, a much fuller picture of Australian urban politics needs to be developed before we can conclude that questions involving production and investment in land and buildings are regularly settled through corporatist forms of interest intermediation. In the State of Victoria for about six years, as Saunders admits, the question of redevelopment of Melbourne's central area was dealt with by highly consultative and typically pluralist processes. These processes were certainly no less pluralist and involved much more open conflict than those described by Dahl in the redevelopment of New Haven. Only when decision-making seemed paralysed, and with the emergence of extraneous party-political issues (such as the changing balance of power in Melbourne City Council) did the State Government of Victoria act to replace the elected local council with a board of appointed commissioners. Strictly speaking, the behaviour of this board was far from corporatist, since it did not seek any concertation of interests, merely acting on behalf of the frustrated would-be developers of the central area. The extreme unpopularity of the action of the State Government in sacking the Melbourne City Council was undoubtedly one of the factors that soon afterwards brought the Government down. The unpopular board was immediately dismissed by the new Labor Government and the City Council was reinstated under boundaries that ensured the Council's domination by local resident and Labor Party interests.

However, with a somewhat looser definition of corporatism, it becomes easier to find evidence of its existence. Cawson, in recent work, postulates that different forms of corporatism occur at different levels (Cawson, 1986). 'Macro-corporatism' refers to the institutionalized extension of governance to peak organizations representing social classes, the classic example being that of Austria. 'Meso-corporatism' refers to the integration of economic 'sectors' cutting across class boundaries. Sectors are structural divisions arising from the industrial division of labour, e.g. types of industry: agriculture, the steel industry, the car industry; or divisions within the state: functional domains such as education, housing or transport. Micro-corporatism refers to the integration of the interests of individual firms and other local interests with those of the state through a process of private bargaining. Corporatism is thus a term describing a particular type of intermediation among class, sectoral and group interests through the agency of the state. The process of 'bargaining', which Healey *et al.* found so prevalent in British land-use planning, Cawson defines as micro-corporatism. Under Section 52 of the UK Town and Country Planning Act of 1971 local authorities could strike bargains with developers to grant permission or give concessions on, for example, the density of development in exchange for 'social' benefits such as car-parking provision, local conservation work or local open space, sometimes on sites unconnected with the original development (Hawke, 1981). 'This kind of "planning gain"', writes Cawson, 'is in effect a tax on land development assessed according to rules which are fashioned for each case, often in secret and always well insulated from democratic processes at the local level' (Cawson, 1986, p. 121).

In Australia both the Federal Government and the governments of some States, in a period of unprecedented Labor Party domination of politics in the 1980s, moved some way along Cawson's version of the 'corporatist' path. Macro-corporatism is evident in the concertation of the organized interests of labour through close collaboration between the peak organizations of the trades union movement and Federal and State governments. What is lacking, however, is the concertation of business interests whose peak organizations are, on the whole, weak and divided. Business views are advanced through close personal contacts between government leaders (particularly the Prime Minister) and certain prominent businessmen, but these businessmen are not in a position to represent, let alone command, the class to which they belong (Keating and Dixon, 1989). The attempt by the Federal Government to plan the development of certain economic sectors (the car and steel industries, for example) with the participation of unions and business through an Economic Planning Advisory Council is typical of 'meso-corporatism'. It is noteworthy that the plan for the steel industry, which is dominated by one massive transnational corporation (BHP) has met with considerably greater success than the plan for the car industry, which involves several competing corporations. State level meso-corporatism has been taken furthest in Victoria, where the Labor Government, from 1982, has moved to subject all the functional divisions of the bureaucracy, including urban planning, to a long-term economic strategy.

At the 'micro' level, provisions similar to those of the British Town and Country Planning Act existed in the Town and Country Planning Act of Victoria (Victoria, 1971) and are perpetuated in the Planning and Environment Act (Victoria, 1987). A minister may call in (from the local authority) an application for permission to develop land or amend a planning scheme, to be decided at his or her own discretion. When the Labor Party took office in Victoria in 1982 the power to control major development was not returned to Melbourne City Council, even though the Council itself was reinstated. The State Government has conducted closed consultations with developers on major projects and has established a special unit under the direct supervision of a minister for that purpose. Yet the State Government has brought the power over metropolitan planning (formerly residing with a quasi-autonomous statutory Board, the Melbourne Metropolitan Board of Works) directly under the control of a minister. This action could be regarded as a move away from corporatism, since it sheets home the responsibility for planning to an elected official. Moreover, in seeking to facilitate development, the Government has on occasion been sensitive to pressure from well organized interest groups such as the National Trust of Australia and local residents' groups. It is possible that some of these interests have been co-opted into the policy process. But the Government has backed away on a number of occasions from supporting major developments in the face of strong external pressure-group activity. A recent 'back-down' was over the construction of a new electricity power line through inner city neighbourhoods in Melbourne. Electricity supply, it should be noted, is a functional domain in which Saunders would expect corporatist intermediation to take place.

Turning to the wider question of why corporatist intermediation occurs, Marxist neo-corporatists argue that the need for corporatist structures arises from the contradictory fact of the rising political power of the working class and its remaining subjection to the yoke of private property and the labour contract. Because labour is organized and, therefore, has certain weapons at its disposal, such as the strike and the vote, capital can be forced to negotiate. But so long as capital retains the power it acquires from the state (guaranteeing the rule of private property) it can always extract a bargain which, at least, maintains the process of private accumulation. This is because, given that condition, it is in the short-term interest of labour to maintain accumulation. This is why Schmitter (1974, p. 107) can suggest as a 'macrohypothesis' that the 'corporatization of interest representation is related to . . . the needs of capitalism to reproduce the conditions for its existence', and why Panitch (1980, p. 176) can contend that corporatism is 'specific to those groups which are class-based'. The thrust of corporatism is to direct attention to the 'dominant state' (Williamson, 1985). But the boundaries of the state become clouded and arbitrary. Are incorporated groups inside or outside the state? The direction in which corporatism points is towards increased domination in society *through* the state.

Schmitter has since modified his ideal type of corporatism. Streeck and Schmitter (1985) suggest that different societies may be organized on the basis of different mixtures of 'guiding principles'. They outline three such principles: community, market and state, or bureaucracy; the first characterized by 'spontaneous solidarity', the second by 'dispersed competition' and the third by 'hierarchical control'. To these they add a fourth: 'associative order', to which neo–corporatist theory points. The growth of the principle of associative order within a nation requires certain enabling conditions to exist. Interest associations need to have developed a certain symmetry in the resources (membership, funds, organization) they control and the degree of control over their members, and they must have obtained an effective monopoly of representation for a class, industrial sector or profession (i.e. sector in the division of labour). When such conditions exist, interest associations are able to calculate the outcome of pacts among them and between each and the appropriate sector of the state. Therefore, there will be a strong incentive to enter into a process of negotiation with a view to compromise. However, the growth of associative order is precarious. Market forces may be too strong to be contained by associational compromise; electoral competition may bring to power parties opposed to associational rule and intent upon reinstating the dominance of either the bureaucratic or the market principle. Or the bureaucratic agents themselves may try to reverse the delegation of 'their' authority to the interest associations.

The authors claim that there is enough empirical evidence of what they term 'private interest government' (the existence of strong institutions for inter-associational conflict regulation) to suggest that the principle of associative order is making headway in a significant number of European nations, although its progress has been checked in others such as Britain. Private interest government is the result of 'an organizational dynamic by which pluralist interest representation is transformed into corporatist interest intermediation' (Streeck and Schmitter, 1985, p. 17). Rather than the conveyers of individual interests, the authors argue that interest associations should be seen as the producers of interests and shapers of 'collective identity'. Disputes between pressure groups and state agencies lead the latter to relinquish some of their regulatory power in exchange for voluntary self-regulation. This, in turn, leads to a closer relationship of the association with the state in which the association attains 'political status', the sharing in the state's authority to make and enforce binding decisions. Finally, state agencies may then try to 'design' interest associations in specific policy areas, which, in the pursuit of their own 'categoric' interests, will produce 'public goods'. There is a choice between setting up large 'encompassing' organizations capable of absorbing conflict of interest internally or creating inter-organizational structures mandated to take decisions through bargaining. (Here it is worth referring to Olson, 1986, and Hechter, 1987, for 'rational choice theory' explanations for the emergence of solidary groups).

Private interest government has advantages for the maintenance of public order in an expanding and increasingly complex society (*vis-à-vis* interests). It eases the problem of legitimation both by removing some of the burden from the state and by enabling decisions to be legitimated by different interest groups with reference to different rationales. It also provides a collectivist alternative as states reach the limits of bureaucratic, étatiste planning. The appeal of the associative principle, argue Streeck and Schmitter, lies in its capacity to supply pragmatic solutions to specific problems of policy-making and implementation, rather than in its intrinsic ideological attractiveness. Therefore, they suggest, those societies in which the appropriate conditions exist tend to move towards the associative principle through a series of pragmatic adjustments within the liberal, democratic, capitalist system of government rather than through its wholesale replacement by a corporatist system.

It may be that the entire institution of urban planning in capitalist countries is an instance of the growth of associative order. Through a series of pragmatic adjustments, the conflicts between occupiers of small parcels of land have forced into existence new methods of allocating resources and resolving disputes, involving what we might term discursive practices, practices involving discourse and talk (bargaining) as well as political manoeuvring, rather than either hierarchy and coercion on the one hand or market exchange on the other. Faludi's latest conception of strategic planning (1986) rather supports this view. In such a conception the meaning of 'corporatism' is stretched rather beyond what the term can reasonably stand. But perhaps it is time to transcend the concept anyway.

Most of the writers discussed so far are Europeans. We must ask, therefore, whether corporatism, rather than being a universal phenomenon of the twentieth century, is instead a mainly European phenomenon.

Corporate pluralism and the American and European polity

As we have seen, a strong non–Marxist critical tradition flourished in the postwar years in America alongside mainstream liberal pluralism. Some of these critics drew attention to the way in which governance extended deep within civil society, linking private associations and corporations with the state. Reagan (1963, p. 210) wrote of the United States economy as a 'marbled mixture of private and public forces and institutions'. Galbraith ([1967] 1971) portrays a society in which

much of the culture as well as the economy centres on the large corporations, the aggregate of which he calls the 'planning system'. The
corporations share with the state the task of regulating and organizing
society: 'the planning system, in fact, is inextricably associated with
the state. In notable respects the mature corporation is an arm of
the state. And the state, in important matters, is an instrument of
the planning system' (p. 307). The work of the 'educational and
scientific estate' is also shaped by the needs of the 'planning system'.
McConnell (1967) argued that the liberal notion of a clear demarcation
between the state and civil society (the ectopic state) was fictitious.
The private association, the trade union and the business corporation
were extensions of government, the last in particular being unchecked
by democratic norms of accountability. Pluralists, said McConnell,
assumed that powerful dispersed organizations would check one other
and the power of the state. But pluralism did not address the question
of individual liberty within the organization, and chose to ignore the
tendencies towards internal oligarchy, hierarchical managerial control
and monopoly representation of interests. Such portrayals depict an
organic state in which the functions of government spread like a
network of filaments throughout society.

Lowi (1969, p. 71) drew attention to the function of groups in
organizing and governing American society. He picks out three main
assumptions of what he calls a vulgarized version of the pluralist
model: i) organized interests are homogeneous and easy to define,
sometimes monolithic; ii) organized interests fill up and adequately
represent 'most of the sectors of our lives'; iii) the role of government
is to ensure access to public decision-making for the most effectively organized groups and to ratify the agreements and adjustments
worked out among their competing leaders. He considers the term
'corporatism' to describe this model of state–society relations, but
rejects it in favour of 'interest group liberalism' on the grounds
of the 'unwanted' association of the former term with conservative
Catholicism and Italian Fascism. However, Lowi was particularly
disturbed at the growth of the 'corporate city' in America. This
structure combined fragmented territorial authority with functionally specific professionalized agencies to which 'legitimised clientele
groups' enjoyed privileged access. Territorial fragmentation enabled
the residents of new suburbs to exclude the poor and the blacks; the
functional bureaucracies took power out of the hands of the elected
political leaders. Thus, Lowi writes, 'There are now many publics but
no polity . . . The modern city is now well run but badly governed
because it is now comprised of islands of functional power before
which the modern mayor stands impoverished' (p. 197).

R. J. Lustig (1982), going back over the work of the American
analytical pluralists as well as some of their critics, finds a theme not

fully developed. He reconsiders the role of organization and association in the American polity and interprets 'group theory' in politics in terms of its opposition to individualism and atomism. Emphasis on the social and political function of the business corporation and trades unions and the enthusiasm of Justice Oliver Wendell Holmes for corporate life, Lustig argues, can be linked to the theme of social solidarity, which can be found in the work of the pluralists, Arthur Bentley, John Dewey, Mary Parker Follett and Herbert Croly. On McConnell, Lowi and Reagan, Lustig comments that, putting their faith in a strengthened federal system and a stronger presidency (essentially the ectopic state), 'they failed to examine the structures of private power and the larger social formations in which federal institutions are rooted' (Lustig, 1982, p. 254). His point, however, is not really that these writers failed to *observe* the structures of 'private' power, but that they did not go far enough in their conclusions about the political functions of these structures in creating a form of governance that went far beyond the bounds of the 'official' public sphere. Yet Lustig acknowledges that there is a profound contradiction in American society: 'Modern American society thus captures the worst of both modern and medieval worlds. Corporatist to its core, it creates mechanistic rather than organic social relations. It forces agglomeration, but without community. It mandates corporatism, but without trust. And it justifies hierarchy without enforcing accountability. The irony is that where medieval society extended the mantle of the common good over obvious heterogeneity, modern society farms out sovereignty over an increasingly homogeneous terrain to private parties' (Lustig, 1982, p. 247).

This same theme emerges also in the work of sociologist Robert Bellah and his colleagues (1985): the ideology of individualism and fragmentation coupled with the struggle of isolated individuals to create local community, and the pervasive discipline of public and private corporate authority. Some of the characteristics of corporatism have been observed in American society, particularly the interpenetration of private and public authority, the 'pillarization' of society into functional domains, and oligarchy and hierarchy within these domains. But the American polity does not by any means fit the ideal types constructed by European theorists such as Schmitter and Winkler. Wilson (1982) argues that the American polity is very far from meeting the conditions of Schmitter's model on two main grounds. First, there exists no single interest group or close coalition of interest groups to which most people in each social or occupational category belong. There may be some pillarization, but there is no monopoly of representation. Nor is it widely accepted that organizations representing social or occupational groups are truly representative of *all* in the group and capable of making binding commitments on their behalf. It follows that the more demanding conditions of corporatism cannot be met: for example, major decisions being made by the government only after close consultation with major economic interests and such decisions strongly influencing the behaviour of *both* government *and* interest group members.

Heisler and Kvavik (1974) have sought to identify, in terms of the state–society relationship, more precisely where the difference lies between the American and European political systems. Their point of departure is David Easton's *Systems Analysis of Political Life* (Easton, 1965). This work is a useful reference point, because it attempts to construct a neutral framework for the consideration of different political systems. However, Heisler and Kvavik detect a flaw in its neutrality traceable to Easton's contact with the empirical reality of American political life. This flaw provides the key to the difference between the American and European polity. In Easton's framework, they say, 'it is difficult to escape the conclusion that "input-type behaviour" (e.g. voting, party and interest group activity) is the principal source of influence on outputs (i.e. on authoritative decisions, rules and laws). Second, and in part as a corollary of the problem identified in the last sentence, there is a clear assumption of the preeminence of inputs over what Easton has termed "withinputs" in terms of substantive – i.e. policy-influencing, output-determining – importance and volume' (Heisler and Kvavik, 1974, p. 35).

By contrast, the authors, drawing on a large body of European literature, identify three main elements of a model, which they claim describes the typical European as against American polity. First, although there are high levels of social and political mobilization in European society, the outputs from society do not translate directly into inputs into the state. The relationship of inputs to outputs is complex. The European polity is marked by increasing consensus, institutionalized participation and managerial-style policy-making. The authors call on Mostafa Rejai (1971 pp. 18,19) to sum up: 'The most important changes [in societies manifesting a decline of ideology] revolve around economic development and its attendant consequences: an increasing general affluence; an increasing reliance on science and expertise; and increasing attenuation of class and party conflict; a gradual attainment of political and economic citizenship by the lower classes; a gradual emergence of a vast, homogeneous, professional–managerial middle class; a gradual transformation of laissez faire capitalism into the welfare state; *and a gradual institutionalization of stable political processes for resolution of political issues*' (Heisler and Kvavik, 1974, p. 41). These developments are coupled with a decline in the importance of the institutional role of parliaments compared with other branches of government (e.g. cabinets, bureaucracies).

Secondly, the growth and thorough politicization of interest groups ('highly articulated pluralistic structures') in Europe has led to their being increasingly incorporated directly into the governmental decision-making process. This incorporation of interest groups was described by Rokkan (1966) as 'corporate pluralism' and by Lijphart (1977) as 'consociational democracy'. The degree to which incorporated interest groups are able to claim a monopoly of representation or even crowd out alternative groups would seem to be an important measure of 'corporatism'. Incorporation was accompanied by an implicit agreement on the part of the leadership of interest groups to desist from open competition. 'Each interest seeks security and protection for the position it has already acquired, and together they rob political conflict of its dynamics' (Dahrendorf, 1967, pp. 277–8). Interest groups tended to be vertically structured, and communication between sectors tended to be restricted to the upper echelons, a form described as 'pillarized'. On the other hand, at the elite level a 'horizontal, cross-sectoral leadership structure . . . must be established and maintained' (Heisler and Kvavik, 1974, p. 46). The leaderships of potentially conflicting groups are brought together to reach agreement on the basis of non-zero-sum bargaining. Participants are seen as 'sharers' rather than 'winners and losers'. This elite dialogue helps to prevent the groups from becoming rigid in their attitudes and policies, because they have to adapt to one another constantly. Interest group leadership is thus co-opted into the decision-making process and the committees established become institutionalized in the structure of government.

Thirdly, the political importance of 'administration' has increased in everyday life. Formal bureaucracy has grown by the 'adhesion' of mixed public bodies, that is, formally mandated authorities consisting of politicians, bureaucrats, professional 'experts' and interest group leaders. These bodies are increasingly involved in the implementation of comprehensive economic plans. A by-product of the growth of the welfare state has been that more political issues revolve around the actions or inactions of the administration. The tendency, however, is to question outcomes rather than processes: *what* is done rather than *how* it is done. In general, the influence on policy outcomes of the 'mass public' 'can be said to have been effectively removed' (Heisler amd Kvavik, 1974, p. 70). Heisler and Kvavik stress that the above three main elements reinforce one another and must be read together as a whole. Their point is that the European polity, in contrast to other types, is primarily to be understood in terms of what is already inside the system rather than by reference to what is put into it from its environment. As Zeigler (1980, p. 16) has put it, 'governmental and non-governmental experts develop policy proposals which are then *responded to* by broader segments of the public including the

most visibly responsive interest groups. A few groups, those with
technical resources, are involved in the development of policy. Most
groups participate only in response to policy.'

In a later paper, Heisler (1979) reflected critically on the way in
which the concept of 'corporatism' had been employed. Taking a
typically pluralist–empiricist epistemological stance, he objected to
the idea that 'corporatism' could represent a distinctive socio-political
system and claimed that the value of the neo-corporatist work had
been to add to the complex set of variables describing relationships
among private and governmental interests: 'the attention drawn to the
more prominent, institutionalized roles of organized sectoral (and/or
territorial or segmental) interests and their intricate and thorough
intertwining with the decision-making and administrative aspects of
governments was the major corrective provided in this literature' (p.
278). Heisler also objected to the functionalist interpretation of the
role of the state, and indeed to the whole concept of *the state*: in the
neo-corporatist literature 'public elites (and sometimes even interest
organization leaders) are seen as agents of the *state*, purposively
orchestrating structurally determined and rigidified, abiding, class
interests – rather than, for instance, as hapless politicians who are
temporary incumbents of *government* offices and who walk tightropes
of narrow coalitions above deep societal divisions, shallow sectoral
demands, and intra-sectoral conflicts and problem-imposing environments' (p. 284). Heisler thus views government primarily as a *role*,
denies the importance of the demarcation between state and 'civil
society' and consequently denies the existence of regularities in the
deployment of power in society that could be interpreted as structural
parameters limiting and channelling the behaviour of the state and
its agents. 'The evidence', he says, 'indicates that roles and utility
schedules shift (and the former are sometimes interchanged); governments are far from content simply to mediate; and the outcomes of
the interplay of multiplex role-interest sets are not at all predictable
from assumptions derived from the status and comprehensiveness of
organizations, the postulated interests of citizens, or a posited division
of functions' (p. 286). Continuing the theme that neo-corporatism
simply pointed to the emergence of a more complex pattern of
plural interest group relationships, Jordan (1981, p. 113) asks, 'But
if an increasingly complex form of pluralism does emerge, because
of the growth of government and the interventionist economy, does
the response have to be seen as corporatism? *Isn't it merely pluralism
in a new environment?*'

The answer very much depends on what 'pluralism' is taken to be.
If pluralism is no more than the view that the theoretical treatment
of political phenomena must be decomposed into the specific behav-
iours of individuals and groups, then all politics can be regarded as

'pluralist'. Pluralism is merely a level of theory, a view of society and politics from close at hand. If, on the other hand, pluralism is taken as saying something distinctive about the political organization of society, a view we have tried to elaborate in chapter 5 of this book, then corporatism does seem to be saying something different. There is a difference in the way each theory views interest groups and their relationship with the state. Pluralist theory assumes that the dominant function of interest groups is to *represent* interests and make demands on the state. Corporatist theory views the dominant function of interest groups as one of governance, ensuring compliance with bargained policy. As Grant (1985, p. 21) points out, 'Intermediation means that group leaderships have to ensure that their memberships comply with the agreements they have arrived at with the state or other organised interests.'

Conclusion

Corporatism developed as a theory of how society both *is* organized and *ought* to be organized politically. The normative element of the theory was discredited following its adoption by fascist and other authoritarian regimes, and its fate was sealed for a time by the defeat of fascism in the Second World War. The idea was revived in the 1970s in modified form as descriptive of modern states, in contrast with the pluralist description of interest representation and articulation of demand and the norm of open, competitive contestation of public policy. Selective incorporation of non-state elites into government decision-making was counterposed against the ideology, which is popularly associated with pluralism, of equal access to the decision-making forums of the state.

The central theme of neo-corporatist theory is the intermediation between core interests in civil society and those of the state. It is clear that in this respect there is considerable overlap between corporatist theory and the more institutionally minded varieties of pluralism. The incorporation of interests in civil society into the sphere of the state is a tenet of both perspectives. Whereas pluralism, on the whole, postulates a weaker, less decisive, less centrally organized and 'planned' state than corporatism, this does not seem to be the critical distinction between the two. It is possible to imagine a form of centrally directed, presidential or cabinet government whose stance towards external interests is entirely pluralist. The key difference between pluralist and corporatist theory is, rather, in the emphasis of the latter on the extension of legitimate coercive power to organizations in civil society, which are then endowed with the right to monopolistic representation of functional interests. We might call this 'concertation' rather than 'incorporation'; looking towards the organic rather than the ectopic state. It seems that there is more evidence for this occurring in some European states than in the American polity. In the field of urban planning there is plenty of evidence of bargaining behind closed doors and incorporation of interests into state policy-making. There may also exist more or less permanent structures for such incorporation. But there is little evidence of concertation.

It does seem, then, that the models of corporatism and plural-ism as distinctive types of polity may not be particularly useful in conceptualizing actual observable events and structures. For comparative work, we may have to go beyond these types to identify key dimensions along which the behaviour of states vary. In this respect we have already identified three: decisiveness, incorporation and concertation. States may vary in the degree to which they attempt to co-ordinate their activities by dominating bureaucratic agencies and interests from a central authority: top-down policy-making. They may also vary in the degree to which they endeavour to incorporate dominant interest groups (interest associations, pressure groups, firms) into their own decision-making. Finally, they may differ in the degree to which incorporated interests become, in effect, channels of state power or sub-governments situated in civil society. The last two dimensions may in fact be elided, so that incorporation is regarded as an intermediate stage between competitive intermediation and full concertation. Such a step would be in line with the recent work of Streeck and Schmitter (1985) and Cawson (1986). The distinction between decisiveness and concertation, however, must remain. In the next chapter we shall see that neo-liberal theory argues in favour of a strong (or decisive) ectopic state, whose stance towards interests in civil society is that they compete for political power as they do for economic domination in the market.

On political values, pluralism is explicit but neo-corporatism is vague. The original rationale for corporatism as 'a system of functional representation designed to foster class harmony' was discredited by the experience of fascism. It seemed that fascism put corporatist theory into practice. The appearance of class harmony, sometimes accompanied by frightening demonstrations of mass-hysterical fer-vour, was achieved only by state repression and naked terror directed primarily 'against the indigenous organizations of the working class' (Panitch, 1980, pp. 161, 165). Schmitter's very reasonable attempt to separate 'state corporatism' of the type displayed by fascist and other right authoritarian regimes from the 'societal corporatism' more characteristic of left reformist regimes is an attempt to quarantine the former and preserve for the latter some semblance of legiti-macy. But neither Schmitter nor any other corporatist writer to date has been able to codify the virtues of corporatism or even to do for corporatism what Dahl, with 'polyarchy', did for pluralism.

The normative deficiency is most acutely felt in those versions of corporatism that depict it as a distinctive mode of social organization. To take Winkler's model as the paradigm, the virtues of systems of private *or* public ownership and control of the means of production are well known, but what could possibly be the virtue of a system of state control and private ownership in which the power structure embodied in the ownership of wealth remains unchanged, yet the powerful owners are reduced to mere functionless, parasitical rentiers? The same deficiency is present, though less obviously, in the type of analysis which depicts corporatism as an evolving social form within capitalism, whether this form ultimately functions to mediate among opposing interests (Schmitter), to shore up the crumbling integration of capitalist society (Panitch), to reinforce state domination (Williamson) or some combination of the three.

The convergence of planning, consensus-building and mediation inevitably gives rise to an uncomfortable dilemma for the planner. On the one hand, pluralism embodies the norm of free contestation and openness of access, but provides little opportunity for the consistent implementation of plans and no opportunity for change in the power structure. Corporatism, on the other hand, at least permits consistent implementation of plans, but only at the cost of limited contestation and openness. Institutionalized exclusive bargaining merely substitutes one structural means of protecting existing power structures for another: centralized for decentralized bargaining. The particular outcome of pluralist or corporatist approaches to planning, however, is contingent upon the actual balance of class and interest group power in a particular place and time, as well as the attitude of the state bureaucrats and politicians towards the distribution and redistribution of resources in society. Neither pluralism nor corporatism as ideal types provides an intrinsically preferable norm for the planner. The bias in favour of the former is a matter of history and ideology and any normative judgement must remain contingent on other circumstances.

7 Neo-liberalism and the strong state

Changes in dominant ideology seem to be closely connected with economic crises. With the crisis of the 1930s' Depression and the Second World War came the ascendancy of ideas of economic planning and reconstruction in which the state played a central role (see Cole, 1935; Mannheim, 1940; Wootton, 1934, [1945] 1979; Ward, 1976). After the war, the capitalist world entered a period of unprecedented growth in which the programmes of the state greatly expanded and the idea of state intervention in the economy became widely accepted. The public came to hold governments responsible for national economies. Urban planning, which embodied intervention in the land market, benefited greatly from the ascendancy of these ideas.

After the oil shock of 1974, growth faltered and the downturn in growth was accompanied by sustained inflation. From the early 1970s for about ten years, the average rate of inflation in the world's leading economies exceeded the rate of growth (see Figure 7.1). From the late 1970s, conservative ideas, the ideas of the 'new right', enjoyed a resurgence. The ideas were not new. Their development had proceeded steadily since the war, but the election of radical conservative regimes in Britain and America allowed these ideas to dominate political discourse and replace the Keynesian compromise that had held sway in the postwar period up to that time.

The ideas of the 'new right' are diverse and it is not possible to do justice to them in the space of one chapter. What is most important for our present purposes, however, is the philosophical critique of state planning from the 'neo-liberal' perspective. This critique was first unfolded in the seminal work of one man: *The Road to Serfdom* of F. A. von Hayek, published in 1944 in response to the socialist ideology of the 'planned society'. The essence of Hayek's critique is that planning is both dangerous, leading to totalitarianism, and ineffective, in being unable to produce an increase in individual utility. This critique is based on the prescriptive idea of strengthening the market through the action of a strong but restricted state. The restriction of freedom necessitated by the action of the strong state is justified by the increase in freedom that a strong market is thought to produce.

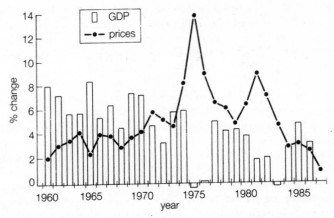

Figure 7.1 Average annual percentage change in gross domestic product (at constant prices) and average annual percentage change in consumer prices for the world's leading capitalist economies: the United States, Japan and West Germany

(*Source*: Norton and Aylmer, 1988, Table S.18, pp. 208, 209.
Original Sources: GDP: National accounts of OECD Countries, Vol. 1, Paris: OECD; Prices: International Financial Statistics, Washington DC: International Monetary Fund.)

Hayek's critique of planning

Hayek was writing at a time when the world had reason to fear the growth of strong centrally directed governments in Europe: fascism in Italy and Spain, Nazism in Germany, and Stalin's brand of communism in the Soviet Union. The democracies were at war and Hayek attempted to show how the origins of Nazism in Germany lay in the acceptance of collectivist ideas in the 1930s. He laments the passing of the 'liberal' age:

> For at least twenty five years before the spectre of totalitarianism became a real threat, we had been progressively moving away from the basic ideas on which European civilisation has been built. That this movement on which we have entered with such high hopes and ambitions should have brought us face to face with the totalitarian horror has come as a profound shock to this generation, which still refuses to connect the two facts. We have progressively abandoned that freedom in economic affairs without which personal and political freedom has never existed in the past. Although we had been warned by some of the greatest political thinkers of the nineteenth century that socialism means

slavery, we have steadily moved in the direction of socialism. And now that we have seen a new form of slavery arise before our eyes, we have so completely forgotten the warning it scarcely occurs to us that the two things may be connected (Hayek, 1944, p. 16).

This statement reveals two of Hayek's most fundamental assumptions: that it is ideas that shape human history ('a change of ideas and the force of human will have made the world what it is now'; Hayek, 1944, p. 18); and that personal and political freedom are impossible without economic freedom. Economic freedom, for Hayek, meant the freedom of the market, the freedom to exchange goods and services and profit from the exchange: 'It is necessary in the first instance that the parties in the market should be free to sell and buy at any price at which they can find a partner to the transaction, and that anybody should be free to produce, sell and buy anything that may be produced or sold at all' (p. 40). Hayek sometimes comes close to defining the free market as an end in itself. But there is, in fact, a higher end which the market serves: the 'co-ordination of individual effort': 'any attempt to control prices or quantities of particular commodities deprives competition of its power of bringing about an effective co-ordination of individual efforts, because price changes then cease to register all the relevant changes in circumstances and no longer provide a reliable guide for the individual's actions' (Hayek, 1944). The question of 'co-ordination of individual effort' is clearly an extremely important one because this is precisely what *planning* appears to be about. It also concerns the relationship between the state and civil society. We shall return to this question but, first, we must look at Hayek's juxtaposition of individualism and collectivism.

Individualism and collectivism

Hayek argues that the idea of individualism, which lies at the heart of Western civilization, is gradually being replaced by collectivism. Modern socialism is abandoning not just eighteenth and nineteenth century liberalism but the individualism inherited from 'Erasmus and Montaigne, from Cicero and Tacitus, Pericles and Thucidides' (Hayek, 1944, p. 20). Yet classical individualism had to await the arrival of commerce before the rigid hierarchy of feudalism gave way to a system 'where men could at least shape their own life, where men gained the opportunity of knowing and choosing between different forms of life' (p. 21). Here Hayek is reinforcing his point about the relationship between political ideas and economic processes. First, he says, there existed the philosophical foundations of individualism.

These foundations underpinned the gradual growth of political freedom which, in time, gave rise to the free growth of economic activity as an 'undesigned and unforeseen by-product' of political freedom. This economic activity in turn led to 'the elaboration of consistent argument in favour of economic freedom' (p. 22). Political freedom of the individual is thus seen to depend upon economic freedom, which, in turn, depends upon and is supported by the philosophy of individualism.

In his discussion of individualism Hayek advances two further postulates: that human freedom in general means the free exercise of human ingenuity in the satisfaction of an ever-widening range of desires – more prosaically the production of goods and services – and that what is crucially important is the *idea* of freedom rather than the actual lack of freedom of some people in society. Individualism means 'the respect for the individual man *qua* man, that is the recognition of his own views and tastes as supreme in his own sphere, *however narrowly that may be circumscribed*, and the belief that it is desirable that men should develop their own individual gifts and bents' (Hayek, 1944, pp. 20,21; emphasis added). The ideas developed by Marx and Engels a hundred years earlier in the *German Ideology* contain a similar view of freedom as the power to work creatively, although of course Marx and Engels took a different view of the origin of 'views and tastes' and portrayed humankind as essentially social. But what divides Hayek most strikingly from Marx and Engels is their respective views of how society as it exists promotes or crushes individual freedom. Hayek saw a society of individual entrepreneurs creatively working to produce new goods and services for the use of consumers in their own individual pursuit of creative activity. Marx and Engels saw a society full of virtual slaves who had to sell their labour for a survival wage, enabling their employers to extract a surplus from that labour out of which both investment and luxury consumption of the employer was drawn. They saw that not only the 'views and tastes' of the majority but their whole life's activity was utterly circumscribed.

Hayek's argument rests on the conservative view that existing democratic capitalism is good and must be preserved. Therefore, freedom to produce according to the rules of this form of society has to be protected and nurtured, even though the very application of the principle may circumscribe the actual freedom of some sections of the population. Hayek placed great emphasis on the dynamic growth under nineteenth-century capitalism:

The result of this growth surpassed all expectations. Wherever the barriers to the free exercise of human ingenuity were removed man became rap:dly able to satisfy ever-widening ranges of desire. And while the rising standard soon led to the discovery of dark spots in society, spots which men were no longer willing to tolerate, there was probably no class that did not substantially benefit from the general advance (Hayek, 1944, p. 23).

Somehow, however, the collective efforts of the working population to improve their standard of living have been discounted. For Hayek, these are not part of capitalism. For the 'new right' today the collectivist philosophy of the welfare state that accompanied the postwar boom – far surpassing that of the nineteenth century – is also discounted. This too is not part of capitalism. Rather, it is axiomatic that economic growth follows from individualism and market competition in all fields.

A recent enthusiast for capitalism, Peter Berger (1987, p. 21), is more circumspect. He writes: 'There can be no doubt that no society commonly classified as capitalist (including all of North America and Western Europe) remotely resembles what Adam Smith would have recognised as a "free" society. In other words, in these societies mechanisms of political allocation are constantly intervening to modify (the critics would say to distort) the working-away of the market.' Berger defines capitalism, in brief, as 'production for a market by enterprising individuals or combines with the purpose of making a profit' (p. 19). But he goes on to define actual capitalist *societies* as located on a continuum between two poles, which are ideal types of pure socialism and pure market societies, neither of which exist in reality. He is prepared to draw a dividing line somewhere in the middle. He then extols the virtues of 'capitalist societies' that fall on the market side of the continuum. For example, he says: 'An economy oriented toward production for market exchange provides the optimal conditions for long-lasting and ever-expanding productive capacity based on modern technology' (p. 37). The problem, however, is that the real societies in the middle of the continuum may actually represent a type different from both 'socialist' and 'market' societies. There may be a further element (or elements) that is not accounted for in the construct 'socialist–market' expressed as a continuum.[1] Alternatively, it may be precisely the mixture of socialist and market principles that leads to the very successes Berger talks about.

Such an idea was anathema to Hayek, who thought that a mixed society would have the worst of both worlds. The universal struggle against competition would lead to something that would satisfy 'neither planners nor liberals': a sort of syndicalist or corporative organisation of industry in which competition is more or less suppressed but planning is left in the hands of the independent monopolies of the separate industries. Such an outcome would combine the

1 For an account of the concept of a bi-polar construct see Kelly (1955).

dictatorial features of planning with the lack of public accountability of large-scale industry (Hayek, 1944, p. 44). Clearly, Hayek is foreshadowing corporatism and complaining about something that seems to have been one of the most salient features of postwar capitalism: monopolistic production.

Hayek contrasts the principle of individualism with that of collectivism. The collectivist idea of freedom (and unfreedom or 'alienation') is clearly elaborated in the works of Rousseau ([1762] 1973), Marx and Engels ([1846] 1976). But it is to the more authoritarian philosophers Saint Simon and Comte that Hayek turned for illustration of collectivism and its translation into modern socialism. 'Where freedom was concerned, the founders of socialism made no bones about their intentions. Freedom of thought they regarded as the root-evil of nineteenth century society and the first of modern planners, Saint Simon, even predicted that those who did not obey his proposed planning boards would be treated as cattle' (Hayek, 1944, p. 29). Only under the influence of the democratic currents of thought preceding the 1848 revolution in France, said Hayek, did socialism ally itself with the forces of freedom. But this new demand for freedom disguised the true demand for an equal distribution of wealth. And, for reasons that will be discussed below, the redistribution of wealth, he thought, was in direct conflict with the principle of individual liberty.

Although Hayek's critique of the early planners is amply justified, his argument is inconsistent. In view of his insistence on the primacy of individual tastes, why should he assume that the taste for equality is somehow less acceptable than the taste for, say, microwave ovens? The answer is that Hayek, as a conservative, deplored political struggle over material goods. Equality is not a commodity that can be obtained in the market; equality can only be sought through political struggle. It is not the taste for equality that Hayek so dislikes but the political struggle to attain this value. Struggle must only be allowed to occur in the context of the rule of the market, in which the existing distribution of material goods is not challenged and where struggle only appears as 'healthy competition'. This point was elaborated in a later book: 'Once politics becomes a tug-of-war for shares in the income pie, decent government is impossible. This requires that all use of coercion to assure a certain income to particular groups (beyond a flat minimum for all who cannot earn more in the market) be outlawed as immoral and strictly anti-social' (Hayek, 1979, p. 150). So, according to Hayek, people fail to understand that it is not in their own best interest to carry on political struggle over material goods, and such struggle must be branded 'immoral and anti-social'. Here, then, is an extremely restricted vision of political freedom and a conservative's version of false consciousness.

Hayek then moved from principle to practice and the critique of the working out of collectivism in a certain kind of planning. He is not, he says, opposed to planning, only to the socialist form of planning that necessarily means a 'planned society'.

The choice between socialist and libertarian planning

It is against centrally directed 'blue-print' planning (cf. Faludi 1973b, pp. 133–6) that Hayek's critique is directed. What he has to say is eminently sensible:

> The dispute between the modern planners and their opponents is, therefore, *not* a dispute on whether we ought to choose intelligently between the various possible organisations of society; it is not a dispute on whether we ought to employ foresight and systematic thinking in planning our common affairs. It is a dispute about the best way of so doing. The question is whether for this purpose it is better that the holder of coercive power should confine himself in general to creating conditions under which the knowledge and initiative of individuals is given the best scope so that *they* can plan most successfully; or whether a rational utilisation of our resources requires *central* direction and organisation of all our activities according to some consciously constructed 'blueprint'. The socialists of all parties have appropriated the term 'planning' for the latter type and it is now generally accepted in this sense.(Hayek, 1944, pp. 38, 39; author's emphasis).

Hayek adds that central 'blue-print' planning requires extraordinary knowledge by planners of the values held by the people on whose behalf the plan is made, a point made also by pluralist critics of planning such as Charles Lindblom (1959). Furthermore, central planning makes it necessary to make detailed choices among ends and means years in advance of action being taken. These choices then determine what activity is possible under the plan. Even supposing that people can agree on such choices, the result will be a rigid set of rules. Yet, says Hayek, as civilization has progressed, there has been 'a steady diminution of the sphere in which individual actions are bound by fixed rules. The rules of which our common moral code consists have progressively become fewer and more general in character' (Hayek, 1944, p. 59). Hayek's fear is that this progressive trend, which can be observed over the long term, has been reversed in the twentieth century. This is a fear he shares with Weber (recall Weber's metaphor of the 'iron cage'; see chapter 4). 'Blue-print' planning restricts future choices. To simplify the point, if one person were to be required to decide in advance all her activities for the year ahead and required to stick to that plan, her activities would be severely restricted. How much more so for millions of people over a number of years? Markets sensitively register continual changes in present preferences. Urban planning, where it consists in tying future developments to a preconceived plan devised by central authority, slows down the response of the producers of developed land to the preferences being expressed in the land market. The result is a pattern of land use, which represents only the preference of bureaucrats and of government officials responding to the demands of whichever group (inside or outside the state) is able to exert the most political muscle at the time the plan is made (see Hayek, 1960, pp. 349–54).

A further criticism of planning made by Hayek (1944, pp. 88–9, 114–5) stresses the connection between economic and political freedom. Economic planning takes away the freedom of individual households and firms to distribute economic gains and losses to the margin of their preferences. The attempt to provide economic security for all merely means that individuals are to be protected from the necessity of solving their own economic problems and facing 'the bitter choices which this often involves'. Such freedom and the corresponding discipline and responsibility it entails can only be ensured by allowing economic choices to be made by the market.

Hayek does not reject planning, but conceives of a libertarian form of planning. He writes: 'It is important not to confuse opposition against this kind of planning [blue-print planning] with a dogmatic laissez-faire attitude. The liberal argument is in favour of making the best possible use of the forces of competition as a means of co-ordinating human efforts, not an argument for leaving things just as they are' (Hayek, 1944, p. 39). Hayek's point is that the complexity of the division of labour in society has made it impossible to co-ordinate all activities from a central point. What is required is a form of co-ordination 'which leaves the separate agencies free to adjust their activities to the facts which only they can know, and yet bring about a mutual adjustment of their respective plans' (p. 51).

The means of accomplishing the task of co-ordination is, of course, the free, competitive market, for a market in effect mobilizes the knowledge held *throughout* society rather than relying on the necessarily limited knowledge that can be collected and processed centrally. In a competitive market the price mechanism is the means of recording and integrating all the effects of individual actions. The price mechanism 'enables entrepreneurs, by watching the movement of comparatively few prices, as an engineer watches the hands of a few dials, to adjust ttheir activities to those of their fellows' (p. 51). Competition acts as a discipline that forces activities to be adjusted to one another 'without coercive or arbitrary intervention of authority'

(p. 39). Private property guarantees this freedom from coercion 'because the control of the means of production is divided among many people acting independently [so] that nobody has complete power over us' (p. 100).

The market requires a carefully thought-out legal framework, which will protect its institutions: the price mechanism, competition and private property. This protection is accomplished by 'the rule of law'. The rule of law means that a government lays down rules, which are fixed and the same for everybody. These rules allow producers and consumers to know with 'fair certainty' how the public authority will use its powers, and thus to plan their own affairs on the basis of this knowledge. (Hayek, 1944, p. 72). There must be no *ad hoc* action by governments. Laws must be universal, consistent and non-retrospective. No law should single out a particular place and time because, in that case, the law would be unpredictable. Hence the 'more the state "plans" the more difficult planning becomes for the individual' (p. 75). The state must be completely impartial. Predictability applies in general terms, but not to specific individuals and groups. Where the precise effects of government policy on particular people are known, the government cannot help taking sides and imposing its own values on people, that is, choosing those whom it will assist and those it will restrict.

One consequence of the application of this principle is that as few cases as possible should be decided by governments 'on their merits', or in terms of what is 'fair and reasonable'. And there must be as little as possible discretion for people in government to deviate from or interpret the law. Urban development, therefore, should be controlled only by pre-set rules. Wage relativities should be decided only by the market and not by arbitration systems and judges. More fundamentally, Hayek argues that there is an irreconcileable conflict beween application of the rule of law and 'attempts to realise substantive justice and equality' (Hayek, 1944, p. 79). Formal equality before the law precludes governments from aiming at redistribution, because this would obviously mean treating some people differently from others.

Robert Nozick (1974) developed his justification for a minimal state on similar foundations. 'Things', says Nozick (1974, p. 160), 'come into this world already attached to people having entitlements over them.' Clearly *entitlement* is dependent on law, or at least on custom. If we accept that this law or custom establishing entitlement is just, and if it can be shown that every step by means of which initial entitlements are altered is just (e.g. by fair exchange and contract), then the final outcome must also be just. So no attempt through political struggle employing the apparatus of the state to correct inequality, alleviate poverty or to provide what is not provided through economic (market) exchange is justified.

Urban planning

Where Hayek deals specifically with the problem of cities and the regulation of land use he admits that the question of externalities ('neighbourhood effects' both positive and negative) presents real difficulties for a market system, and that: 'the city which is the source of nearly all that gives civilization its value and which has provided the means for the pursuit of science and art as well as of material comfort, is at the same time responsible for the darkest blotches on this civilization' (Hayek, 1960, p. 341). He suggests that some territorial unit larger than the parcel of land under the control of an individual owner may need to be given rights over land in order to take into account the costs and benefits imposed (upon a landowner), which arise beyond the boundaries of the territory owned. Hayek proposes that such a wider unit might either be a local municipality or the private developer of an estate. He argues that the primary business of such an authority is to 'expropriate' the full social costs of any activity on private land and to use the amount expropriated to compensate all those adversely affected by such land use. Indeed he goes further and proposes that all gains and losses resulting from 'town planning' (including the provision of government services such as roads) accrue to the planning authority, 'who must be able to accept the responsibility of charging the individual owners for the increase in the value of their property (even if the measures causing it have been taken against the will of some owners) and of compensating those whose property has suffered' (Hayek, 1960, p. 351). He has no objection to the use of compulsory purchase powers by the planning authority in support of the above actions, provided that the purchase price is the full market value of the property.

When it comes to doing something about the 'darkest blotches', the slums or ghettos, Hayek believes that there are two solutions: either let the social costs of slums (negative externalities) be borne in full by the slum landlords, or restrict the influx of population seeking cheap housing. Hayek is concerned that the insanitary conditions of slums pose a threat to the health of the whole urban population. In the first solution the developers or landlords must be made to pay to bring these conditions up to a minimum standard. If this places the price of slum housing beyond the means of slum dwellers, then the slums and their inhabitants will disappear. Where these former slum dwellers will go Hayek does not tell us, but he seems to think that everyone will be better off if they are accommodated in the countryside, for: 'Life at a level of poverty which is still bearable in the country not only is scarcely tolerable in the city but produces outward signs of squalor which are shocking to fellow men' (Hayek, 1960, p. 341).

Hayek is less concerned about the effects of poverty on the poor themselves than on the rest of the population. The thrust of his argument is that slums are the consequence of the concentration of large numbers of poor people in cities. Relative poverty, consequent upon inequality, is inherent in a free market society and in such a society the poor will be less poor than they would be in an egalitarian society. Bad housing, bad environments and unpleasant locations are simply the sorts of housing, environments and locations that the poor can afford. So no attempt must be made to improve them beyond the minimum standard required to protect the rest of the population from disease and other health hazards. Any other action by planners would interfere with a distribution of resources arrived at by market forces and which is, therefore, just. The overall distribution of environmental quality throughout a city must be made to reflect the overall distribution of wealth (and therefore command over material resources) of its citizens.

The case against government intervention to relieve the social and economic problems of cities has been made by other new right critics of planning such as Banfield (1968, 1974), Kristol (1972), and Bradbury, Downs and Small (1982). People and economic activities, it is argued, should be allowed to distribute themselves over space through market exchanges with a minimum of interference from planners or planning. If efficiency is defined as the maximum satisfaction of all preferences (given the existence of such economic constraints as the need of people to seek employment and of firms to make profit), such an arrangement will result in the most efficient spatial distribution of people and functions.

Urban planners in a democratic state are always accountable to the population of a given territory, and in most countries urban planning is, to a very large extent, a function of local government. Planners, therefore, try to solve the problems arising within their local territory. For example, if there is poverty resulting from high unemployment, they may try to attract new employment and provide incentives to industries to remain in the area. If the locality is suffering from a 'fiscal crisis' caused by a declining tax base and rising demand for welfare and other services, planners may try to stem the flow of people and firms out of the area by offering financial incentives. If all localities try to solve their problems in this way, the unintended result will be merely to increase the level of subsidies to people and firms across the board (a point also made from a socialist perspective by Bluestone and Harrison, 1982). If only certain localities do this, the result will be to discourage firms from moving to where their locational, environmental or space needs can be met most efficiently, and to discourage households from moving to where their particular mixture of preferences can best be met, a mixture that balances price against both environmental quality and accessibility to various activities, including employment. Of course, neither poverty nor environmental squalor will be abolished by such an approach. But the living conditions and spatial location of the population will come to reflect the preferences of the population coupled with their material resources. If there are poor and rich areas it is because there are poor and rich people in the society.

Banfield (1968, 1974) is particularly pessimistic about the prospects of planning to relieve urban problems, on the grounds that these problems stem almost entirely either from middle-class 'politics' or from the existence of a 'lower-class' culture coupled with the altruism and guilt of the upper class. Banfield postulates a four-tier stratification in society defined with reference to a particular culture. The class culture is in turn defined with reference to a particular orientation towards planning for the future, organized on a simple continuum from the most future-oriented (the upper class) to the most present-oriented (the lower class) via two classes with middle-distance horizons (the middle and working classes). The middle and upper classes are politically active and constantly seek their own advantage. Urban planning problems occur when the interests of one middle-class group conflict with those of another. For example, says Banfield, the rush-hour traffic problem could be readily solved by staggering working hours. But the business community kills that option because it prefers the traditional nine-to-five pattern. Or: 'When a mayor says that his city is on the verge of bankruptcy he usually means that when the time comes to run for re-election he wants to be able to claim credit for straightening out a mess that was left to him by his predecessor' (Banfield, 1968, p. 9).

The most obviously worrying feature of urban life, the poverty and physical degradation of the ghettos, occurs because of the existence of a 'lower class' which constantly creates the conditions that upper-class altruists define as problems. The lower-class person is 'radically improvident', living from hand to mouth and day to day: 'His bodily needs (especially for sex) and his taste for "action" take precedence over everything else – and certainly over any work routine. He works only as he must to stay alive, and drifts from one unskilled job to another, taking no interest in work' (Banfield, 1968, p. 53). Remove the lower class and the problems of the ghetto would disappear. The immensely expensive efforts to relieve poverty and improve the living conditions of the lower class are doomed to failure and may actually worsen the problem by reinforcing the dependent culture. Banfield therefore concludes that planning is ineffective and too much time and money is spent on solving problems that are insoluble either because they are political in origin or because they result from an unchangeable culture of poverty.

Banfield's contentions about the existence of a 'culture of poverty' have been challenged by Vedlitz (1988), who points out that the empirical evidence on personal values shows that there is very little difference between poor people and those with higher incomes. More important, however, even if evidence could be found of the sort of 'hand-to-mouth' orientation described by Banfield as characteristic of the very poor, there is simply no way to prove that such an orientation is a cause of poverty rather than its effect. Vedlitz explains the influence of Banfield's book in terms of its contribution to a convenient myth, which relieves the loss of legitimacy of the state's accompanying failure to deal adequately with the problem of the ghettos.

In spite of his willingness to allow some form of urban planning, Hayek argues that there is no effective 'middle way' between totalitarian, blueprint planning and the free market society: 'both competition and central direction become poor and inefficient tools if they are incomplete; they are alternative principles used to solve the same problem, and a mixture of the two means that neither will really work and that the result will be worse than if either system had been consistently relied upon. Or, to express it differently, planning and competition can only be combined by planning for competition, but not by planning against competition' (Hayek, 1944, pp. 44–5). Any planning that interferes with the freedom to produce, buy and sell anything in any place is, therefore, to be resisted. When the world economy entered a period of crisis after 1973, Hayek's words began to carry weight. In the crisis, it was possible to forget the years of stable growth. The problem for planners is that the demand for planning arises precisely because of the negative effects of a free market society. One of these negative effects is great inequality. However, Hayek argues that it makes no sense to strive for distributive justice or even *greater* equality. Socialist movements, he says, do not aim for complete equality, which would make some sense, but for *increased* equality. But increased equality merely means that we should 'take from the rich as much as we can'. We are then left with the problem of rationally planning the distribution of the spoils. This is an impossible task, according to Hayek, without a totalitarian system of centrally directed planning. As with planning, so with equality, for Hayek it is either all or nothing (pp. 105–6). Once you take the first step towards collectivist planning you have to go all the way down the road, a road that leads ultimately to serfdom.

The popular image projected by neo-liberal philosophy is of a society of free individuals interacting freely in a free market. But there is another and equally important aspect of the philosophy, which argues for the market as a powerful organizing and co-ordinating mechanism and for the state as a strong authority upholding the 'public good'.

The strong market

As will have become apparent, Hayek placed considerable emphasis on the organizing function of markets. This theme was developed more fully, however, by Hayek's mentor, Ludwig von Mises. Mises ([1949] 1963, p. 257) at first claims that 'there is in the operation of the market no compulsion and coercion'. If this were so, however, there would be no necessity to bring anything to market. Later, Mises says that there is no *direct* compulsion. 'What pressure is needed to impel an individual to contribute his share to the cooperative effort of production is exercised by the price structure of the market. This pressure is indirect. It puts on each individual's contribution a premium graduated according to the value which the consumers attach to this contribution' (p. 288). Thus inequality of wealth and income is essential in a market to bring about a system of co-operative production. What ultimately forces producers to the market is the need to obtain the means of subsistence.

The market is a system for organizing production and co-ordinating the efforts of individuals. The freedom of the individual in this system is justified by his place in the collective effort: 'The member of a contractual society is free because he serves others only in serving himself' (Mises, [1949] 1963, p. 283). This system is 'steered' by the 'entrepreneurs': 'The direction of all economic affairs is, in the market society, a task of the entrepreneurs. Theirs is the control of production. They steer the ship' (p. 269). But these entrepreneurs are accountable to 'the consumers'. The enterprise will not succeed if the consumers do not buy the product. And if the enterprise does not succeed, investors will not invest in the stock and bonds it issues. Here, it should be noted that Mises stresses that the managers of a firm should always be subservient to the entrepreneurs. In particular, a manager should never be paid a share of the profits because the manager does not share the risks of entrepreneurship, which are, of course, an essential element of the accountability imposed by the market (p. 306). The whole system is organized by the entrepreneurs, the managers, the investors, who function as consumers of stocks and shares, and the consumers of products. It is enforced by the price system and inequality of wealth and income.

Such a system is not self-justifying. It relies on a further assumption that 'the consumers', to whom the whole system is accountable, are the population at large. The legitimacy of the system rests on the idea of *consumer sovereignty*. Both Hayek and Mises generally write as though 'the consumers' were an undifferentiated mass, the people, 'us'. We 'vote' for a product or firm by buying its output. But because Mises views inequality of wealth as essential to the organizing function of the market, he cannot avoid dealing with the effect of inequality on consumer sovereignty. In the market, he says, the various consumers do not all have the same 'voting' right: 'the rich cast more votes than the poorer citizens' (p. 271). Here Mises acknowledges that 'the consumers' are stratified by wealth.

We can take this point further. In a *pure* market system, the consumers may, in fact, be quite a small minority. The majority may consume at subsistence level while a wealthy minority consumes a large volume of luxuries produced by the majority. If this is not the case in advanced capitalist societies today, if there is mass consumption of what would in earlier times have been considered luxuries, this occurrence does not follow from the logic of the market. The market serves the consumers, and if the consumers happen to be a rich minority, then production will be geared by the market to the demands of that minority. Mises argues that the rich became rich by successfully serving the needs of consumers, but he does not say which consumers. It is true that the wealthy minority may employ people to service their needs, and this employment provides for some measure of spreading of wealth, but there is nothing in a market system to ensure that this spreading occurs to a substantial degree, rapidly or even at all. A market system can operate in conditions of the most extreme wealth and poverty and, in the absence of political struggle (including the struggle of organized labour at the workplace), these conditions need never change. Although a market system is deficient in *redistributing* wealth, it provides very well for the *accumulation* of wealth. Hobbes understood that the power conferred by wealth increases exponentially. The more wealth a person accumulates, the more power it provides to accumulate more wealth and more power. 'For the nature of Power, is in this point, like to Fame, increasing as it proceeds; or like the motion of heavy bodies, which the further they go, make still the more hast' (Hobbes, [1651] 1909, pp. 66–71).

Mises observes that capitalism, the market economy, is no recent phenomenon, it is the product of a long historical process going back many centuries (Mises, [1949] 1963, pp. 266–7). But, if capitalism has a long history, we might want to ask why it is only recently that it has provided for mass consumption. Braudel (1984), using data of Phelps-Brown and Hopkins (1955) has shown that, until this century, periods of economic growth in Europe coincided with periods of decline of the living standards of the majority of the population. Only in the period that saw the success of political struggles for democracy, followed by increased political intervention in the market, did living standards of the mass greatly increase (for contrasting views of the welfare state, see Rothbard, 1973, and Maddison, 1976, p. 442).

Murray Rothbard has been described as an 'anarcho-capitalist' (see King, 1987, p. 12) because he has advocated the complete abolition of the state: 'The ultimate libertarian program may be summed up in one phrase: the abolition of the public sector, the conversion of all operations and services performed by the government into activities performed voluntarily by the private enterprise economy' (Rothbard, 1973, p. 201). But Rothbard is not advocating the abolition of the organizing and governing function of the state. This function would simply be transferred to the strong market. Those who desire justice, safety, protection from violent crime, education, the cure of disease, even defence against external aggressors must buy these services on the market. The rules of the market are to be enforced through private courts and private police forces. In effect, the power to command armed force, a power resting on the ownership of wealth, would finally determine the outcome of all disputes.

Since wealth, the power to command material resources, is unevenly distributed, this vision is one of absolute domination by the rich through the organising mechanism of the market, not polyarchy but plutarchy. Note, however, that, if we take Weber's definition of the state as an agency that commands the monopoly of the use of coercive force within a given territory, the transfer of all state functions to the market would not really do away with the state. The 'state' would merely be fragmented into the multitude of parcels of land in the *ownership* of individuals, groups and organizations. Every owner would make the laws for the land in his or her possession. Eventually, the market would ensure the gradual consolidation of parcels of land into larger and larger units. Eventually, something resembling nation states would reappear. The formation of states from private 'protective associations' through the 'invisible hand' of the aggregate of individuals pursuing their own best interest is elaborated by Nozick (1974) in his justification of the minimal state. Rothbard's view of governance, since it dispenses with the state, also dispenses with democracy, for he has nothing to say about the hierarchical, bureaucratic or autocratic government of 'private' corporations.

These corporations present a problem for the more moderate neo-liberals. Hayek (1979, p. 80) acknowledges as worthy of 'serious consideration' the argument that 'the great size of an individual corporation confers great power on its management, and that such power of a few men is politically dangerous and morally objection-able'. But, in an argument that recalls the socialist apologists of *state* power, he portrays the power wielded by the large corporation as power over material things and only to a limited degree over people

– those who join the corporation 'for their benefit'. Thus, as long as the option of leaving the employment of the corporation exists, its power over its employees is sufficiently limited. This view, as we have seen in chapter 5, was vigorously disputed by Dahl and Lindblom. Irving Kristol (1983, ch. 15) reflects that an economy dominated by vast corporations does not fit the model of a free market society, 'the system of natural liberty' advanced by such founders of liberalism as Adam Smith and James Madison. Kristol points out that the corporate empires are opposed in America by populist fears of their power. But, says Kristol, one of the consequences of the existence of large corporations is to create 'orderly markets': 'What businessmen disparagingly call "cutthroat competition", with its wild swings in price, its large fluctuations in employment, its unpredictable effects upon profits – all this violates the very *raison d'être* of a large corporation, with its need for relative stability so that its long range investment decisions can be rationally calculated' (Kristol, 1983, p. 206). Kristol concedes that even though the corporation is a 'quasi-public institution, it is publicly largely unaccountable even to the stockholders. Management may talk piously about its obligations to the stockholders, but, in practice, management generally wishes to have as little to do with them as possible 'since their immediate demands are all too likely to conflict with management's long term corporate plans'. Kristol's view is that the corporate sector will have to change in response to the reasonable demand for greater public accountability. But for Kristol, as for Hayek, the order of a strong market includes the security that large bureaucratic organizations, looking to their own wider and longer-term interest, provide. Unlike Dahl (1985; see chapter 5), neo-liberals and neo-conservatives see no need for democratic government of these corporations.

The simplistic assumption of 'consumer sovereignty' begs the question of the complex structures of interest that can be observed in society, structures linking the economic interests and cultural perceptions of individuals (race, colour, class, gender, locale) and structures enabling individuals to act collectively (family, pressure group, corporation, state). If we set aside the assumption of 'the consumers' as vacuous, it appears that the space can be filled by either a Marxist 'class' perspective or a pluralist 'pressure group' perspective. Neither are incompatible with the neo-liberal view of the market as itself a strong organizing structure.

The strong state

Neo-liberalism is associated with the idea of the minimal state. Hayek argues that the functions of government should be reduced to those

where consensus can be reached through free discussion on the policies
to be adopted: 'it is the great merit of the liberal creed that it reduced
the range of subjects on which agreement was necessary to one which
was likely to exist in a society of free men' (Hayek, 1944, p. 70).
Hayek's vision of politics is one of rational discussion concluding in
firm and lasting agreement. The contrast with the pluralist vision of
the state could not be more marked. Whereas pluralism regards the
state as subject to the play of political struggle, the neo-liberal vision
regards the state as above political struggle. The state represents the
public good and only those matters on which the public good can
emerge through the enlightened deliberation of a political elite are
the business of the state.

The question of what constitutes that body of affairs on which
consensus could reasonably be expected to occur has been a major pre-
occupation of some neo-liberal philosophers. Buchanan and Tullock
(1965) seek a higher 'public interest' in the constitutional decision
rules that determine the scope of such games as politics and markets.
In the manner of Pareto optimality, they argue, only those changes
can be admitted as better 'that are observed to be approved unani-
mously by all members of the group [society]' (p. 285). However,
they acknowledge that this criterion is politically unpractical and
instead adopt as a criterion what they call the 'Kantian solution'
in dealing with questions of public expenditure.[2] According to this
criterion, no collective activity should exceed the expenditure level
equal to the median preference in a community for an expenditure
determined by each person's assessment of the balance of marginal
costs to him or herself. The authors then deduce that the operation of majority rule, taken with the capacity of interest groups to
enter into logrolling bargains, results in a higher level of expenditure than the 'Kantian solution'. The bargains that individuals
and groups make to maximize their short-term advantage tend to
increase the overall level of government expenditure. There is a
spiral of mutual exploitation. Such arguments are part of an extensive
'public choice' critique of pluralist politics and the way in which such
politics contributes both to unending growth and ever-increasing

2 Kant held that individuals were ends in themselves and their interests
   required no justification other than that decided internally by each
   person. This principle is sometimes used by conservatives to argue
   that the interests of the powerful cannot legitimately be interfered
   with by the state. It may equally be argued, however, that the
   self-determined interests of one person may not legitimately interfere
   with the self-determined interests of another and that some force,
   namely the state, is required to protect the interests of the powerless.
   Faced with this point, conservatives tend to revert to the argument
   that the powerful are in fact powerless.

ungovernability or 'overload' of the public sector (see King, 1975; Brittan, 1975; Huntington, 1975; Douglas, 1976). Self (1985, pp. 18, pp. 56–69) comments on 'the increasingly black picture of political and bureaucratic perversions painted by Tullock (1965), Niskanen (1971), Ostrom (1973), Breton (1974) and others. The point here, however, is not the critique itself but what lies behind it, the quest for a clearer definition of the public interest, which would support and legitimate strong, decisive government, albeit over a severely restricted range of activities.

Buchanan explores the nature of 'the public interest' in a later book (1977), in which a value position favouring strong, paternalistic authority clearly emerges. He writes: 'a family example may be helpful. A mother may find it too emotionally painful to spank a misbehaving child. Yet spanking may be necessary to instill in the child the fear of punishment that will inhibit future misbehavior' (Buchanan, 1977, p. 175). Later (p. 184), he deplores the fact that 'as incomes have increased, and as the stock of wealth has grown, men have increasingly found themselves able to take the soft options. Mothers can afford candy to bribe misbehaving children.' By means of a variation of the prisoners' dilemma game, which he calls 'the Samaritan's dilemma', Buchanan seeks to show that, logically, a series of distributional exchanges between unequal parties acting in their immediate interest (without anticipating the long-term outcome) will inevitably result in the reduction of the initial power differential between the two. Strong government is required to correct this state of affairs, to counteract the terrible egalitarian tendency. 'Modern man', says Buchanan, 'has become incapable of making the choices that are required to prevent his exploitation by predators of his own species, whether the predation be conscious or unconscious'. Of course, the efficacy of Buchanan's critique of 'welfare statism' and anti-poverty programmes depends on prior assumptions about who is predator and who prey. For Buchanan the predators are those who live off social welfare programmes. Changing the assumption only slightly, it might be said that the predators and parasites are those who draw income without having to work themselves, or those who work but draw incomes grossly disproportionate to their utility to society. In such a light, Buchanan's logic is as supportive of a strong socialist as of a strong capitalist state. In Buchanan there is a 'looking glass' reflection of Marx: 'a species that increasingly behaves, individually and collectively, so that it encourages more and more of its members to live parasitically and/or deliberately to exploit its producers faces eventual destruction' (Buchanan, 1977, p. 185).

Hayek uses the concept of the 'rule of law' to justify strong action on the part of the state:

Of course, every state must act and every action of the state interferes with something or other. But that is not the point. The important point is whether the individual can foresee the action of the state and make use of this knowledge as a datum in forming his own plans, with the result that the state cannot control the use made of its machinery, and that the individual knows precisely how far he will be protected from others, or whether the state is in a position to frustrate individual efforts. The state controlling weights and measures (or preventing fraud and deception in any other way) is certainly acting, while the state permitting the use of violence, for example, by strike pickets, is inactive (Hayek, 1944, p. 80).

A liberal state acting according to the rule of law may legitimately use coercion to enforce operation of the free market. This sentiment was echoed by Margaret Thatcher (1980) when she said: 'In our Party we do not ask for a feeble State. On the contrary, we need a strong State to preserve both liberty and order . . . to maintain in good repair the frame which surrounds society' (quoted by Hall, 1986, p. 127). Subsequently, as has been noted by several commentators (Gough, 1983; Krieger, 1986; Jones, 1986; Hall, 1986; Gamble, 1988), Thatcher set about strengthening the apparatus of the state and its direction from the political centre. Likewise, in America, a major part of the agenda of the Reagan presidency was the strengthening of the steering capacity of the executive branch, through the consolidation of the budgetary process and the installation of political appointees in key positions in the Federal bureaucracy (Moe, 1985; Krieger, 1986; Gormley, 1989; Aberbach and Rockman, 1989). The interpretation given to neo-liberalism by the Thatcher and Reagan governments is profoundly conservative. Gamble (1988, p. 170) argues that, 'The most basic task of all Conservatives is to uphold the authority of the state.' For conservatives the state is an end in itself embodying the unity of the nation, authority in society and the dominance of the ruling class. The central problem of the welfare state was its ungovernability. 'Rolling back the state' means at the same time reducing the scope of state functions and strengthening the power of the central government to direct the state apparatus (see Gamble, 1988, p. 171).

The idea of the strong and active state is not something that conservative politicians have tacked on to neo-liberalism. It is part of neo-liberal philosophy itself, though a somewhat contradictory part. Both Hayek and Buchanan postulate a government above politics. Hayek (1979, pp. 145,149) deplores centralist planning and argues for the 'dethronement' of politics. Forsyth, a critic of Hayek, has pointed out that Hayek's vision of the Great Society demands that people obey unquestioningly a set of abstract rules. These rules are at once a spontaneous 'natural' order occurring as humankind adapts to its 'hostile' environment and an order to be willed to exist:

> Quite unconscious of irony or paradox, he [Hayek] pushes onwards and proceeds to 'construct' models of government which will ensure that the right people with the right insight will make the right kind of rules for the Great Society to proceed uninterrupted on its way, models that would do credit to the most rational of all eighteenth century rationalists. The spontaneous order has now suddenly lost its spontaneity. We must will it to exist and make it happen. But by this same token we have lost hold of its very raison d'être. Why should we will it to happen, now that we can see it is not the spontaneous product of nature? (Forsyth, 1988, p. 250).

Politics is the way political systems are constructed and changed. In the tradition of parliamentary democracy, change to a political system is wrought through strong action from the centre. If there is another way, the philosophers do not tell us what it is. Questions of the constitution of the state and the 'law' that is to rule are just as much political questions as questions about the distribution of resources via government programmes. In stressing the end and ignoring the political means, Hayek unwittingly mounts the very same argument that socialists have used to justify the creation of their vision of a fair and classless society. By dethroning politics, Hayek's road leads to serfdom just as surely as the road of centralist planning.

Critique of the core of new right philosophy

In the 1970s and early 1980s much of the critical energy of those who opposed the political agenda of the right was spent in attacking the social democratic state, an attack that unwittingly reinforced the attraction of the alternative offered by the right. To be effective today, critique has once again to address the central philosophical premises of the right that a market order is necessarily superior to one that mixes markets, politics and planning. There is a literature that addresses this premiss. We have already discussed Dahl's work (1985). We must now consider Lindblom's *Politics and Markets* (1977).

Lindblom attacked the central contention of the right that the market invariably supports liberty. He pointed out that 'a hidden assumption in the conventional argument is that private property, on which exchange [in a market] rests, does not itself constitute a barrier to freedom and is, in addition, noncoercively established and perpetuated' (Lindblom, 1977, p. 46). In Lindblom's view neither of these propositions is true. The freedom of the propertyless is severely restricted by virtue of their (propertyless) condition. Nevertheless, in the rightist's view, 'a world of exchange is conflict free. Everyone does what he wishes.' But this is only possible because the political conflicts over who gets what have already been settled through a distribution of property rights in a society. 'Was that distribution conflict free?', Lindblom asks, "Was it non-coercively achieved? Obviously not. The distribution of wealth in contemporary England, for example, is a consequence of centuries of conflict, including Viking raids, the Norman Conquest, the early authority of Crown and nobility, two waves of dispossession of agricultural labor from the land, and the law of inheritance' (p. 46).

Lindblom goes on to argue that the proposition that the market is a non-coercive institution is also false. Where people are dependent for their livelihood on the exchange of their labour for a wage, the threat of termination of this exchange relationship is, in fact, highly coercive. Even where alternative work can be found, the 'friction' of change is unaccounted for in approaches advocating pure market exchange. People cannot move from job to job without incurring economic costs (of retraining, for example). This is especially so in cases of spatial relocation. The poorer the people, the greater (proportional to their income) will be the transfer costs of spatial relocation. There are also non-monetary costs. All people tend to build up and rely to some degree on social networks. The more that these networks are important and valued, the higher will be the psychological cost of moving to a new job or to a distant neighbourhood in search of work. The costs are multiplied where households of more than one person are involved. But often the costs incurred by spouses and children, where the 'breadwinner' is required to relocate, are ignored. The friction of change applies to capital as well as to labour. The use of land involves very large-scale and long-term investments in, for example, roads, public transport and other physical infrastructure, as well as buildings on a site. The dynamic of the market demands constant change and adjustment. But, of course, what is built cannot be quickly adjusted. The built environment imposes itself as a forceful restraint on the movement of capital.

The justice of the existing distribution of property is implicit in Nozick's 'entitlement' theory of justice. Nozick's logic supports a view of justice exclusively in terms of process. An outcome is just if it results from a just process. The weakness of his argument is that it fails to establish convincingly that the initial position from which any redistribution departs must be regarded as just. This is Lindblom's point. To illustrate the justice of market distributions Nozick chooses an example in which many people each pay a small amount to watch a star basketball player in action. The basketball player thus becomes rich, and Nozick asks whether he is entitled to his wealth. In Nozick's example the consumers are initially on a more or less equal footing. Almost everyone can afford a dollar to see a basketball game. But there are some markets in which the consumers are grossly unequal: for example, in housing, education, and health. Some consumers may be unable to enter the market at all. Are we to believe that the condition of these consumers has been caused solely by a series of exchanges, each of which involves a choice by the parties to the exchange? The answer may lie in a continuation of Nozick's parable. An equally successful basketballer decides to spend his earned wealth in conspicuous consumption and riotous living rather than invest it wisely. He is entitled to do this for that is his sovereign preference. He spends nothing on his children's education and, when the money is all spent, these children end up poor. Although we might not say that the behaviour itself (though selfish) was 'unjust', we might well say that the victims of such behaviour suffered an injustice. That is, we might not be inclined to blame this basketballer's children for the poverty that is inflicted on them. They did not choose poverty and, being poor, they are not able to pay for the training that would enhance their potential skills in basketball so as to enable them to compete for the dollars of the spectators.

Nozick is also taken to task by Cohen (1989). Cohen wishes to set aside the historical question of how property was actually formed in order to tackle Nozick on the more fundamental question of how property *could* legitimately be formed. The crux of Nozick's argument is that unequal distribution of property could be justified, provided that the position of others no longer at liberty to use the thing is not thereby worsened. Cohen shows that such a condition is not necessarily true. This is because Nozick fails to take account of the possibility that, initially, people might have owned property in common. To impose private ownership is not necessarily to put into the hands of individuals what was previously not owned by anyone. It could also mean expropriating objects in common ownership. It cannot be argued by means of deductive logic that such expropriation necessarily makes people better off. The question is an empirical one.

The case of 'ownership' of land illustrates Cohen's point. Common ownership of some land at some times in some societies is a historical fact, and we cannot know that the owners-in-common of such land would have been worse off if the land expropriated to private ownership had been left in common use. Even where land has been privatized, the matter of ownership is never finally settled. An ongoing source of conflict in Australia has been over the use of the same land by farmers and miners. Throughout Australia ownership of land does not prevent any individual or firm from staking a claim to the minerals under the soil and mining them; naturally, farmers who 'own' the land strongly object to the devastation that mining imposes on 'their' agricultural property. More importantly, perhaps, it is now widely recognized by governments that, prior to white settlement, the aboriginal people owned the land in common. An assertion that the aborigines are unequivocally better off as a result of the expropriation of their land would today be regarded as laughable by anyone familiar with the present condition of aborigines in Australia.

It must also be recognized that land contains broad values, which ought to be preserved on behalf of the public. A system that works by means of the division of a whole (land) into multiple parcels, each individually 'owned', cannot take account of needs that each individual somehow *assumes* will be met *outside* the parcel owned. For example, people living in cities frequently assume that they will always have access to a countryside or a coastline or mountains where they can escape from the pressures of city life. But under a pure market system no such guarantee can be given. The same can be said of any environment publicly regarded as of high quality, including all buildings and places of historic or aesthetic significance. To put the matter in this way is to go somewhat beyond the discussion of 'neighbourhood effects' or 'externalities'. We are not talking about *post hoc* 'effects' here but of prior values, or, in the language of economics, preferences. The real point here is that preferences are evanescent. The decisions we make today we may well regret tomorrow; or our successors on the planet may regret them. The preferences of the unborn do not enter market transactions. Certain preferences of the living are not strongly held because they discount the future; the abuse of drugs (alcohol, tobacco and narcotics) is a case in point, but all pollution of the planet results to some degree from the same 'future-discounting' tendency. To say that there are broad values attached to land is a way of reminding ourselves to think of the future. But the definition of these broad values cannot be above politics. That point is itself a universal truth arising from the knowledge of politics. The question of who should be given charge of preserving broad values and on what political conditions is of course highly problematic. Can we trust the state to do so? Whatever the answer, there is no compelling reason to trust private owners, who are politically unaccountable to the public, any more than a government, which is.

We are entitled to evaluate the wider social conditions we find in this world here and now, conditions that include poverty, squalor, lack of health, crime, environmental degradation, traffic congestion, overcrowded cities, bad design. This evaluating activity implies that we have a better situation in mind. Whether we use the term 'unjust' to describe the bad situation or another term, this does not alter the fact that we feel entitled to join with others to put right what we regard as wrong. Political action is the way we go about this 'putting right'. If we deny the legitimacy of political action we would have to deny the legitimacy of the new right itself as a political movement, for its own ideology is embedded in political action. It is interesting that some admirers of Hayek agree that the planner will continue to play an important role in such action, but: 'The libertarian perspective does not comprise a theory of government and has nothing to say on how conflicts raised by the introduction of government into market transactions will work out in practice. Thus there will remain numerous areas of conflict requiring planning skills' (Sorensen and Day, 1981).

Conclusion

Despite the optimistic assessment of new right ideology by Sorensen and Day, the message of Hayek's critique contains little comfort for planners. In essence, the argument is that planning by the state is dangerous and ineffective; therefore, the less of it the better. But there is a sense in which planning is permissible and, in fact, desirable: that is, planning to facilitate to the maximum the operation of the market. The market may be supported by state intervention in the form of laws. But the making and implementing of these laws entails long term plans devised centrally and backed by coercive measures. Rightist analysts disagree about the permissible extent of state action to solve urban problems. Banfield would rather see inaction by the state on urban poverty and environmental squalor. Rothbard wants to see the state abolished in its entirety, though such abolition would itself require action by the state of the toughest possible kind. Some of Hayek's prescriptions for urban planning, it could be argued, contradict his strictures on the absence of a 'middle way'. If problems arise in co-ordinating the effects of action on single 'owned' parcels of land, why should they not occur with equal force between larger units of territory?

Many of the criticisms levelled at planning by the most thoughtful of its right-wing critics, such as Hayek, may be conceded, indeed were already conceded before the new right agenda gained ideological dominance. It has long been agreed that centralist 'blueprint' planning is highly ineffective, that bureaucratic decision-making frequently fails to respond to legitimate public desires, and that markets are capable of translating into practical effect the balance of an enormous and complex range of preferences, provided always that people have the resources to participate in the market. These points have not always been fully appreciated by planners. In particular, the value of a market as a tool for planning has not been grasped, and planners often seem to want to resist the action of a market without realizing that it may produce a better result than planning is capable of. However, conceding these points does not require that planning by the state be either abandoned or completely subordinated to the order of the market. Rather, these concessions could be the stimulus for a renewed search for *better* planning, a search that might be considered to be itself a necessary component of 'good planning'. But such a renewal is not on the agenda of the new right, for planning opens up a possibility that the right wishes to eradicate. This is the possibility of redistribution of material resources or 'life chances' through political action. While it is true that such redistribution may favour the rich and powerful, this is not necessarily the case. Better planning and not less planning would ensure that egalitarian goals are implemented. But the right is opposed to egalitarianism.

The right also complains that planning threatens freedom. Of course, this is true in the sense that all order reduces freedom. This is the central problem of politics: how can order be reconciled with freedom? The right, even so-called anarcho-capitalists such as Rothbard, does not prescribe a reduction of order in society, rather the reverse. In claiming to have discovered a truth higher than politics, the right denies the existence of alternative truths, alternative sources of authority. There is in this a danger of authoritarianism, which has not been realized in practice only because *pluralist* traditions and practices are deeply entrenched in society. Even corporatist orders, which recognize multiple sources of authority, seem to have more to offer in the way of freedom than the order of the strong market and the strong state. So at the core of the rightest critique of planning there is a critique of democracy. We are invited to choose between democratic politics and the market as the means of deciding who gets what, when and how.

The new right critique is strongly normative. It poses the question: 'Should planning by the state be improved or abandoned?' The answer depends on an understanding of what planning is, what it does and why it takes place. Different political perspectives provide different responses, and it is premature to try to sum up these responses here. There is more to be said about planning and about the state, which is to be found in what we termed in chapter 1 'dissenting theory', which is the subject of the next two chapters.

Part 3

Dissenting theory

8 Neo-Marxist theory and the philosophy of praxis

In the first half of the nineteenth century, nascent capitalism faced a political crisis caused by mass poverty, starvation, disease and social dislocation. As Hobsbawm (1969, p. 24) put it, 'waves of desperation broke time and again over Britain'. At the same time the working population began to organize on its own behalf. In 1831 a National Union of the Working Classes was formed in London and other such 'working men's associations' were organized in industrial cities throughout Britain. These associations formed the Chartist movement, demanding an extension of democracy: adult male suffrage, annual parliaments, the secret ballot, equal electoral constituencies, payment of members of parliament and the abolition of property qualifications for parliamentary candidature. Militant working-class movements developed all over Europe. In the 1840s the Communist League spread its influence as an international revolutionary organization. In France, 'under the forbidding eye of the Minister of the Interior, French workers, peasants, bourgeois and political activists persisted in forming clubs, secret societies, compagnonnages, associations for mutual aid, rudimentary trade unions and parties' (Tilly, 1975, pp. 40, 41). In the 1840s violent protest broke out all over Europe.

Dissenting political theory of the eighteenth and nineteenth centuries culminated in the work of Marx and Engels, whose ideas took shape against this background of revolutionary struggle. Marx was not just a philosophical observer of the events of his time but also an activist, whose writing had the purpose of inspiring and organizing a political movement as well as analysing the political economy of society. Limited democracy had added political power to the economic power of the new capitalist class. The political critique undertaken by Marx and Engels is based on the premiss that values such as freedom and justice cannot be attained simply through the democratization of the state. Such values pertain to the entire organization of society, especially the aspect of society that is so crucial to everyone's wellbeing: work, production or praxis. In Marxian theory, politics is inseparable from economics, so, in order to concentrate on Marxian politics, we shall have to assume that the reader knows something of Marxian economics.

Neo-Marxist political theory contains many different strands. The principal lines of cleavage are between those that emphasize the development of capital (and its various forms) and those that emphasize class struggle. Plainly the two overlap to a considerable degree. Within each perspective are to be found analyses that view politics as largely determined by economic forces or structures and those that allow to politics a more independent role in shaping economic structures, so that the latter, although still recognizable as 'capitalism', are dependent on multiple national and local institutional variables. For ease of reference, the first will be termed 'structural' Marxism and the second will be termed 'institutional' Marxism.

Collective 'planning' is a Marxist concept, but Marx did not develop the idea. Centralist 'blueprint' planning, which became associated with the practice of Marxism, has been discredited, and it is important for the left to reformulate a much more sophisticated approach to planning. If a Marxist conception of planning is to be developed it is more likely to be grounded in the institutional than in the structural perspective, since the latter directly addresses the question of political action and, as has been argued, planning is a political activity. In what follows we shall first look at the central normative concepts to be found in the work of Marx and Engels, which must underpin any Marxist ideological reconstruction. We shall then introduce the neo-Marxist debates on the state and politics. The thought of Antonio Gramsci has greatly influenced the development of 'institutional' Marxism. Therefore, we shall, look at Gramsci's theory before considering the reformulation of the problematic of class and of the state. In chapter 9 we shall pursue a different and quite distinctive strand of dissenting theory also inspired by Marx, the 'critical theory' of the Frankfurt school and its successors, particularly the theory developed by Jürgen Habermas.

Freedom and justice in the work of Marx and Engels

Marx and Engels held that human everyday life, as it has existed throughout history, is what is important and not just the cultural life of the elite, which finds its way into history books. More fundamental to humanity than 'consciousness' or 'rationality' is human productive activity (praxis): the active interchange between human beings and nature. Marx and Engels ([1846] 1976, p. 31) argued that people express and create themselves through the process by which they transform physical objects for their use. This is why the process of production is so important. People begin to distinguish themselves from animals when they produce their material means of life.

Marx and Engels were thinking here not just of the production of economic necessities but of all human creative activity: economic, social, artistic and scientific. This activity is social. It has to occur with other people. Production, even in science and art, can never be accomplished by some mythical 'isolated individual'. Further, people are able to distinguish their activity from themselves and make that activity subject to their conscious will. But consciousness 'can never be anything else than conscious being'. And such being is social being. People's conduct and thoughts are conditioned by the society they find themselves in. They are the producers of their conceptions 'as real active men, as they are conditioned by a definite development of their productive forces and of the intercourse [political, economic] corresponding to these' (Marx and Engels, [1846] 1976, p. 36). Thus the capacity for the practical, *social* construction of an objective world, in which humanity sees itself reflected, defines the human species. This capacity is, of course, the capacity for collective planning.

All of Marx's work contains the idea of freedom, but the realization of freedom, liberation, would be achieved through the working out of humanity's material historical destiny and not through the *idea* of freedom: It is not, in fact, ideas that dominate and repress people, and therefore it is not ideas that will liberate humanity. 'People cannot be liberated as long as they are unable to obtain food and drink, housing and clothing in adequate quantity and quality. "Liberation" is a historical and not a mental act and it is brought about by historical conditions' (p. 38).

According to O'Rourke (1974) two concepts of freedom are to be found in Marx's writings, the anthropological and the historical. Marx's anthropological concept of freedom consisted in the ability of human beings to express themselves through praxis to the limits of their potential (see Fischer, [1968] 1973, p. 30). Sometimes this concept is expressed as the 'freedom to' (positive freedom) as against the liberal conception of 'freedom from' (negative freedom): freedom to work creatively as opposed to freedom from the 'tyranny of the majority' (see pp. 85, 113, chapter 5). As to the historical conception of freedom, Marx believed that he had discovered certain patterns or laws in the history of mankind. He felt that humanity was progressing inevitably towards its self-realization and freedom (in the anthropological sense). As a believer in progress he was very much a man of the nineteenth century. The driving force of history, for Marx, was the dialectical struggle between opposing social forces in the sphere of production. So Marx was able to say in the *Communist Manifesto*, 'the communists merely express in general terms, actual relations springing from an existing class struggle, from an historical movement going on under our very eyes'.

How, then, could people be regarded as having free will and the capacity to act if they were caught up in the dialectical processes of history? Marx believed that a person's freedom of will and freedom to act would always be limited until the dawn of the period of complete self-realization under communism (true communism, not state socialism). The social and economic environment in which people found themselves would always act as a constraint on their freedom of thought and action. Probably the clearest expression of the Marxian position on this matter was written by Engels, some years after Marx's death:

> Men make their own history, whatever its outcome may be, in that each person follows his own consciously desired end, and it is precisely the resultant of these many wills operating in different directions and of their manifold effects upon the outer world that constitutes history. Thus it is also a question of what the many individuals desire. The will is determined by passion or deliberation. But the levers which immediately determine passion or deliberation are of very different kinds. Partly they may be external objects, partly ideal motives, ambition, 'enthusiasm for truth and justice', personal hatred or even purely individual whims of all kinds. But, on the other hand, we have seen that the many individual wills active in history for the most part produce results quite other than those intended – often quite the opposite; that their motives, therefore, in relation to the total result are likewise only of secondary importance. On the other hand, the further question arises: what driving forces in turn stand behind these motives? What are the historical causes which transform themselves into these motives in the brains of the actors? . . . To ascertain the driving causes which here in the minds of acting masses and their leaders – the so-called great men – are reflected as conscious motives, clearly or unclearly, directly or in ideological, even glorified form – that is the only path which can put us on the track of the laws holding sway both in history as a whole and at particular periods in particular lands (Engels, [1888] 1962. p. 391).

Here Engels is saying that people have motives that result in actions that change things. But these purposeful actions also have determinants of which the actors themselves may be unaware, and these actions may have unintended consequences. Marx and Engels regarded the hidden determinants of action as 'laws of history'. Unfortunately, if motives and purposes are subject to the laws of history, which have already been discovered, it is all too easy for Marxist actors to give up thinking for themselves: for whatever they think will be predetermined by the laws. No doubt this is an unintended consequence of Marxian theory. This consequence can be avoided if it is conceded that underlying determinants may exist without being 'laws of history'. First, many determinants may be operating quite weakly. Secondly, if there are many determinants, they may not all press in the same direction. In either case there is scope for some freedom of action and choice on the part of individuals and groups (though not, of course, complete freedom). Furthermore, we may prefer to regard the nature of the underlying determinants as the subject of debate. No one, especially such politically motivated people as Marx and Engels, can be regarded as free from hidden determinants. Therefore, they cannot free themselves to take up a scientifically detached (and privileged) position outside the society of which they are part. Therefore, the political struggle informed by political thinking must go on, and no theory is outside it or beyond it.

Returning to the anthropological concept of freedom, Marx developed the idea of 'alienation' as its antithesis. In primitive society people were unfree because they were oppressed by nature itself. They had to struggle against the elements just to survive. Under capitalism nature had been conquered. Marx perceived the immense productive power unleashed at the climax of the industrial revolution. He was witness to the vision of never-ending growth of that period. But mankind was nevertheless not free but alienated. People in capitalist societies are alienated in four ways. They are alienated from the product of their work, from the process of working, from their fellow human beings, and, in summary, from the very 'species-being' (*Gattungswesen*) of humanity itself.

There is an inverse relation, Marx believed, between the growing amount of goods produced and the amount appropriated by the worker. Productivity grows and, in the short term, increases the rate of profit (in the long term the rate of profit tends to fall), but the worker becomes poorer the more wealth he produces. He is alienated from his own product, which assumes an independent existence and becomes a power on its own. Thus Marx began his major work, *Capital*, with an analysis of the commodity. A commodity is a product whose primary purpose under capitalism is not its use value (though every commodity must have a use) but its ability to be exchanged on the market. Marx lets commodities speak for themselves: 'our use-value may interest men, but it does not belong to us as objects. Our own intercourse as commodities proves it. We relate to each other merely as exchange values' (Marx: [1867] 1976 p. 177). Producers are related to one another in the capitalist mode of production by exchanging commodities for another universal commodity, money. Individual producers, workers, are typically isolated from one another except in this one form of social relation: buying and selling. To the producers, therefore, the social relations between their private labours 'do not appear as direct social relations between persons in their work, but rather as "thing-like" (*dinglich*) relations between persons, and social relations between things' (pp. 165–6).

Finally, therefore, workers themselves become ('thing-like') commodities, whose principal function for capitalism is to generate profit (through surplus value) and to be exchanged. Work is performed not as an end in itself nor for an end set voluntarily by workers, but in the service of commodity production. The workers' activity ceases to be truly their own: 'the worker feels himself to be freely active only in his animal functions' (Marx, manuscripts quoted by O'Rourke, 1974). In their properly human functions of directing the aim and purpose of their work, workers are not free at all. So firmly is this principle established that through the education system children are trained to accept orders, to think what they are told to think and not to act on their own initiative. Only the elite are encouraged to take the initiative. Workers, therefore, are alienated both from the product of their work and from the process of production.

The product of labour and the activity of labour have been dispossessed of the worker and the dispossessor is another person. Under capitalism, people are fundamentally divided at the most basic level (that of productive activity) between those whose interests lie with capital and those whose interests lie with labour. The worker and the capitalist stand to each other as opposed and alien forces. Because of this fundamental conflict of interest in society there can be no affirmation of persons as individuals with their own intrinsic value. There can be no real consensus, only that which is designed to legitimate the activities of the dominant class. The basis of genuine social relations is destroyed and people are alienated from their fellow human beings. The vicious circle of alienation is closed, in that people fail to recognize their own alienation. People suffer from a 'false consciousness', which is created by all the ideas generated by the capitalist establishment. In the interests of the dominant class, these ideas conceal the truth of the human condition. The wool is pulled over the eyes of the workers. Marx said: 'The veil is not removed from the countenance of the social life process, i.e. the process of production, until it becomes production by freely associated men and stands under their conscious and planned control' (Marx: [1867] 1976, p. 173). Here, quite explicitly, appears the concept of collective planning as the antidote to alienation.

Marx and Engels thus set out their conceptions of freedom and justice. A free society is one in which all people have the opportunity to reach their maximum potential for self-expression through work. A just society is one that allows this to happen, and from which the injustice of mutual exploitation and alienation is removed. This critique is not a wholesale condemnation of market exchange. Marx and Engels only condemn the application of market principles to the exchange of labour: to market labour is to reduce what is fundamental about human beings to the status of a thing. In the three volumes of *Capital* Marx shows in fine historical detail how, under capitalism, labour becomes the commodity that is valued solely for its capacity to produce a surplus for the owners of capital.

The positive conception of freedom is important for urban planning, because it provides a philosophical justification for collective action to improve the quality of life of a given population. The very term 'quality of life' is given meaning by Marx's and Engels' interpretation of freedom as the capacity of individuals to live life to the full extent of their potential. This idea is also contained in the essay *On Liberty* by the liberal John Stuart Mill ([1859] 1910). As Norman Geras (1983) has pointed out, acknowledging that human beings are social creatures does not mean denying that individual 'human nature' is the measure of human need. Marx and Engels remind us of the central importance of *productive work* in the development of human potential and this is something that liberal political philosophy greatly neglects. Marx and Engels, however, neglected the danger of collective power, whether exercised by the state or by any other agency, and the contradiction between this power and the needs of the individual. Implicit in Marx's and Engels' work (and occasionally explicit) is the belief that collective planning would automatically solve the problem of freedom. It does not. It is the virtue of pluralism that it recognizes that human needs are many and contradictory, and that any planned solution can only be temporary and provisional.

The state and politics

According to Marx, the central feature of any capitalist society is the conflictual relationship between capital and labour, a relationship engendered by the exploitation of humans by other humans in the process of organizing material survival, namely the process of production. 'Historical materialism' holds that it is this fundamental conflict around which capitalism has deposited layer upon layer of structure as the oyster does around the original grain of sand' (Aronson, 1985). In Aronson's words capitalism 'has become a staggeringly complex system – its many layers and blockages stemming in part from ever-renewed attempts to defend itself against its opponents and contradictions. But it remains one whose original and fundamental exploitation is *not* done away with even if it is pacified and softened' (p. 89). The contradictions inherent in the capitalist mode of production produce an accumulation of crises that lead to the breakdown of the capitalist system and its eventual transformation into socialism. In the process of this transformation the state comes to play an increasing role.

In contrast to the theory of the pluralists or that of Weber, the hallmark of Marxist state theory is its reference of the question of power to the relationship between people in the sphere of production, that is, to *class*. Therborn (1982) observes that pluralist studies of power ask questions like: 'who has power?' Who rules? How much power do different groups have? These questions are framed with reference to a *subject* of power – either an individual or group. Marxists, on the other hand, view power, which on the face of it seems to be something individuals can get their hands on, as at root a structural property of the class relationship constituted in the process of production. Whereas Weber defined class as a power relationship based on the *ownership* of wealth, which was realized in the market, Marx pointed to the essentially exploitative *production* of wealth. The class relationship necessitated a 'state'. In the Marxist view, the state *is* the structure deposited by a class-based society and built up around it. When classes disappear under communism, the state will wither away because there will be no need for the state.

Jessop (1982) discusses the capital-theoretic and class-theoretic perspectives of the state in Marxian theory. The most interesting analysis in the capital-theoretic perspective seeks to elaborate the laws of development of capital that underlie the changing relationship between capital and the state: the way the organization of the one interacts with the organization of the other. An important formulation is that of 'state monopoly capitalism' (stamocap). This is 'a distinct stage of capitalism characterized by the fusion of monopoly forces with the bourgeois state to form a single mechanism of economic exploitation and political domination ' (Jessop, 1982, p. 32). As capital is centralized into vast corporations operating in oligopolistic rather than purely competitive markets, production capacity grows at an explosive pace, the division of labour is intensified and the different branches of production become increasingly interdependent. In short, the forces of production are increasingly socialized. The revolution in technology also increases the importance of links between material production and the non-material sphere of education and research.

The prosperity of individual fractions of capital becomes more dependent on the health of capital accumulation in the nation as a whole. There is, therefore, a growing developmental need to match the degree of organization ('socialization') of the *forces* of production with organization of the *relations* of production: the relations among individual capitals, between capital and labour, and among various class fractions. The pressures of this need are realized in crises, for example of uneven development (see Smith, 1984), across different sectors and areas of production, disproportions between exchange value and use value, periodic excess of capital relative to the available opportunities for the creation and realization of surplus value (see Boccara, 1977), overproduction of commodities, and working-class underconsumption. Working-class pressure and the interpenetration of business and state political elites ensure that the state responds to these crises.

Most stamocap theorists endeavour to show how state–capital relations have passed through a number of distinct periods punctuated by waves of crises. For example, Fine and Harris (1979) postulate three stages in the restructuring of the social relations of production: *laissez faire*, monopoly capitalism and state monopoly capitalism. Fine and Harris observe that, politically, the appearance of state monopoly capitalism is characterized by absorption into the state of working-class economic struggles over wages and conditions of work: 'In all cases it involves building a system where the political struggle of the working class is contained. Its most developed form is the establishment of bourgeois social democracy so that political parties based on working class support become part of the state apparatus' (Fine and Harris, 1979, p. 125).

Stamocap theory, Jessop points out, is not strictly a theory of the state but a theory of the latest stage of capitalism, in which the state plays a decisive role. The theory suggests a possible causal explanation of 'corporatism', as the development of capitalist exploitation requires some accommodation between the needs of capital and the contradictory demands of labour (see Westergaard, 1977). But it also allows rather too much to depend on a single economic causal relationship. It fails to explain the variety of state structures that exist in capitalist societies, apparently at similar stages of development. If the relationship between monopoly capital and the state is indeed *the* crucial one, stamocap theory does not show how other causal factors (pressures from labour, the bureaucracy, other fractions of capital etc.) are subordinated to that single dominant relationship (see Jessop, 1982, pp. 67, 69).

The class-theoretic perspective places emphasis on the role of the state in shoring up the domination of the ruling class, the bourgeoisie. In an exposition of state theory written in the summer before the 1917 Revolution, Lenin drew together ideas in the work of Engels and Marx portraying the capitalist state as an instrument in the hands of the ruling class (Lenin, [1917] 1964). Lenin viewed the state as the 'public coercive power', typically the standing army, police and state bureaucracy. This power, he constantly emphasized, must be 'smashed' and 'destroyed' (pp. 388, 416 and *passim*.). But he also used this 'instrumentalist' perception to justify the creation of a new proletarian state apparatus. Although he preferred not to portray this apparatus in terms of 'state' (a term he reserved for the bourgeois form of political power), the new apparatus would also have its coercive core. He said: 'It follows that the "special coercive force" for the suppression of the proletariat by the bourgeoisie, of millions of working people by handfuls of rich, must be replaced by a "special coercive force" for the suppression of the bourgeoisie by the proletariat' (p. 397). At a time when coercive socialist states have broken up all over Europe, we need hardly labour the dangers inherent in such a concept.

Later 'instrumental' theorists, who might not agree with Lenin's prescription for a coercive socialist state, argue that 'the ruling class of capitalist society is that class which owns and controls the means of production and which is able, by virtue of the economic power thus conferred upon it, to use the state as its instrument for the domination of society' (Miliband, [1967] 1973, p. 23). There has been much debate in Marxist circles about the nature of the nexus between the dominant class and the State (see, for example, the debate between Poulantzas and Miliband: Poulantzas 1969, 1976; Miliband 1970, 1973; Laclau, 1975). Poulantzas ([1968] 1973) presented a *political* analysis of the role of the superstructure, the state, in reproducing the mode of production. In his view the capitalist state *isolates* workers (direct producers or 'agents of production') by treating them juridically as individual subjects, i.e. individual voters, individuals before the law, in contract, etc. But, on the other hand, the state stands for the *unity* of the nation, thus reassembling on non-class lines what it has first fragmented. This 'double function' is no mere ideological mirage, for isolation and reunification is constituted by concrete political practices and institutions. At the same time, the state also functions to unite the isolated and divergent interests of the dominant class by ensuring the economic conditions appropriate to profitable accumulation and by portraying (by means of liberal economic ideology) the specific interest of the dominant class as the collective interest of the nation as a whole. The state thus functions 'to disorganize the dominated classes and, at the same time, to organize the dominant class' (Poulantzas, [1968] 1973, p. 189).

Both Poulantzas and Althusser regarded the political domain of the state as 'relatively autonomous' from the economic. In other words, although political developments are connected ultimately to developments in economic relations they are not determined by them. Politics is dependent on human action and develops in its own particular way. In his well known essay on 'Contradiction and Overdetermination', Althusser argued that the multiplicity of social forces at work in society does not permit the derivation of political (superstructural) phenomena from economic contradictions, even though these contradictions provide the motive force for social change. Quoting Engels (1890) Althusser ([1965] 1979, p. 112) stated: 'Here, then, are the two ends of the chain: the economy is determinant but *in the last instance*, Engels is prepared to say: in the long run, the run of History. But History "asserts itself" through the multiform world of the superstructures, from local tradition to international circumstance!'

In these formulations of the state, political action is subsumed within 'class struggle'. One element of class struggle that has, increasingly, been viewed as important is ideology. Larrain (1983) has pointed out that the Marxist conception of ideology underwent an important change in the twentieth century. Marx and Engels, in *The German Ideology*, had contrasted the socially determined forms of consciousness (political ideas) thrown up by a particular economic system with their own 'scientific' understanding, which revealed material contradictions for which these political ideas could not account. Systems of political ideas, ideas embedded in the superstructure of society, were thus given a negative connotation of mystification and illusion, an 'inverted consciousness' which concealed a different underlying *reality*.

But a programme of political action, especially revolutionary action for which exceptional sacrifices were required, made it necessary to put forth alternative political practices, which embodied alternative political ideas. These ideas could hardly be portrayed as alternative illusions. Ideas, therefore, had to be allowed a positive force and reality of their own and the ideological sphere accorded the status of a battleground of the class struggle. Lenin dealt with the problem by simply welding together the concepts of ideology and science. Some ideologies were scientific and these ideologies corresponded to an objective truth in nature (Lenin, [1909] 1972, p. 153). Gramsci and, later, Althusser, however, approached the view that political criteria cannot be reduced to the truth criteria governing science. Thus ideology had to be accorded a separate validity. Althusser ([1965] 1979, p. 235) wrote that 'ideology (as a system of mass representations) is indispensable in any society if men are to be formed, transformed and equipped to respond to the demands of their conditions of existence'.

In summary, thus far, Marxists have viewed power as a structural property of the social relations of production (i.e. in capitalism). The state has been regarded as derivative either of the development of capital or of class struggle. The state has been reified and separated from politics, which, in turn, has been reduced to class struggle. There is, however, a tension between the structural analysis of power and the needs of political practices, which require political ideas, ideology, both to motivate and organize the political forces and to provide direction and some concrete vision of an alternative social order.

This tension is apparent in Marxist urban studies. Neo-Marxist structural theory casts the urban planner, as an agent of the capitalist state, in a conservative role. David Harvey (1985, p. 175) well expresses this point of view. If society reduces ultimately and essentially to the domination of labour by capital, then the state has to be viewed as the instrument that stabilizes the power structure inherent in the mode of production, and counteracts the destabilizing effects of class struggle. Therefore, the state in capitalism 'should' (i), help to stabilize an otherwise rather erratic economic and social system by acting as a 'crisis-manager', (ii), strive to create the conditions for 'balanced growth' and a smooth process of capital accumulation, and (iii), contain civil strife and factional struggles by repression (police power), co-optation (buying off politically or economically) or integration (trying to harmonize the demands of warring classes or factions). The urban planner occupies 'just one niche within the complex of instrumentalities of state power'. From this perspective, the role of planning and its ideology is to maintain stable urban development.

Marxists differ on the question of what can and should be done. For Harvey (1985) current urban planning theory merely 'plans the ideology of planning', whereas a better planning practice is dependent upon the reconstruction of society. If we 'step aside' and reflect critically on the supposed 'harmony' (and real contradictions) of the capitalist world, then we might begin to plan such a reconstruction of society. Critique therefore plays an important part in changing things. Scott and Roweis (1977) proposed that a theory of planning practice should be grounded in the Marxist critique of the process of urbanization. Fainstein *et al.* (1986, p. 250) suggest that 'the absence in the daily press and television of any left-oriented critique of urban programs [in the USA] was enormously important in legitimating the political force behind them'. But critique by itself is plainly not enough. Scott and Roweis (1977, p. 1118) state that 'urban planning is today in the process of becoming increasingly politicized as urban life becomes increasingly mediated by the State'. But they offer no political strategy beyond the formation of some sort of grand coalition between the labour movement, the women's movement and the 'citizens' movement'.

Fainstein *et al.* (1986, pp. 270–4), on the other hand offer a more politically oriented, institutional perspective. They argue that a 'counterstrategy' must be based on the political representation of 'lower and working class interests' in governmental policy-making. The implication is that, if the lot of the working class (in, for example, the inner neighbourhoods of American cities) is to be improved, then this class must be organized and represented. It is not at all clear whether planners can make such representation their *goal* and seek to achieve it (planning *with* the poor rather than planning *for* the poor), or whether such organization and representation has to come from within the ranks of the working class itself. Either way, the planner has a positive role: in the first instance as an activist and organizer, in the second by responding sympathetically to local signs of working-class mobilization. But the ameliorative possibilities of such mobilization are limited by the power of capital over investment and its location.

While the strength of neo-Marxist structural analysis is its critique, its weakness is in making the transition from critique to action, from analysis to prescription. Although Marxist urbanists usefully interpret the context in which political struggle occurs, their prescriptions for action add little to what has been already said by pluralists and their critics. Important questions relating to 'class' and 'the state' remain unanswered. For example: how are the various social strata, movements and organized groups encountered in day-to-day political life and planning practice, in specific localities, related to class? To what class do state agents such as planners belong? Is the state and state policy (e.g. land-use policy) a proper target for political struggle in the interests of social justice, equality and freedom?

These are questions to which answers must be provided if theory is to guide practice. It may be that neo-Marxist theory provides no clear prescriptions. However, a doctrine that cannot take the step from critique to action remains, against its best intentions, profoundly conservative. Among the founders of neo-Marxist theory, Antonio Gramsci was the most acutely aware of this point. His is the theory that comes closest to developing a genuinely Marxist political theory and strategy.

Gramsci and the philosophy of praxis

The most obvious criticisms of the Marxian programme are, first, that it tells us little about the politics of transition to socialism, particularly in advanced capitalist societies and, secondly, that it supplies only an indistinct and utopian account of the politics of socialism itself. Antonio Gramsci was involved in the political organization of the workers' struggles in Italy before the Second World War, and he saw that behind the socialist rhetoric of his contemporaries lay 'the absence of real political activity, rejection of mass initiative and pessimism'. 'Left-wing phrases covered a politics that was in fact "a fatalistic and mechanical conception" of Marx's politics' (Buci-Glucksmann, [1975] 1980, p. 2, quoting Gramsci, 1971b). During his eleven years of imprisonment under Mussolini's fascist regime, Gramsci had time to reflect on his experiences and to formulate a theory that is arguably the most 'political' of all Marxist theories of the state. This theory tells us that the transition to socialism requires an understanding of the conditions specific to different countries, that political action is required to match those different conditions and that an important part of that political action is ideological struggle. The dictatorship of the proletariat would emerge from the eventual overthrow of the bourgeois state and lead to a truly democratic society, with the withering away of both class conflict and the state. We shall look first at what Gramsci had to say about 'hegemony' and the power of the capitalist state, and then turn to the question of ideology and political strategy.

Hegemony and state power

Lenin used the term 'hegemony' to describe the organized consent of the masses to the domination of a particular class. In a preliminary analysis, Gramsci (1971a, p. 12) identified two levels of class domination:

> One that can be called civil society, that is the ensemble of organisms commonly called 'private', and that of 'political society' or 'the State'. These two levels correspond on the one hand to the function of 'hegemony' which the dominant group exercises throughout society and, on the other hand to that of 'direct domination' or command exercised through the State and 'juridical government'.

The radical conceptual separation of 'the state' from 'civil society', politics from economics, was the product of capitalist ideology. The virtue of Marxist thought was that it viewed the two as a dialectical unity: thus hegemony could not be limited to civil society nor could the concept of 'the state' be limited to that of government. Hegemony, in Gramsci's conception, on the one hand was the active construction of mass political support and, on the other, the acting out of modes of life: mass participation in actions that involved compliance. Therborn (1982) compares the Marxian conception of capitalist 'reproduction' with Weber's concept of legitimacy, pointing out that people may be quiescent not because they regard the state as legitimate but because they do not know what kind of domination they are subjected to. But in the idea of 'hegemony' Gramsci developed a more active interpretation of capitalist reproduction than this. To establish hegemony, consent has to be mobilized; genuine inducements have to be offered rather than mere deception and coercion. Therefore, 'a dominant class is hegemonic in its progressive historical phase because it really does carry the whole of society forward' (Buci–Glucksmann, [1975] 1980, pp. 57, 58).

Hegemony is an educational relationship. From childhood we learn about 'markets', 'competition', dependency, family, authority and status. We are taught to construe these terms in a particular way and we enact roles that embody these constructions. The knowledge that supports hegemony is held and cultivated by the 'intellectual strata' of society, a grouping in which Gramsci included not just the producers of knowledge but also the users, the clerks and functionaries, the teachers and managers. In this analysis, urban planners would form part of the hegemonal structure.

Hegemony is not formed merely through the dissemination of knowledge but originates at the heart of the work process. Writing of the United States, Gramsci said: 'hegemony here is born in the factory and requires for its exercise only a minute quantity of professional political and ideological intermediaries' (Gramsci, 1971a, p. 83). In his discussion of 'Americanism and Fordism' he postulated that the new 'American' systems of mass production and scientific management created a whole nexus of domination in which new social strata were formed, roles were prescribed and rules of private morality were laid down. Taylorism, he observed, expressed 'with brutal cynicism the purpose of American society – developing in the worker to the highest degree automatic and mechanical attitudes, breaking up the old psycho–physical nexus of qualified professional work, which demands a certain active participation of intelligence, fantasy and initiative on the part of the worker and reducing productive operations to the mechanical physical aspect' (Gramsci, 1971a, p. 302). The process of work required clearly demarcated gender roles and sexual mores and created new strata within the working class: the unskilled and deskilled, the high-wage labour aristocracy. In capitalism, the domination embodied in the work process was paralleled by a moral ideology outside work, which spoke constantly of the sanctity of the family and monogamous marriage. Stressing the point that different political cultures had different ways of generating hegemony, he said that the American system provided a sharp contrast with that of most European countries, in which the 'intellectuals' played a much larger role.

Gramsci challenged reductionist conceptions of the state. The state was not a thing to be captured and used as an instrument by a ruling class or fraction, nor was political struggle mechanically geared to the economic process. At the same time, the state and politics were not to be seen in voluntaristic terms because hegemony and the constitution of hegemonic apparatuses were rooted in the economic base. The intellectual strata, whose function was to organize consent, were themselves constituted by aspects of production. Here we might say that the production of developed land and struggles over land use constitute the need for planning and planners.

There are two senses in which Gramsci speaks of the state: as the apparatus of coercive power in a strict sense and in a broader sense as 'the entire complex of practical and theoretical activities with which the ruling class not only justifies and maintains its dominance but manages to win the active consent of those whom it rules' (Gramsci, 1971a, p. 244). In modern Western societies state power is protected by 'the trenches and fortifications' of hegemony in civil society. Real change in society could only be brought about if the 'trenches and fortifications' surrounding state power had first been seized. One might nominally control the state apparatus but one could not use it to bring about socialism without having first changed the wider complex of institutions, ideologies, practices and agents constitutive of hegemony. Conversely, the apparatuses of hegemony were entrenched by the coercive power of the state, so that it was also possible to conceive of the state as 'political plus civil society, in other words hegemony protected by the armour of coercion' (Gramsci, 1971a, p. 263).

Political strategy

Opportunities for political action occur because hegemony is never stable. Hegemony itself involves contradictions. In organizing the consent of the subordinate classes, the hegemonic class leaves open the possibility for the subordinate classes to form themselves into an autonomous political force (Lenin, [1919] 1964, p. 486; Buci-Glucksmann, [1975] 1980, p. 57). Moments of potential for funda-mental change in society occur when the energy and commitment necessary for class struggle are accompanied by a certain freedom to organize. In order to take advantage of such moments, the primary political task is the construction of a socialist counter-hegemony.

First, the working class itself must be organized. This requires the practical action of the proletariat's own 'organic' intellectuals. Gramsci's conception of the intellectuals of the proletariat was based on his view of the party (the vanguard party of the proletariat) as embodying the practical organizing and thinking activity of the working class. A person was an 'organic intellectual of the proletariat' not by virtue of his or her opinions but through participation in the intellectual life of the proletariat, centring on the party. The political party was responsible for 'welding together' the organic intellectuals of any dominant group. It trained the leaders of this group and turned them 'into qualified political intellectuals, leaders and organizers of all the activities and functions inherent in the organic development of an integral society both civil and political' (Gramsci, 1971a, p. 15). The party of Labour must, therefore, become an organizing and organized force parallel to the hegemonic bourgeois state and capable ultimately of replacing it.

Within the party, leadership and education did not mean laying down and enforcing from the centre a dogmatic and rigid framework of ideas, but constant engagement with the concerns of the masses. Gramsci sought 'a dialectic of spontaneity and conscious organized leadership'. This principle Gramsci regarded as necessary to any true democracy. The hegemony of the working class in the construction of socialism could not be based on 'a military coercive model'. Leadership and education had to be a two-way process. The intellectual must address 'the elementary passions of the people, understanding them and therefore explaining and justifying them in the particular historical situation and connecting them dialectically to the laws of history and to a superior conception of the world, scientifically and coherently elaborated – i.e. knowledge. One cannot make politics–history without this passion, without this sentimental connection between intellectuals and people–nations' (Gramsci, 1971a, p. 418).

The democratic solidarity of the working class only marks the beginning of the construction of socialist hegemony. The next task is to look beyond the revolutionary 'core' and analyse the political forces operating in the specific region or nation where the political action takes place, that is, the interests, factions, organized groups and political parties. The party of the working class has to find ways of forming a new coalition of these groups and of establishing its leadership of this coalition through political struggle (Gramsci, 1971a, p. 181). Because Gramsci was concerned at first hand with practical political action – through the party, through the factory councils – he saw the dangers in too rigid an interpretation of Marx's conceptual distinction between structure and superstructure, material production and the world of ideas. His project was to reunite these elements and to demonstrate that if both political stability and revolutionary change were at all the product of human action, such action was necessarily constructed around ideas. In so far as a state had attained hegemonic rule there would be associated with it supportive ideologies, forms of consciousness, conventional wisdoms, customs, habits of thought, accepted methods of knowledge, patterns of work and social relations, all of which added up to an integration of structure and superstructure in a 'historic bloc'. 'The complex, contradictory and discordant ensemble of the superstructures is the reflection of the ensemble of the social relations of production' (Gramsci, 1971a, p. 366). There is a reciprocity between structure and superstructure 'which is nothing other than the real dialectical process'.

Ideas developed in response to practices but also fed back into and enhanced those practices. Gramsci attacked socialist 'economism' and the failure of its left exponents in Italy to take advantage of the moment presented to them by structural conditions. The problem was partly a failure to organize the working class for the task of seizing power, but also a failure to mobilize ideology in the service of action. Gramsci maintained that although specific ideologies can be criticized, others are 'historically necessary'. That is, they organize human activity. They 'create the terrain on which men move, acquire consciousness of their position, struggle etc.' (p. 377). Gramsci argued that it is necessary to conceive of an alternative form of society in order to generate the will to change; also that ideologies have to be confronted on their own terms. Unlike military struggle, in which the weakest points provide the opening for successful advance, the ideological struggle always requires one to 'engage battle with the most eminent of one's adversaries'. The aim must be to concentrate on what is *centrally* attractive about the opposing ideology, because it is that core rather than peripheral points that inspires political action and mobilizes mass support.

The ideological struggle takes place on two fronts – that of philosophy, which influences the masses only indirectly through the mediation of the intellectuals; and that of common sense in day-to-day political struggles. The problem for Marxist philosophy is to bring the two together 'holding firmly to both ends of the chain, internal and external hegemony, i.e. what directly affects the popular masses and what affects them only indirectly through the way it organizes the hegemony of the leading classes' (Buci-Glucksmann, 1980, p. 226). Here, Gramsci was referring to the need for ideological conviction on the part of the elite, and the translation of ideology into popular symbols and acts readily understood by the mass. Ideology, then, provides 'a general conception of life, a philosophy . . . offering those who subscribe to it a dignity, providing a principle of differentiation from the old ideologies which dominated by coercion and an element of struggle against them' (Gramsci, 1971a, pp. 103, 104).

The political strategy Gramsci developed to organize the proletariat and prepare for socialist counter-hegemony he called the 'war of position'. He used this term to draw a contrast with the attempts of the German Communist Party after the First World War to emulate the armed insurrection of the Bolshevik Revolution in Russia: the 'war of movement or manoeuvre'. These adventures were disastrous for the communist cause in Germany, resulting in savage repression by the Prussian state and the total loss of momentum of the Party (see Anderson, 1976/1977, pp. 56, 57). Lenin himself had to remind the Third Congress of the International Communist Movement (Comintern) that the revolution in Russia had been accomplished because of the mass support for the small Bolshevik party by the majority of Soviets (councils) of workers and peasant deputies throughout the country and by more than half the army. How much more necessary was it to achieve mass support in Western nations, where bourgeois hegemony was so much more firmly entrenched and where the state could reliably call upon massive coercive resources – a loyal army and police? Significantly, Gramsci's images of the relationship between the state (in the restricted sense) and the apparatuses of hegemony in civil society depict the former as the outer shell and the latter as the core. Remember that the state in the wider sense was 'hegemony protected by the armour of coercion'.

The 'war of position' was the strategy aimed at forging a 'national–popular collective will' in opposition to the bourgeois hegemonic state (Gramsci, 1971a, pp. 131, 242). Its task was the education of the spontaneous and practical movements of the masses, which would give them 'a "theoretical" consciousness of being creators of *historical* and institutional *values*, of being founders of a State'. 'Conscious leadership', therefore, meant being able to demonstrate how the specific problems which different movements of the masses were concerned with were traceable to the same root cause in the economic structure of capitalism, thus enabling the formation of a broad-based coalition of interests.

From certain orthodox Marxist viewpoints this 'war of position' looks like reformism – fighting for socialism within the ground rules established by the dominant bourgeois class and imposed by the bourgeois state. Anderson (1976/77, p. 69) writes: 'Gramsci never relinquished the fundamental tenets of classical Marxism on the ultimate necessity for violent seizure of state power, but at the same time his strategic formula for the West fails to integrate them. The mere counterposition of "war of position" to "war of manoeuvre" in any Marxist strategy in the end becomes an opposition between reformism and adventurism.' But, in the light of Gramsci's practical activity in the factory councils, this criticism seems unfair. The struggle in Turin was directed precisely *against* the ground rules of bourgeois democracy. Therefore, essential to the concept of war of position is the call for new rules for the representation of interests, new political processes in general, backed by a new ideology of democracy.

Naturally enough, the bourgeois state could be expected to resist such developments with every resource at its disposal. However, the use of force tended to destroy the belief, necessary for bourgeois hegemony, that rule was exclusively by consent. Gramsci depicted the stage of opposition as a 'mutual siege' and suggested that the most likely bourgeois strategy would be to entice and co-opt the newly formed hegemonic organizations of the proletariat and its allies into the power structure. Therefore, to resist this incorporation, the discipline of the opposition forces was crucial. Buci-Glucksmann (1980, p. 160) observes: 'cohesion, discipline, unity, organization: these are terms that recur perpetually in all of Gramsci's and Togliatti's articles'.

Here, however, the contradiction of hegemony is revealed within the socialist camp. The discipline required to besiege the ruling class and to withstand counter-pressures could destroy the very values of proletarian democracy which the revolution was fighting for and which would form the ideological spine of proletarian hegemony. This seems to be a terminal antinomy of *all* politics, in as much as politics is a power struggle, as Weber was keenly aware. The solution can only be a pragmatic one, based on some kind of human judgement about an appropriate balance between the opening up of possible courses of action and their closure and resolution upon a single path forward. Gramsci's judgement stressed the active collaboration and dialogue between a centrally organized party and its mass supporting base organized in local cells. 'A matching of thrusts from below with orders from above', a 'practical' and 'experimental' process and not the result of 'a rationalistic deductive, abstract process' (Gramsci, 1971a, p. 189).

'Every state is a dictatorship' Gramsci wrote ([1924] 1978, p. 209). Every state entails the coercive leadership of a small group of people at the top. The central question for the 'dictatorship of the proletariat' is the relationship between the government leaders and the party of the proletariat and between the party and the wider class. The leaders are selected by a process of extended political struggle among the factions of the class ('a struggle of factions and small groups; it was also an individual struggle; it meant splits and fusions, arrest, exile, prison, assassination attempts'; p. 210). The relationship between the leaders and the class must be organic rather than hierarchical and military. The leader and the party must represent the vital interests and aspirations of the working class. They must not be 'an excrescence or simply a violent imposition' (p. 209).

Gramsci evidently wanted central planning to be modified by something like pluralist politics, but he was not prepared to specify the institutional forms in which these principles would be embodied. 'Democratic centralism' was, rather, an 'elastic formula' which could take many forms arising out of practical necessity. Gramsci's vision of the socialist state presupposed majoritarian principles, popular self-government and organized consent (see Buci-Glucksmann, 1980, p. 155). But, initally, a coercive state apparatus would continue to be necessary, occupied as it would be with ensuring the transition from the capitalist to the socialist mode of production (see Gramsci, 1971a, p. 263). The socialist state would go through its own process of development over many years from the 'economic corporative' phase (see chapter 6, pp. 137–41) to the 'nightwatchman' phase, in which the principal task was to safeguard the emergence of a regulated and increasingly self-regulating society, in short an ethical state. As complex self-regulating mechanisms and customs developed in civil society in accordance with a socialist reality, so the coercive function of the state would gradually 'wither away'. As for the state institutions that would accompany these developments, 'they will inevitably be few in number and have a character of foresight and struggle but as yet few "planned" elements. Cultural policy will above all be negative, a critique of the past; it will be aimed at erasing from the memory and at destroying. The lines of construction will as yet be "broad lines", sketches, which might (and should) be changed at all times, so as to be consistent with the new structure as it is formed' (p. 265). Looking forward to socialism thus meant *not* setting out a fixed utopia but rather keeping to the principle of theory growing out of practice, allowing space for the design of institutions to emerge from the ideas of the makers of the new society themselves.

What does Gramsci's formulation of the state and politics say to the urban planner? Although it is true that professionals within the state are part of the state's fortifications, part of the 'city trenches' in Katznelson's (1981) Gramscian phrase, it is also true that hegemony is contradictory. Certain kinds of urban policy are a concession to the working class and help to mobilize opposition to capitalist exploitation. This puts planners in a contradictory position. Viewed as 'problem solvers' planners may adopt ends of equality and social justice but, in order to serve these ends, they must adopt means (such as encouraging investment) that serve capital. They may also seek to co-opt the leaders of oppositional groups that coalesce around planning policy, in order to facilitate a compromise between these groups and development interests. Nevertheless, planners are also workers and members of a class themselves. They are not outside the class struggle or simply servants of the bourgeoisie. They have some choice in the use of what power and knowledge they possess. If, as Harvey puts it, they can 'step outside' their given social role, if they can recognize the progressive political forces (classes and class alliances), then they can, perhaps, put their power at the disposal of those forces. They can play a different role in developing an ideology that will inform a new, socialist form of planning. The question, however, remains: what are the progressive forces? To answer this question we must look more closely into the matter of class.

The reformulation of class

The Marxian concept of class as a social grouping arising from the exploitative nature of the process of production is, of course, central to Marxian politics. Yet the concept has been acknowledged to be highly problematic by many neo-Marxist scholars, the more so as the prospect of a revolutionary industrial proletariat has receded in the twentieth century (Gorz, 1985). Debates in the 1970s centred on the relationship between class as an abstract relationship between exploiters and exploited in the process of production, and class as descriptive of organized groups of people sharing common economic interests and engaging in political struggle. Political and economic developments in the twentieth century strongly indicated that the transformation of the *economic* class of labour ('class in itself') into a consolidated *political* 'class for itself', led by the revolutionary proletariat, was unlikely to occur. Furthermore, it appeared that political classes could neither be derived from nor reduced to the economic contradiction in capitalism between capital and labour. In the light of Gramsci's analysis a certain consensus on the need to decouple the political from the economic emerged among Marxist critics of class reductionism.

The abandonment of the categories 'capital' and 'labour' as uniquely descriptive of class permits the conceptualization of a variety of distinctive classes, not just 'fractions' or 'factions'. The existence and mode of operation of political actors and the political means by which these actors structure society can be conceptualized independently of economic class. The existence of non-class structures that are far from peripheral can be admitted, and even the connection between person and class can be decoupled so that the possibility can be allowed of a person belonging to more than one class. However, if the whole framework of historical materialism is not to be abandoned some alternative explanation of the dynamic relationship among these elements must be provided. In this respect the concepts of structuration and overdetermination have taken the place of 'forces' in the analysis.

The Marxian critique of reductionism takes the form of alternative readings of Marx, which arguably provide accounts of the phenomena that are consistent with Marx's theory but are more empirically and conceptually plausible than the reductionist reading of the same phenomena. Poulantzas was among the first to decouple political from economic conceptions of class. Although he states that, for theoretical purposes in defining a mode of production 'in a pure and abstract fashion' we find that modes of production involve two classes, the exploiting and exploited, he also disconnects this economic abstraction from the concrete reality of actual class societies. First, he says that wage labour by itself does not constitute classes. Wage labour is merely a judicial form and part of the superstructure: 'a form of distribution of the social product' (Poulantzas, 1975, p. 20). Class positions are designated by the economic 'division of labour' in society. Secondly, he argues that any actual society will be characterized by alliances between classes. But he denies that the classes that can be found in a particular conjuncture (actual society) are factions or fractions of bourgeoisie and proletariat: 'the concepts of "class" and "people" are not coextensive: according to the conjuncture, a class may or may not form part of the "people", without this affecting its class nature.' (p. 33).

Actual groups of people and their interests and perceptions of themselves are shaped by political and ideological factors as well as (and to some degree independently from) the economic division of labour manifested in class positions. This decoupling of the political from the economic conception of class leads Poulantzas to suppose that certain occupational groups may occupy a 'contradictory class position'. For example, technicians and engineers, according to Poulantzas' economic criteria, are part of the working class because they increasingly contribute directly to the production of commodities. Yet political and ideological criteria assign them to a position of special authority in overseeing the labour process and its despotic organization (Poulantzas, 1975, p. 35). Therefore, to that extent they are part of the bourgeoisie. This contradictory position is not a subjective matter concerning which class particular technicians and engineers believe or feel themselves to belong to, but an objective fact of their contradictory position in the economic division of labour.

Hall (1977), in a penetrating and careful analysis of 'the political' in Marx's own works, arrives at three conclusions. First, Marx never intended to imply that political structures (or indeed any observable strata and groupings) necessarily corresponded with the 'objective determinations' of the economic level: 'that the terms and contents of the one [political level] are fully given in the conditions and limits of the other [economic]' (p. 40). The latter merely 'establishes the outer limits, the determinations, the horizons within which the forms of the political arise and appear'. Secondly, there are certain political forces to which no clear class designation corresponds, although their role and support is pivotal. In Marx's *Eighteenth Brumaire* (according to Hall) these are the army, the press, the intellectual celebrities, the priests and the rural population (see Marx,[1848] 1962).

Thirdly, a political grouping (such as a political party or pressure group) may represent the interests of a particular class through the role it plays on the political stage, even though the members of the group may occupy a variety of class positions. A political group is usually a coalition of class interests, but the action the group takes may support or oppose the interests of a class. The example Hall uses is the

Social Democratic Party in France (of the *Eighteenth Brumaire*), which cemented a coalition of proletarian and petty bourgeois interests. This 'party' had its immediate determinations: it advanced, temporarily, the interests of those left aside by the forceful regrouping of bourgeois forces. It had its contradictory internal structure: through their subordination within it the proletariat lost 'their revolutionary point' and gained 'a democratic twist'. Social democracy also had its objective political content: weakening the antagonism between capital and wage labour and transforming it into harmony. It was 'democratic' reform within the limits of bourgeois society. If there is no necessary correspondence between economic class positions and organized groups, it follows that we must be prepared to account for non-class structures or structures in which many class positions are represented. Nevertheless, at any given conjuncture, the political role of such a (non-class) group may (though not 'must') represent a particular class interest.

E. O. Wright explained the plurality of middle-class groups primarily in terms of their structural locations. In his initial formulation of the problem (1976, 1980) he built on Poulantzas' concept of objective structural determination of contradictory class positions. In his analysis of economic class positions he made use of three polar types: bourgeoisie, proletariat and petty bourgeoisie. The last of these he regarded as more than a mere anomalous remnant of an earlier mode of production. Indeed, the three poles emerged from the economic dimensions of domination and subordination within production itself. Wright thus introduced an active and 'political' higher order concept, domination, to explain the nature of class. This strategy enabled him to generate multiple interests from quite simple elements.

In response to criticism that an emphasis on domination moves his analysis away from Marx and towards Weber, and in order to maintain the integrity of a specifically Marxist position, Wright has employed an analysis of class in his more recent work (1984) based on unequal possession and exploitation. Following Roemer (1982), he explains the observable complexity of class positions by the existence of contradictory modes of production in modern capitalism. Roemer argues that class and exploitation inevitably arise from free choice in a system with unequally distributed assets. Class is not dependent, therefore, on the labour contract (see also Roemer, 1988). Capitalist exploitation based on inequality in the distribution of the means of production exists alongside bureaucratic exploitation, based on unequal control of organizational assets, and socialist exploitation based on unequal control of scarce skills.

Political phenomena can then be discussed in terms of coalitions and alliances of class locations and contradictory class locations based on relations not of domination but of exploitation. This reformulation of the problem of the middle classes enables Wright to dispense with the need to introduce non-structural (in the economic sense) concepts to explain the complex phenomena of class structure. However, Wright's new conception of class structure leads him to a radical possibility: that the new middle class and not the proletariat is today's revolutionary class. In feudalism, the critical contradictory location is constituted by the bourgeoisie, the rising class of the successor mode of production. Within capitalism, the central contradictory location within exploitation relations is constituted by managers and state bureaucrats. They embody a principle of class organization that is quite distinct from capitalism and that potentially poses an alternative to capitalist relations. This is particularly true for state managers, who unlike corporate managers are less likely to have their careers tightly integrated with the interests of the capitalist class.

In this conception there is more than one possible historical transition between capitalism and socialism. If this analysis is correct, then urban planners, with other members of their managerial class, are not mere passive supporters of capitalism but, potentially at least, bearers of a new mode of production. This is not altogether far-fetched, for the production of serviced, developable land is already subject to a process that is very different from simple commodity production and exchange.

Wright's argument does not deny the existence and possible importance of non-structural and non-class political groupings of the sort referred to by Hall (1977). Indeed, he observes that it remains problematic whether workers will be formed into a class or into some other sort of collectivity based on religion, ethnicity, region, language, nationality or trade: 'The class structure may define the terrain of material interests upon which attempts at class formation occur, but it does not uniquely determine the outcome of those attempts' (Wright, 1984, p. 404). Taking this point only a small step further, we can say that classes as groups of peopple with political interests are partly, but only partly, shaped by the economic positions that can be deduced from analyses of the power relations inherent in the mode of production. These positions, in all their complexity, are also reciprocally created as a result of actual class and non-class struggles. Even in Marx's day, class struggles between organized groups whose political interests corresponded with their economic position (classes) took place in the context of struggles among groups with no clear 'class' designation. These class and non-class struggles resulted in agreements, pacts, conventions, rules, norms and (with reference to the state) policies, which created new groupings of political interest and constantly shuffled the boundaries among existing groups. The struggle among these new groups in turn produced new responses (agreements, conventions, rules, etc.), which gradually entrenched the position of the dominant class in a hegemonic system. So urban planning practice, even though it contains the elements of an alternative mode of production, can also be viewed as part of a hegemonic system.

But, as Gramsci tells us, a hegemonic system, as opposed to a functionally determinate system, contains contradictions. Przeworski (1980) argues that the hegemonic system of institutionalized rules, acted out daily, shapes the perception and expression of interests. Hegemony becomes constituted when struggles over the realization of material interests become institutionalized in a manner rendering their outcomes to some extent indeterminate with regard to positions that groups occupy within the system of production. It is this kind of organization of social relations that constitutes 'democracy'. Capitalist democracy is a particular form of organization of political relations, in which outcomes and conflict are within certain limits uncertain and, in particular, in which these outcomes are not uniquely determined by class positions (p. 28).

The kinds of struggle that are stimulated by the constitution of pluralist democracy also bring into existence real material interests (things worth struggling for) and actual political groups sharing these interests, which are independent of class interests but are none the less real. At the same time certain kinds of political action are ruled illegitimate and open to being legitimately ignored or suppressed. However, Przeworski's analysis is not aimed primarily at explaining the relationship between class and non-class interests but at demonstrating that 'class compromise' provides the conditions of existence both of a plurality of material interests and of the state. The basis of the compromise is that 'workers consent to the perpetuation of profits as an institution in exchange for the prospect of improving their material welfare within some future period' (Przeworski and Wallerstein, 1982, p. 217). The latter prospect is guaranteed by institutions that would permit workers to process their claims with some chance of success: unions, parties and a relatively autonomous state. In short, 'workers consent to capitalism, capitalists consent to democracy' (p. 218).

In this analysis consent is not a matter of subjective perception nor is compromise a goal. Consent is inherent in action and compromise is an unintended consequence of class struggle. A compromise holds if and only if it is continually in the best interest of workers and capitalists, and only if it is repeatedly remade. A compromise is not a commitment for some indefinite or even limited future; it is an outcome of strategies chosen today, which today appear optimal. If the compromise is to last the day after, it must be made again the day after, and it will be made only if it constitutes the best solution the day after. (Przeworski and Wallerstein, 1982, pp. 218, 219). Capitalist democracy is precarious precisely because it depends on day-to-day compromise, but it is not, as Marx thought, inherently unstable. Although society may be transformed either into forms of capitalist dictatorship or state socialism, the stability of capitalist democracy (such as it is) rests on the constitution of multiple material interests and the capacity of the state to organize the form of compromise and broad electoral support for its particular outcomes.

Resnick and Wolff (1987) argue that, immanent in plural conflict of interest are structures of economic power, and immanent in these structures is the 'class process': 'that in which unpaid surplus labor is pumped out of the direct producers' (Resnick and Wolff, 1987, p. 115). Resnick and Wolff regard the class process as one among many distinctive social processes, which together provide the conditions of existence of each other; in short, each of the distinctive processes in society is 'overdetermined' by the multiple influence of all the rest. Resnick and Wolff do not claim, as many Marxists seem to, that Marxist theory can provide a complete understanding of society. They also locate Marx firmly in the political struggle for human emancipation and against self-perpetuating inequalities of wealth and social standing that constrict and distort the potentialities of human life (p. 279). Marx's contribution, they say, lay in defining, locating and connecting the class process to all the other processes comprising the social totality (p. 279).

The working out of the class process produces a number of economic positions. Classes are 'subdivisions among people according to the particular position they occupy in the class process. People participate in class processes; they therefore occupy class positions' (Resnick and Wolff, 1987, p. 117). The positions are given not only by the pure extraction and receipt of surplus labour and its products but by their distribution and receipt for services rendered in the process: to the landowner, for example, for the supply of land and accommodation, or to the agent of the state (including the urban planner), who mediates between consumption and production or otherwise regulates the process. Class structure (according to Resnick and Wolff) includes both classes and 'subsumed classes', the latter referring to persons occupying the positions of distributors or receivers of the portions of surplus value allocated in order to secure the conditions of existence of the extraction of surplus labour and the accumulation of capital.

Finally, there is an important school of Marxist thought, which postulates that the processes of circulation, reproduction and consumption, rather than production, are responsible for class formation in contemporary capitalism. Thrift and Williams (1987, pp. 7–8) state: 'What is clear, then, is that any analysis of class formation as a historically contingent process arising out of reciprocal actions must step outside the social relations of production and venture into social relations of reproduction. Further, these social relations of reproduction cannot be seen in the narrow sense as just concerned with the reproduction of labour power. Many of them are bent towards reproducing practices which may only tangentially interact with class practices, or, indeed may be divorced from them; culture rears its problematic head'.

John Urry is among the leaders of this school of thought. Urry (1973) began by trying to find in Marx's work a structural explanation for the existence of the middle class. This he found in the proposition that there are two fundamental conditions for the survival of any capitalist system: a mechanism that ensures the realization of profits by maintaining consumption at a higher level than production, and a mechanism for reducing the costs of circulation 'and more specifically the need to have efficient administration of the growing capitalist economy' (p. 178). But, as he says, this proposition is insufficient by itself to explain why middle classes, in particular, arise to fulfil these functions. In subsequent work (Urry, 1981; Abercrombie and Urry, 1983), Urry develops a theoretical formulation of the process of class formation in the course of political struggle in the spheres of circulation of capital and the reproduction of labour. Together these 'spheres' constitute 'civil society'. Civil society is 'that set of social practices outside the state and outside the relations and forces of production in which agents both are constituted as subjects and which presuppose the actions of such subjects – first, in the sphere of circulation directly; second, in those social relations within which labour-power is reproduced economically, biologically and culturally; and, third, in the resultant class and democratic forces' (Urry, 1981, p. 31).

According to Urry it is erroneous to characterize 'class' as pertaining to abstract economic positions. Classes only exist 'at the level of' civil society. That is, the term 'class' only comes to have meaning in the context of the circulation of capital, when buyers and sellers of commodities, including labour, interact with one another. Despite Urry's claim to a position 'having more affinities to the Marxist than the Weberian position' (Urry 1981, p. 26), this formulation is a reinterpretation of Weber in Marxist language. Accordingly, Urry has no difficulty in demonstrating that many different factors bear on the formation of political interests and political groups: (in descending order of importance) spatial organization of labour and residence; sexual division of labour; religion/ethnic/racial 'allocation of subjects'; differentiation on the basis of secondary groups such as trades unions, professional associations and voluntary groups; and 'general allocation of subjects', a category which is presumably intended to allow for individual distinctions (p. 70). The family is at once a refuge from capitalist competitive social relations and one of the non-capitalist forms of production that makes capitalism possible by subjecting women to marginalized labour and the domination of men.

Abercrombie and Urry (1983) discuss the distinction between classes as economic positions (class places) and classes as groups of people. The authors reject a radical distinction between 'places' and 'persons' as postulated by Poulantzas, arguing instead that 'although classes are constituted as places, class practices are partly determined by the characteristics of persons who fill those places, characteristics determined by a number of determinants outside class places' (p. 109). Additionally, both market (exchange relations) and work situations (production relations) determine class places. Thus 'the mechanisms of the capitalist mode of production require the functions of conceptualization, control and reproduction to be performed and they produce sets of places comprising specific market and work situations which we call classes' (p. 126). So both a plurality of functions and a plurality of non-class factors combine to produce a plurality of groups of persons.

Urry is really saying that classes are constituted of acting subjects, individuals in effect. The subject's consciousness of her/his political position is given by many social factors, including the social relations stemming from the capitalist mode of production and, in particular, the culture and ideology of the society. Urry's analysis both works down to the individual from the social level and up to the social from the individual level. Marrying collectivism with individualism in this way makes it permissible to consider that an individual may have interests in both capital and labour simultaneously as well as in other non-class structures. Therefore, since there is no such thing as a 'pure' individual, there is also no such thing as a pure class. In keeping with Marxist language, however, Urry turns the matter round: 'Capitalists and workers are categories of subject produced within civil society and such classes are fissured by the bases of structuration present within civil society. There are no pure classes of capitalists and workers existing outside the forms of differentiation effective within civil society. And further, within civil society there are other 'classes-in-struggle' [a concept of Laclau's] and popular democratic forces and struggles' (Abercrombie and Urry, p. 106).

Unfortunately, this is confusing. If there are no pure classes, and if classes cannot exist outside the political domain of acting subjects, can it be said that there really are such things as classes, in the Marxian sense, at all? The only way out of this conceptual problem is to postulate, via realist epistemology, an underlying 'mechanism' similar to Resnick's and Wolff's 'class process', which acts on individuals. However, the mechanism need not be considered 'underlying' or hidden at all. It would be much simpler to say that class is one of the many institutionalized relationships in which individuals are enmeshed. 'Class' is the term given by Marxist theory to a cluster of very fundamental social rules structuring work and property relationships. If we take this step we should reserve the term 'class' for that cluster alone. Therefore, it would be incorrect to talk of 'consumption classes' or indeed a 'service class' (Abercrombie and Urry, 1983; Thrift, 1987). Rather, we should say that capitalism, in the course of its development, with state 'polyarchy' (Dahl and Lindblom, 1953) and mass consumption, has constituted many different organized groups and social strata, but the fundamental work and property relationships remain unchanged. In all this we have returned more than half way to Weber and pluralism.

The political role of the planner cannot be fully understood simply as legitimating capitalism and smoothing the process of capitalist exploitation. The role of urban planners as state officials need not be viewed as derivative of the relationship between the bourgeoisie and proletariat. Indeed, Wright (1984) argues that managers and state bureaucrats occupy the pivotal contradictory class location in late capitalism. Because this managerial class represents an alternative mode of exploitation to that of capitalism, its members (and not the proletariat) constitute the revolutionary class. Such a view is obviously debatable, not least because state and private sector bureaucrats would seem to share little in the way of economic interest. Hoff (1985) points out that the capitalist state apparatus is itself divided on class lines between the 'classical' bureaucracy concerned with the efficient development, management and control of capitalist economies (the army, the law, public finance, etc.) and the 'welfare' bureaucracy, including health, educational and social services and environmental agencies. This view recalls the earlier arguments of Cawson and Saunders (1983) on the 'dual state' (see chapter 6 p. 147). At all events the political role of the state bureaucrat seems both pivotal and problematic in the light of a non-reductionist class perspective.

The reformulation of the state and politics

The economic crisis of the 1970s, which led to the replacement of the 'Keynesian consensus' by neo-liberalism in the United States, Britain, West Germany and elsewhere, also gave rise to a reformulation of Marxist theory of the state. Capitalism survived the crisis, as it had survived all previous crises, and analytical attention turned from the crisis tendencies and inherent contradictions in capitalism to its capacity to survive and regenerate in new forms. What has become known as the 'regulation' school (initiated by Aglietta, 1979) asked 'how capitalism could survive even though the capital relation itself inevitably generated antagonisms and crises which made continuing accumulation improbable' (Jessop, 1988, p. 149). Jessop continues: 'They found an answer in specific institutional forms, societal norms, and patterns of strategic conduct which both expressed and regulated these conflicts until the inevitable tensions and divergencies among these various regulatory forms reached crisis point.' A particular mode of regulation is 'the outcome of social and political struggles which stabilise to form a *hegemonic* system – class alliances, based on consensus armoured by coercion, which shape the interests both of the ruling and dominated classes into conformity with the accumulation regime' (Jessop, 1988, p. 150). An 'accumulation regime' is a particular combination of modes of production and consumption, which can be sustained in particular circumstances despite conflictual tendencies (see Lipietz, 1985, pp. xvi, xvii). Aglietta (1979) based his initial analysis on the flowering of 'Fordism' in the United States after the Second World War, but this was later extended to include the experience of France and West Germany (Aglietta, 1982). Other Marxist scholars have used a regulationist approach in different ways to explain the different forms of capitalism arising in different nations (see, for example, Boyer, 1979; Gordon, 1980; Lipietz, 1982; Davis, 1988; Ominami, 1986; Beaud, 1987; Jessop, 1988, pp. 163–5).

Bonefeld (1987) connects regulationist theory with the 'reformulation' of state theory developed by the German theorists Hirsch, Esser and Roth (see Hirsch, 1980, 1983, 1984; Esser, 1982; Esser and Hirsch, 1984; Hirsch and Roth, 1986). Crisis tendencies in capitalism act as the motive force for the construction of varying forms of state and varying institutionalized relationships between the state, capital and labour. A particular mode of domination 'corresponds' to a particular regime of accumulation. This historical 'correspondence' is, following Gramsci, characterized as a 'historic bloc': 'a peculiar ensemble of class relations and social forms, together with a particular hegemonic structure or hegemonic project' (Bonefeld, 1987, p. 102). The state is viewed as central to the reproduction and integration of capitalist society. The state rather than the capital relation becomes the main generator of struggle and resistance. Therefore, social movements arising in response to state initiatives tend to replace classes as the main political actors. Here we can see a link with Weber and the institutional pluralists. Bonefeld criticizes reformulation theory for its economic determinism, pointing out that the German theorists identify Marx's law of the tendency of the rate of profit to fall as being at the core of the development of the state. The role of class struggle is separated from that of structural (economic) development, with the implication that the former is always subordinated to the latter: 'In this view the scope of struggle is subordinated to the law-determined path of development which provides the "environment" for struggle' (Bonefield, 1987, p. 105). The state appears as a functional necessity for the reproduction of capitalist social relations, which underplays the role of state institutions as mediating contradictory social relations (pp. 106, 107).

Jessop defends regulation theory and the reformulation of state theory on three main grounds. First, he argues that the theory postulates a real material-dialectical process, involving both 'structure' and 'struggle', which is expressed in Gramsci's concept of 'historic bloc': 'a configuration of economic base and political and ideological superstructures that are mutually supportive and co-evolving and whose coherence depends on specific practices rather than deriving from the objective laws of capitalist development' (Jessop, 1988, p. 152). Accumulation regimes and modes of regulation are always the product of past struggles and always penetrated with current struggles. Once accumulation regimes have become relatively stable they form the terrain on which particular forms of struggle take place. But there is no guarantee that struggles will always be contained within these institutional forms and/or resolved in ways that reproduce them. So 'regulation involves a set of temporary institutional solutions which contain and limit the basic conflicts of capitalism but cannot do so for ever' (p. 151). Secondly, Jessop argues that the German reformulationists *avoided* deriving the form of the capitalist state from the functions it must perform in correcting market failure, compensating for economic crisis and mediating class struggle. On the contrary, 'the activities of the state are determined in the first instance by political considerations and need not coincide (even in the last instance) with the 'needs' of the economy' (p. 155). There are, in fact, no unambiguous economic needs. The needs of capital must be assessed strategically in relation to complex conjunctures rather than formally in terms of an abstract, purely economic circuit of capital (Jessop, 1988, and Jessop *et al.*, 1984). Such a view opens the way to analysis (as Gramsci suggests) of every nation or region in terms of its peculiar social, political and institutional characteristics.

Thirdly, pursuing his own contribution to reformulation theory, Jessop proposes a 'dialectic between structure and strategy'. Jessop uses the terms 'strategy' and 'project' to denote types or levels (which is not entirely clear) of intentional political action. An accumulation regime and hegemonal structure are the complex outcome of many strategies and projects, which have been implemented in the past and are currently under way. Jessop, therefore, prefers the term 'ensemble' to denote the accretion of the institutional outcomes of the strategies and projects of political actors. There can be no general strategy on the part of the bourgeoisie or any other class to maintain an accumulation regime; indeed there are always competing strategies (which may, presumably, be advocated by different groups). The accumulation regime, the hegemonal structure or ensemble is simply what emerges, with its unintended consequences, from past political struggle and is what provides the ground rules of current political struggle. Thus, says Jessop (1988, pp. 157, 158):

> Both the structural and the strategic moments are complex and changeable: the boundaries and articulation of structural ensembles are unstable, the world of strategies is pluralistic and conjunctural. Their dialectic is nothing more (and nothing less) than the structural conditioning of strategies (both as explicit reference points for strategic calculation and as a partly and partially unacknowledged set of structural constraints and conjunctural opportunities) and the strategic transformation of structural ensembles (both through deliberate, if often unsuccessful, attempts to modify them and through unanticipated consequences of interaction among patterns of strategic conduct with other objectives).

The 1970s and 1980s appeared to many Marxists to be a period of fundamental transition, not merely in the political superstructure and dominant ideology but in the capitalist mode of production and consumption itself. Lash and Urry (1987) viewed the transition as a movement from 'organized' to 'disorganized' capitalism. They argue that, with the rise of a new middle class, a service class, the working class has become fragmented; the integration of the interests of capital and labour via the agency of the state has begun to break down and corporations have been thrown back into market competition. The term 'disorganized', however, seems problematic when applied to capital. Lash and Urry do not regard the market as an organizing institution. They note that the effectiveness of the nation state as an organizing force has been reduced, but that new sub-national and international institutions are appearing. They claim that within nations the process of concentration of capital has been reversed but, on the other hand, 'a central role has been played by the emergence of giant corporations within certain industrial sectors, corporations whose attachment to any national territory is limited and who are able to subdivide their operations so taking advantage of variations in operating conditions across the globe' (Lash and Urry, 1987, p. 306). This does not sound like disorganization but reorganization. Claus Offe's analysis of the rules regarding capital–labour relationships (1985) lends some support to Lash's and Urry's contention of the disorganization of the working class. But Offe also challenges the postulate of an 'organized capitalism' (originally put forward by Hilferding in 1910). He shows that capitalist rules institutionalize an asymmetry of power between workers and firms, so that the latter have (and have always had) a greater need to organize and a smaller capacity to do so.

A more political view of the transition than that of Lash and Urry is offered by the reformulationists. Aglietta (1979, p. 382) used Gramsci's term 'Fordism' to characterize the postwar development of an intrinsically capitalist mode of consumption, 'formed and structured by the mass production of standardized commodities' made possible by the intensive Taylorist organization of assembly-line work. The specifically Fordist form of the state is the Keynesian, corporatist, statist, welfare state, which emerged to secure the expanded reproduction of the workforce during the crisis of Fordist accumulation (Bonefeld, 1987, p. 110). The welfare state integrates society on the basis of individual claimants: home owners, tenants, unemployed, car drivers, etc. (London Edinburgh Weekend Return Group, 1980). Its policies tend to channel class struggle into a pluralist struggle for distributive shares.

In the 1980s capitalism was seen to be moving into a post-Fordist phase, though quite what post-Fordism might mean, whether it is possible yet to discern the features of a new regime of accumulation, or even whether the future direction of capitalism is yet determined, are matters of debate. In Britain, Thatcherism was interpreted by Stuart Hall (1983) as a new hegemonic project, which he terms 'authoritarian populism', and by Jessop *et al.* (1984) in terms of a 'two nations' hegemonic strategy. Hall (1983, p. 29) observes, 'Thatcherite populism is a particularly rich mix. It combines the resonant themes of organic Toryism – nation, family, duty, authority, standards, traditionalism – with the aggressive themes of a revived neo-liberalism – self-interest, competitive individualism, anti-statism'. Jessop *et al.* warn (and Hall, 1985, concedes) that Thatcherism should not be regarded as an achieved project but rather 'as an alliance of disparate forces around a self-contradictory programme' (Jessop *et al.*, 1984, p. 38). However, others point to the disorganization of the Labour opposition (Hobsbawm, 1978) and argue rather that Thatcherism merely represents the return of class politics (Jacques and Mulhern, 1981; Benn, 1985). Hirsch (1985) finds in 'post-Fordism' a characteristic division of the workforce into a well qualified and well paid core and an individualized, marginalized, non-unionized mass, with low income, short-term employment contracts and poor working conditions. He thus agrees with Jessop in portraying a new polarization of society. The Post-Fordist state, despite its rhetoric, is a strong state deeply penetrating society; politics is transformed into a marketing strategy and parties into public relations agencies.

Bonefeld (1987, p. 121) criticizes the reformulationists' analysis of post-Fordism for attempting to generalize from what are in reality very varied experiences of the state and politics in different countries. Both Fordism and post-Fordism become, in his view, abstractions, which gloss over important differences among, for example, the British, American, Japanese and German systems. Further, in identifying a new phase of capitalism, there is a danger of reifying what is merely an analytical category and thereby closing off certain avenues of class struggle because they do not fit the new reality. The British miners' strike, for example, was represented by Hirsch as 'an anachronistic attempt to preserve the old unionism which is inadequate in the world of populist new realism' (Hirsch, 1985, p. 117; for a contrary view, see Holloway, 1987). Jessop (1988) is sympathetic to Bonefeld's criticism, agreeing that there is no single model either of Fordism or post-Fordism; the abstractions must be specified in terms of national models of capitalist growth. Until they are specified, it should be added, and until we know more precisely what different nations have in common, we cannot know for sure whether the abstract terms have any real meaning. Also, Jessop points out, 'If national roads and the eventual form of national post-Fordism depend on the course of class struggle within the structural conditions established by an initial starting point, then there may be nothing inevitable about the transition at all' (p. 161).

The significance of the reformulation of state theory for urban planning is its attempt to theorize the relationship between structural conditions and political agency, and how each determines the other. The practice of urban planning in particular places and cultures feeds into the structure, which conditions that practice. But, of course, the precise nature of this structure is determined by many other inputs from many other practices. This understanding resonates with the recognition by pluralists of the relationship between 'the game' and 'the rules'. The understanding that practices determine structure (as well as vice-versa) accounts for the many geographical variations in forms of capitalism. It also returns to the practitioner, in this case the urban planner, a degree of responsibility for what happens. Certainly, planners are faced with appalling dilemmas, but recognition of these dilemmas need not lead to paralysis, because the possibilities of improvement remain open: that is, improvement of the urban condition in the light of the values of freedom, justice, equality and democracy. Planners sympathetic to Marxist analysis can engage in the struggle over ends and means without feeling that the outcome is predetermined or that their own position is tarnished by their class location. All that Marxist theorists demand is that the urge to immediate action should be balanced by a reflective critique of its structural conditions, conditions that always include the economic exploitation of society by the owners and controllers of wealth.

Conclusion

In the first section of this chapter some of the basic normative positions of Marx and Engels were discussed. It was argued that a certain conception of freedom and justice is embedded in Marxian thought. This conception ultimately concerns the emancipation of the individual. For Marx and Engels, class solidarity and revolution are the political means to individual emancipation, but not ends in themselves. They are, however, *not* the means that have characterized political action in the advanced industrial societies in the twentieth century. Marxist analysis has gradually come to terms with the plural politics and the varying institutional outcomes that *are* characteristic of these societies. In subsequent sections, we considered the way in which Marxian analysis has dealt with a changing capitalist dynamic, which Marx and Engels themselves did not and could not have foreseen. This analysis reconciles a plural reality with the central perceptions of Marx concerning the source of exploitation and domination, namely, in the relationship known as 'capital'. Like all other political analysis, Marxist analysis is fraught with debates and arguments. There is no comforting consensus. Yet such a consensus would hardly be Marxian.

Marxist urban analysis seeks to explain how it is that injustice, exploitation and concomitant poverty, environmental squalor and degradation enter into the process of urban development. But there is no message in Marxism about how to be a better urban planner. When urban planners reach the conclusion that there is nothing substantial that they can do, within the current rules and norms of their particular part of capitalist society, to improve urban conditions and solve urban problems, Marxists (e.g. Harvey, 1985, p. 184) invite them to step outside the roles given to them by those rules and norms. Such a step may well be demanded by conditions in some of the cities in America and Britain today. This is not just a failure of planning, but a wholesale failure of political structures that are supposed to enable people through legitimate political struggle to improve their conditions of life. Gottdiener (1987) has announced the death of democratic politics at the local level in the United States. Without intervention by the state, as occurred in the 1960s, people living in extreme poverty have little hope of mobilizing to press demands for improvement. Existing democratic structures simply reflect the biases in society in favour of the powerful.

'Stepping outside' their role does not, of course, mean that planners should give up their jobs, simply that planners should start thinking of the city as citizens. This extends planners' thinking beyond their job descriptions. Marxism suggests three further steps that the urban planner should take. First, become aware of the societal rules that limit the possibility of action and that define and constrain the role of the planner. These rules must become the target for change. Second, become aware of the class to which you belong: that is, look to the people, in the widest sense, who share your values and interests. Third, mobilize for action (in accordance with those values and interests) with members of your class and all available allies, with all the power at your disposal, including the power, however circumscribed, that the institution of urban planning affords. The strong implication of modern Marxist thought (influenced by Gramsci) is that, if society is to be changed, those who wish to change it must themselves be prepared to fight for what they believe in and not wait for some other 'force' or other actors, such as the working class, to do it for them.

Such political action is, of course, always problematic. As Gottdiener (1987, p. 268) observes: 'When local political culture has died, it can only be resurrected from outside. All other changes are doomed to be coopted within the encapsulating, totalizing logic of State power. As with the case of mobilization against capital, how one gets outside a globalizing system while being caught within it is a puzzle of some magnitude.' But when it comes to political action, there is no 'outside'. The only hope for change is to work with whatever political resources exist in the surrounding environment of the political actor. Marxism draws our attention to the importance of periods of crisis in capitalist economies in creating conditions in which structural change involving re-negotiation of the rules becomes easier. In the next chapter, we turn to a school of thought that casts a different light on the problematic of capitalism and its crises, on the role of 'critique', and on the nature of human emancipation and its ethic.

9 Critical theory: state, politics and rationality

We have seen how Gramsci wanted to re-establish the position of the political actor, the acting subject, in the historical process of social development. He did so from the perspective of one who was constantly involved in political action. From quite a different practical standpoint, this same theme unites the very varied work of the critical theorists. Critical theory is, however, the product of a contemplative, scholarly and academic practice. Its central concern is the theory of political action and the relationship of 'action theory' to the critique of society.

The unfolding of events in the Soviet Union and in Western capitalism in the first half of this century made such a project unavoidable. On the one hand, a Marxist revolution had produced a society that was patently unfree and undemocratic. On the other, capitalism, which was portrayed by orthodox Marxism as in the last stages of imperialist decay, had gained a new momentum that apparently provided greater prosperity and permitted greater freedom than Soviet society. Critical theory had to confront these developments with honesty and integrity if any fundamental opposition to capitalism was to be kept alive in the West. In particular, the relationship between theory and practice had to be reconsidered and this, in turn, necessitated a re-examination of the epistemological status of theory. The project of retrieving the role of the subject and reconstituting the terrain of political action was not to be undertaken at the cost of a return to the idea of transcendental consciousness. A new and closer relationship had to be worked out between the objective world with its causal explanations and functional systems, and the intersubjective 'lifeworld' with its moral arguments and practical reason. But the one must not be submerged into the other, either with primacy being given to the material world, as in Marx, or to consciousness, as in Hegel. These 'philosophies of identity' were precisely what seemed most to threaten subjective autonomy.

Critical theory is relevant to urban planning in its reflexive examination of the critique of society. It explores the meaning and purpose behind dissenting theory and warns planners against the tendency to believe too uncompromisingly in their own images of social improvement. Culture and language are brought into central focus as well as the rules and procedures constituted in the practice of planning. In Habermas's 'systems' view, conflict over the production and consumption of developed land is thrust upon the state. Urban planning is the structure that has evolved to enable the state to cope with this conflict by depoliticizing it and rendering it a 'professional' matter. In his 'lifeworld' critique of rationality, Habermas develops new universal criteria for political interaction, based on the assumptions inherent in the practice of communication. Some of the prescriptive implications of these criteria for planning have been explored by Forester and others, although the danger exists of such prescriptions, like other formulae for 'public participation', turning into a new ideology of planning practice, legitimating an unequal power structure. Ultimately, a radically different planning practice is unlikely to emerge until there is radical change in the political organization of the economy.

The Frankfurt School

In 1923, still only a short time after the Bolshevik Revolution and the revolutionary insurgency in Europe, a wealthy grain merchant, Felix Weil, put together the means to establish the Institute for Social Research at Frankfurt in Germany. Although financially independent, thanks to Weil, the Institute was formally attached to the University of Frankfurt, which gave it academic status. The Institute's first director was Carl Grünberg, a Marxist who had previously held a chair in law and political science at the University of Vienna. In his six years as director, Grünberg set out an academic strategy for the Institute, which was broadly followed and built upon by his successor and early member of the Institute, Max Horkheimer.

This strategy, derived from Marx's conception of society, brought together scholars of many different disciplines who shared a belief in Marx's principles and a desire to develop and extend them. Many scholars made their own quite distinctive contributions to the work of the Frankfurt Institute and took varying and, in some cases, conflicting methodological and substantive positions on a number of topics. Yet there emerged a definite school of thought in the neo-Marxian tradition, that of 'critical social theory', which united them. No doubt this overall coherence owed something to both Grünberg's and Horkheimer's specification of the central questions to be addressed and the philosophical and empirical treatment of these questions.

Horkheimer wished to place the 'great philosophical questions' concerning the relationship between the individual and society, the meaning of culture, etc., in their proper historical, social and economic context. But he did not regard social phenomena, including meanings and ideas, as deducible from 'material being' – that is, from economic production. He believed that no single disciplinary perspective could provide an adequate interpretation of society and that no one method could produce 'definitive results'. He insisted that the Institute's members must explore the question of the 'interconnection between the economic life of society, the psychic development of the individual and transformations in the realm of culture . . . including not only the spiritual contents of science, art and religion, but also law, ethics, fashion, public opinion, sport, amusement, life-style, etc' (Held, 1980, p. 33, quoting Horkheimer, 1931).

Two major themes are to be found in critical theory that are relevant to the theory of the state and of planning: the critique of freedom and the stabilization of capitalism. In the first place, planning is seen as a component of the political action necessary to realize freedom. In the second, capitalist planning is seen as a means of consolidating bourgeois domination through bureaucratic procedures and ideology. These interwoven themes are most systematically developed in the work of Marcuse, but we shall also have to consider, by way of warning, Adorno's critique of critique.

Adorno and Marcuse

In critical theory we see a shift in neo-Marxist thought from the offensive (as in Gramsci) to the defensive: from the struggle *for* communism to the struggle *against* domination. The Marxist struggle had hitherto been about changing society in order to usher in an era of self-evident human freedom and self-determination. For the critical theorists, the struggle against domination required not so much ideological struggle as 'immanent critique', that is, the critique of systems of political ideas on the basis of the axioms on which these systems were themselves founded. For both Adorno and Marcuse this project meant exposing the gap between a concept – such as freedom – and the reality. If capitalist society or Soviet socialism purported to enable people to be free, then how free were they really, and if they were not, what prevented them from being free? These two theorists, however, differed in their understanding of the nature of critique and in their critical strategy.

Marcuse took 'freedom' to be a transcendental concept, which he could use as a yardstick against which to evaluate a particular historical reality. This approach distanced him somewhat from Marx. Adorno viewed a 'materialist philosophical critique' as problematic and somewhat paradoxical. 'No philosophy', he observed, 'not even extreme empiricism can drag in the *facta bruta* and present them like cases in anatomy or experiments in physics' (Adorno, [1966]

1973, p. 11). Nevertheless, all philosophical concepts referred to a non-conceptual reality in some way. Philosophy necessarily operated with concepts, but there was a constant tendency to 'fetishize' the concept, to assume an *identity* of the concept with the reality, and it was this 'identity thinking' that a genuine critique had to struggle against. Such thinking, both in capitalist and Soviet society, assumed an identity of the *concept* of freedom inherent in their respective ideologies with the *reality*. Plainly, a 'materialist' critique could be as guilty of this naïve fetishism as any transcendental idealism.

A materialist critique must, therefore, always let us know that 'the concept is a concept even when dealing with things in being'; and that on its part a concept is entwined with reality (Adorno, [1966] 1973, p. 12). Adorno's discussion of freedom illustrates this approach to critique. 'Freedom' and the principle of 'individuality' in capitalist societies are closely associated concepts. They are not primary facts, but arise from a particular material historical context. But neither are they mere illusions, for they have real consequences. One consequence is the real separation of the person from society. Given that the person opposes himself to society as a being capable of rationally pursuing his own interest, the 'genuine' question arises 'whether society permits the individual to be as free as it promises; and thus . . . the question whether society itself is as free as it promises' (p. 219). These are, Adorno says, genuine questions, because they invite exploration of the distance between the concept and the reality. However, implicit in this very exploration – and herein lies the danger of transcendental critique – is the conclusion that the individual is *really* separable from the social context, from society. The assumption of a 'windowless isolation' of the individual helps to reproduce a society whose very social operation is predicated upon just such isolation. From this point of view, *any* conceptualization, even one employed in critique, has a tendency to reproduce the historical context in which it occurs. Only by constantly subjecting critique to critique in a ruthless reflexivity of argument could we hope to shine some light between concept and reality without giving rise to new ideological justifications of new forms of domination.

This project Adorno pursued by means of a particular style of writing, which organized a series of commentaries from different viewpoints around a central theme. This style makes for a certain repetitiveness and lack of development. As Jay (1984, p. 162) remarks, 'a lengthy journey through the thicket of Adorno's prose does give the impression of passing the same landmarks with uncomfortable frequency'. Adorno's prose style and his assumption of a broad knowledge of philosophy on the part of the reader make his work difficult to cope with. What is important is the warning it sounds against all closed systems of ideas. This warning is the more convincing because it was consistently applied to his own work.

Marcuse's critical strategy was more traditionally didactic and, perhaps for that reason, more easily grasped. Marcuse sought to expose the reasons for the degeneration in practice of the idea of freedom in the Soviet Union and in Western capitalism. He considered the claim of liberal political economy that objective rationality would be realized through the competition of 'reasonably freely functioning' individual enterprises (Marcuse, 1958). The qualities required of the individual: autonomy, foresight, perspicacity and so forth, had to be learned 'not only in the actual business of living but in the preparation for it: in the family, in school, in the privacy of thinking and feeling'. However the rational organization of nature by means of technological 'progress' threw up an exactly opposite tendency. Mass labour was increasingly subjected to a work process shaped by the requirements both of the machine and 'factory discipline' (cf. Weber's views on bureaucracy). Time was now freed by increased productivity, but this time was defined as 'leisure'. The increased time available to the individual was not spent by the masses in creative self-development through work but in 'relaxation from and preparation for labour in conformity with the apparatus'. Therefore, the time seemingly gained for the individual was immediately subjected to the same domination inherent in the organization of the work process.

For Marcuse, then, class domination in the mode of production was less salient than technological domination in the process of production. In this respect Weber seems to have been a greater influence than Marx. The reduction of individual autonomy and subjective reason to the collective rationality of a socio-political apparatus, he thought, was common to all advanced industrial societies, both socialist and capitalist, though in different ways. On the socialist side, class conflict had produced a revolution in Russia which, far from resulting in the increased level of individual autonomy promised by communism, had succeeded only in creating an even more oppressive and total conformity. Marcuse traced the direction of the post-revolutionary phase in Russia to the explicit intentions and beliefs of the philosophers and leaders of the Revolution. He cited Marx's observation that: 'The first phase of socialism still chains the worker to his specialized function, still preserves the "enslaving subordination of individuals under the division of labour", and thereby the antagonism between rationality and freedom' (Marcuse, 1958, p. 20, quoting Marx, [1875] 1962).

The suppression of individual self-realization in pursuit of the most rational way of developing society led Lenin and subsequently Stalin to give first priority in the development of Soviet society to raising industrial productivity to the level of the Western nations. This entailed developing the means of production and the means of military self-sufficiency and security. In so doing, Soviet society became entrapped in a dynamic of competition with Western nations, which tied it ever more closely to the technological demands of production. Meanwhile, capitalism had changed in ways that enabled it to endure crises and further develop its productive capacity. The growth of Soviet military and industrial power played a continuing role in unifying the capitalist nations and rationalizing the peace-time growth of the armaments industry.

Unlike Gramsci's socialism, Soviet socialism never seriously involved dialogue with the working class. Rule was from above by way of a hierarchical party–state apparatus. The only permitted action was obedience to that apparatus. Therefore, the transformation of Soviet socialism into communism could easily be 'performed' by proclamation of the authorities, thus postponing indefinitely its real occurrence. Indeed, as Marcuse observed, in the Soviet Union the withering away of the coercive state was portrayed by Stalin in terms of the necessity for *increased* state power and control.

Turning to the critique of capitalist society, Marcuse endeavoured to show how the freedom proclaimed as the ethical basis of Western liberalism was cancelled in practice 'by the rigidity of prescribed behaviour patterns, by the standardization of required work performance; or it involves a risk which the majority of the people cannot afford to take (risk of unemployment, of falling behind, of becoming an outsider and so forth)' (Marcuse, 1958, p. 205). Freedom in Western society had been, in practice, *redefined* and had entailed 'the surrender of the "natural" liberty of the individual to the civil liberty of being able to do what is not prohibited by law . . . The standards of freedom are shifted from the autonomous individual to the laws governing the society which governs the individual' (p. 206). The rationality of the whole was in fact not the rationality of freedom but that of *security*. Paradoxically, although security was necessary for freedom, the pursuit of security also conflicted with freedom. Freedom was inhibited in Western society not only by residual insecurity and the unjust sharing out of freedom but also by the very organization that guaranteed a certain level of security.

In *Soviet Marxism* (1958) Marcuse took the view that there was still a live conflict in Western capitalism that ensured the preservation of a certain domain of autonomy for the individual. In the later *One Dimensional Man* (1964,) which was oriented more towards cultural than economic aspects of capitalist society, he was much more pessimistic and depicted capitalist society as gripped by a positive, rosy image of itself, which paralysed criticism and rendered acceptable the most appalling underlying facts of existence: 'Auschwitz continues to haunt not the memory but the accomplishments of man – the space flights; the rockets and missiles; the labyrinthine basement under the Snack Bar; the pretty electronic plants, clean, hygienic and with flower beds; the poison gas which is not really harmful to people; the secrecy in which we all participate' (Marcuse, 1964, p. 193). The one-dimensional illusion was constructed and maintained in every cultural and political domain by the linguistic reconciliation of opposites, the positive solution of every problem, the absorption of every protest, the resolution of every antinomy. In this constructed reality true opposition was presented as false and irrational. The dynamics of a class-based society produced a type of enslavement to technology that draws into its net even those societies (such as the Soviets) that have put an end to class rule. In this respect, Marcuse regarded capitalism as a global rather than just a hemispheric economic system.

Problem-solving and the resolution of conflict in a positive manner leading to *solutions* is, of course, precisely what 'planning' does, in the sense of a purposive rationality. Marcuse's critique is, to that extent, a critique of planning. Yet he did not seek to abolish planning. On the contrary, he said that those who opposed central planning in the name of liberal democracy did so merely to further their own class interests. 'The goal of authentic self-determination by the individuals depends on effective social control over the production and distribution of the necessities' (Marcuse, 1964, p. 196). The critical theorists who approached the subject of a new radical democracy, particularly Marcuse and Horkheimer, avoided specifying its structure. To do that, they thought, would impinge on the rights of the citizens who would be fully involved in its creation. 'Plans cannot be forced on others through power or through routine, but must be arrived at through free agreement' (Horkheimer, 1973, p. 17, quoted in Held, 1980, p. 46). Nevertheless, they had a definite image of such a society.

A machine-like productive system under central control, and therefore no longer the site of class conflict, would routinely satisfy all the material requirements of life with the maximum use of technology and the minimum of human labour. This productive machine would be accountable to a decentralized network of councils representing workers and consumers. Marcuse had in mind a society of groups of people with voluntary membership; people who, being attracted to one another, would join together to pursue goals they themselves would collectively decide upon and enjoy pursuing; a society where co-operation, work and sensuous pleasure would be combined. Marcuse refers to Fourier's conception of '*attraction passionnée*' in human nature, which drew people together for purposes of luxury, sensuous pleasure and the delight in joint endeavour (Marcuse, [1955] 1969, p. 174). Taking the USA as the paradigm, Marcuse came to believe that radical social change under capitalism was only a remote possibility, 'given the power and efficiency of the system, the thorough assimilation of mind with fact, of thought with required behaviour, of aspirations with reality' (Marcuse, 1964, p. 196). The only conceivable revolutionary subject was the substratum of outcasts and outsiders, the exploited and persecuted of other races and colours, the unemployed and unemployable. However, Marcuse's hope, which he pinned on the protest movements of the 1960s, was not in the end realized and, arguably, could not be.

The themes that formed the basis of Marcuse's critique were all fore-shadowed by other members of the Frankfurt Institute. In Pollock's work (1941a, 1941b) there is the suggestion that new forms of state capitalism both fascist and democratic were potentially capable of overcoming the inherent contradictions of capitalism. The rise of technical rationality, bureaucratic structures and comprehensive planning by the state would enable capitalism to survive its tendencies towards economic crisis. There is an awareness of Keynesian planning, sympathy with Weber's prognosis and parallels with the neo-corporatist analyses of Schmitter and Lehmbruch and the Marxist 'regulationist' school, rather than with the more orthodox Marxist theories of state monopoly capitalism. Horkheimer (1974) observed the growing division in the ranks of the German working class between the unemployed (or underemployed), whose miserable conditions gave them the greatest incentive for revolutionary action, and the majority of workers, who now enjoyed a certain security of life. The former might gain from revolution, but were disorganized and lacked leadership and class consciousness. The latter, organized labour, came to fear unemployment and, at least in the short run, faced uncertainty and risk in revolution.

Cultural solidarity in capitalism was underpinned by what critical theorists called the 'culture industry'. The term displayed a concern with the commodity production of so-called 'popular' culture, rather than with the organizational and intellectual culture dealt with by Gramsci and Althusser. The culture industry shaped mass attitudes, encouraging acceptance of society and its commodities through images and myth and dulling criticism. In popular culture, public problems such as the effects of economic crises, inflation and unemployment were internalized and individualized. Commercial entertainment offered escape from the world, diverting attention from the need to change it. Communication among individuals was increasingly standardized and trivialized. Stereotyped models of the successful person were purveyed, demonstrating the paradoxical achievement of individuality through conformity: that is, through consumption of standardized commodities each of which 'affects an individual air' (Horkheimer and Adorno, 1972).

The Frankfurt School undertook three projects of importance both to dissenting theory and to urban planning. First, the question of culture was brought firmly on to the agenda of dissenting thought. The concern with culture has since become something of an obsession with 'post-modernist' dissenters (see Nelson and Grossberg, 1988), but as Harvey (1989, p. 355) observes, the development was a positive one for Marxist theory: 'Aesthetic and cultural practices matter, and the conditions of their production deserve the closest attention.' Urban planners have always had to deal with images and have produced quite a few of their own: green belts and new towns, city centres recalling Italian city squares and hill towns, the romance of the rural lifestyle, 'spaceship Earth' and 'the environment'. These images cannot be dismissed as some product of false consciousness. Urban planners have to accept that images represent quite a large part of what a reasonably prosperous population wants and is prepared to pay for or fight to get.

Secondly, critical theory set out to establish a permanent place for critique in political life. Cultural imagery is also a commodity whose production serves to draw a veil over the black side of capitalism. It is the purpose of critique to balance the anodyne messages of capitalist culture with a negative thrust; to keep alive the *denial* that all is for the best in the best of all possible worlds. However distasteful, this is necessary to urban planning, which is always liable to become complacent, to believe in its own construction of reality, that it is succeeding, that problems can be solved. Here, however, there is a dilemma. Immanent critique takes the values of a political system and subjects them to scrutiny, asking how and why these values are not met. This evaluative activity is obviously quite consistent with good planning practice. Political decision-makers should never feel completely comfortable with their solutions, and it is the business of critique to keep them feeling uncomfortable. But at some point this uncomfortable feeling becomes self-defeating. Decision-makers depend for their legitimacy not on critique but on solutions, and planners are expected to provide them. Critique can easily turn to cynicism, discomfort to despair or, more likely, a refusal to listen to any more critique. Ultimately, critique cannot survive on its own without at least an equal focus on new solutions, new utopias, alternative directions. Such directions as were given (by Marcuse, for example) remained näive, undeveloped and politically uninformed. But the critical theorists were right in one respect: that new solutions would have to be discovered and worked out in political struggle.

Thirdly, like Weber, the critical theorists confronted the tension in the idea of rationality and hence in planning. Though they did not succeed in answering the questions they posed, the search opened up new debates concerning the norms of rationality and freedom and the relationship between the individual and society. Jürgen Habermas, in particular, has recognized that the step from critical analysis to action must involve the development of new political norms. These have been interpreted by Forester(1980, 1982a, 1982b) as a guide to the urban planner. Habermas, one-time assistant to Adorno at Frankfurt, has continued the tradition of critical theory, systematically reconstructing its philosophical foundations and gathering around him a new generation of critical scholars.

Habermas: system and lifeworld

If we are to understand Habermas, we need to grasp his view of how the 'co-ordination' of society may be understood according to two different perspectives, that of 'lifeworld' and that of 'system'. Here, Habermas is grappling with the relationship between values and facts, the action perspective and the observation perspective, ideology and social analysis; problematic relationships that continually re-emerge in the discussion of the acquisition and use of political knowledge. The 'life-world' of a social group refers to the co-ordination of social action through shared practical knowledge about what is to be done in given circumstances. This knowledge includes ethical and moral precepts as well as expectations of chains of consequences that shape the definition of means–ends hierarchies. In the system perspective, social action occurs because of the interplay of power and interest. There is an analogy with the working of machines or biological or ecological systems.

As a critical theorist, Habermas has followed in the steps of Marx, Weber, Horkheimer and Adorno, and he has undertaken an exhaustive reconstruction of their work. Their analyses, Habermas states, contained implicit criteria of rationality, which they used to assess the rationalization of society. Marx posited that the class-based relations of production 'fetter' the process of rationalization, which is proceeding in the development of the productive forces. Weber regarded the bureaucratization of society on purposive-rational lines as resulting in the reification of social relationships, which 'stifles' a truly value-rational conduct of life. For Horkheimer and Adorno (and later, Marcuse) 'the rationality of mastering nature merges with the irrationality of class domination. Fettered forces of production stabilize alienated relations of production' (Habermas, 1984, p. 144). But, says Habermas, these analyses contain an important inconsistency:

> On the one hand, Marx, Weber, Horkheimer and Adorno identify societal rationalization with expansion of the instrumental and strategic rationality of action contexts; on the other hand,

they all have a vague notion of *an encompassing societal rationality* – whether in the concept of an association of free producers, in the historical model of an ethically rational conduct of life, or in the idea of fraternal relations with a resurrected nature – and it is against this that they measure the relative position of empirically described processes of rationalization. But this encompassing concept of rationality would have to be confirmed at the same level as the forces of production, subsystems of purposive rational action, totalitarian carriers of instrumental reason. This does not happen (p. 144).

In other words, while they investigated in very specific terms the ways in which society is rationalized, they did not develop the criteria of rationality to the same specific level. These remain vague notions. From Weber on, however, the rationalization theme had at least been freed from the amalgamation of the ideas of scientific with those of moral progress inherited from 'philosophy of history' and social evolutionism. Habermas wishes to maintain that distinction and raise the analysis of the 'lifeworld' to the sophistication and complexity of social analysis achieved by his philosophical mentors from the system perspective.

System and lifeworld are metatheoretical concepts and not, as in Talcott Parsons' work, analyses of different types of sub-system. Parsons' theory tended to reduce lifeworld to system, whereas for Habermas lifeworld reflexively involves the analyst and his own ethical precepts. These precepts must be developed as part of the analysis of the social system: an account of the lifeworld both in terms of reflexive criteria of rationality and the connection between cultural rationalization and system function. For the latter purpose, Habermas adopts a fictionalist stance, arguing that it is methodologically useful to conceive of the lifeworld as a system, thus projecting it into the object domain (Habermas, 1987, Vol. 2, pp. 348, 349).

Habermas's theory seeks to draw together the critique of society and the critique of rationality, the analysis of the rational development of the forces of production and that of communicative practice. The success of this attempt, as well as some of the key distinctions he makes – for example, between productive work and communicative practice – have been questioned by his critics (see Giddens, 1982). The theme of integrating certain clearly articulated categories has emerged constantly in Habermas's work, but integration has until recently been a secondary focus in works that have adopted either (mainly) the system or the lifeworld perspective. The specific problem of their relationship has only recently been dealt with in depth (Habermas, 1984). Here we shall look first at Habermas' analysis of 'late capitalism' from a system perspective and then at his critique of rationality.

Crises of capitalism

Unlike Marcuse, Habermas does not regard capitalism as a stabilized and closed system. On the contrary, he argues that capitalism is subject to various tendencies towards structural crisis, rooted in class conflict, which result in the developmental change of the capitalist system. Such tendencies may or may not erupt into actual crises. Habermas does not regard the outcome as in any way certain: 'The same system modification can be conceived of equally well as a learning process and change or as a dissolution process and collapse of the system. It cannot be unambiguously determined whether a new system has been formed or the old system has merely regenerated itself (Habermas, 1975, p. 3).

Nevertheless, in exploring the crisis tendencies of late capitalism, Habermas's interest lies in the possible emergence of a 'post-modern' society: 'a historically new principle of organization and not a different name for the surprising vigor of an aged capitalism' (Habermas, 1975, p. 17). A crisis is not just a disturbance of the system's equilibrium, but one in which the consensual foundations of the society are shaken and people experience a rupture 'through which the interpretive systems that guarantee identity lose their social integrative power' (p. 4). Thus what happens to social institutions impinges upon individuals and, at the same time, the actions of individuals shape what happens to social institutions.

Habermas argues that, in order to cope with the problem of integrating a mass society that has broken away from traditional (e.g. feudal) norms and institutions, capitalism has had to generate mechanisms that reduce the need for actors to reach agreement through direct 'face to face' communicative practices. These are standard routines or rules of behaviour for 'steering' social interactions on purposive-rational lines. These 'steering media' governing remote social interactions form partially autonomous functional networks or sub-systems (McCarthy, 1984, p. xxx). The economy (the market, civil society) and the politico-bureaucratic 'state' are sub-systems in which money and political power are deployed as the steering media. Crises propagate through the economic and political subsystems at the institutional level, resulting in identity crises at the level of the individual. These then develop as 'motivation crises' in a third sub-system, the socio-cultural.

Following the logic of systems theory, Habermas postulates a complex causality in the generation and propagation of crises in which the output of one sub-system is the input of another. The economic sub-system requires an input of work and capital and its output consists of consumable values (products and services). The political system requires an input of mass loyalty and has an output of 'sovereignly executed decisions', decisions which regulate and reproduce the economy and the socio-cultural sub-system as well as ensuring that material inputs are provided. The socio-cultural system receives its input from the economic and political systems in the form of 'purchasable and collectively demandable goods, services, legal and administrative acts, public and social security, etc'. Its output of work, capital and loyalty completes the circuit of inputs and outputs. As a result of the fluid circuitry of this self-sustaining system, crises can build up as imbalances in any part of it and may be enhanced or dampened by positive or negative feedback.

Within this framework Habermas discusses a number of 'theorems' of crisis in the inputs and outputs of the three sub-systems resulting from the contradictory requirements of system (boundary) maintenance. From this discussion, he draws conclusions about four types of crisis: economic, rationality, legitimation and motivation crises, in which conceptions of planning and rationality are enfolded.

Economic crisis

In market liberalism, the legitimacy of class-based relations of production was sustained by the depoliticized 'freely' contracted exchange of wage labour for capital. But, in the face of class struggle, the device of the wage contract could not bear the entire load of 'legitimation'. Universal suffrage was gradually introduced, and this step, in turn, pressed the state to become involved in satisfying the needs of the population (Habermas, 1975, p. 58). The function of legitimation was, therefore, added to the prior function of the capitalist state in maintaining the legal and institutional framework for class-based commodity production. So the state, in advanced capitalism, undertakes contradictory functions. On the one hand, it *constitutes* and *adapts itself* institutionally to the mode of production, seeking to disturb as little as possible class or market exchange relations. On the other, it *replaces* the mode of distribution (the market), which upsets class relations and compensates for the dysfunctional consequences of the mode of production. Indeed, as Habermas says, it is characteristic of the advanced capitalist state as against its earlier liberal capitalist manifestation that the mode of production can only be reproduced *in so far* as the state 'simultaneously fills functional gaps in the market, intervenes in the process of accumulation and compensates for its politically intolerable consequences' (p. 55).

The state, then, has been involved in a fundamental change in the relations of production. First, the application of science and technology to the production process indirectly contributes to the production of increased surplus value. But the development of science requires labour power. The state, in organizing education to this end, assists the extraction of relative surplus value.[1] Secondly, stemming from the coalition of interest between the most organized sections of capital and labour (unions in key industries and monopoly capital), the state has become more and more involved in the determination of wage levels. This is partly a result of its steering functions and partly because of the increased representation of labour in the state through its political organization. Thirdly, the replacement of market exchange relations in substantial areas of distribution by administrative mechanisms increases the need for legitimation. 'Because a class compromise has been made the foundation of reproduction, the state apparatus must fulfill its tasks in the economic system under the limiting condition that mass loyalty be simultaneously secured within the framework of formal democracy and in accord with ruling universalistic value systems (freedom, justice, etc.) These pressures of legitimation can be mitigated through a depoliticized public realm (Habermas, 1975, p. 58).

Here, Habermas is thinking of the purposive rationality of a bureaucratized public realm (state enterprise, public corporations, functional agencies and the like) under nominal 'parliamentary' control. However, he points out that, contrary to the theory of 'state monopoly capitalism', the possibility of an overall rational co-ordination of the various bureaucracies is strictly limited. Bureaucratic planning takes the form of reactive avoidance of crisis and, because of their 'deficient capacity for perceiving and planning', bureaucracies are dependent on the influence of their clients. Conflicts of interest among individual capitalists, between the interests of individual capitalists and the collective capitalist interest, and between interests specific to the maintenance of the capitalist system and generalizable interests (of the population) are thus 'displaced into the state apparatus' (Habermas, 1975, p. 60).

Rationality and legitimation crisis

A more or less permanent, if unstable, pact between capital and labour interests (class compromise) follows the class struggle waged in the state arena. This pact, together with the desire to exploit the possibilities opened up by science and technology, leads to increased state operations, expenditure and taxation in the interest of maintaining the core elements of the system: private property and accumulation. But this means acting against the interests of specific capitals, and capital in general in certain respects, by reducing the sphere (the market) within which the owners of capital can exercise the power of their wealth in order to increase it. Class struggle is temporarily converted

1 Surplus value accumulating thorough the use of machinery.

into chronic inflation and a 'permanent crisis' in state finances. Also, we might add, in so far as capital retains and increases its power to disinvest, sporadic acute economic crises are bound to appear. Just what form they take and where (spatially) they appear – in which nations, regions, etc. – depends on the nature of disinvestment and reinvestment whose conceptualization requires a spatial and temporal dimension that Habermas's theory does not contain.

A rationality deficit is the outcome of the inability on the part of the state to resolve the conflicting functions with which it is burdened. 'The mutually contradictory imperatives of expanding the planning capacity of the state with the aim of a collective capitalist planning and, yet, blocking precisely this expansion which would threaten the existence of capitalism' (Habermas, 1975, p. 62). But this economic contradiction is not the only possible cause of rationality deficit. Relevant also are the limits to the rational co-ordination of any bureaucratic system pursuing multiple goals on behalf of conflicting interests. Several tendencies in advanced capitalism make effective administrative steering of the market system more problematic. The range of variables now in the control of the management of large corporations means that their own investment decisions can be planned internally rather than simply responding to extraneous 'market' pressures (see Rugman, 1981, on 'internalization'). The state is increasingly involved in the production and supply of use values (e.g. education, transport, housing, health care). And the proportion of the population who do not owe their livelihood to participation in labour markets has increased (school children, students, the unemployed, pensioners, etc.). These tendencies remove large areas of social production and reproduction from the private economy, opening them up more and more to processes of conscious choice and increasing the demands on the capacity of the state for resolution of political conflict.

If the state cannot develop adequate strategies within its systemic constraints, the eventual result will be a breakdown in policy and planning operations, in other words a rationality crisis (Held, 1980, p. 290). However, crisis may not develop for three reasons. First, there is considerable tolerance of irrationality in administrative systems because clear evaluative criteria for the social consequences of policy failure are, on the whole, not available. Secondly, various conflicts of interest, particularly between the more generalizable interests of labour and capital and specific interests of organized groups, can sometimes be resolved by bargaining. Thirdly, the inherent tendency towards escalation of unintended consequences characteristic of the collective 'rationality' of the private economy is not present in administrative systems that pursue strategies of crisis avoidance. The state has developed a variety of strategies for dealing with the manifestations of latent class conflict: personalization of substantive issues (e.g. the vilification of the victims of economic recession as dole cheats and welfare scroungers), the symbolic use of public hearings (see Kemp, 1985), expert judgements, the use of the courts (e.g. forcing industrial relations into the legal arena), advertising techniques, secretive managerialist and corporatist administration and open 'public participation'. There are also periodic appeals to patriotism and nationalism. The state, as Habermas says, attempts selectively to create and manage the themes of public debate.

The expansion of the state's administrative apparatus into production and distribution means that 'more and more areas of life are seen by the general population as politicized, as falling within its (via the government's) general control' (Held, 1980, p. 291). Failure to satisfy the demands and expectations thus generated leads to legitimation deficits. The repoliticization of production gives rise to an increasing danger that the asymmetrical class power relations inherent in 'capital' will be exposed. Habermas seeks to show that the legitimation deficits temporarily kept in check by the postwar class compromise will eventually outstrip the state's capacity to handle them and a legitimation crisis will result.

Legitimation and motivation crisis

In order to deal with its problems of legitimation the state attempts to act on the cultural sphere. But the cultural system is 'peculiarly resistant to administrative control' (Habermas, 1975, p. 70). As soon as the attempt to procure legitimacy is seen as such it loses its effectiveness. Hegemonic relations are those established through unconscious acceptance of the status quo, that is, through universalistic cultural values, which are *not* seen in terms of their reinforcement of class domination.

The core values, which Habermas regards as motivating individuals to accept the system, are 'civil privatism' and 'familial–vocational privatism'. The former denotes an interest in the output of the political system with minimal political participation. The latter is the orientation to the family, leisure and private domesticity, on the one hand, and to the forward-looking competitive pursuit of a career rising in status and income, on the other. Condensing Habermas's argument greatly, there are two main points: that the above-mentioned core value orientations are being eroded and that no replacement for them is emerging from bourgeois culture. Habermas points out that the bourgeois ideology of individualism leaves the person isolated in the face of the basic risks of existence (guilt, sickness and death) and without access to relations of emotional solidarity. Such 'pre-bourgeois' values as mutual support and affection have been entirely displaced from the public realm and reduced to mere subjective opinion. Habermas's analysis of public dissatisfaction with bourgeois morality seems today somewhat dated, a product of the late 1960s. Orientation to individual achievement, possessive individualism and the virtue of distribution of the social product by means of market exchange are values that have been rampantly reasserted since he wrote. Yet the contradiction between mutuality and individualism remains. Bourgeois liberalism has itself established universal values of equality and justice, which provide the basis for an immanent critique of society. These tendencies, says Habermas, cannot be reversed without a regression to authoritarianism, with corresponding costs to the system's legitimacy.

Habermas's concept of crisis is a complex one. First of all, there are latent contradictory tendencies in the capitalist system, some of which (but not all) are traceable to class conflict. Secondly, there are crisis tendencies in the system, which if they are not damped down and managed in various ways will result in actual crisis. Sometimes Habermas portrays the balancing act by which governments constantly struggle to maintain equilibrium as 'permanent crisis' – for example in the state's finances (fiscal crisis; see O'Connor, 1973). Thirdly, there is the concept of actual crisis in the system, which results in its breakdown and transformation. Crisis in this sense is only realized at the individual level, in the breakdown of motivation to accept and support the system. At the institutional level this breakdown is manifested as legitimation crisis.

The planner, of course, participates in both system and lifeworld. Urban planning, its professional institutions, interests and networks are part of a politico–economic system riven with contradictions and constantly prone to crises of varying form and dimension. Marxist explorations of these crises are contained in Gottdiener and Komninos (1989); a pluralist and more finely detailed analysis of the crises of governance in Britain is conducted by Rhodes (1988). Habermas's perspective, and 'dissenting' crisis theories generally, may be helpful to the planner in that they explain the dilemmas planners confront in terms of inherent attributes of the capitalist politico–economic system. For example, a planner dealing with the question of whether or not to permit or promote a development proposal in the face of opposition from local pressure groups will realize that the dilemma is inherent in the capitalist system and does not necessarily indicate a failure of planning. Pluralist or neo-corporatist analyses are more likely to conclude that the dilemma is inherent in *any* democratic politico–economic system and is characteristically dealt with in different ways in different locales. Either way, the decision is necessarily a political one contingent upon the local circumstances of each case.

Habermas argues that through repeated decisions of this kind the politico–economic system moves through crises and generates new structures (social rule systems) to enable it to survive. Urban planning with all its professional and bureaucratic apparatus and its capacity to enshrine new rights and form new interest groups is an example of just such a structure. The questions remain, however, whether or not the direction of movement is benign and what part planners and other political actors can play in ensuring that it is. Obviously, the planner need not and should not simply abdicate responsibility for planning decisions to politicians. As a bureaucrat, the planner is in a position to give advice and is expected to do so. Are there, then, general guidelines that can be adduced for the giving of advice, interaction with the public and the performance of the bureaucratic role? To answer these questions we must turn to Habermas's lifeworld conception and the theory of communicative rationality.

The critique of rationality

The assumption of philosophers such as Descartes and Kant was that their own consciousness, representative of human consciousness in general, provided a universal point of reference or criterion from which to evaluate the world. This is 'modernism': still our common-sense view of things and the unstated assumption behind most undertakings of modern natural and social science. It was the assumption on which the political philosophy of the Enlightenment was based, directed, as it was, towards the emancipation of the individual.

Hegel, and even more Marx, began to overturn this very basic assumption by arguing that consciousness was shaped by the social world. The radical implications of their argument – that there was no point outside the social world from which to observe, evaluate or change it – were not fully apparent to Hegel or Marx. Hegel turned the idea of 'the state' into a universal expression of consciousness and an ultimate criterion. While criticizing Hegel, Marx continued to write and think as though his own thought were somehow exempted from social-historical determination. He presented his analysis as the truth and regarded historical materialism as 'science', capable of penetrating false consciousness, in exactly the Cartesian manner of thought.

This strategy had great practical significance for Marx. Although he considered that society changed as a result of the unfolding of the historical process, he also believed that people played an important part in making change happen. His own 'science' was the tool that would help people work out what to do, what to aim for, who to look to for action and so forth. But its usefulness as a tool depended on its being not just relatively true – relative, for example, to its author's particular material circumstances -- but absolutely true.

Marx's science, therefore, was an archimedean point from which to shift the world.

But, of course, this is precisely what, on Marx's own account of social reality, does not exist. And not only Marx's philosophy but also that of Nietsche, Heidegger and the later Wittgenstein pointed in this same direction. A similar paradigm shift was also under way in physics, with the science of quantum mechanics throwing doubt on the 'detachedness' of the observer from the reality observed. Some of the critical theorists, particularly Adorno, were deeply concerned about this radical inconsistency in the entire project of critique, which threw doubt on the truth of the very values they were striving for, values that gave social critique its practical point.

Habermas's argument, in a nutshell, is as follows. Let us accept that consciousness is socially conditioned. Although ideas help to reproduce the social world, they are primarily shaped by the material processes of social existence, which are external to consciousness. To quite a large extent consciousness (e.g. political ideas) is shaped by that universal human activity 'work'. The social organization of work goes through a historical process of development and, as it develops, it plays a part in generating supportive systems of political ideas. Although we may criticize the details of Marx's analysis of this process of development we can accept the principle. But work is not the only universal human activity. If it were, we would have to accept that all political knowledge was of secondary importance in social organization and social change. The experience of change in the first half of the twentieth century showed that this was not so. Ideas about existing social relations stemming from religion and historical tradition at every level of consciousness, from the intellectuals to the uneducated mass, were necessary to the constitution of society. And political ideas were just as necessary for fundamental change to social structures, both to motivate the human agents of change and to guide the reconstruction of society.

The changed view of ideology and the renewed importance accorded to the concept of the state and its institutions by twentieth century Marxists indicated a reinstatement of political knowledge. Habermas takes this reinstatement further by positing a number of 'interests' that go beyond 'men dominating men' (namely 'class'), and domains of social existence other than work. These 'interests' are basic orientations to the world, forms of life constitutive of forms of knowledge. They determine the categories of knowledge (see Habermas, [1968] 1978). There is the *technical* interest in controlling the natural environment and using it to produce useful goods. And there is a *practical* interest in furthering human co-operation, without which no technical progress would be possible. Various co-ordinating devices have emerged throughout history, but these have involved the use of force in different ways, for example, from the feudal institutions of the middle ages to the modern bourgeois state and its institutions of private property and the market. The technical interest is grounded in instrumental action, work, the practical interest is grounded in communicative action or language. The natural sciences developed from the pursuit of the technical interest. The historical/hermeneutic forms of knowledge, the study of history and political and social philosophy, developed out of pursuit of the practical interest. But there is a third interest, which has gradually developed since the Enlightenment, the *emancipatory* interest in freedom from repression, in human autonomy and in undistorted communication. The emancipatory interest constitutes the study of power and hence 'critical knowledge'. This interest, says Held (1980, p. 317), is rooted in their [human beings'] capacity to act rationally, to reason self-consciously and to make decisions in the light of available knowledge, rules and needs. This is an interest in self-formation and self-understanding through *free* social interaction.

This, then, is the core of Habermas's theory of rationality. People have an interest in developing their own identity, their sense of selfhood, of self-worth not only, as Marx thought, by producing useful things but by communicating with other people. Co-operative practices and communicative practices are universal domains of social existence distinguishable from work practices. The interest in emancipation is the general practical interest in pursuit of which the critique of society has emerged (including, of course, Marx's critique). 'It is in human beings' ability to reflect on their own development and, as a consequence, to act with greater consciousness and autonomy that the emancipatory interest can be uncovered' (Held, 1980). This interest in growth and change through self-reflection in conditions of mutual interaction finds expression at all levels from the individual to the societal. By focusing on communication as praxis we can begin to understand how the domain of political action (social interaction) is today still systematically distorted in a way comparable to Marx's conception of the alienation of work practice.

Habermas's first full treatment of communication (in *Communication and the Evolution of Society*, 1979) parallels Marx's method of historical–theoretical analysis. He explores the developmental logic of social interaction leading to emancipation. From this historical investigation he endeavours to reconstruct criteria of undistorted communication, which are implicit in the practice of communicative action and which make communication possible. As Marx postulated the historical emancipation of the producer as a social being, so Habermas postulates the emancipation of the 'communicator' as a social being. In this sense, 'producing' and 'communicating' are understood as human social roles.

Habermas inquires into the assumptions we make about each other when we communicate. He limits the part of communication he is talking about very precisely to statements designed to convey information from one person to another (1979, pp. 39, 40). He acknowledges, however, that this is not all there is to communication. In this kind of communication, he says, we try to reach agreement on the basis of reciprocal understanding, shared knowledge, mutual trust and accord with one another. Implicit in this attempt are at least four claims concerning the validity of our communication – without which we could not claim to be communicating at all. They are the *truth* of propositions about external reality (external to ourselves as subjects), the *rightness* of our interpersonal relations with the other person, *truthfulness* about our internal, subjective state and the *comprehensibility* of our language.

We can of course fail to find and share the truth about external reality and about our internal subjective states (hate, love, fear, anger or whatever). But communication implies the attempt. Likewise, communication demands that our language be comprehensible. These claims are relatively unproblematic from the point of view of political knowledge. But *rightness* as to our interpersonal relations, our social world, is the central problem of politics. Can we ever agree on what constitutes right social relations? Or is the essence of politics that we do not and never can agree? This is the question that Habermas dwells upon in greater depth in his second treatment of communication: *The Theory of Communicative Action* (1984 and 1987). This work is both an immanent critique of the practice of communication and a reconstruction of critical theory where it touches on rationality, from Marx and Weber to the Frankfurt theorists and the modern systems and linguistic philosophers.

Habermas develops further the contrasting validity claims of *truth* when we are acquiring knowledge and *effectiveness* when we are using it. These appear to us as radically different: an assertion (a speech act), in so far as we desire it to be considered rational, contains the claim to be *true*. An intervention in and on the world (a teleological act) to be considered rational must contain a claim to be *effective*, that is, successfully achieving what it sets out to do. We tend to fetishize truth and effectiveness and thus fail to see their connection at the level of communicative praxis. For intervening rationally in the world also implies knowledge of the world, and knowing about the world stems from the desire for 'instrumental mastery' of the world. More fundamentally, however, truth and effectiveness are connected in the process by which these claims are realized and tested. This is a social process directed towards *reaching understanding*. Neither rational thought nor rational action are conceivable, in the sense in which we understand these terms today, in an isolated individual. Rationality arises from purposive communication among people.

Habermas disputes Weber's conception of rationality because Weber's theory grew from an understanding of meaning based on the Kantian–Cartesian idea of consciousness. Weber regarded rationality as 'the purposive activity of a solitary acting subject' (Habermas, 1984, p. 279). Habermas shows that Weber's fourfold typology of action can be reduced to a single dimension, with value rational, affectual and traditional types being imperfect realizations of purposive rationality. However, he acknowledges that Weber also had an 'unofficial' typology. Habermas claims to have clarified and extended this unofficial version by distinguishing between solitary 'strategic' action oriented to success and mutual 'communicative' action oriented to 'reaching understanding'. This distinction is made possible on the basis of the idea of a socially constructed consciousness.

Of course there are many different reasons for human communication, but the *underlying* purpose of the construction of rational knowledge and action is reaching mutual understanding – on the one hand, about what is in the world and how it works and, on the other, about what is to be done. This purpose is to be distinguished from that of 'settling disputes'. Habermas uses the term 'consensus' which, in normal usage, covers both reaching understanding and settling disputes. Disputes about action can be settled in a variety of ways: institutionally through the law (and quasi-legal structures), through organizations, political processes and the market; by reference to traditional norms, by brute force or by power bargaining and compromise. Most of our instrumentally rational institutions and processes (including practices of planning) contain built-in methods of settling disputes that involve a mixture of force and procedures directed towards reaching understanding.

It is the latter (the procedures aimed at reaching understanding), which constitute the rationality of the Enlightenment and which have gradually been introduced alongside the continuing use of force in human affairs. These procedures Habermas describes by the term 'argumentation'. Not only does the rationality of the validity claims of truth and effectiveness depend on their being susceptible to criticism and disputation but also this same process of 'argumentation' lies at the heart of what we regard as the civilized life.

This concept of communicative rationality carries with it connotations based ultimately on the central experience of the unconstrained, unifying, consensus-bringing force of argumentative speech, in which different participants overcome their merely subjective views and, owing to the mutuality of rationally motivated conviction, assure themselves of both the unity of the objective world and the intersubjectivity of their lifeworld (Habermas, 1984, p. 10).

In Habermas's scheme, argumentation is conceptually opposed to coercion of every kind and, therefore, must be clearly differentiated also from the kind of discourse designed to *win* arguments. He says:

> Participants in argumentation have to presuppose in general that the structure of their communication, by virtue of features that can be described in purely formal terms, excludes all force – whether it arises within the process of reaching understanding itself or influences it from outside – except the force of the better argument (and thus that it also excludes, on their part, all motives except that of a co-operative search for truth), (Habermas, 1984, p. 25).

It is essential to grasp the difference between an argument designed to win and an argument designed to reach understanding. In ordinary speech as well as political speech the two are mixed up all the time. But the former is the deployment of coercion by another means, and coercion is for Habermas the antithesis of rationality. Habermas's point, however, is that even coercive argument draws on the general form of argument designed to reach understanding. The latter constitutes the basic criterion of judgement in a variety of different institutional dispute-settling contexts. This may not be the only criterion by which decisions are reached, but it is the criterion by which arguments are judged better or worse. Conversely, once the nature of an argument is exposed as coercive it loses its force.

What then of conflict of interest? Our (Kantian) common sense understanding of conflict of interest stems from an individualistic interpretation of interest, in which people are presumed to have fixed interests that are exclusively determined internally by themselves as isolated individuals. This is the point of view generally adopted by neo-liberalism. According to Habermas, this position is a defence against the coercion of the individual by the state rather than an ontological truth. Once we remove coercion from the scene we can allow ourselves to think that individual interests may be determined in interaction with our social world. As McCarthy (1984, p. xxi) puts it, 'Habermas is after a notion of ego identity that centers around the ability to realize oneself under conditions of *communicatively shared intersubjectivity.*' With such a conception, conflict of interest is much more susceptible to resolution through argument in which interests are capable of redefinition.

What Habermas is aiming at is a philosophical solution to a practical problem of central importance to planning and the state. Pluralists conflate rationality with the outcome of competitive power play, even if it is one conducted by way of argument and persuasion. Orthodox Marxists tend to assume away the problem of reaching agreement under the solution of changing the mode of production: political rationality will follow with the emergence of economic rationality. Habermas disagrees with both these points of view. Against pluralism, rationality in politics and, therefore, in planning means reaching agreement on action *without* force of any kind; against Marxism, however, there will always be an irreducible level of difference in values, goals and interests among individuals. For Habermas the key to rational politics lies in the process of argumentation under conditions of truth (outer world), truthfulness (inner world), effectiveness (social world) and comprehensibility (language). Effectiveness can be achieved only in so far as differences are resolved, *not* through compromise, which is the outcome of power play, but through mutual adjustment and redefinition of goals, values and interests. This becomes possible only where force is absent and hence where power is equal. Equality, therefore, is connected with rationality via effectiveness. People are able to discover both what they are and what they really want and need, through mutual interaction in conditions of power equality. This end, which is emancipation, is the end towards which humanity in its communicative practice is haltingly evolving.

Critical theory and planning practice

Exploration of the implications of critical theory for planning practice has proceeded very slowly. One of the first attempts to absorb Habermas's theory of communicative action was that of Forester (1980). Forester (p. 277) gives examples of typical speech acts of planners: warning of problems, presenting information, suggesting new ideas, agreeing to perform certain tasks, arguing for policies, reporting events, offering opinions, commenting on ideas and proposals. He then interprets Habermas's criteria in terms of planning practice. Planners, he says, ought to speak *comprehensibly*: that is, in such a way as to be fully understood by the audience to whom the communication is addressed. They should speak *sincerely*: that is, not manipulate, mislead, fool or misguide their audience. They should speak *legitimately*: that is, not overreach or abuse the role permitted to a bureaucrat in a democratic society. And they should speak the *truth*: that is, provide all the evidence at their disposal. From these criteria, Forester derives a list of prescriptions for practice that resembles the old-style liberal pluralist formula: cultivate community networks, listen carefully to all participants in the planning process in order to gauge their interests and concerns, pay special attention to notifying the less organized interests (the poor) of proposals, educate citizens about 'the rules of the game', supply technical and political information to enable effective and informed participation by individuals and groups, ensure access of community groups to public planning information, encourage community groups to press for open and full information about proposals, develop skills to work with groups in conflict situations 'rather than expecting progress to stem mainly from isolated technical work', make negotiations over proposals equitable to professionally unsophisticated groups, encourage independent project reviews, anticipate external political pressures and be prepared to mobilize counter-pressures ('pressures we can use').

There are problems both with Forester's interpretation of Habermas and with the application of Habermasian criteria to planning practice. Most problematic are Forester's interpretation of Habermas's 'rightness of our interpersonal relations' as 'legitimacy', and 'truthfulness about our internal state' as 'sincerity'. In the first case, although Habermas is very much concerned with 'legitimacy', it must be noted that he defines a basis for right interpersonal relations that transcends any locally established political legitimacy. Critical theory challenges rather than takes as given existing norms of legitimacy. Habermas demands nothing less than an end to domination, which means that relations between the planner and the planned must be conducted on the basis of equality of power. Very rarely is such a situation likely to occur, and if inequality exists it is often very difficult to change. In the second case, truthfulness about internal states demands that planners have some insight into their 'internal states'. Some planners may develop such insight, but if they do it is a matter of chance. Few planning educators understand the need for self-awareness and the ethical application of psycho-social skills. The mastery of these skills requires a very different approach to planning education from that which is normally adopted in urban planning courses (see, for example, Argyris and Schön, 1974). The literature of group practice from Freud and Lewin onwards explores in depth the ramifications of 'right interpersonal relations' and 'truthfulness about internal states'. The 'Tavistock' approach to group dynamics appears to parallel at the level of the small group the critical approach of the Frankfurt School (see Bion, 1961; Shaffer and Gralinski, 1974, ch. 9). Although Lewin saw the connection between this work and democratic practice, in general the connection between political philosophy and group practice has not been stressed (however, see Little, 1985, Tyson and Low, 1988). The political climate of the late 1980s was unfavourable for the advancement of innovative approaches to planning education that emphasize experiential learning, interpersonal relations and group dynamics.

Hoch (1984b) recommends a radical pragmatism, which recognises the terrain of power within which the planner must operate. Instead of acting under the illusion that he performs a role as 'honest broker' or mediator between developer interests and the public, 'the critically-oriented planner would recognise that the privilege of private property rights and the priority of private economic interchange structures the encounter between himself and the developer in a biased fashion' (Hoch, 1984b, p. 93). The radical planner would insist on identifying the problem in terms of the distributive effects a development might have on local residents. The planner would advise the decision-takers of alternative possibilities and become an advocate for 'a critical public interest', that is to say from the point of view of shared values of fairness with respect to the distribution of material goods (health, food and shelter, work and leisure – quoting Walzer, 1983, p. 82) in the context of a local community. Hoch insists that it is only within the confines of a limited local polity and culture that the formation of a democratic consensus becomes possible. Only through the experience of conflict as political argument, confrontation, and negotiation will diverse groups and factions change their positions without the use of force. Just *how* local, and how *local* polities might be integrated in some way with, say, national or Federal polities, Hoch does not say.

Albrecht and Lim (1986) begin their appropriation of Habermas from the perspective of his theory of knowledge. This theory, they claim, throws light on the divergence between the political and technical roles performed by planners, and the gap between theory and practice, both matters that we have discussed in chapters 2 and 3. Functional, or purposive, rationality (see chapter 4) and the use of scientific knowledge based on theories in social science are features of knowledge guided by the 'technical interest'. The technical interest specifies a rational-bureaucratic role for the planner, based on instrumental action. This role operates on the assumption that knowledge of how the city (and other presumed entities of concern to the planner) 'works' is sufficient to specify various means by which solutions to problems can be arrived at. It is then only necessary to specify the ends in sufficient detail to arrive at an optimal solution. The specification of ends and the political rules for deciding upon ends are regarded by technocrats not merely as unproblematic, but as unworthy of being viewed as knowledge. The specification of ends is the field of the 'practical interest' and practical reason, which specifies a political role for the planner based on communicative action. Since planning is a political activity, planners cannot avoid playing a role in politics. In doing so, they are engaging in the pursuit of the practical interest, operating with language, and performing the kind of speech acts referred to by Forester. Critical knowledge, as Habermas explains, is based on the 'emancipatory interest'. Albrecht and Lim (1986, p. 122) argue that, 'Planning practice should be a combination of instrumental and communicative action directed by emancipatory interests – planning as an enlightened social process.' The specification of functional rationality along Weberian lines and the specification of politics along pluralist lines can be brought to the formation of knowledge serving the technical and practical interests. But what of the emancipatory interest? Critical theory is directed primarily at exposing relations of *power*, which prevent the attainment of human emancipation. For Habermas, the drive for emancipation is written into human history; what are problematic are the complex self-deceptions and social deceptions that restrict the emancipatory drive. It is the business of critical theory to reveal these deceptions through critique of ideology both at the personal and at the social level. Discourse directed at reaching understanding and, hence, mutually agreed definitions and solutions of problems should be the aim of planning.

Albrecht and Lim draw conclusions for planning from three functions of discourse. First, knowledge about the city and planning emerges from on-going argumentative inquiry among a community of equal inquirers. The planner is not in a privileged position in respect to other actors with stakes in the development of knowledge. No one actor, academic, professional or political, and no one theorist is in a position to say: 'I know best'. Secondly, the results of theoretical discourse always have implications for action. Concepts lead to action; learning occurs when reflection on action leads to a modification of concepts. In this sense, critical theory invites self-reflection not only in an academic and theoretical but also in a completely *personal* sense. The person cannot be separated from the person's knowledge. In order to become aware of such matters as the manipulation of others and power play through communicative action, the planner must cultivate a high degree of *self*-awareness. Thirdly, 'critical theory is retrospective', its objective is to initiate self-reflection in order to achieve insight into past influences. Theory cannot justify what is to be done in future: 'the only possible justification at this level [of future action] is consensus achieved in practical discourse' (Albrecht and Lim, 1986, p. 127). In working to reach consensus the criteria of the 'ideal speech situation' apply (truth about the external world, rightness of interpersonal relations, truthfulness about internal states and comprehensibility of language). Albrecht and Lim warn of the danger of technical domination by the planner. But it is not by any means always the planner who dominates the discourse about urban development. Planners are often dominated by politicians, who are in turn dominated by those with political and economic power.

Critical theory seeks to expose the sources of unequal power and to examine the political arguments justifying such inequality. Where unequal power cannot be justified steps must be taken to correct the situation.

Unfortunately, it is all too easy for an alternative theoretical framework, including even critical theory itself, to become an orthodoxy. Marxist analysis in urban studies can become merely another avenue for technical domination, an alternative means of mystification. This is especially the case where analysis is devoid of political content and fails to pay attention to the needs of political struggle. In this respect critical theory, which has always been a reflective academic practice, pays too little attention to the critical potential of active politics. It is not enough to reflect, it is also necessary to act. And action of any sort brings one back to the contradiction between the need for coercive authority of some sort in order to act collectively and the goals of freedom and emancipation which such action may aim at. No theory can abolish that dilemma.

Conclusion

The members of the Frankfurt Institute set a new and distinctive direction for critique in the tradition of historical materialism. But it was one that both extended and broke away from classical Marxism. Perhaps the most obvious break was with the total emphasis on class in the sphere of production, which dominated all questions of politics in the Marxian scheme. The critical theorists took for granted the class–defining nature of the relationship between capital and labour, but they did not think that class analysis exhausted the analysis of domination. Although they did not redefine Marx's conception of class in the way that Weber did, they moved closer to Weber's critique of the rationalization of society brought about by mass production technology and mass organization. Their emphasis on the stabilization and reproduction of capitalism and on the analysis of politics and culture in modern society pointed towards a tenuous connection between the sphere of production and developments in politics and culture.

Critical theorists made various attempts to confront the contradiction in planning for security and planning for freedom: freedom requires security but planning for security stifles freedom. There are not two kinds of freedom – freedom *to* pursue one's own self-development through work (Marx) and freedom *from* external coercion (Mill). Freedom is as indivisible as the material existence of a human being. However, individualist philosophy and ideology blinds us to the social being of humanity, in which neither interests nor needs nor freedom are properties of isolated individuals.

Critical theorists have envisaged a possible society in which, on the one hand, basic material needs are met through automatic mechanisms from which class domination has been eliminated and, on the other, the higher needs of self-realization are met through an infinitely variable, co-operative and sensuous practice. In such a truly post-modern society, distribution of the means of existence would be 'uncoupled' from labour; production and praxis would be recoupled with need. Habermas's theory is attractive because it offers a convincing alternative to the subjective individualism of pluralist orthodoxy while recognizing the plurality of opinions and interests. It says in effect that, through collaboration under certain conditions, we can make *better* plans. However, Habermas's prescriptions are rather too easy to transplant *uncritically* into planning practice. Before planners pack them into their toolbox of organizational strategies, they should remember that the aim of critical theory is the *critique* of the kind of society in which planners organize people. As Adorno warned, critical theory can all too easily become part of some ideology of domination. Under what conditions does undistorted communication become possible? It becomes possible in the *absence* of domination, repression and ideology. These conditions generally do not exist in any interaction between state planners and the people they have dealings with; those who feel the effect of their policies. Domination is part of the operational rules of society in which planners are enmeshed. Therefore, we should perhaps take note of Bernstein's (1978, p. 225) words of caution against the uncritical use of critical theory:

> If one is to fulfill the promise of developing a critical theory that has practical intent, then it is not sufficient to recover the idea of self-reflection guided by an emancipatory interest. It is not sufficient to develop a critique of ideology and contemporary society which exposes the powerful tendencies to suppress practical discourse and force all rationality into the form of instrumental reason. It is not sufficient even to show that a critical theory can serve to further enlightenment and effect a transformation in political agents. All the preceding is necessary. But, as Habermas so acutely shows, the very idea of practical discourse – of individuals engaged in argumentation directed toward rational will formation – can easily degenerate into a 'mere' ideal, unless and until the material conditions required for such discourse are concretely realized and objectively instituted.

10 Political theory, the state and planning

Political theory opens up a region of knowledge that planners may find confusing. Many would not even regard it as 'knowledge', because it seems to say nothing certain. But that is as it should be. The criteria of knowledge in the region of political theory are different from the criteria of truth to which we are accustomed, based on the paradigm of natural science. There is disagreement in the natural sciences on truth criteria (see Harré, 1972), but these do not form part of the broad public conception of 'science', which still tells us what *really* constitutes knowledge. It is this public face of science that gives us the belief that science deals in certainties. Natural science, however, is derived from the praxis of operating on inanimate objects and transforming them for our use. Politics is a study of people, their actions and their relationships. There can be certainty about things, not because things are somehow less changeable or mysterious than people but because things do not appropriate human knowledge for their own use. Moreover, we do not (ethically) operate on people and transform them for our use. We communicate with them, debate with them, enter into dialogue with them. Political knowledge is defined by this ethical standpoint.

Debate can never be concluded in the field of political knowledge, because knowledge is attached to interests. People use knowledge in pursuit of their interests and, where interests are in conflict, people disagree. Conflict of interest cannot be disentangled from other sorts of disagreement central to the interpretation and understanding of society and its organization. The human pursuit of interests, however, does not prevent the emergence of truths that transcend the particularities of personal or class interest, time and place.

The best way of approaching these 'universals', as Habermas does, is to view them as being attached to the shared interest in human emancipation that is the project of all modern societies: 'modern', that is, as opposed to 'traditional' and not to 'post-modern'. There are societies today whose members believe in the subordination of human beings to the will of some supernatural authority expressed on earth through a clerical power structure. These are traditional societies. We have to agree with Weber that there is no authority to which we can appeal to enable us to judge whether such societies are better or worse than societies based, however inadequately, on the ethic of human emancipation and sovereignty on earth. This is not a matter of theism versus atheism. The idea of human emancipation itself has theistic roots even though the idea strikes at the power of hierarchies.[1] The distinction between the modern and the traditional cuts across all creeds, theistic and atheistic. A 'post-modern' society may gradually wish to share with things some of the dignity reserved in 'modern' society for human beings, but it will not give up the idea of human emancipation. Only in so far as readers share the ethic of human emancipation will the ideas discussed in this book have any claim to 'universality'. Within the bounds of this ethic, however, there are certain ideas that are true. Of course, just as in natural science these truths are provisional. They stand only until disproved by the force of better argument. There are also contrary material facts of human political organization, which derive from the practical application of this ethic. The term 'contradiction' is scarcely adequate to cover these facts if all that is implied by the term is the dictionary definition: 'denial' or 'opposition'. 'Dilemma', that is the term used by Dahl (1982), captures the notion of a choice between alternative courses of action. Politics is about the choices which combine in different ways the contrary facts of human political organization.

In the first part of this final chapter we shall summarize the truths and dilemmas that emerge from the foregoing discussion of political theory. We shall also consider what political theory has to say about the roles of planners and the rules that both limit and shape role performance. Some ideas on the theory of the state will then be distilled, which are both of general relevance and relevant to urban planning as a policy field.

Truths, dilemmas, roles and rules

Let us retrace our steps. Urban development is inevitably the target of political will (influence, manipulation) and the object and product of political struggle (the use of power). The professionalization of decision-making about urban development was an attempt to depoliticize the struggle. In many places urban planning was absorbed into the state as a bureaucratic function. However, depoliticization could only be temporary because, in modern societies, neither political will nor political struggle can be permanently suspended. The profession of urban planning thus developed with two faces. Planning must serve political will yet present a technical face to the general public, for technique is the basis of professional legitimacy. Technical information about the city (and management technique)

1   The original meaning of hierarchy is rule by the priesthood.

serves specific political ends within the state apparatus, and as a general device for legitimating decisions in the eyes of the public. However, depoliticizing decision-making about urban development means removing such decision-making from the immediate power struggle among the actors on the urban scene. It does not mean taking the politics out of planning. For, as Jacques Ellul (1967) pointed out, 'to become apolitical is to make a political choice, and as a result, apolitism hides some very definite political choices'. 'Choice' is too voluntaristic a word, but political dilemmas are resolved in practices such as urban planning and each such resolution is a political act. What then are the 'choices' which apolitical planning hides?

Assenting theory

The approach that best corresponds with the principle of human emancipation, the democratic approach, is squarely to confront the dilemmas of politics and not to succumb to the comforting myth that this or that political (or apolitical) solution will finally do away with them. Weber makes clear that all political (collective or social) action involves the use of force. But the use of force restricts human freedom. The modern sublimation of force into the rationalism of the market, the legitimate state and bureaucratic rule (and rules) provides for a certain limited sphere of freedom within a collective order, but only at the cost to the public realm of the expressive values of human affection and solidarity.

Weber specifies the nature of the bureaucratic role that the urban planner typically occupies, and sets out its internal dilemmas – the cultivation of expertise versus the 'iron cage' of hierarchical organization. He also specifies the threefold contradiction between bureaucratic rationality, the market and political leadership. Modern 'mass' societies require a combination of these three factors, the particular combination varying with the social rules generated by different societies. The form urban planning takes in a particular society reflects a resolution of this threefold dilemma. Modern Weberians (see, for example Healey *et al.* 1988; Cawson and Saunders, 1983; Campbell and Peters, 1988) through the device of 'ideal types', seek to characterize the combinations and trade-offs that are made in different societies at different times.

Contrary to the arguments of some planning theorists, the 'rational paradigm' cannot be superseded. The breakdown of rationality is simply an aspect of the dilemma generated by the professionalization (and hence rationalization) of decision-making about something, urban development, which is the subject of political struggle. In order to be effective in the achievement of their goals, planners must enlist the support of the powerful (economically, politically). But if they do so, the goals they are pursuing may be changed in accordance with the interests of the powerful. Political leaders, on the other hand, are to some degree dependent on the bureaucrat for information and technical knowledge as well as for the legitimacy that this knowledge supplies. As a distributional mechanism Weber believed that the market was generally superior to bureaucratic decision, but the market performs at least four functions: it distributes goods and services, regulates production, transmits economic power and functions as a lottery to facilitate accumulation of wealth. Bureaucratic decision may be required to mitigate the negative effects of unequal power, which the market both transmits and creates. Planning may thus be required to achieve goals that have to do with human emancipation – freedom, increased choice, equality, quality of life; but planning, as an instrument of change by bureaucratic means, is also an iron cage, restricting freedom. However painful, planners must keep this dilemma ever in mind.

Weberian theory takes 'the state' as its point of departure (see Evans, Rueschemeyer and Skocpol eds., 1985). Pluralist theory starts with the politics of society and only later returns to the state. Whereas Weber assumed a strong European-style state, pluralism grew in the context of a weak and fragmented state in the United States and, in a different governmental context, in Britain. Pluralism stemmed from several themes of liberal theory: individuals should be regarded as having certain natural rights, although a structure of rules was necessary for mutual security and collective action; individual liberty had to be defended against majoritarian power focused in the state; interest group membership educated people in democratic conduct and created mutual solidarity. Analytical pluralism regarded the conglomerate of political structures known as 'the state' as emerging from group formation and competition. Institutional pluralism turned the theoretical attention to the prior structural rules embodied in the constitution of the state, which make group formation and competition possible.

Pluralist theory hinges on the truth that freedom to form and join groups in the pursuit of interests (economic and political) is an indispensable component of democracy. But the theory also reveals the contradiction between that principle and the equally indispensable principle of majority rule. The fragmentation of political power acts as a check on the possibility of the majoritarian state redistributing power in society. In pluralist theory, planners' authority is not exclusively drawn from their bureaucratic position in the legitimate state but also from the political process that allows free interaction among many minorities. Planners are viewed as one among many contending interest groups in the political arena; thus, planning comes to mean the pursuit of the interests of planners. The goals of policy vary with the balance of group pressures; there are multiple 'clients'; and, since different groups have varying interpretations of 'the urban problem', there are also multiple and possibly conflicting criteria of success.

Critics accused the pluralists of glossing over fundamental power structures in society, which gave political power to entrenched economic and social as well as political elites. Wealth, they said, conferred power. Moreover, by concentrating on descriptive analysis of manifest power, the pluralists drew attention from important normative questions concerned with class-variable political participation, the exclusion of certain programmes and decisions from the political agenda, the exclusion of significant minorities from the decision-making process, and the undemocratic nature of industrial corporations viewed as political structures. Others disputed the democratic claims of pluralism, arguing that 'group theory' portrayed a corporatist polity structured by organized interests that held a large share of political power. Some versions of institutional pluralism pointed to the tendency for state policies and programmes to bring organized groups into existence.

Although Dahl's critics viewed his concept of 'polyarchy' as a watered-down version of democracy, the principles of 'polyarchy' established an important minimum benchmark based on current practices. If polyarchy did not provide a goal for the advancement of democracy, it at least provided a minimum position from which retreat could be measured. Recently, Dahl has acknowledged the dilemmas inherent in capitalist democracy and has pursued a theme identified by himself and Lindblom in their earlier work: the overwhelming power of wealth and the need to apply the criteria of democracy to political structures outside the state, in particular to business corporations. In this, Dahl argues for a redefinition of the public and private domains, including corporate enterprises in the former. We might say that, in order to accommodate the new realities of power in corporate capitalism, the public domain should now be conceived as consisting of two major sources of structured power: an ensemble of organizations within the state and an ensemble of organizations within civil society – the so-called 'private sector' major industrial corporations at the peak of which are some 500 to 1000 transnational corporations. Much has been written about this ensemble, which cannot be covered in this book. Smith and Feagin (1987, p. 6) write: 'These major organizations have created an integrated, worldwide network of production, exchange, finance and corporate services arranged in a hierarchical system of cities.' Dahl's point is that this is a system of control and authority, and thus a political system. To level the political playing field, normative democratic theory must be applied equally to the whole of the public domain (Figure 10.1).

Recognizing the importance of political struggle, pluralism enjoins planners to engage in the political process and, therefore, prescribes a

	Public domain	Private domain
Competitive capitalism	The state	Individuals, households, firms, organized groups
Corporate capitalism	The state ensemble, The corporate ensemble	Individuals, households, voluntary associations

Figure 10.1 Redefinition of public and private domains

number of political roles. These were grouped under four headings: advocate, negotiator, activist (or entrepreneur) and mediator. These roles are arguably the basic role clusters of all political action in a democratic society. In so far as planners wish to extend their activity beyond the limitations of traditional bureaucracy, they must learn to play these four roles (and variations on them) effectively. If they do so, however, they will be immediately confronted by the dilemmas of politics. In order to overcome these dilemmas, albeit temporarily and provisionally, they must be prepared to make personal judgements based on well worked out *political* values concerning what is fair, whom they wish to help, who are their allies in political struggle, what constitutes a 'just process' of decision-making, and what dis-tributive mechanisms (e.g. bureaucracy, the market) will give the best results.

Ultimately, the pluralist concern with the political game brings a renewed concern with the rules of this game. A major part of urban planning action is concerned with setting, implementing and changing the rules governing urban development. Pluralist theory assents to capitalism and, therefore, contains an initial assumption that the basic rules are fair. But there is a strong critical tradition within pluralism, which challenges that assumption. It also seems that there are different levels of rules. For example, there are the rules encompassed by planning practice. These operate within systems of rules defining the territorial boundaries and functional limits of the local state as well as the relations between organized groups in the state and civil society, and in the private and public domains. Such (more or less) specified rules operate within ill-defined but influential sets of cultural norms. In the background lie the basic rule-laden conditions of economic power: property, contract, the wage relation, the bias of capitalism which permits authoritarian relations in the corporations (themselves subject, at least partially, to the discipline of the market) while insisting on forms of democratic accountability everywhere else (e.g. through elections of the executive, voting, etc.). The Weberian and pluralist schools of theory effectively address the more immediate rules of capitalism, but do not provide as powerful a conception of the deeper bias of capitalism as does the Marxist theory of class.

Although corporatist forms of political life have been identified in the United States, corporatist theory originated in Europe out of the organic conception of the state. In chapter 6 two ideal types of state were postulated: the organic and the ectopic. Whereas, in the latter, political power and authority in society are displaced into a crisply defined separate entity, 'the state' (especially its modern representative form), in the former, political power is spread throughout society, culminating in the state. The terms 'ectopic' and 'displaced' intentionally suggest a somewhat artificial, mythical or fantastic conception of the location of power and authority. The main achievement of corporatist theory is arguably the exposure of this fantasy for what it is. While the organic state is too extreme an image of reality, pluralism, at least in its traditional form, fails to come to grips with the interpenetration of state and civil structures of power.

Neo-corporatist theory is most immediately relevant to urban planning when it addresses interest intermediation. Corporatist intermediation is secretive and exclusive. Organizations in civil society are used for the implementation of state policy. This policy, however, is arrived at by prior bargaining among those actors who are able to bring into play resources of power (e.g. control over investment, the co-operation of organized labour or of other communities of interest). A plan represents a pact among these players: a pact that contains the promise of implementation. The central role defined by neo-corporatism for the planner is that of mediator. However, neo-corporatist theory, for the most part, contains no implication that this is a desirable role in the secretive and exclusive setting of its performance. Neo-corporatists tend to contrast 'bad' corporatist intermediation with a somewhat idealized 'pluralist' intermediation. The attraction of corporatist intermediation, however, is that it offers an accountable majoritarian government some real power to implement policy. If pluralism exposes the weakness of the majoritarian state in the face of necessarily dispersed power, corporatism offers a way back to strength within the limitations imposed by the existing power structure. Pluralism provides for widespread consultation and open contestation of policy – which is a necessary ingredient of democracy – but little opportunity for implementation of policy. Corporatism permits consistent implementation, but only at the expense of openness. Pluralist intermediation means that the powerless in society can (if they are organized) compete with the powerful for the attention of the state. Corporatism, by selecting and llimiting the numbers of the players, means that the powerful will always be selected and the powerless usually excluded. We come back to the Machiavellian dilemma, referred to earlier, which the planner faces in dealing with power.

Neo-corporatism challenged the reality of the ectopic state, postulating in effect a form of political order, 'associative order' in Schmitter's words, between the organic and market forms. This is a conclusion to which much recent pluralist thought also points, so it is reasonable to postulate a convergence between neo-corporatist and neo-pluralist theory. Neo-liberal thought, in the conservative tradition, holds on to the idea of the ectopic state. The most important contribution of neo-liberal theory is its insistence on the virtues of the market as a distributional and co-ordinating mechanism, and its ability to throw into sharp relief the dilemma between market and bureaucratic decision-making ('blueprint' planning). The virtue of markets is real. Hayek's argument that the market is a co-ordinating mechanism that allows *the individual* to plan is convincing. The market is a system of incentives encouraging people to engage in service to each other. These are truths planners have sometimes been reluctant to accept. The fact that it is land markets modified by rules of land-use regulation and interest intermediation and not blueprint plans determined by bureaucratic rule that have determined the form of cities is too often incorrectly regarded as a failure or negation of planning.

Neo-liberalism also highlights the contrast between the 'rule of law', which is universally applicable, and political or bureaucratic judgements pertaining to individual cases. For individuals to plan they must be able to rely on clearly specified and known rules being applied by the state. The pluralist, and especially the corporatist modes of decision-making seem to fly in the face of the rule of law, since each case is decided 'on its merits', or on the balance of power among the key players. Here, there is an interesting dilemma. Rules must be stated in general terms. To do otherwise would constitute a 'blueprint' plan. But the more generally stated is a rule, the more it is open to interpretation. Interpretation, according to neo-liberals, is the function of the law courts. But use of the courts to settle matters of interpretation of law merely substitutes a competitive process (usually involving the expenditure of large sums on lawyers fees) for a more collaborative process of negotiation or bureaucratic decision. Although the existence of universal laws stated in general terms is a requirement of a just polity, certainty on the outcome of a dispute can, in fact, never be guaranteed by such laws.

However, neo-liberal theory goes much further than this. First, the dilemma between markets and planning is interpreted as a choice between freedom and 'serfdom'. For reasons already stated, this is far too extreme an interpretation. It overlooks the characteristic of markets as a means for the realization and transmission of vastly unequal economic power and the function of bureaucratic decision-making in correcting this inequality. From the point of view of urban planning, it also ignores the special characteristic of land as an indivisible nexus; moreover, markets only respond to presently expressed preferences, and the use of land, as an irreplaceable resource, must somehow accommodate the desires of future populations.

Secondly, the existing distribution of wealth and power is regarded by neo-liberals as just, therefore political struggle to alter that distribution is viewed as profoundly immoral. Nozick, in fact, turns the matter round, saying that no change to existing distributions of wealth can be carried out without breach of 'just process'. Those who want to understand the debate between a conception of justice as 'just process' and a conception of justice as 'fair outcomes' would do well to read Pitkin's brilliant discussion of Plato's dialogue between Socrates and Thrasimachus (Pitkin, 1972, pp. 169–92, Plato: *Republic*, Book 1). Pitkin's Wittgensteinian view is that both conceptions are true in a different sense, and that we need to value the dialectic between the two concepts more than each in its pure form. There is a dilemma. While the importance of 'just process' must be acknowledged, the principle of human emancipation, and thus democracy, necessarily entails equality. Dahl's (1985, 1989) reasoning can be contrasted with that of Nozick (1974). Dahl (1989, pp. 311–12) writes: 'The close association between democracy and certain kinds of equality leads to a powerful moral conclusion: if freedom, self-development, and the advancement of shared interests are good ends, and if persons are intrinsically equal in their moral worth, then opportunities for attaining these goods should be distributed equally to all persons.' The legitimacy of political struggle over material resources was correctly established in the twentieth century as a fundamental condition of democracy. Additionally, those who laud the virtues of modern capitalism in serving the legitimate desires of mass populations conveniently forget the historical role of political struggle in creating the conditions for the redistribution of economic power necessary to bring this about.

Thirdly, the strong ectopic state, as the only legitimate representative of the public interest, is counterposed against the 'associative orders' of pluralism and corporatism. Conservatives take up varying positions combining the strong, if functionally restricted, state, and the strong market as the proper form of order. The danger of all these positions is their tendency to institutionalize 'plutocracy', the rule of wealth.

Neo-liberalism postulates that the task of the planner is to establish markets for all feasible products and services. The role prescribed for the planner is something like that of an umpire, ensuring that the rules of market exchange are properly observed and correcting departures, created by unavoidable bureaucratic decisions, from the outcomes that would be achieved by market exchange if a market could be established. Thus, the planner apportions costs in such a way as to balance the effects of 'externalities' – negative against positive.

Dissenting theory

Dissenting theory challenges the assumption that capitalism, even democratic capitalism, is a benign system. Through their concept of alienation, Marx and Engels formulated a radical critique of freedom under capitalism. They pointed out that workers, the real producers of wealth, were unfree in various different ways. By contrast, freedom consisted in the freedom of people to express themselves through collaboratively organized work; work, that is, for themselves and not on behalf of an exploiting employer. In capitalism, workers were reduced to mere commodities to be exchanged like mere things on the labour market. Conflict between the working class and the property-owning class was the fundamental conflict around which capitalism deposited 'layer upon layer of structure' (Aronson, 1985). Thus the complex of structures known as 'the state' or the 'political superstructure' (which includes its 'bourgeois' ideology) developed to cope with the conflicts created by inequality in the ownership of property.

However, critique of capitalism is insufficient as a theory of action. Marx and Engels wanted not only to explain the world but to change it. The political questions are how, and to what? The answers to these questions are closely tied together, because the political regime established in the course of 'changing the world' becomes the political regime to which the world is changed. Marx and Engels envisaged a world of collaborative work. But inherent in work there is a dilemma between working for self and working for others. Marx and Engels assumed that this dilemma would be resolved when the class system of production was overturned. The method of resolving it was through the control of production by a workers' state: the dictatorship of the proletariat. Central planning by the state, therefore, figured both as a ready-made solution to the problem of social organization of work and as an alternative to the capitalist mode of production. In many ways, central planning is the counterpart of the market in liberal theory. Both mechanisms were thought of as sufficient substitutes for politics. Unfortunately, the alternative of central planning turned out to be a dismal failure when compared with a capitalism *modified* by the political struggle of the working people. Marxian critique, therefore, had to become a critique of Marxism as well as a critique of capitalism.

In chapter 8 three forms of this critique were examined: Gramsci's critique of political praxis, the reformulation of class theory and the reformulation of state theory. Gramsci sought to conceptualize civil society and the state as a 'dialectical unity'. The state penetrates civil society through the apparatus of hegemony. To establish hegemony, it is necessary to mobilize the consent of the mass of the population. Economic crisis in capitalism would not be sufficient to produce revolutionary change. Nor would capture of the state be sufficient to guarantee working-class power. As to political strategy, moments of potential for fundamental change occur when the energy and commitment necessary for class struggle are coupled with a certain freedom to organize. The party of labour is the vehicle for the creation of a working-class hegemony. The organization of the party is the model for the organization of the 'dictatorship of the proletariat'. The party would become the leader and core of a coalition of classes and factions in a 'war of position' with the bourgeoisie. In order to maintain both leadership from the centre and contact with the periphery, the party leadership would conduct a continuous dialogue with its mass base ('dialectic of leadership and spontaneity') directed at education of the mass and resolution on a course of action. Critique would need to be directed at the strongest points of capitalist ideology. If this formula is taken seriously as a mode of dispersal of political power, it is evidently a pluralist strategy, for the validity of differing viewpoints and interests must be acknowledged. The strategy works by mobilizing consent and not, at least in the first instance, by coercion. It may be necessary to seize power by force, but only when such seizure already has mass approval.

Gramsci assumed that an industrial proletariat would form the vanguard of a widespread progressive working-class movement. Subsequent thinking by Marxists on 'class', along Gramscian lines, throws doubt on that assumption. The concept of 'class' as descriptive of the basic relationship in a mode of production is uncoupled from 'class' as descriptive of a political structure in which people with shared interests act together. 'Non-class' (in the economic sense) structures play a significant role in political struggle. Indeed, under capitalism non-class structures proliferate. The Marxist reformulation of the 'class' concept does not deny the reality of a basic exploitative 'class' relationship inherent in the mode of production, but the adaptive strategies that arise under capitalism create new interests crystallized around classes and groups other than the traditional class enemies in industrial capitalism, proletariat and bourgeoisie. Marxist political strategies must come to grips with a real plurality of political actors and interests, a plurality that is not reducible to 'class' or 'class fraction'.

We can say, therefore, that class is to do with *interests*, arising from exploitation in the process of production, which certain widespread groups of people have in common – but this is not the only or even necessarily the strongest thing they have in common. Or we can say that class is some sort of grouping of *people* who happen to share certain interests arising from a variety of sources (for example, from culture, locale, the consumption process, politics). These are two different ways of using the term 'class'. What we can no longer assume is that the formation of interests in the process of production will necessarily generate organized groups of people around these interests. Capitalism divides and spreads interests, creating pluralist hegemony. Maybe, however, a socialist hegemony would have to do likewise – so that it comes to be in the interest of capitalists to give concessions that will ultimately change the mode of production.

Examination of the outcome of economic crisis turned the Marxian attention to the capacity of capitalism to survive. The state plays a pivotal role in that survival, for it is because both the broad economic interests of capital and labour are represented in the state, even though the balance of power favours the former, that hegemony is possible. As Ellul (1967, p. 13) puts it, 'The expansion of the state's encroachment upon all our affairs is exactly paralleled by our conviction that things *must* be that way.' Regimes espousing neo-liberal ideology do not appear to have weakened that conviction. In a capitalist hegemonic system, the state becomes the main generator of struggle and resistance. The activities of the state are determined by political considerations and need not coincide with the 'needs' of capital. In any case, 'capital' does not have unambiguous 'needs'. There are always competing strategies in defence of a particular 'regime of accumulation'. Structure is simply what is established as the outcome of past struggle and what now forms the ground rules of present struggle (Jessop, 1988). Some Marxists have tried to identify a new 'post-Fordist' form of capitalism, which reasserts the power and command over consumption of a new capitalist class together with a new set of myths, illusions and ideologies. Others question the unity and coherence of the most recent developments in capitalism.

Urban planning drew strength from the idea that there eexisted a viable form of central planning. But Marxist theory tended to view 'capitalist' planning in a negative light. Until a new mode of production was established, urban planning could do no more than support and maintain the unjust system of power. If it is agreed that centralist 'blueprint' planning can no longer be considered viable, the ideology of planning may be weakened but so is the Marxist critique of planning in capitalism. If Marxism does not provide a viable alternative, then we can only look to so-called bourgeois practices and ideologies to provide one. It is also possible that planners themselves, occupying a contradictory class position within the state ensemble, may be part of the progressive class of today or at least part of a progressive coalition; though who will lead this coalition remains to be seen. To realize such a possibility, planners will have to 'step aside' (as Harvey, 1985, puts it) from their given roles, reconsider the 'rules of the game' and conceptualize how these may be changed in order to accord better with their political values and economic interests. Marxism draws attention to the most basic rules of capitalism embedded in cherished assumptions about property, contract and wage labour. The roles prescribed are those of critic and activist.

Critical theory in the tradition of the Frankfurt School shifted the dissenting perspective from Marx to Weber (or rather, as Habermas, 1987, p. 232, says, to 'the interpretation of Marx stemming from Western Marxism's reception of Weber'). In both Adorno and Marcuse the struggle is against domination rather than, as in Gramsci, for communism. Aware that all political ideas and prescriptions could become formulae for legitimating domination, Adorno set out to expose as false all claims that the 'good' or 'just' society had been achieved – even to the point of turning critique against itself. Marcuse sought to expose the totally enveloping cultural shroud of capitalism in which freedom in America was wrapped. In both capitalism and Soviet socialism, freedom was redefined in terms of obedience to cultural norms or bureaucratic rules. In Marcuse's work the dilemma is revealed between freedom and security. Planning is necessary to ensure security for the individual or nation. The goal of authentic self-determination by individuals depends on effective social control over the production and distribution of necessities. But planning inhibits freedom.

The standard that critical theory sets for planning is, therefore, in the process of decision-making. Plans must be arrived at through a consensus-seeking process, a discursive process in which the full range of interests affected are represented and the bearers of these interests freely reach agreement. But Marcuse's prescription begs important questions. How is power to be redistributed without the use of force? Once force is used, how can it be prevented from becoming institutionalized and misused? Marcuse had in mind a system in which production would somehow be removed from politics (something Marx also envisaged under communism). But this is a central problem of political economy: how can production be adapted to the full range of human desires without the process of production and distribution being used to accumulate economic power, thus fatally biasing the expression of demand in favour of the rich? Dissenting theory is not alone in assuming a simple answer to these questions. Neo-liberalism with its faith in the market is equally guilty of the glib answer. In reality there are many different answers, which is why 'capitalism' takes many different forms. But more understanding is needed of how people actually co-operate successfully, and under what cultural, institutional and economic conditions.

Habermas, perhaps the most remarkable successor of the Frankfurt School, has tried in his work to integrate two concerns: the critique of society and the criteria of political action. He does this by postulating two distinct domains of knowledge: 'system' and 'lifeworld'. In the terms discussed in chapter 3, these can be regarded as arising out of different forms of praxis: critique of society, and political struggle (involving critique of rationality). There are crisis tendencies in any mass society, produced by dilemmas of the sort already referred to, which sometimes eventuate in actual crises. This constant tension in mass society is the force behind social change, a force which, in response, creates political structures such as those of the state, and presumably also the 'associative order' noticed by the pluralists and neo-corporatists.

'Modernism' postulated the existence of an external point from which to observe and criticize. 'Post-modernism' rejects such a postulate. Ideas serve interests and emerge from praxis – practical human activity. Marx proposed work as the material praxis that unites the human species. Habermas, very much in the tradition of Wittgenstein, postulates 'communication' as an equally universal praxis, equally formative of human identity. The assumptions contained in the praxis of communication, assumptions which we have to adopt in order to communicate, provide the criteria for 'communicative action'. In so far as an ethical politics eschews coercion, these can become criteria of political association. Communicative action is directed towards reaching understanding. The substitution of communicative action for force is the product of a universal interest in human emancipation. 'Reaching understanding' occurs through argument from which all force (power play) is absent. There must be no prior distinction based on bureaucratic hierarchy, social status or wealth. Thus, intrinsic equality of the participants is a necessary but not sufficient condition. Equally necessary is the adoption by the participants of certain norms: of truth (outer world), truthfulness (inner world – sincerity), effectiveness (social world) and comprehensibility (language). Habermas does not explore the psycho-social implications of his argument to any great extent, but undoubtedly they are immense. Starting at the level of the group, a group may espouse norms such as those proposed by Habermas but its practice may differ from its espoused theory (Bion, 1961; Argyris and Schon, 1974). Just how does a group work without unconscious fears and hopes distorting its decision-making praxis? Internal critique seems necessary on the basis of Freudian psycho-social theory, which, as Marcuse recognized, has its place alongside Marx's critique of society.

Forester and others have derived practical prescriptions for urban planning from critical theory, particularly from Habermas. Planners engage constantly in communicative practices, political discourse, with individuals and groups. Habermas's criteria provide an ethical basis for such practices. Habermas's theory provides a theoretical foundation for a radical pluralism, a pluralism that can already be implemented under present conditions and as a means of transforming those conditions. The problems of implementation may, however, be greater than the critical planning theorists suppose.

So far, then, we have reviewed some of the political theory in the assenting and dissenting schools that provide foundations for planning thought. Although they may not do so explicitly, different political theories ask their readers to make up their minds in favour of diverging choices when faced with the dilemmas of politics. The present book also contains its biases, which are, it is hoped, explicit. But the choices are the reader's. In what follows we shall draw some more convergent conclusions about the nature of the state and planning suggested by the theory discussed.

State theory and planning

Urban social theory has been much taken with the work of the sociologist Anthony Giddens (1979, 1984). This is no doubt because Giddens confronts head-on the problem, which has concerned pluralist and Marxist theorists alike, of the relationship between the very obvious and much reported facts of individual and pressure group activity and the less visible 'structures' that both limit and shape such overt political activity. Giddens has reconstrued the idea of social structure in terms of an active process, which he calls 'structuration'. Society structures itself through the purposive action of multiple subjects organized in various ways, both in terms of the rules under which they are associated and how they interpret their world. Syntactically, therefore, 'structuration' indicates a reflexive form of the verb 'to structure'. Although action is by definition purposive, structuration is not, for the structures set up as a result of action include 'unintended consequences' (see also Merton, 1936, Vernon, 1979). As a sociologist, Giddens views society as continually being reconstituted by people following their conceptions of the world and acting out the rules and customary norms that have developed as a result of the aggregate of all previous actions. This perspective, although fruitful, fails to give sufficient emphasis to the distinction between the active and passive dimensions of structure. In so far as the study of politics is about structure, it is about a kind of structure by means of which people actively seek to transform nature and organize themselves.

Mann (1987, p. 16) characterizes society in terms of 'organized networks of power': 'Human beings do not create unitary societies but a diversity of intersecting networks of social interaction.' Equally, social structures are not discrete objects, they overlap and interweave. Some structures are simply collections of people with shared interests at some level, others are groups of people actively working together under certain norms or rules. Both 'interests' and 'norms and rules' are defined by means of systems of belief, ideology. But the distinction between simply sharing interests (so perceived) and actively and collectively working to achieve them is an important one. Marxists have recognized this distinction with the concepts 'class in itself' and 'class for itself' (e.g. Poulantzas, [1968] 1973). Pluralists make the distinction between 'interest groups' and 'pressure groups' or organizations (e.g. Truman, [1951] 1965). In order to conceptualize the state in society this distinction can be generalized. The passive dimension of structure we will call 'social' and the active dimension 'political'. A society is thus a self-sustaining (self-reproducing) and, sometimes, self-transforming system with a degree of secular stability, consisting of social and political structures.

Political structures are forms of association in which rules are made, interpreted, acted upon, acted out, changed, enforced or obeyed. They are, therefore, structures of domination. Examples in modern 'Western' society are the state, the organization, the business corporation, the market, the 'pressure' group, and the family. Social structures are people associated by common interest. Examples are classes, strata and interest groups. Social structures may be formed by culture, 'locale', the division of labour or technology (see, for example, Massey, 1984; Gregory and Urry, 1985). They may also be acted on and sometimes formed by political structures. Through their rule-making activity (including the making of norms and 'criteria'), political structures may constitute social structures. For example, neither women nor blacks are inherently 'structural' groups in any meaningful sense. Yet the norms given by the family and the state in certain societies create these groups as social structures of gender and race. These social structures have in turn thrown up a variety of political structures, groups that struggle against the existing order or form up in support of it. While it is no doubt true that the organization of societies reflects the power of interests within them, it is also true that societies, even the most authoritarian, are never monolithic. As Mann (1987) says, there are always interstices in the power structure in which new alliances can be formed, new wedges driven in and from which new structures can emerge.

In current ideology markets are portrayed as something like natural phenomena. There is reason to dispute this view. Weber ([1924] 1968) argued cogently that the market was a legally sanctioned institution for the conduct of struggle for the means of existence among groups and individuals with varying economic resources. Money was not only an index of price and the key to formally rational accounting but also the means by which economic power was concretized and wielded. Karl Polanyi ([1944] 1975) pointed out that markets are political structures in which property relations are realized in action. More recently, Peter Hall in his examination of state intervention in the economies of Britain and France concluded that, 'Markets are themselves institutions whose effectiveness varies with their configuration, just as the effectiveness of public policy does. Moreover, many markets depend on an ancilliary network of social institutions, often generated and sustained by state action, in order to function effectively' (Hall, P., 1986, p. 282). From a viewpoint further to the right, the market appears as a means of co-ordination quite independent of its state supports (Mises, [1949] 1963, p. 257; Hayek, 1944, pp. 39, 40, 51). Mises ([1949] 1963, pp. 287–9) points out that the function of inequality of wealth, which finds expression in the market, is to compel social co-ordination. Economic domination may be preferable to naked force or bureaucratic coercion, but it is domination just the same. The term Hayek and Mises use to describe the order of the market is 'catallactic'. 'Catallaxy' is order brought about by multiple transactions or exchanges. The market is thus a political structure, an order of orders.

The establishment of markets demands a strong state to maintain the rules that permit the transmission of inequalities in ownership of resources into material effects (Hall S., 1983; Gamble, 1988). If the strong, decisive state is a requirement of the market, might it not also be said that the increasing efficacy of the market tends to produce strong, decisive states? When the market organizes by throwing its participants into competition, the state, like any other participant, must respond by acting in a decisive and unified way. The state is forced to behave more like a corporation.

The state is an ensemble of political and social structures. However, the state may be regarded as a single political structure in one important sense. Modern states have come to be regarded as *the* political structure through which collective action can be taken on behalf of society as a whole. A state can deliberately and purposively enact rules for the conduct of its subjects. Through its monopoly of violence these rules can then be enforced; though in a state that is widely regarded as legitimate the threat of force need only rarely be actually invoked. The most perfect embodiment of this image of the state as the political arm of society is the democratic (or at least 'polyarchic') state. Through democratic processes, pressures exerted in civil society are transmitted to the state. Politicians respond to what they perceive to be demands emerging from civil society. If those demands are multiple and contradictory, the logical response of the state will be multiple and contradictory. Many different programmes will be created to meet the demands. If, on the other hand, the demands are strongly organized and point in one direction, be it through the catallactic process of the market or by virtue of the dominance of a particular group or coalition, the logical response of the state will be to organize itself to move in a single direction.

Political structures occur both inside and outside the domain of 'the state'. Therefore, while the state may be regarded as itself a political structure, it is useful to maintain the common distinction between the state and civil society as separate domains of action. Even though the boundary between the two may be difficult to distinguish, the conceptual distinction between 'the state' and the rest of society is characteristic of modernity (see Poggi, 1978; Bendix, 1964). What we have to consider is the relationship between these two domains. In terms of action how 'decisive' are the political structures in the state as against political structures in civil society? By 'decisive' we do not mean the degree of influence exerted by a particular group on the outcome of a particular event. We are speaking here of decisiveness in general, the tendency to engender action of some lasting structural consequence; the tendency for the forces exerted by political structures to become aligned in a single direction instead of counteracting each other. Decisiveness necessarily entails domination, whether or not it is willingly supported. Usually, however, this domination is accompanied by legitimacy. In this respect popular knowledge (or ideology) establishes the basis of legitimacy both for action and domination.

We need not assume that there is a straightforward trade-off between the decisiveness in civil society and in the state. It may be that neither are decisive. There may be a lack of 'decisiveness' all round in a particular society at a particular time. This lack of collective decisiveness signifies a corresponding increase in personal freedom. People are not constrained to act collectively to change anything, but their freedom remains constrained by all the existing social and political structures without which a society could hardly be said to exist. Nevertheless, the loss of freedom entailed by increased collective decisiveness is perhaps one of the principal normative issues facing us today. Whereas the danger of a weak and highly fragmented polity is ungovernability and a kind of inertia, the danger of too much collective decisiveness is authoritarianism.

Figure 10.2 shows the state and society as two axes or dimensions scaled according to weak or strong collective decisiveness. If we set the two axes off against one another we have the means of generating some ideal types of polity, which can then be used to make sense of empirical data. At the extremes we find the *bureaucratic*

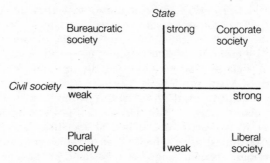

Figure 10.2 Collective decisiveness in state and civil society

society, dominated by a strong, hierarchical state in the presence of a weakly decisive civil society; the *plural* society, in which decisiveness is minimal on both sides; the *liberal* society, organized collectively by the catallaxy of the market in the presence of a weak state; and the *corporate* society dominated by the strong market and the strong state.

This model, however, is insufficient to characterize the interaction between political structures in the state and in civil society. It is necessary to add a second dimension, a relational dimension. This relational dimension has been much discussed in the debates between pluralist and neo-corporatist theorists.

In order to develop a clearer picture of the relational dimension, let us briefly consider the two ideal types of polity that have already been foreshadowed. The first is the market polity. Here, the main organizing principle in civil society is the market, which involves many individuals in simple trading or exchange relationships. The status of the relationships in this universe of colliding atoms is established by laws of property and contract. The ideology is one of 'philosophical individualism'. Of course authority is needed to enforce the rule of law, but this authority is concentrated in the ectopic state. The state is entirely separate from civil society and is related to civil society only by controlling the fundamental rules of exchange among 'free' individuals. This is the polity of Hobbes and Hayek.

The second ideal type is the organic polity. In this concept authority is spread throughout society. The state is merely the pinnacle of the authority structure, or as Hegel puts it, the highest (but not the unique) expression of universality. Contrary to the image portrayed by modern neo-corporatists, the state does not need to delegate or share 'its' authority with the corporations, because political authority is not the unique property of the state. The idea of the organic polity can be traced to feudal society and its successor, the Ständesstaat or the society of the estates. Hegel ([1821] 1967, p. 152, para 251) and

Durkheim ([1902] 1949, p. 5), reacting to what they perceived as the threat of a purely atomized society of free-floating egoists ruled by an ectopic state, developed new conceptions of the organic polity. The organic polity embodies the principle of collectivism, which is to be found in all socialist thought and especially in the normative themes in the work of Marx and Engels.

Both of the above ideal types capture something of the truth of modern capitalist societies. But they remain poles to which societies tend, rather than descriptions of actual societies. We should then consider a third ideal type, which we shall call the interactive polity, which describes a certain range between these poles. The interactive polity is the type that is suggested by the convergent traditions of institutional–pluralist and neo-corporatist thought. The interactive polity is one in which political structures settle their differences mainly through political interaction, manoeuvring and talk. 'Negotiation' and 'bargaining' are terms frequently used, but these seem rather too narrow. Mediation occurs not just by actors coming together and talking through their differences but by the talk being structured by certain concepts, principles and ideologies (see Roweis, 1983; Friedmann, 1987) The principles and practices of urban planning are very much a case in point. The negotiation of conflict over land use takes place within a fluctuating set of implicit assumptions and 'knowledges' that structure the discourse: concepts of 'amenity', 'participation', 'third party rights', 'environmental externalities', 'efficiency', 'equity' (which means something quite different to planners from the legal meaning of 'equity'), and so forth. The question of who has access to forums of intermediation is also most important, and, therefore, what constitute the criteria for access (see Healey, McNamara, Elson and Doak, 1988). 'Associative order' (Streeck and Schmitter, 1985), the network of 'interest systems' (Lehmbruch, 1989), the 'differentiated polity' (Rhodes, 1988) are all ways of conceptualizing the overlapping systems of authority and order that span between state and civil society.

At least four 'positions' can be identified along the relational continuum. At the market (ectopic state) end of the spectrum we have a lobbying relationship between the state and organized interests. Groups outside the state make demands upon it, and the state responds to these demands in whatever way its leaders and lower level officials think will serve their purposes best. This is the type of demand-oriented 'input' politics which, according to Heisler and Kvavik (1974) is reasonably characteristic of the American polity (others would disagree that it is so characteristic; see Lustig, 1982). Easton (1965) points to the importance of 'gatekeepers' in the system, who filter the demands (see also Pahl, 1977). We should also note that standardized rules may be applied to deal with demands. This is particularly the case in land–use planning where those wishing to carry out development of prescribed types must apply for a permit to do so. The front desk of the planning authority is, for some developers, the boundary between themselves and the state.

A second position on the way towards the organic polity is when those making demands or putting forward proposals (for example, concerning urban development) enter into protracted, non–public negotiations with the ultimate decision–makers in the state. Cawson (1986) has described such a relationship as 'micro–corporatist'. Healey *et al.* (1988) describe this relationship as 'bargaining'. They do not regard such a relationship as corporatist on the grounds that it does not extend to 'a range of issues over time'. In other words, while there may be protracted negotiations between a government and a developer over a particular project, the same developer (or its representative) is not consulted on other projects. However, it might be asked rhetorically, if the state makes a permanent practice of consulting developers behind closed doors about urban development, what else is this but corporatism? We shall adopt the term used by Healey *et al.*, bargaining, to describe this position on the continuum.

A further step towards corporatism (or the organic state) is when a group or corporation outside the state is consulted about policy on a more or less permanent basis. Here, there may be structures created specifically to legitimize such consultations: consultative councils or committees. The groups represented on these committees do not necessarily have a monopoly of representation of a particular sphere of interest in society, nor is the issue of command of their members particulary salient. In order to reduce open conflict, which the political leaders of the state regard as electorally debilitating, it is usually enough to co–opt the leadership of the external group. Selznick (1966, p. 13) defines 'coöptation' as 'the process of absorbing new elements into the leadership or policy–determining structure of an organisation as a means of averting threats to its stability or existence'. The term 'incorporation', which has been more widely used in neo–corporatist work, will be used to describe this position.

Finally, there is the position of full-blown neo–corporatism, in which key organizations representing interests that are in conflict at the most fundamental level (e.g. capital and labour) are inserted into the steering mechanisms of the state at the highest level. It is imperative that the bargains struck at this level, facilitated by the state (with its own interests firmly in mind), are complied with. Therefore, these organizations must be equipped with a degree of coercive authority over all the groups and individuals within their purview. This authority is usually supplied by the state. To this end the state may seek to restructure the organizations to create more effective hierarchies and/or to outlaw deviant organizations.

Frequently, this process is accompanied by a rhetoric of nationalism, economic success, consensus and class reconciliation. In line with neo-corporatist terminology, we call this position concertation. Just as lobbying stops short of the pure market polity in which the state merely exists to uphold the rule of law, so also concertation stops short of the organic society in which political authority is spread throughout society (Figure 10.3). None of the above is inconsistent with Marx's view of the fundamentally exploitative nature of the relationship between capital and labour in the process of production. What is disputed is the instrumentalist and capital-reductionist view of the state. The state is formed by political dynamics, which respond to and are influenced by the conflict of interest over production. But the form of the state in society cannot be derived from this conflict alone (see chapter 8 pp. 220–5).

Looking to the future, the 'interactive' polity may be contrasted with a hypothetical 'discursive polity' postulated by Habermas. Although the interactive polity is organized by communicative practices, these practices are not, as yet, structured on ethical lines. The 'discursive polity' will emerge from the interactive polity through political struggle. It will be shaped by the nature of the struggle. There is no perfect polity waiting to emerge once the struggle has been 'won'. The general form of polity will be shaped both by the norms and structures of democracy already in existence and the extension of democracy into the corporate ensemble. New norms of communicative practice, such as those discussed by Habermas, will have to become entrenched before the 'discursive polity' can be realized. If Habermas is right, the establishment of such norms follow

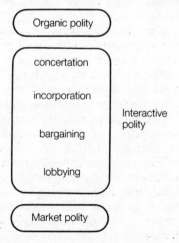

Figure 10.3   Elements of an interactive polity

naturally from the imperatives of communication itself. They are not ideological superimpositions at odds with practical reality. If he is right, the establishment of such norms will seem a natural response to economic and political crises. So too will the extension of democracy to the corporate ensemble. But these developments will not occur without human agency. They must be struggled over, debated and fought for. Democracy has to be defended as well as extended. State power will be involved. Planners, as political agents, and agents in the state, can expect to play active roles in pursuit of the values of the discursive society, roles already delineated by pluralist theory. But the performance of these roles must be informed by those very values (see Forester, 1980, 1982a and 1982b).

Land-use planning is one of many institutions and practices through which the particular character of a polity is realized. Whenever the state enacts a rule some new stratum or interest group may be formed. Land-use planning was instituted as a result of the perceived inadequacy of the market, not only to produce a socially acceptable physical environment but also to resolve conflicts among landowners. Property in land could not be defined simply in terms of absolute ownership rights over territorial parcels, because the value of a particular parcel of land was tied in with the value of all neighbouring land. Professionalism and bureaucracy eventually came to be employed in conjunction with the land market to form a new hybrid institution for the mediation of interests and the resolution of conflict.

The institution of land-use planning is, however, something more than a static device mediating among powerful interests in land. It is a growing and changing political structure in its own right, which also plays a certain role in changing the polity of which it is a part. As was argued in chapter 4 p. 76, the decision to institute land-use planning sets in motion a sequence of events whose course is contingent on political conditions in different countries. In the process of its development, land-use planning defines new interests and new pressure groups; creates new bureaucratic organization; new rules for decision-making are laid down; new knowledge is created, which sets up public expectations of the state. Each step in its development has consequences that, in aggregate, gradually change the nature of the polity in a particular sphere. The distinction between the collective 'steering' dimension (decisiveness) and the 'relational' dimension is an important one. The common assumption seems to be that a high degree of incorporation or concertation always goes with a high degree of internal organization and planning (decisiveness) on the part of the state. It is suggested here that the two dimensions, in fact, have quite separate dynamics. By analysing urban planning or land-use control, as a political field, we may be able to record the operation of these dynamics in particular places.

A final word

Political theory provides the foundations of planning knowledge. The truths of politics provide the ingredients of real and tolerable political systems. No single ingredient on its own is ever sufficient. For example, the reader may rightly conclude that three principles can be deduced from the arguments put forward in this book: the more open debate the better, the more informed debate the better, the more equal the opportunity to participate in the debate the better. These principles are threatened by the drive for decisiveness. Yet it is not a matter of one or the other, debate or decisiveness, but of how decisiveness can best be combined with debate, for a society that spent all its time in debate would produce nothing but words and would be politically moribund. In the twentieth century, through the peoples' political struggle, many capitalist regimes have come a long way towards a better, fairer polity. But there is still far to go before we leave barbarism behind for good. And there is an ever-present danger of regression.

Towards the end of the nineteenth century urban planning was seen as a vehicle for real social reform. Utopian ideas for the planning of cities centred on the creation of new built form, but within the existing framework of the (as yet new) democratic polity. One hundred years later the radical possibilities of urban planning are exhausted. We can see clearly that it is the rules constituted ultimately by the state that impress on cities their built form and the distribution of good and bad locations to rich and poor people. If further social reform is to be achieved, action has to be directed at the present rules rather than at the design of future cities. Planners need a new utopian vision, but it will not resemble the utopias of the early years. It will be a vision that centres on the ensembles of political structures that produce the city. In particular, attention must be given to extending democracy to the 'corporate ensemble', to the complex of firms whose pursuit of profit and entrepreneurial activity leads to the development of land. This extension is a necessary but not sufficient condition for real reform. A new role for the state must also be generated. Such changes, however, are unlikely until a major crisis occurs with which existing structures in the corporate and state ensembles cannot cope. Perhaps the changes will not occur at all in the capitalist nations of 'the West' but in the formerly planned economies of the former 'Eastern bloc'; if, that is, those nations do not wholly embrace liberal capitalism. It is not within the scope of this book to explore such visions and their implications for planning. However, let us end by noting that a better, fairer built form can only be achieved by a better, fairer polity.

Bibliography

Aberbach, J. D. and Rockman, B. A. (1989), 'Administration, interest groups and the changing political universe in Washington – Perceptions and behavior'. Paper prepared for the International Political Science Association Conference on the Structure and Organization of Government: 'Government and Organized Interests', Zurich, 27–30 September 1989.

Abercrombie, N. and Urry, J. (1983), *Capital, Labour and the Middle Classes* (London: Allen and Unwin).

Adorno, T. ([1966] 1973), *Negative Dialectics* (New York: The Seabury Press).

Aglietta, M. (1979), *A Theory of Capitalist Regulation: The U.S. Experience* (London: New Left Books).

Aglietta, M. (1982) 'Avant-propos à la deuxième édition', *Régulation et crises du capitalisme: L'Expérience des Etats Unis* (Paris: Calmann Levy).

Albrecht, J. and Lim, G-C. (1986), 'A search for alternative planning theory: use of critical theory', *Journal of Architectural and Planning Research*, vol. 3, pp. 117–131.

Albrow, M. (1970), *Bureaucracy* (London: Pall Mall Press).

Alexander, E. R. (1981), 'If planning isn't everything, maybe it's something', *Town Planning Review*, vol. 52, pp. 131–42.

Alexander, E. R. (1982), 'A rejoinder', *Town Planning Review*, vol. 53, pp. 72–7.

Alexander, E. R. (1984), 'After rationality, what?, A review of responses to paradigm breakdown, *Journal of the American Planning Association*, vol. 50, no. 1, pp. 62–9.

Alford, R. R. and Friedland, R. (1985), *Powers of Theory: Capitalism, the state and democracy* (Cambridge: Cambridge University Press).

Alinsky, S. D. ([1946] 1969), *Reveille for Radicals* (New York: Vintage Books).

Alinsky, S. D. (1971), *Rules for Radicals: A practical primer for realistic radicals,* (New York: Random House).

Almond, G. and Verba, S. (1963), *The Civic Culture* (Princeton, NJ: Princeton University Press).

Althusser, L. ([1965] 1979), *For Marx* (London: Verso).

Altshuler, A. A. (1970), *Community Control: The black demand for participation in large American cities* (New York: Pegasus).

Anderson, P. (1976/77), 'The antinomies of Antonio Gramsci', *New Left Review*, no. 100, pp. 5–80.

Andreski, S. (ed.) (1983), *Max Weber on Capitalism, Bureaucracy and Religion* (London: Allen and Unwin).

Arendt, H. (1967), 'Truth and politics', in P. Laslett and W. G. Runciman, (eds) *Philosophy, Politics and Society*, Third Series, (Oxford: Blackwell).

Argyris, C. and Schön, D. (1974), *Theory in Practice: Increasing professional effectiveness* (New York: Jossey Bass).

Arnstein, S. R. (1969), 'A ladder of citizen participation', *Journal of the American Institute of Planners*, vol. 35, pp. 216–24.

Aronson, R. (1985), 'Historical materialism, answer to Marxism's critics', *New Left Review*, no. 152, pp. 74–94.

Arrow, K. (1951), *Social Choice and Individual Values* (New Haven, Conn.: Yale University Press).

Bachrach, P. (1967), *The Theory of Democratic Elitism: A critique* (Boston: Little, Brown).

Bachrach, P. and Baratz, M. S. (1962), 'The Two Faces of Power', *American Political Science Review*, vol. 56.

Badcock, B. (1984), *Unfairly Structured Cities* (Oxford: Blackwell).

Banfield, E. C. (1968), *The Unheavenly City: The nature and future of our urban crisis* (Boston: Little, Brown).

Banfield, E. C. (1974), *The Unheavenly City Revisited: A revision of the unheavenly city* (Boston: Little, Brown).

Bardach, E. (1977), *The Implementation Game: What happens after a bill becomes a law* (London and Boston: MIT Press).

Barr, D. A. (1972), 'The professional urban planner', *Journal of the American Institute of Planners*, May 1972, pp. 155–9.

Barrett, S. and Fudge, C. (eds) (1981), *Policy and Action. Essays on the implementation of public policy* (London: Methuen).

Bay, C. ([1965] 1970), 'The concern with pseudopolitics', in H. S. Kariel, (ed.), *Frontiers of Democratic Theory* (New York: Random House), pp. 164–88.

Beaud, M. (1987), *Le Système National Mondial Hiérarchisé* (Paris: La Découverte).

Beauregard, R. A. (1980), 'Teaching planning theory: dilemmas beyond the rational model', *The Bulletin of the Association of Collegiate Schools of Planning*, vol. 18, no. 1 pp. 1–4.

Beauregard, R. A. (1984), 'Making planning theory: a retrospection', *Urban Geography*, vol 5, no.3, pp. 255–61.

Beauregard, R. A. (1986), 'Planning practice', *Urban Geography*, vol. 7, no. 2, pp. 172–8.

Beckman, N. (1964), 'The planner as bureaucrat', *Journal of the American Institute of Planners*, vol. 30, no. 4, pp. 323–7.

Beetham, D. (1985), *Max Weber and the Theory of Modern Politics* (Cambridge: Polity Press).

Bellah, R. N., Madsen, R., Sullivan, W. M., Swidler, A. and Tipton, S. M. (1985), *Habits of the Heart: Individualism and commitment in American life* (Berkeley: University of California Press).

Bendix, R. (1964), *Nation-building and Citizenship: Studies of our changing social order* (New York: Wiley).

Bendix, R. (1978), *Kings or People: Power and the mandate to rule* (Berkeley: University of California Press).

Benevolo, L. (1967), *The Origins of Modern Town Planning*, tr. J. Landry (London: Routledge and Kegan Paul).

Benn, T. (1985), 'Who dares wins', *Marxism Today*, vol 29, no. 1, pp. 12–14.

Benson, J. K. (1975), 'The interorganizational network as a political economy', *Administrative Science Quarterly*, June 1975.

Benson, J. K. (1980), 'Interorganizational networks and policy sectors: Notes towards comparative analysis' (unpublished).

Benson, J. K. and Weitzel, C. (1985), 'Social structure and social praxis in interorganizational policy analysis', in K. Hanf and T. A. J. Toonen, *Policy Implementation in Federal and Unitary Systems: Questions of analysis and design* (Dordrecht: Martinus Nijhoff).

Bentley, A. ([1908] 1935), *The Process of Government*, (Evanston, Ill.: Principia Press) (also the Harvard University Press edition of 1963 with an 'Introduction' by P. H. Odegard).

Berger, M. S. (ed.) (1981), *Dennis O'Harrow: Plan talk and plain talk* (Washington DC: Planners' Press, American Association of Planners).

Berger, P. L. and Neuhaus, R. J. (1977), *To Empower People: The role of mediating structures in public policy* (Washington, DC: American Enterprise Institute for Public Policy Research).

Berger, P. L. (1987), *The Capitalist Revolution: Fifty propositions about prosperity, equality and liberty* (Aldershot, Hants.: Wildwood House).

Berger, S (ed.) (1981), *Organizing Interests in Western Europe: Pluralism, corporatism, and the transformation of politics* (Cambridge: Cambridge University Press).

Bernstein, R. (1978), *The Restructuring of Social and Political Theory* (Philadelphia: University of Pennsylvania Press).

Bernstein, R. (1983), *Beyond Objectivism and Relativism* (Oxford: Blackwell).

Bhaskar, R. ([1975] 1978), *A Realist Theory of Science* (Leeds: Leeds Books).

Bion, W. R. (1961), *Experiences in Groups* (London: Tavistock).

Blau, P. M. (1963), *The Dynamics of Bureaucracy: A study of interpersonal relations in two government agencies* (Chicago: Chicago University Press).

Blowers, A. (1980), *The Limits of Power: The politics of local planning policy* (Oxford: Pergamon).

Bluestone, B. and Harrison, B. (1982), *The Deindustrialization of America* (New York: Basic Books).

Boccara, P. (1977), *Etudes sur le capitalisme monopoliste d'état, sa crise et son issue* (Paris: Editions Sociales).

Bonefeld, W. (1987), 'Reformulation of state theory', *Capital and Class*, vol. 33, pp. 96–127.

Bookchin, M. (1974), *The Limits of the City* (New York: Harper and Row).

Bourdieu, P. ([1972] 1977), *Outline of a Theory of Practice* (Cambridge: Cambridge University Press).

Bowles, S. and Gintis, H. (1986), *Democracy and Capitalism: Community and the contradictions of modern social thought* (New York: Basic Books).

Boyer, M. C. (1983), *Dreaming the Rational City: The myth of American city planning* (Cambridge, Mass.: MIT Press).

Boyer, R. (1979), 'Wage formation in historical perspective: the French experience', *Cambridge Journal of Economics*, vol. 3, pp. 99–118.

Boyte, H. (1980), *The Backyard Revolution* (Philadelphia: Temple University Press).

Bradbury, K. L., Downs, A. and Small, K. A. (1982), *Urban Decline and the*

Future of American Cities (Washington DC: The Brookings Institution).

Braudel, F. (1984), *The Perspective of the World, (Le Temps du Monde)*, Vol. 3 of Braudel, F. *Civilization and Capitalism* (London: Collins). Translated by S. Reynolds.

Brecht, A. (1959), *Political Theory: The foundations of twentieth century political thought* (Princeton, NJ: Princeton University Press).

Breheny, M. and Hooper, A. (eds) (1985), *Rationality in Planning: Critical essays* (London: Pion).

Breton, A. (1974), *The Economic Theory of Representative Government* (Chicago: Aldine).

Briggs, A. (1963), *Victorian Cities* (London: Odhams).

Brittan, S. (1975), 'The economic contradictions of democracy', *British Journal of Political Science*, vol. 5.

Brubaker, R. (1984), *The Limits of Rationality* (London: Allen and Unwin).

Bryson, J. M. and Roering, W. D. (1987), 'Applying private-sector strategic planning in the public sector', *Journal of the American Planning Association*, vol. 53, no.1, pp. 9–22.

Buchanan, J. M. (1977), *Freedom in Constitutional Contract: Perspectives of a political economist* (College Station, Tex.: Texas A and M University Press).

Buchanan, J. M. and Tullock, G. (1965), *The Calculus of Consent* (Ann Arbor, Mich.: University of Michigan Press).

Buci–Glucksmann, C. ([1975] 1980), *Gramsci and the State*, tr. David Fernbach (London: Lawrence and Wishart).

Burke, E. (1979), *A Participatory Approach to Urban Planning,* (New York: Human Sciences Press).

Campbell, C. and Peters, B. G. (1988), *Organizing Governance: Governing organizations* (Pittsburgh, Pa.: University of Pittsburgh Press).

Cardoso, J. P. (1958), *Questoes Corporativas – Doutrino e Factos* (Lisbon: Gabinete de Estudos Corporativos de Centro Universitario de Mocidade Portuguesa).

Carr-Saunders, A. M. and Wilson, P. A. (1933), *The Professions* (Oxford: Oxford University Press).

Castells, M. (1983), *The City and the Grass Roots* (London: Edward Arnold).

Catanese, A. J. (1978), 'Learning by comparisons: Lessons from experiences', in A. Catanese and P. Farmer (eds), *Personality, Politics and Planning: How city planners work* (Beverly Hills, Calif.: Sage), pp. 179–207.

Catanese, A. (1984), *The Politics of Planning and Development* (Beverly Hills, Calif.: Sage).

Cawson, A. (1978), 'Pluralism, corporatism and the role of the state', *Government and Opposition*, vol. 13, no. 2, Spring 1978, pp. 178–98.

Cawson, A. (1982), *Corporatism and Welfare* (London: Heinemann).

Cawson, A. (1986), *Corporatism and Political Theory* (Oxford: Blackwell).

Cawson, A. and Saunders, P. (1983), 'Corporatism, competitive politics and class struggle', in R. King (ed.) *Capital and Politics* (London: Routledge and Kegan Paul).

Checkoway, B. (1983), 'Forum on the future of planning practice', *Journal of Planning Education and Research*, vol. 3 pp. 51–60.

Cherry, G. E. (1974), 'The development of planning thought', in M. J. Bruton (ed.) *The Spirit and Purpose of Planning* (London: Hutchinson).

Cherry, G. E. (1982), *The Politics of Town Planning* (London: Longman).

Christensen, K. S. (1985), 'Coping with uncertainty in planning', *Journal of the American Association of Planners*, vol. 51, no. 1, pp. 63–73.

Clark, G. L. and Dear, M. (1984), *State Apparatus: Structures and Language of legitimacy* (Boston, Mass.: Allen and Unwin).

Clawson, M. and Hall, P. (1973), *Planning and Urban Growth, an Anglo-American Comparison* (Baltimore and London: Johns Hopkins University Press).

Cogan, M. L. (1953), 'Toward a definition of profession', *Harvard Educational Review*, vol. 23, pp. 33–50.

Cohen, G. A. (1989), 'Are freedom and equality compatible?', in J. Elster and K. O. Moene (eds), *Alternatives to Capitalism* (Cambridge: Cambridge University Press).

Cohen, J. and Rogers, J. (1983), *On Democracy* (Harmondsworth: Penguin).

Coit, K. (1978), 'Local action, not citizen participation', in W. Tabb and L. Sawers, *Marxism and the Metropolis* (New York: Oxford University Press).

Colby, P. W. (1983) 'The organization of public interest groups', *Policy Studies Journal*, vol. 11, no. 4, pp. 699–706.

Cole, G. D. H. (1935), *Principles of Economic Planning* (London: Macmillan).

Colebatch, T. (1989), 'Tax break for the super-rich', *The Age*, Melbourne, 16 December 1989, p. 1.

Collins, J. (1985), 'Education for practice, a local authority view', *Town Planning Review*, vol. 56, no. 4 pp. 458–67.

Connolly, W. (1969), *The Bias of Pluralism* (New York: Lieber-Atherton Press).

Cooke, P. (1983), *Theories of Planning and Spatial Development* (London: Hutchinson).

Cooke, P. and Rees, G. (1977) 'Faludi's "Sociology in Planning Education": a critical comment', *Urban Studies*, vol. 14, pp. 215–18.

Coser, L. (1956), *The Functions of Social Conflict* (London: Routledge and Kegan Paul).

Crouch, C. (1977), *Class Conflict and the Industrial Relations Crisis* (London: Heinemann).

Crouch, C. (1979), *The Politics of Industrial Relations* (London: Fontana).

Crozier, M. (1964), *The Bureaucratic Phenomenon* (London: Tavistock Publications).

Dahl, R. A. (1956), *A Preface to Democratic Theory* (Chicago: The University of Chicago Press).

Dahl, R. A. (1961), *Who Governs? Democracy and power in an American city* (New Haven, Conn.: Yale University Press).

Dahl, R. A. (1971), *Polyarchy: Participation and opposition* (New Haven, Conn.: Yale University Press).

Dahl, R. A. (1976), *Modern Political Analysis* (Englewood Cliffs, NJ: Prentice-Hall).

Dahl, R. A. (1982), *Dilemmas of Pluralist Democracy: Autonomy versus Control*

(New Haven, Conn.: Yale University Press).

Dahl, R. A. (1985), *A Preface to Economic Democracy* (Berkeley and Los Angeles: University of California Press).

Dahl, R. A. (1989), *Democracy and Its Critics* (New Haven, Conn.: Yale University Press).

Dahl, R. A. and Lindblom, C. E. (1953), *Politics, Economics and Welfare* (New York: Harper and Row).

Dahrendorf, R. (1967), *Society and Democracy in Germany* (Garden City, NY: Doubleday).

Dahrendorf, R. (1987) 'Max Weber and modern social science', in W. J. Mommsen and J. Osterhammel (eds) *Max Weber and his Contemporaries* (London: Allen and Unwin).

Danielson, M. N. and Doig, J. W. (1982), *New York: The politics of urban and regional development* (Berkeley: University of California Press).

Davidoff, P. and Reiner, T. (1962), 'A choice theory of planning', *Journal of the American Institute of Planners*, vol. 28, pp. 103–15.

Davidoff, P. (1965), 'Advocacy and pluralism in planning', *Journal of the American Institute of Planners*, vol. 31, no. 4, pp. 331–8.

Davis, M. (1986), *Prisoners of the American Dream* (London: Verso).

De Neufville, J. I. (1983), 'Planning theory and practice', *Journal of Planning Education and Research*, vol. 3, pp. 36–45.

De Neufville, J. I. (1987), 'Knowledge and action, making the link', *Journal of Planning Education and Research*, vol. 6, pp. 86–92.

Dennis, N. (1970), *People and Planning* (London: Faber and Faber).

Dennis, N. (1972), *Public Participation and Planners Blight* (London: Faber and Faber).

Dewey, J. (1927), *The Public and Its Problems* (New York: Henry Holt).

Dewey, J. and Tufts, J. M. ([1908] 1932), *Ethics* (New York: Henry Holt).

Domhoff, G. W. (1967), *Who Rules America?* (Englewood Cliffs, NJ: Prentice Hall).

Domhoff, G. W. (1983), *Who Rules America Now? A view for the eighties* (Englewood Cliffs, NJ: Prentice-Hall).

Dotson, F. (1951), 'Patterns of voluntary membership among working class families', *American Sociological Review*, vol. 16, p. 687.

Douglas, J. (1976), 'Review article: The overloaded crown', *British Journal of Political Science*, vol. 6, pp. 483–505.

Downs, A. (1967), *Inside Bureaucracy* (Boston: Little, Brown).

Duncan, G. (1973), *Marx and Mill: Two views of social conflict and social harmony* (Cambridge: Cambridge University Press).

Dunleavy, P. and O'Leary, B. (1987), *Theories of the State: The politics of liberal democracy* (London: Macmillan).

Durkheim, E. ([1902] 1949), *The Division of Labour in Society*, (Glencoe, Ill.: Free Press).

Dyckman, J. (1961), 'What makes planners plan?', *Journal of the American Institute of Planners*, vol 27, no. 2, pp. 164–167.

Dye, T. R. and Zeigler, L. H. (1972), *The Irony of Democracy: An uncommon introduction to American politics*, 2nd edn (Belmont, Calif.: Duxbury Wadsworth).

Easton, D. (1965), *A Systems Analysis of Political Life* (New York: Wiley).

Eckstein, H. (1960), *Pressure Group Politics* (Stanford, Calif.: Stanford University Press).

Edelman, M. (1977), *Political Language: Words that succeed, policies that fail* (New York: Academic Press).

Eden, R. (1987), 'Why wasn't Weber a nihilist?', in K. L. Deutsch and W. Soffer, (eds) *The Crisis of Liberal Democracy: A Straussian perspective* (New York: State University of New York Press), pp. 212–41.

Elkin, S. L. (1974), *Politics and Land Use Planning: The London experience* (Cambridge: Cambridge University Press).

Elliott, P. (1972), *The Sociology of the Professions* (London: Macmillan).

Ellul, J. (1967), *The Political Illusion* (New York: Knopf).

Emmet, D. (1966), *Rules, Roles and Relations* (Boston: Beacon Press).

Engels, F. ([1888] 1962), *Feuerbach and the End of Classical German Philosophy*, in K. Marx and F. Engels: *Selected Works*, Vol. 2, (Moscow: Foreign Languages Publishing House).

Engels, F. ([1884] 1962), *The Origin of the Family: Private property and the state*, in K. Marx and F. Engels, *Selected Works*, Vol. 2 (Moscow: Foreign Languages Publishing House).

Engels, F. ([1844] 1971), *The Condition of the Working Class in England in 1844*, tr. W. O. Henderson and W. H. Chaloner (Oxford: Blackwell).

Engels, F. (1890), *Letter from Engels to J. Bloch, 21 September 1890* in K. Marx and F. Engels (1962), *Selected Works* Vol. 2, (Moscow: Foreign Languages Publishing House) pp. 488–9.

Esser, J. (1982), *Gewerkschaften in der Krise* (Frankfurt: Suhrkamp).

Esser, J. and Hirsch, J. (1984), 'Der CDU Staat: Ein Politisches Regulierungsmodell für den Nachfordistischen Kapitalismus', PROIKA, vol. 56.

Evans, P. B., Rueschemeyer, D. and Skocpol, T. (eds) (1985), *Bringing the State Back In* (Cambridge: Cambridge University Press).

Eversley, D. (1973), *The Planner in Society: The changing role of a profession* (London: Faber and Faber).

Fainstein, N. I. and Fainstein, S. S. (1979), 'New debates in urban planning: The impact of Marxist theory within the U.S.', *International Journal of Urban and Regional Research*, vol. 3, no. 3. September 1979.

Fainstein S. S. *et al.* (1986), *Restructuring the City: the Political Economy of Urban Redevelopment* (New York: Longman).

Faludi, A. (1973a), *Readings in Planning Theory* (Oxford: Pergamon).

Faludi, A. (1973b), *Planning Theory* (Oxford: Pergamon).

Faludi, A. (1986), 'Towards a theory of strategic planning', *The Netherlands Journal of Housing and Environmental Research*, vol. 1, no 3, pp. 253–68.

Faludi, A. (1987), *A Decision-Centred View of Environmental Planning* (Oxford: Pergamon).

Festinger, L., Schachter, S. and Back, K. (1950) Social Pressures in Informal Groups, A Study in Human Factors in Housing (New York: Harper Bros.).

Fine, B. and Harris, L. (1979), *Rereading Capital* (London: Macmillan).

Fischer, E. ([1968] 1973), *Marx In His Own Words* (Harmondsworth: Penguin).

Fishman, R. (1977), *Urban Utopias in the Twentieth Century: Ebenezer Howard, Frank Lloyd Wright and Le Corbusier* (New York: Basic Books).

Foglesong, R. E. (1986), *Planning the Capitalist City* (Princeton, NJ: Princeton University Press).

Foley, D. L. (1960), 'British town planning: One ideology or three?' *British Journal of Sociology*, Vol. II.

Ford, G. B. (1913), 'The city scientific', in *Proceedings of the Fifth National Conference on City Planning*, pp. 31–40 (Cambridge, Mass.: Harvard University Press).

Forester, J. (1980), 'Critical theory and planning practice', *Journal of the American Planning Association*, July 1980, pp. 275–85.

Forester, J. (1982a), 'Planning in the face of power', *Journal of the American Association of Planners*, vol. 48, pp. 67–80.

Forester, J. (1982b), 'Understanding planning practice: an empirical, practical and normative account', *Journal of Planning Education and Research*, vol. 1, pp. 59–71.

Forester, J. (1987), 'Planning in the face of conflict: negotiation and mediation strategies in local land use regulation', *Journal of the American Association of Planners*, vol. 53, pp. 303–14.

Forsyth, M. (1988), 'Hayek's bizarre liberalism: A critique', *Political Studies*, vol. 36, pp. 235–50.

Frazer, R. D. L. (1972), 'Planning and government in the metropolis', *Public Administration* (Sydney), vol. 31, no. 1, pp. 123–47.

Freidson, E. (1970a), *Professional Dominance* (New York: Atherton Press).

Freidson, E. (1970b), *Profession of Medicine* (New York: Dodd, Mead and Co.).

Friedmann, J. (1967), 'A conceptual model for the analysis of planning behavior', *Administrative Science Quarterly*, vol. 12, no. 2, September 1967.

Friedmann, J. (1987), *Planning in the Public Domain: From knowledge to action* (Princeton, NJ: Princeton University Press).

Friend, J. K. and Jessop, W. N. (1969), *Local Government and Strategic Choice* (London: Tavistock Publications).

Friend, J. K., Power, J. M. and Yewlett, C. J. L., (1974), *Public Planning: The Intercorporate Dimension* (London: Tavistock Publications).

Galbraith, J. K. ([1967] 1971), *The New Industrial State* (Boston: Houghton Mifflin).

Gamble, A. (1988), *The Free Economy and the Strong State: The politics of Thatcherism* (London: Macmillan).

Geras, N. (1983), *Marx and Human Nature: Refutation of a legend* (London: Verso).

Gerth, H. H. and Mills, C. W. (1953), *Character and Social Structure* (New York: Harcourt Brace).

Giddens, A. (1979), *Central Problems in Social Theory* (London: Macmillan).

Giddens, A. (1982), *Profiles and Critiques in Social Theory* (London: Macmillan).

Giddens, A. (1984), *The Constitution of Society* (Cambridge: Polity Press).

Goldthorpe, J. H. (1984), *Order and Conflict in Contemporary Capitalism* (Oxford: The Clarendon Press).

Goodman, R. (1972), *After the Planners* (Harmondsworth: Penguin).

Gordon, D. (1980) 'Stages of accumulation and land economic cycles', in T. K. Hopkins and I. Wallerstein (eds), *Processes of the World System* (London: Sage).

Gormley, W. T. (1989), *Taming the Presidency* (Princeton, NJ: Princeton University Press).

Gorz, A. (1985), *Farewell to the Working Class* (London: Pluto Press).

Gottdiener, M. (ed.) (1986), *Cities in Stress* (Beverly Hills, Calif.: Sage).

Gottdiener, M. (1987), *The Decline of Urban Politics* (Beverly Hills, Calif.: Sage).

Gottdiener, M. and Komninos, N. (1989), *Capitalist Development and Crisis Theory: Accumulation, regulation and spatial restructuring* (London: Macmillan).

Gough, I. (1983), 'The crisis of the British welfare state', *International Journal of Health Services*, vol. 13, no. 3, pp. 459–77.

Gramsci, A. (1971a), *Selections from the Prison Notebooks*, Q. Hoare, and G. Nowell-Smith (eds) (New York: International Publishers).

Gramsci, A. (1971b), *La Costruzione del Partita Comunista* (Turin: Einaudi).

Gramsci, A. ([1924] 1978), *Selections from Political Writings 1921–1926* translated and edited by Quintin Hoare (New York: International Publishers).

Grant, W. (ed.) (1985), *The Political Economy of Corporatism* (New York: St Martin's Press).

Greenwood, E. (1965), 'Attributes of a profession', in (ed.) Zald, M. *Social Welfare Institutions* (New York: Wiley).

Gregory, D. and Urry, J. (eds) (1985), *Social Relations and Spatial Structures* (Basingstoke: Macmillan).

Habermas, J. (1975), *Legitimation Crisis, tr. T. McCarthy* (Boston: Beacon Press).

Habermas, J. ([1968] 1978), *Knowledge and Human Interests* (London: Heinemann).

Habermas, J. (1979), *Communication and the Evolution of Society*, tr. T. McCarthy (London: Heinemann).

Habermas, J. (1984), *The Theory of Communicative Action*, Vol. 1, tr. T. McCarthy (Boston: Beacon Press).

Habermas, J. (1987), *The Theory of Communicative Action*, Vol. 2, tr. T. McCarthy (Boston: Beacon Press).

Hall, P., Gracey, H., Drewett, R. and Thomas, R. (1973), *The Containment of Urban England* (London: Allen and Unwin).

Hall, P. (1986), *Governing the Economy: The politics of state intervention in Britain and France* (Cambridge: Polity Press).

Hall, S. (1977), 'The "political" and the "economic" in Marx's theory of classes', in A. Hunt, (ed.), *Class and Class Structure* (London: Lawrence and Wishart).

Hall, S. (1983), 'The Great Moving Right Show' in S. Hall and M. Jacques (eds), *The Politics of Thatcherism* (London: Lawrence and Wishart).

Hall, S. (1985), 'Authoritarian populism: A reply', *New Left Review*, no. 151, pp. 106–113.

Halmos, P. (ed.) (1973), *Professionalization and Social Change*, Sociological

290 *Bibliography*

Review Monograph, No. 20 (Keele: University of Keele Press).
Hambleton, R. (1978), *Policy Planning and Local Government* (London: Hutchinson).
Harré, R. (1972), *The Philosophies of Science* (Oxford: Oxford University Press).
Harrington, M. (1964), *The Other America: Poverty in the United States* (New York: Macmillan).
Harrington, M. (1985), *The New American Poverty* (New York: Viking–Penguin).
Harris, B. (1978), 'A note on planning theory', *Environment and Planning A*, vol. 10, pp. 221–4.
Hartman, C. W. (1984), *The Transformation of San Francisco* (Totowa, NJ: Rowman and Allanheld).
Harvey, D. (1985), *The Urbanization of Capital* (Oxford: Blackwell).
Harvey, D. (1989), *The Condition of Post-Modernity: An enquiry into the origins of cultural change* (Oxford: Blackwell).
Hausknecht, M. (1962), *The Joiners – A sociological description of voluntary association membership in the United States* (New York: Bedminster Press).
Hawke, J. N. (1981), 'Planning agreements in practice', *Journal of Planning and Environment Law*, pp. 5–14, 86–97.
Hayek, F. A. von (1944), *The Road to Serfdom* (Sydney: Dymock's Book Arcade, Ltd.).
Hayek, F. A. von (1960), *The Constitution of Liberty* (London: Routledge and Kegan Paul).
Hayek, F. A. von (1979), *Law, Legislation and Liberty, Vol 3, The Political Order of a Free People* (London: Routledge and Kegan Paul).
Healey, P. (1983), '"Rational method" as a mode of policy formation and implementation in land-use policy', *Environment and Planning B, Planning and Design*, vol. 10, pp. 19–39.
Healey, P. (1985), 'The professionalization of planning in Britain', *Town Planning Review*, vol. 56, no. 4, pp. 492–507.
Healey, P., Davis, J., Wood, M. and Elson, M. (1982), *The Implementation of Development Plans*, Report for the Department of the Environment, UK (Oxford: Oxford Polytechnic, Department of Town Planning).
Healey, P., McNamara, P., Elson, M. and Doak, J. (1988), *Land Use Planning and the Mediation of Urban Change* (Cambridge: Cambridge University Press).
Hebbert, M. (1983) 'The daring experiment: social scientists and land-use planning in 1940s Britain', *Environment and Planning B*, vol. 10, pp. 3–17.
Hechter, M. (1987) *Principles of Group Solidarity* (Berkeley: University of California Press).
Hegel, G. W. F. ([1821] 1967), *The Philosophy of Right* tr. T. M. Knox with notes (Oxford: Oxford University Press).
Heisler, M. O., with Kvavik, R. B. (1974), 'Patterns of European politics: The "European Polity" model, in M. O. Heisler (ed.), *Politics in Europe: Structures and processes in some post-industrial societies* (New York: David McKay).
Heisler, M. O. (1979), 'Corporate pluralism revisited: Where is the theory?'

Scandinavian political studies, vol.2, no.3, pp. 277–97.

Held, D. (1980), *Introduction to Critical Theory: Horkheimer to Habermas* (Berkeley and Los Angeles: University of California Press).

Held, D. (1984), 'Beyond liberalism and Marxism', in G. McLennan, D. Held and S. Hall, *The Idea of the Modern State* (Milton Keynes: The Open University Press).

Held, D. (1987), *Models of Democracy* (Cambridge: Polity Press).

Held, D *et al.* (1983), *States and Societies* (Oxford: Martin Robertson).

Hesse, M. (1980), *Revolutions and Recruitments in the Philosophy of Science* (Brighton, Harvester Press).

Hilferding, R. (1910), *Das Finanzkapital: eine Studie über die Jüngste Entwicklung des Kapitalismus* (Vienna: Brand).

Hill, R. C. (1974), 'Separate and unequal: Governmental inequality in the metropolis', *American Political Science Review*, vol. 68, no. 4 pp. 1557–68.

Hirsch, J. (1980), 'On political developments in West Germany since 1945', in R. Scase (ed.), *The State in Western Europe* (London: Croom Helm).

Hirsch, J. (1983) 'Fordist security state and new social movements', Kapitalistate, vol. 10/11, pp. 75–88.

Hirsch, J. (1984), 'Notes towards a reformulation of state theory', *in* S. Haenninen and L. Paldan, *Rethinking Marx* (Berlin: Argument Verlag).

Hirsch, J. (1985), 'Fordismus und Postfordismus', *Politische Vierteljahreszeitschrift*, 2/85.

Hirsch, J. and Roth, (1986), *Das Neues Gesicht des Kapitalismus, Vom Fordismus zum Postfordismus*, (Hamburg: VSA Verlag Hamburg).

Hobbes, T. ([1651] 1909), *Leviathan* (Oxford: The Clarendon Press).

Hobsbawm, E. J. (1969), *Industry and Empire*, Vol. 3 in *The Pelican Economic History of Britain* (Harmondsworth: Penguin).

Hobsbawm, E. J. (1978), 'The forward march of Labour halted', *Marxism Today*, vol. 22, no. 9, pp. 279–87.

Hoch, C. (1984a), 'Doing good and being right, the pragmatic connection in planning theory', *Journal of the American Planning Association*, vol. 50, no. 3, pp. 335–43.

Hoch, C. (1984b), 'Pragmatism, planning and power', *Journal of Planning Education and Research*, vol. 4, pp. 86–95.

Hoff, J. (1985), 'The concept of class and public employees', *Acta Sociologica*, vol. 28, pp. 207–26.

Holloway, J. (1987), 'The red rose of Nissan', *Capital and Class*, vol 32, pp. 142–64.

Homans, G. C. (1951), *The Human Group* (London: Routledge and Kegan Paul).

Horkheimer, M. (1931), 'Die gegenwärtigen Lage der Sozialphilosophie und die Aufgaben eines Instituts fur Sozialforschung', *Frankfurter Universitätsreden*, (reprinted in *Sozialphilosophische Studien*, 1972).

Horkheimer, M. (1973), 'The authoritarian state', *Telos*, no. 15, Spring 1973.

Horkheimer, M. (1974), 'Die Ohnmacht der Deutschen Arbeiterclasse', in *Notizen 1950 bis 1969 und Dammerung*, (Frankfurt: S. Fischer).

Horkheimer, M. and Adorno, T. (1972), *Dialectic of Enlightenment* (New York: Herder and Herder).

Howard, E. ([1902] 1946), *Garden Cities of Tomorrow*, being the second edition of *Tomorrow, a Peaceful Path to Real Reform* (London: Faber and Faber), first published as *Tomorrow, a Peaceful Path to Social Reform* (1898).

Howe, E. (1980), 'Role choices of urban planners', *Journal of the American Planning Association*, vol. 46, no. 4, pp. 398–409.

Howe, F. C. (1913), 'The remaking of the American city', *Harpers Monthly*, no. 127, pp. 186–97.

Hudson, B. M. (1979), 'Comparison of current planning theories: counterparts and contradictions', *Journal of the American Planning Association*, October 1979, pp. 387–98.

Hunter, F. (1953), *Community Power Structure: A study of decision-makers* (Chapel Hill, NC: University of North Carolina Press).

Hunter, F. (1963), *Community Power Structure: A study of decision makers* (Garden City, NY: Doubleday, Anchor Books).

Hunter, F. (1980), *Community Power Succession* (Chapel Hill, NC: University of North Carolina Press).

Huntington, S. P. (1975), 'The United States', in M. Crozier, S. P. Huntington and J. Watanuki, *The Crisis of Democracy* (New York: New York University Press).

Illich, I. (1974), *Deschooling Society* (London: Calder and Boyars).

Jacques, M. and Mulhern, F. (eds) (1981), *The Forward March of Labour Halted?* (London: Verso).

Jay, D. (1947), *The Socialist Case* (London: Faber).

Jay, M. (1984), *Adorno* (Cambridge, Mass.: Harvard University Press).

Jessop, B. (1979), 'Corporatism, parliamentarism and social democracy', in P. C. Schmitter and G. Lehmbruch (eds), *Trends towards Corporatist Intermediation* (Beverly Hills, Calif.: Sage).

Jessop, B. (1982), *The Capitalist State: Marxist theories and methods* (Oxford: Martin Robertson).

Jessop, B. (1988), 'Regulation theory, post Fordism and the state: more than a reply to Werner Bonefeld', *Capital and Class*, vol. 34, pp. 147–68.

Jessop, B., Bonnett, K., Bromley, S. and Ling, T. (1984), 'Authoritarian populism, two nations, and Thatcherism', *New Left Review*, no. 147, pp. 87–101.

Johnson, T. J. (1972), *Professions and Power* (London: Macmillan).

Jones, G. W. (1986), *The Crisis in British Central–Local Relationships*. Paper presented at the conference of the International Political Science Association, 12 December 1986, Pittsburgh, Pa., 'Governing in the midst of change').

Jordan A. G. (1981), 'Iron triangles, woolly corporatism and elastic nets: Images of the policy process', *Journal of Public Policy*, vol. 1, no. 1 pp. 95–123.

Jordan, A. G. (1983), *Corporatism: The unity and utility of the concept*, Strathclyde Papers on Government and Politics, no. 13, (Glasgow: Strathclyde University).

Kariel, H. S. (1961), *The Decline of American Pluralism* (Stanford, Calif.: Stanford University Press).

Kariel, H. S. (ed.) (1970), *Frontiers of Democratic Theory* (New York: Random House).

Katzenstein, P. (1985), 'Small nations in an open international economy: The converging balance of state and society in Switzerland and Austria', in P. B. Evans, D. Rueschemeyer and T. Skocpol (eds), *Bringing the State Back In* (Cambridge: Cambridge University Press).

Katznelson, I. (1981), *City Trenches: Urban politics and the patterning of class in the United States* (New York, Pantheon Books).

Keat, R. (1981), *The Politics of Social Theory: Habermas, Freud and the critique of positivism* (Oxford: Blackwell).

Keating, M. and Dixon G. (1989), *Making Economic Policy in Australia, 1983–1988*, (Melbourne: Longman Cheshire).

Keller, S. (1963), *Beyond the Ruling Class: Strategic elites in modern society* (New York: Random House).

Kelly, G. A. (1955), *The Psychology of Personal Constructs*, Vols 1 and 2 (New York: Norton).

Kemp, R. (1977), 'Controversy in scientific research and tactics of communication', *Sociological Review*, vol. 25, no. 3, pp. 515–34.

Kemp, R. (1985), 'Planning, public hearings, and the politics of discourse', in J. Forester (ed.), *Critical Theory and Public Life* (Cambridge, Mass.: MIT Press), pp. 177–201.

King, A. (1975) 'Overload: Problems of governing in the 1970s', *Political Studies*, vol. 23, pp. 284–96.

King, D. S. (1987), *The New Right: Politics, markets and citizenship* (London: Macmillan).

Krieger, J. (1986), *Reagan, Thatcher and the Politics of Decline* (Cambridge: Polity Press).

Kristol, I. (1972), 'An urban civilization without cities', *Horizon*, vol. 14, pp. 36–41.

Kristol, I. (1983), *Reflections of a Neo-Conservative: Looking back. Looking ahead* (New York: Basic Books).

Krueckeberg, D. A. (1983) *Introduction to Planning History in the United States* (New Brunswick, NJ: Center for Urban Policy Research, Rutgers University).

Krumholz, N., Cogger, J. M. and Linner, J. H. (1975), 'The Cleveland Policy Planning Report', *Journal of the American Institute of Planners*, vol. 41, no. 5, pp. 298–304.

Krumholz, N. (1982), 'A retrospective view of equity planning, Cleveland 1969–1979', *Journal of the American Planning Association*, vol. 48, no. 2, pp. 163–74.

Kuhn, T. S. (1977), 'Objectivity, value judgement and theory choice', in Kuhn, T. S. *The Essential Tension: Selected studies in scientific tradition and change* (Chicago: University of Chicago Press).

Laclau, E. (1975), 'The specificity of the political: the Poulantzas – Miliband debate', *Economy and Society*, vol. 4, no. 1, pp. 87–110.

Laffin, M.(1987) '"No, Permanent Head": politician–bureaucrat relationships in Victoria', *Australian Journal of Public Administration*, vol. 46, no.1, pp. 37–54.

Laing, R. D. (1982), *The Voice of Experience, Science and Psychiatry* (Harmondsworth: Penguin).

Larrain, J. (1983), *Marxism and Ideology* (London: Macmillan).

Lash, S. and Urry, J. (1987), *The End of Organized Capitalism* (Cambridge: Polity Press).

Lazarsfeld, P., Berelson, B. and Gaudet, H. (1944), *The People's Choice: How the voter makes up his mind in a Presidential campaign* (New York: Columbia University Press).

Lehmbruch, G. (1989), 'Networks of bureaucracies and organized interests: cross-sectoral and cross-national approaches toward an analytical model'. Paper for the conference 'Government and Organized Interests' of the International Political Science Association Research Committee on the Structure and Organization of Government, Zurich, 27–30 September 1989. (The author is at: Universität Konstanz, Sonderforschungsbereich 221.)

Lenin, V. I. ([1917] 1964), *The State and Revolution*, in Lenin, V. I., *Collected Works*, Vol. 25, pp. 381–493 (London: Lawrence and Wishart).

Lenin, V. I. ([1919] 1964), *The State*. A lecture delivered at the Sverdlov University, 11 July 1919. In Lenin, V. I. *Collected Works*, Vol. 29, pp. 470–88, (London: Lawrence and Wishart).

Lenin, V. I. ([1909] 1972), *Materialism and Empirio-Criticism* (Beijing: Foreign Languages Press).

Lerner, D. and Lasswell, H. D. (eds) (1951), *The Policy Sciences* (Stanford, Calif.: Stanford University Press).

Lewin, K. (1948), *Resolving Social Conflicts: Selected papers on group dynamics* edited by G. W. Lewin (New York: Harper and Row).

Lijphart, A. (1977), *Democracy in Plural Societies: A comparative exploration* (New Haven, Conn.: Yale University Press).

Lindblom, C. E. (1959), 'The science of muddling through', *Public Administration Review*, Spring 1959 (reprinted in Faludi, 1973a, op. cit.).

Lindblom, C. E. (1968), *The Policy-Making Process* (Englewood Cliffs, NJ: Prentice-Hall).

Lindblom, C. E. (1977), *Politics and Markets: The world's political–economic systems* (New York: Basic Books).

Lindblom, C. E. and Cohen, D. K. (1979), *Usable Knowledge: Social science and social problem solving* (New Haven, Conn.: Yale University Press).

Lipietz, A. (1982) 'Imperialism or the Beast of the Apocalypse', *Capital and Class*, vol. 22, pp. 81–110.

Lipietz, A. (1985), *The Enchanted World: Credit and the world crises* (London: Verso).

Lippman, W. (1937), *An Inquiry into the Principles of the Good Society* (Boston: Little, Brown).

Little, G. (1985), *Political Ensembles: A psychosocial approach to politics and leadership* (Melbourne: Oxford University Press).

Locke, J. ([1690] 1970), *Two Treatises of Government*, Laslett, P. (ed.) (Cambridge: Cambridge University Press).

London Edinburgh Weekend Return Group (1980), *In and Against the State* (London: Pluto Press).

Lorwin, L. L. (1945), *Time for Planning: A social-economic theory and program*

for the twentieth century (New York: Harper Brothers).
Low, N. P. and Power, J. M. (1984), 'Policy systems in an Australian Metropolitan Region: Political and economic determinants of change in Victoria', *Progress in Planning*, vol. 22, part 3, (Oxford: Pergamon).
Lowi, T. (1969), *The End of Liberalism: Ideology, policy and the crisis of public authority* (New York: W. W. Norton).
Lukes, S. (1973), *Individualism* (Oxford: Blackwell).
Lukes, S. (1974), *Power: A radical view* (London, New York: Macmillan).
Lukes, S. (ed.) (1986), *Power* (Oxford: Blackwell).
Lustig, R. J. (1982), *Corporate Liberalism: The origins of modern political theory 1890–1920* (Berkeley: University of California Press).

McAuslan, J. W. P. (1980), *The Ideologies of Planning Law* (Oxford: Pergamon).
McCarthy, T. (1984), 'Introduction' in J. Habermas, *The Theory of Communicative Action* (London: Heinemann).
McConnell, G. (1967), *Private Power and American Democracy* (New York: Knopf).
McLoughlin, J. B. (1969), *Urban and Regional Planning: A systems approach* (London: Faber and Faber).
McLennan, G., Held, D. and Hall, S. (eds) (1984), *The Idea of the Modern State* (Milton Keynes: The Open University Press).
McNamara, P. F. (1984), 'The role of state agents in the residential development process', *Land Development Studies*, vol. 1 pp. 101–12.
McNamara, P. F. (1985), 'The control of office development in Central Edinburgh, unpublished PhD thesis, University of Edinburgh.
MacPherson, C. B. (1966), *The Real World of Democracy* (Oxford: Clarendon Press).
MacPherson, C. B. (1977), 'Do we need a theory of the state?' *Archives Européennes de Sociologie*, vol. 18, pp. 223–44.
Maddison, A. (1976) 'Economic policy and performance in Europe, 1913–1970', in C. M. Cipolla (ed.), *The Fontana Economic History of Europe. Part 2, The Twentieth Century*, (Collins-Fontana) pp. 442–501.
Madison, J. ([1787] 1888), *The Federalist, A commentary on the Constitution of the United States,* (New York: G. P. Putnam and Sons).
Mann, M. (1986), *The Sources of Social Power, Vol 1, A History of Power from the Beginning to AD 1760,* (Cambridge: Cambridge University Press).
Mannheim, K. (1940), *Man and Society in an Age of Reconstruction* (London: Routledge and Kegan Paul).
Manoilesco, M. ([1934] 1936), *Le Siècle de Corporatisme: Doctrine de Corporatisme Intégral et Pur* (Paris: Alcan).
March, J. and Olsen, J. (1984), 'The new institutionalism: Organizational factors in political life', *American Political Science Review*, vol. 78, pp. 734–49.
Marcuse, H. (1958), *Soviet Marxism: A critical appraisal* (London: Routledge and Kegan Paul).
Marcuse, H. (1964), *One Dimensional Man: Studies in the ideology of advanced industrial society* (Boston: Beacon Press).
Marcuse, H. ([1955] 1969), *Eros and Civilization* (London: Allen Lane, The Penguin Press).

Marcuse, P. (1976), 'Professional ethics and beyond: values in planning', *Journal of the American Institute of Planners*, vol. 42, no. 3, pp. 264–74.

Marris, P. (1963) 'A Report on Urban Renewal in the United States' in Dahl, L. ed, (1965) *The Urban Condition* (New York: Basic Books).

Marris, P. (1982), *Community Planning and Conceptions of Change* (London: Routledge and Kegan Paul).

Marx, F. Morstein (1957), *The Administrative State: An introduction to bureaucracy* (Chicago: University of Chicago Press).

Marx, K. ([1848] 1962), *The Eighteenth Brumaire of Louis Bonaparte*, in K. Marx, *Selected Works*, Vol. 1 (Moscow: Foreign Languages Publishing House).

Marx, K. ([1875] 1962), *Critique of the Gotha Programme* in K. Marx, *Selected Works*, Vol. 2, (Moscow: Foreign Languages Publishing House).

Marx, K. and Engels, F. ([1846] 1976), *The German Ideology*, in K. Marx and F. Engels, *Collected Works*, Vol. 5 (London: Lawrence and Wishart).

Marx, K. ([1867] 1976), *Capital, Volume I* (Harmondsworth: Penguin).

Massey, D. (1984), *Spatial Divisions of Labour: Social structures and the geography of production*, (London: Macmillan).

Mead, G. H. (ed.) (1934), *Mind, Self and Society, from the Standpoint of a Social Behaviorist* (Chicago: Chicago University Press).

Meller, H. (1980), 'Cities and evolution: Patrick Geddes as an international prophet of town planning before 1914', in A. Sutcliffe (ed.), *The Rise of Modern Urban Planning 1800–1914* (London: Mansell).

Merton, R. (1936), 'The unintended consequences of purposive social action', *American Sociological Review*, vol. 1, p. 894.

Michels, R. ([1915] 1968), *Political Parties: A sociological study of the oligarchical tendencies in modern democracy*, 2nd edn, tr. E. and C. Paul (New York: Free Press).

Middlemas, K. (1979), *Politics in Industrial Society* (London: Andre Deutsch).

Miliband, R. (1970), 'The capitalist state – reply to Poulantzas', *New Left Review*, vol. 59.

Miliband, R. (1973), 'Poulantzas and the capitalist state', *New Left Review*, vol. 82, pp. 83–93.

Miliband, R. ([1967] 1973), *The State in Capitalist Society* (London: Quartet Books).

Mill, J. S. ([1859] 1910), *Utilitarianism, Liberty and Representative Government* (London: J. M. Dent, Everyman's Library).

Mill, J. S. ([1835] 1973), *Essays on Politics and Culture* (Gloucester, Mass.: Peter Smith).

Miller, E. F. (1977), 'The primary questions of political inquiry', *Review of Politics*, vol. 39, no. 3.

Mills, C. W. (1956), *The Power Elite* (Oxford: Oxford University Press).

Mills, C. W. (1966), *Sociology and Pragmatism* (New York: Oxford University Press).

Ministry of Housing and Local Government (1969), *People and Plans*, The Skeffington report (London: HMSO).

Mises, L. von ([1949] 1963), *Human Action: A treatise on economics* (Chicago: Contemporary Books).

Moe, T. (1985), 'The politicized presidency', in E. Chubb and P. E. Peterson (eds), *New Directions in American Politics* (Washington, DC: The Brookings Institution).

Mollenkopf, J. H. (1983), *The Contested City* (Princeton NJ: Princeton University Press).

Mommsen, W. J. and Osterhammel, J. (eds) (1987), *Max Weber and His Contemporaries* (London: Allen and Unwin).

Montesquieu, Charles-Louis de Secondat ([1746] 1900), *The Spirit of Laws* (London: The Colonial Press).

Moody, W. D. (1919), *What of the City?* (Chicago: A. C. McClurg and Co.).

Moreno, J. L. (1947), *Psychological Organization of Groups in the Community* (New York: Beacon House).

Morris, D. and Hess, K. (1975), *Neighbourhood Power: The new localism* (Boston: Beacon Press).

NCDP (National Community Development Project Information and Intelligence Unit) (1977) *Gilding the Ghetto: The state and the poverty experiments* (London: NCDP).

Nathan, R. P. (1986), 'The underclass, Will it always be with us?' (mimeo). Paper Prepared for a Symposium at the New School for Social Research, 14 November 1986.

Neale, W. C. (1982), 'Language and economics', *Journal of Economic Issues*, vol. 16, no. 2, pp. 355–69.

Needleman, M. L. and Needleman, C. E. (1974), *Guerillas in the Bureaucracy: The community planning experiment in the United States* (New York: Wiley).

Nelson, C. and Grossberg, L. (eds) (1988), *Marxism and the Interpretation of Culture* (Champaign, Ill.: University of Illinois Press).

Newman, O. (1981), *The Challenge of Corporatism* (London: Macmillan).

Nicholls, D. (1975), *The Pluralist State* (London: Macmillan).

Niskanen, W. A. jr. (1971), *Bureaucracy and Representative Government* (Chicago: Aldine).

Norton, W. E. and Aylmer, C. P. (1988), *Australian Economic Statistics 1949/50–1986/87* (Canberra: Reserve Bank of Australia, Occasional Paper, no.8a).

Nozick, R (1974), *Anarchy, State and Utopia* (Oxford: Blackwell).

Oakeshott, M. (1962), *Rationalism in Politics and Other Essays* (New York: Basic Books).

O'Connor, J. (1973), *The Fiscal Crisis of the State* (New York: St Martin's Press).

Offe, C. (1984), *Contradictions of the Welfare State* (London: Hutchinson).

Offe, C. (1985), *Disorganized Capitalism: Contemporary transformations of work and politics* (Cambridge: Polity Press).

Olson, M. (1965), *The Logic of Collective Action* (Cambridge, Mass.: Harvard University Press).

Olson, M. (1986), 'A theory of incentives facing political organizations, neo-corporatism and the hegemonic state', *International Political Science Review*, vol. 7, no. 2, pp. 165–89.

Ominami, C. (1986), *Le Tiers Monde dans la crise* (Paris: La Découverte).

O'Rourke, J. J. (1974), *The Problem of Freedom in Marxist Thought* (Dordrecht: Reidel).

Ostrom, E. (ed.) (1976), *The Delivery of Urban Services* (Beverly Hills, Calif.: Sage).

Ostrom, V. (1973), *The Intellectual Crisis in American Public Administration* (Tuscaloosa, Ala: University of Alabama Press).

Pahl, R. E. (1977), 'Managers, technical experts and the state: Forms of mediation, manipulation and dominance in urban and regional development', in M. Harloe (ed.), *Captive Cities: Studies in the political economy of cities and regions*, (London: Wiley), pp. 49–60.

Painter, M. (1987), *Steering the Modern State: Changes in central coordination in three Australian State Governments*, (Sydney: Sydney University Press).

Panitch, L. (1979), 'The development of corporatism in liberal democracies', in C. P. Schmitter and G. Lehmbruch (1979), *Trends Toward Corporatist Intermediation*, (Beverly Hills, Calif.: Sage) pp. 119–46.

Panitch, L. (1980), 'Recent theorizations of corporatism: Reflections on a growth industry', *British Journal of Sociology*, vol. 31, no. 2, pp. 159–87.

Parenti, M. (1970), 'Power and pluralism, the view from the bottom', *American Political Science Review*, vol. 32, pp. 501–30.

Paris, C. (ed.) (1982), *Critical Readings in Planning Theory* (Oxford: Pergamon).

Paris, C. (1983), 'Whatever happened to urban sociology?' *Environment and Planning D, Society and Space*, vol. 1, pp. 217–25.

Parsons, T. and Smelser, N. (1956), *Economy and Society* (Glencoe, Ill.: Free Press).

Partridge, P. H. (1941), 'Some thoughts on planning', *Australasian Journal of Psychology and Philosophy*, vol. 19, no. 3, pp. 236–52.

Pateman, C. (1970), *Participation and Democratic Theory* (Cambridge: Cambridge University Press).

Peattie, L. R. (1968), 'Reflections on advocacy planning', in H. B. C. Spiegel (ed.) *Citizen Participation in Urban Development, vol. II. Cases and Programs* (Washington DC: NTL Institute for Applied Behavioral Science).

Perlman, J. (1979), 'Grassroots empowerment and governmental response', *Social Policy*, vol. 10, no. 2, pp. 16–21.

Peterson, J. A. (1983), 'The City Beautiful Movement: Forgotten origins and lost meanings', in D. A. Krueckeberg (ed.), *Introduction to Planning History in the United States* (New Brunswick, NJ: Center for Urban Policy Research, Rutgers University).

Phelps-Brown, E. H. and Hopkins, S. V. (1955), 'Seven centuries of building wages', *Economica*, August 1955, pp. 195–206.

Pinto, J. M. C. (1955), *A Corporacao* (Coimbra, Portugal).

Pitkin, H. F. (1972), *Wittgenstein and Justice: On the significance of Ludwig Wittgenstein for social and political thought* (Berkeley and Los Angeles: University of California Press).

Piven, F. F. and Cloward R. A. ([1977] 1982), *Poor People's Movements: How they succeed. How they fail* (New York: Pantheon Books).

Poggi, G. (1972), *Images of Society: Tocqueville, Marx, Durkheim* (London: Oxford University Press).

Poggi, G. (1978), *The Development of the Modern State* (London: Methuen).

Polanyi, K. ([1944] 1975), *The Great Transformation* (New York: Octagon Books; Farrar, Strauss and Giroux).

Polanyi, M. (1958), *Personal Knowledge: Towards a post-critical philosophy* (Chicago: University of Chicago Press).

Pollock, F. (1941a), 'Is national socialism a new order?' *Studies in Philosophy and Social Science*, (Frankfurt), vol. 9, no. 3.

Pollock, F. (1941b), 'State capitalism: its possibilities and limitations', *Studies in Philosophy and Social Science*, (Frankfurt), vol. 9, no. 2.

Polsby, N. (1980), *Community Power and Political Theory: A further look at problems of evidence and inference* (New Haven, Conn.: Yale University Press).

Popper, K. (1972), *Objective Knowledge: An Evolutionary Approach* (Oxford: Clarendon Press).

Poulantzas, N. (1969), 'The problem of the capitalist state', *New Left Review*, vol. 58.

Poulantzas, N. ([1968] 1973), *Political Power and Social Classes* (London: New Left Books).

Poulantzas, N. (1975), *Classes in Contemporary Capitalism* (London: New Left Books).

Poulantzas, N. (1976), 'The capitalist state: A reply to Miliband and LacLau', *New Left Review*, vol. 95, pp. 63–83.

Pressman, J. L. and Wildavsky, A. (1973), *Implementation* (Berkeley and Los Angeles: University of California Press).

Prest, W. (ed.) (1987), *The Professions in Early Modern England* (London: Croom Helm).

Prigogine, I. and Stengers, I. (1984), *Order out of Chaos: Man's new dialogue with nature* (London: Heinemann).

Przeworski, A. (1980), 'Material bases of consent: economics and politics in hegemonic systems' *Political Power and Social Theory*, vol. 1, pp. 21–66.

Przeworski, A. and Wallerstein, M. (1982), 'The structure of class conflict in democratic capitalist societies', *American Political Science Review*, vol. 76, pp. 215–38.

Rabinowitz, F. (1969), *City Politics and Planning* (New York: Atherton Press).

Reade, E. (1981) 'The theory of town and country planning', Paper for the Conference: 'Planning Theory in the 80s', Oxford Polytechnic, 2–4 April 1981.

Reade, E. (1982a), 'The British planning system', Unit 19 in *The Open University: Urban Change and Conflict* (Milton Keynes: The Open University Press).

Reade, E. (1982b), '"If planning isn't everything . . . ", a comment', *Town Planning Review*, vol. 53, pp. 65–72.

Reade, E. (1983), 'If planning is anything, maybe it can be identified', *Urban Studies*, vol. 20, pp. 159–71.

Reagan, M. D. (1963), *The Managed Economy* (New York: Oxford University Press).

Rein, M. (1969), 'Social planning, the search for legitimacy', *Journal of the American Institute of Planners*, vol. 35, pp. 233–44.

Rejan, M. (1971), 'Political Ideology: Theoretical and Comparative Perspectives', in Rejan, M. ed. *Decline of Ideology?* (Chicago and New York: Aldine/Atherton).

Resnick, S. A. and Wolff, R. D. (1987), *Knowledge and Class: A Marxian critique of political economy* (Chicago: University of Chicago Press).

Rhodes, R. A. W. (1986), *The National World of Local Government* (London: Allen and Unwin).

Rhodes, R. A. W. (1988), *Beyond Westminster and Whitehall: The sub-central governments of Britain* (London: Unwin Hyman).

Ricci, D. (1971), *Community Power and Democratic Theory* (New York: Random House).

Rich, R. C. (1977), 'Equity and institutional design in service delivery', *Urban Affairs Quarterly*, vol. 12, no. 3, pp. 383–410.

Rich, R. C. (ed.) (1982), *The Politics of Urban Public Services* (New York: Lexington Books, D. C. Heath).

Riesman, D. (1950), *The Lonely Crowd: A study of the changing American character* (New Haven, Conn.: Yale University Press).

Rittel, H. J. W. and Webber, M. M. (1973), 'Dilemmas in a general theory of planning', *Policy Sciences*, vol. 4, pp. 155–69.

Rochberg-Halton, E. (1986), *The Necessity of Pragmatism* (New Haven, Conn.: Yale University Press).

Rodgers, D. T. (1987), *Contested Truths: Keywords in American politics since Independence* (New York: Basic Books).

Roemer, J. E. (1982), *A General Theory of Exploitation and Class* (Cambridge, Mass.: Harvard University Press).

Roemer, J. E. (1988), *Free to Lose: An introduction to Marxist economic philosophy* (Cambridge, Mass.: Harvard University Press).

Rogers, E. (1962), *The Diffusion of Innovations* (New York: Free Press).

Rokkan, S. (1966), 'Norway: Numerical democracy and corporate pluralism' in R. A. Dahl (ed.), *Political Oppositions in Western Democracies* (New Haven, Conn.: Yale University Press).

Rothbard M. N. (1973), *For a New Liberty* (New York: Macmillan).

Rothman, J. (1974), *Planning and Organizing for Social Change: Action principles from social science research* (New York: Columbia University Press).

Rothman, S. (1960), 'Systematic political theory: observations on the group approach', *American Political Science Review*, March 1960.

Rousseau, J.-J. ([1762] 1973), *The Social Contract, and Discourses* (London: J. M. Dent).

Roweis, S. T. and Scott, A. J. (1981), 'The urban land question', in M. Dear and A. J. Scott (eds) *Urbanization and Urban Planning in Capitalist Society* (London: Methuen).

Roweis, S. T. (1983), 'Urban planning as professional mediation of territorial politics', *Environment and Planning D*, vol. 1, pp. 139–62.

Rubinstein, D. (1981), *Marx and Wittgenstein: Social praxis and social explanation* (London: Routledge and Kegan Paul).

Rugman, A. M. (1981), *Inside the Multinationals* (London: Croom Helm).

Runciman, W. G. (1972), *A Critique of Max Weber's Philosophy of Social Science* (Cambridge: Cambridge University Press).

Ryle, G. (1965), 'Categories', in A. Flew (ed.), *Logic and Language* (Garden

City, NY: Doubleday).

Ryle, G. (1966), *Dilemmas* (Cambridge: Cambridge University Press).

Saunders, P. (1980), *Urban Politics: A sociological interpretation* (Harmondsworth: Penguin).

Saunders, P. (1983), *The Regional State: A review of the literature and agenda for research*, Urban and Regional Studies Working Paper No. 35 (Brighton: University of Sussex).

Saunders, P. (1985), 'Corporatism and urban service provision', in W. Grant, *The Political Economy of Corporatism* (New York: St Martin's Press).

Schattschneider, E. E., (1960), *The Semisovereign People* (New York: Holt, Rinehart and Winston).

Schmitter, P. C. (1974), 'Still the century of corporatism', *The Review of Politics*, vol. 36, no. 1, pp. 85–131.

Schmitter, C. P. and Lehmbruch, G. (1979), *Trends Toward Corporatist Intermediation* (Beverly Hills and London: Sage), pp. 53–62.

Schumpeter, J. A. (1943), *Capitalism, Socialism and Democracy* (London: Allen and Unwin).

Scott, J. C. jr. (1957), 'Membership and participation in voluntary associations', *American Sociological Review*, vol. 22, p. 315.

Scott, A. J. and Roweis, S. T. (1977), 'Urban planning in theory and practice: a reappraisal', *Environment and Planning A*, vol. 9, pp. 1097–1119.

Self, P. (1985), *Political Theories of Modern Government: Its role and reform* (London: Allen and Unwin).

Selznick, P. (1966), *T.V.A. and the Grass Roots* (New York: Harper and Row).

Shaffer, J. B. P. and Gralinski, D. M. (1974), *Models of Group Therapy and Sensitivity Training* (Englewood Cliffs, NJ: Prentice Hall).

Sharkansky, I. (1975), *The United States Revisited: A study of a still developing country* (New York: Longman).

Shils, E. (1987), 'Max Weber and the world since 1920', in W. J. Mommsen and J. Osterhammel (eds) *Max Weber and his Contemporaries* (London: Allen and Unwin).

Shirvani, H. (1985), 'Insiders' views on planning practice', *Journal of the American Planning Association*, vol. 51, no. 4, pp. 486–95.

Shonfield, A. (1984), *In Defence of the Mixed Economy*, Z. Shonfield (ed.) (Oxford and New York: Oxford University Press).

Simmel, G. ([1908] 1955), *Conflict, and the Web of Group Affiliations*, tr. K. Wolff (Glencoe, Ill.: Free Press).

Simmie, J. (1974), *Citizens in Conflict: The sociology of town planning* (London: Hutchinson).

Simmie, J. (1981), *Power, Property and Corporatism* (London: Macmillan).

Simmie, J. (1985) 'Corporatism and planning', in W. Grant (ed.) *The Political Economy of Corporatism* (New York: St Martin's Press).

Simmie, J. and French, S. (1989), 'Corporatism, participation and planning: the case of London', *Progress in Planning* (Oxford: Pergamon), vol. 31, pp. 1–57.

Simon, H. A. ([1945] 1976), *Administrative Behaviour* (New York: Free Press).

Sleeper, R. W.(1986), *The Necessity of Pragmatism* (New Haven, Conn.: Yale University Press).

Smith, M. P. and Feagin, J R. (eds) (1987), *The Capitalist City: Global restructuring and community politics* (Oxford: Blackwell).

Smith, N. (1984), *Uneven Development* (Oxford: Blackwell).

Sorensen, A. D. and Day, R. A. (1981), 'Libertarian planning', *Town Planning Review*, vol. 52, pp. 390–402.

Spann, R. N. (1981), 'Fashions and fantasies in public administration', *Australian Journal of Public Administration*, vol. 40, no. 1, pp. 12–25.

Strauss, A. (1978), *Negotations* (New York: Jossey Bass).

Strauss, L. (1953), *Natural Right and History* (Chicago: Chicago University Press).

Streeck, W. and Schmitter, C. P. (1985), 'Community, market, state – and associations? The prospective contribution of interest governance to social order', in W. Streeck and C. P. Schmitter (eds), *Private Interest Government: Beyond market and state* (Beverly Hills, Calif.: Sage).

Sutcliffe, A. (1981), *Towards the Planned City: Germany, Britain, the United States and France 1780–1914* (Oxford: Blackwell).

Taylor, N. (1980), Planning theory and the philosophy of planning', *Urban Studies*, vol. 17, pp. 159–72.

Taylor, N. (1984), 'A critique of materialist critiques of procedural planning theory', *Environment and Planning B*, vol. 11, pp. 103–26.

Ten Broek, J, (ed.) (1966), *The Law of the Poor* (San Francisco: Chandler).

Thatcher, M. (1980), 'The Airey Neave Memorial Lecture', *Commentary*, vol. 1, no. 2, pp. 7–14.

Therborn, G. (1982), 'What does the ruling class do when it rules?' in A. Giddens and D. Held (eds), *Classes, Power and Conflict: Classical and contemporary debates* (Berkeley: University of California Press), pp. 224–48.

Thomas, H. and Logan C. (1982), *Mondragon: an Economic Analysis* (London: George Allen and Unwin in co-operation with the Institute of Social Studies at The Hague).

Thomas, M. J. (1982), 'The procedural planning theory of A. Faludi', in C. Paris (ed.) *Critical Readings in Planning Theory* (Oxford: Pergamon).

Thrift, N. (1987), 'Introduction, the geography of late twentieth century class formation', in N. Thrift and P. Williams (1987), op. cit., pp. 207–53.

Thrift, N. and Williams, P. (1987), *Class and Space: The making of urban society* (London: Routledge and Kegan Paul).

Tilly, C., Tilly, L. and Tilly, R. (1975), *The Rebellious Century 1830–1930* (Cambridge, Mass.: Harvard University Press).

Tocqueville, A. de ([1835] 1945), *Democracy in America* (New York: Knopf).

Tribe, L. H. (1972), 'Policy science: analysis or ideology?', *Philosophy and Public Affairs*, Vol. 2, pp. 66–110.

Truman, D. B. ([1951] 1965), *The Governmental Process* (New York: Knopf). (2nd edn., 1971, with a new 'Introduction' by the author).

Tullock, G. (1965), *The Politics of Bureaucracy* (Washington DC: Public Affairs Press).

Turner, B. (1981), *For Weber: Essays on the sociology of fate* (London: Routledge and Kegan Paul).

Tyson, B. T. and Low, N. P. (1988), 'Experiential learning in planning education', *Journal of Planning Education and Research*, vol. 7, no. 1, pp. 15–27.

Urry, J. (1973), 'Towards a structural theory of the middle class' *Acta Sociologica*, vol. 16, pp. 175–87.

Urry, J. (1981), *The Anatomy of Capitalist Societies: The economy, civil society and the state* (London: Macmillan).

Van Til, J. (1984), Citizen participation in the future, *Policy Studies Review*, vol. 3, no. 2, pp. 311–22.

Vasu, M. L. (1979), *Politics and Planning: A national study of American planners* (Chapel Hill, NC: University of North Carolina Press).

Vedlitz, A (1988), *Conservative Mythology and Public Policy in America,* (New York: Praeger).

Verba, S. (1961), *Small Groups and Political Behavior: A study of leadership,* (Princeton, NJ: Princeton University Press).

Vernon, R (1979), 'Unintended consequences', *Political Theory*, vol. 7, no. 1, pp. 35–73.

Victoria, Parliament (1971), *Town and Country Planning Act 1971* (Melbourne: Government Printer).

Victoria, Parliament (1987), *Planning and Environment Act 1987* (Melbourne: Government Printer).

Waddington, C. H. (1977), *Tools for Thought: How to understand and apply the latest scientific techniques of problem solving* (New York: Basic Books).

Waismann, F. (1965), *Principles of Linguistic Philosophy*, ed. R. Harré (New York: St Martin's Press).

Walker, J. L. (1966), 'A critique of the elitist theory of democracy', *American Political Science Review*, vol. 60, pp. 285–95, 391–2.

Walker, J. L. (1970), 'Normative consequences of democratic theory', in H. S. Kariel (ed.) *Frontiers of Democratic Theory* (New York: Random House) pp. 227–47.

Walzer, M. (1983), *Spheres of Justice* (New York: Basic Books).

Ward, B. (1976), 'National economic planning and policies in twentieth century Europe 1920–1970', in C. M. Cipolla (ed.), *The Fontana Economic History of Europe, Part 2, The Twentieth Century* (Collins/Fontana).

Warren, R. L. (1972), *The Community in America* (New York: Rand, McNally).

Waste, R. J. (1987), *Power and Pluralism in American Cities: Researching the urban laboratory* (New York: Greenwood Press).

Weber, Marianne (1975), *Max Weber, a Biography*, tr. H. Zohn (New York: Wiley).

Weber, M. (1946), *From Max Weber: Essays in Sociology*, H. H. Gerth and C. W. Mills eds (New York: Oxford University Press).

Weber, M. ([1919] 1946), 'Politics as a vocation', in H. H. Gerth and C. W. Mills (eds) *From Max Weber: Essays in sociology,* (New York: Oxford

University Press).

Weber, M. ([1924] 1968), *Economy and Society: An outline of interpretive sociology*, (eds) G. Roth and C. Wittich (New York: Bedminster Press).

Westergaard, J. (1977), 'Class, inequality and corporatism', in A. Hunt, (ed.), *Class and Class Structure* (London: Lawrence and Wishart).

Whyte, W. F. (1947), *Street Corner Society: The social structure of an Italian slum* (Chicago: Chicago University Press).

Wilber, C. K. and Jameson, K. P. (1981), 'Hedonism and quietism', *Society*, vol. 19, pp. 24–28.

Wildavsky, A. (1973), 'If planning is everything, maybe it's nothing', *Policy Sciences* vol. 4, pp. 127–53.

Wilding, P. (1982), *Professional Power and Social Welfare* (London: Routledge and Kegan Paul).

Williamson, P. J. (1985), *Varieties of Corporatism: Theory and practice* (Cambridge: Cambridge University Press).

Wilson, G. K. (1982), 'Why is there no corporatism in the United States?', in G. Lehmbruch and P. C. Schmitter, *Patterns of Corporatist Policy Making* (Beverley Hills, Calif.: Sage).

Wilson, W. J. (1985), 'The urban underclass in advanced industrial society', in P. E. Paterson (ed.) *The New Urban Reality* (Washington, DC: The Brookings Institution).

Winkler, J. T. (1976), 'Corporatism', *Archives Européennes de Sociologie*, vol. 17, no. 1, pp. 100–36.

Wirt, F. M. and Christovich, L. (1984), 'The political world of urban planners: a report from the field', *Journal of Planning Education and Research*, vol. 3, pp. 93–101.

Wittgenstein, L. (1968), *Philosophical Investigations*, tr. G. E. M. Anscombe (New York: Macmillan).

Wittman, D. A. (1973), 'Parties as utility maximizers', *American Political Science Review*, June 1973, p. 491.

Wood, M. (1982), *High Wycombe: The implementation of strategic planning policy in a restraint area in the south east*, Oxford Working Paper No. 67 (Oxford: Department of Town Planning, Oxford Polytechnic).

Wootton, B. (1934), *Plan or No Plan?* (London: Gollancz).

Wootton, B. ([1945] 1979), *Freedom under Planning* (Westport, Conn.: Greenwood Press).

Wright, E. O. (1976), 'Class boundaries in advanced capitalist societies', *New Left Review*, vol. 98, pp. 3–41.

Wright E. O. (1980), 'Varieties of Marxist conceptions of class structure' *Politics and Society*, vol. 9, pp. 323–70.

Wright E. O. (1984), 'A general framework for the analysis of class structure', *Politics and Society*, vol. 13, pp. 383–423.

Zeigler, H. (1980), 'Interest groups and public policy: a comparative revisionist perspective' in R. Scott (ed.), *Interest Groups and Public Policy: Case studies from the Australian states* (Melbourne: Macmillan) pp. 1–16.

Zweig, F. (1942) *The Planning of Free Societies* (London: Secker and Warburg).

Index